Programmer's Guide: STREAMS

Published by P T R Prentice Hall
Prentice-Hall, Inc.
A Paramount Communications Company
Englewood Cliffs, New Jersey 07632

IMPORTANT NOTE TO USERS

TRADEMARKS

20 19 18 17 16 15 14 13 12 11

ISBN 0-13-020660-1

PRENTICE HALL

ORDERING INFORMATION

UNIX® SYSTEM V RELEASE 4.2 DOCUMENTATION

To order single copies of UNIX® SYSTEM V Release 4.2 documentation, please call (515) 284-6761.

ATTENTION DOCUMENTATION MANAGERS AND TRAINING DIRECTORS:
For bulk purchases in excess of 30 copies, please write to:

Corporate Sales Department
PTR Prentice Hall
113 Sylvan Avenue
Englewood Cliffs, N.J. 07632

or

Phone: (201) 592-2863
FAX: (201) 592-2249

ATTENTION GOVERNMENT CUSTOMERS:

For GSA and other pricing information, please call (201) 461-7107.

Prentice-Hall International (UK) Limited, *London*
Prentice-Hall of Australia Pty. Limited, *Sydney*
Prentice-Hall Canada Inc., *Toronto*
Prentice-Hall Hispanoamericana, S.A., *Mexico*
Prentice-Hall of India Private Limited, *New Delhi*
Prentice-Hall of Japan, Inc., *Tokyo*
Simon & Schuster Asia Pte. Ltd., *Singapore*
Editora Prentice-Hall do Brasil, Ltda., *Rio de Janeiro*

AT&T UNIX® System V Release 4

General Use and System Administration

UNIX® System V Release 4 Network User's and Administrator's Guide
UNIX® System V Release 4 Product Overview and Master Index
UNIX® System V Release 4 System Administrator's Guide
UNIX® System V Release 4 System Administrator's Reference Manual
UNIX® System V Release 4 User's Guide
UNIX® System V Release 4 User's Reference Manual

General Programmer's Series

UNIX® System V Release 4 Programmer's Guide: ANSI C
   and Programming Support Tools
UNIX® System V Release 4 Programmer's Guide: Character User Interface
   (FMLI and ETI)
UNIX® System V Release 4 Programmer's Guide: Networking Interfaces
UNIX® System V Release 4 Programmer's Guide: POSIX Conformance
UNIX® System V Release 4 Programmer's Guide: System Services
   and Application Packaging Tools
UNIX® System V Release 4 Programmer's Reference Manual

System Programmer's Series

UNIX® System V Release 4 ANSI C Transition Guide
UNIX® System V Release 4 BSD / XENIX® Compatibility Guide
UNIX® System V Release 4 Device Driver Interface / Driver−Kernel
   Interface (DDI / DKI) Reference Manual
UNIX® System V Release 4 Migration Guide
UNIX® System V Release 4 Programmer's Guide: STREAMS

Available from Prentice Hall

Contents

1 **Introduction**
Introduction to This Guide   1-1

2 **Overview of STREAMS**
What Is STREAMS?   2-1
Basic Streams Operations   2-5
STREAMS Components   2-9
Multiplexing   2-15
Benefits of STREAMS   2-20

3 **STREAMS Mechanism**
STREAMS Mechanism Overview   3-1
Stream Construction   3-3

4 **STREAMS Processing Routines**
Put and Service Procedures   4-1
An Asynchronous Protocol Stream Example   4-4

5 **Messages**
Messages   5-1
Message Structure   5-4
Message Queues and Message Priority   5-15
Service Interfaces   5-34
Message Allocation and Freeing   5-54
Extended STREAMS Buffers   5-60

6 Polling and Signaling

Input/Output Polling	6-1
Stream as a Controlling Terminal	6-9

7 Overview of Modules and Drivers

Module and Driver Environment	7-1
Module and Driver ioctls	7-9
Flush Handling	7-31
Driver-Kernel Interface	7-37
Design Guidelines	7-42

8 Modules

Modules	8-1
Flow Control	8-11
Design Guidelines	8-14

9 Drivers

Drivers	9-1
Cloning	9-18
Loop-Around Driver	9-20
Design Guidelines	9-30

10 Multiplexing

Multiplexing	10-1
Connecting/Disconnecting Lower Streams	10-13
Multiplexor Construction Example	10-16
Multiplexing Driver	10-19

Persistent Links   10-32
Design Guidelines   10-37

11 STREAMS-Based Pipes and FIFOS

STREAMS-based Pipes and FIFOs   11-1

12 STREAMS-Based Terminal Subsystem

STREAMS-based Terminal Subsystem   12-1
STREAMS-based Pseudo-Terminal Subsystem   12-15

A Appendix A: STREAMS Data Structures

STREAMS Data Structures   A-1

B Appendix B: Message Types

Message Types   B-1
Ordinary Messages   B-2
High Priority Messages   B-14

C Appendix C: STREAMS Utilities

STREAMS Utilities   C-1
Utility Descriptions   C-3
Utility Routine Summary   C-22

D	**Appendix D: Debugging**	
	Debugging	D-1

E	**Appendix E: Configuration**	
	Configuration	E-1

F	**Appendix F: Manual Pages**	
	Manual Pages	F-1

G	**Appendix G: Hardware Examples**	
	Hardware Examples	G-1
	3B2 STREAMS-based Ports Driver	G-2
	3B2 STREAMS-based Console Driver	G-10
	3B2 STREAMS-based XT Driver	G-15
	Extended STREAMS Buffers	G-35

	Glossary	
	Glossary	1

I	**Index**	
	Index	I-1

Figures and Tables

Figure 2-1: Simple Stream   2-2
Figure 2-2: STREAMS-based Pipe   2-3
Figure 2-3: Stream to Communications Driver   2-7
Figure 2-4: A Message   2-10
Figure 2-5: Messages on a Message Queue   2-11
Figure 2-6: A Stream in More Detail   2-13
Figure 2-7: Many-to-one Multiplexor   2-15
Figure 2-8: One-to-many Multiplexor   2-16
Figure 2-9: Many-to-many Multiplexor   2-16
Figure 2-10: Internet Multiplexing Stream   2-17
Figure 2-11: X.25 Multiplexing Stream   2-18
Figure 2-12: Protocol Module Portability   2-22
Figure 2-13: Protocol Migration   2-23
Figure 2-14: Module Reusability   2-24
Figure 3-1: Upstream and Downstream Stream Construction   3-3
Figure 3-2: Stream Queue Relationship   3-4
Figure 3-3: Opened STREAMS-based Driver   3-7
Figure 3-4: Creating STREAMS-based Pipe   3-9
Figure 3-5: Case Converter Module   3-13
Figure 4-1: Idle Stream Configuration for Example   4-5
Figure 4-2: Operational Stream for Example   4-7
Figure 4-3: Module Put and Service Procedures   4-9
Figure 5-1: Message Form and Linkage   5-7
Figure 5-2: Message Ordering on a Queue   5-15
Figure 5-3: Message Ordering with One Priority Band   5-16
Figure 5-4: Data Structure Linkage on non-EFT Systems   5-25
Figure 5-5: Flow Control   5-29
Figure 5-6: Protocol Substitution   5-36
Figure 5-7: Service Interface   5-37
Figure 7-1: Flushing The Write-Side of A Stream   7-33
Figure 7-2: Flushing The Read-Side of A Stream   7-34
Figure 7-3: Interfaces Affecting Drivers   7-38
Figure 9-1: Device Driver Streams   9-8
Figure 9-2: Loop-Around Streams   9-21
Figure 10-1: Protocol Multiplexor   10-3

Figure 10-2: Before Link   10-5
Figure 10-3: IP Multiplexor After First Link   10-6
Figure 10-4: IP Multiplexor   10-7
Figure 10-5: TP Multiplexor   10-9
Figure 10-6: Internet Multiplexor Before Connecting   10-16
Figure 10-7: Internet Multiplexor After Connecting   10-17
Figure 10-8: open() of MUXdriver and Driver1   10-33
Figure 10-9: Multiplexor After I_PLINK   10-34
Figure 10-10: Other Users Opening a MUXdriver   10-35
Figure 11-1: Pushing Modules on a STREAMS-based Pipe   11-3
Figure 11-2: Server Sets Up a Pipe   11-11
Figure 11-3: Processes X and Y Open _/usr/toserv_   11-12
Figure 12-1: STREAMS-based Terminal Subsystem   12-2
Figure 12-2: Pseudo-tty Subsystem Architecture   12-16
Figure B-1: M_PROTO and M_PCPROTO Message Structure   B-8
Figure D-1: Error and Trace Logging   D-18
Figure G-1: STREAMS-based XT Driver (before link)   G-16
Figure G-2: STREAMS-based XT Driver (after link)   G-17
Figure G-3: STREAMS-based XT Driver   G-18
Figure G-4: STREAMS-based XT Driver over Starlan   G-20
Figure G-5: STREAMS-based XT Driver Data Flow   G-27
Figure G-6: UNIX I/O on 3B2   G-36
Figure G-7: UNIX I/O on a 386 Box   G-38

1 Introduction

Introduction to This Guide   1-1
Audience   1-1
Organization   1-1
Conventions Used   1-3
Other Documentation   1-4

Introduction to This Guide

This guide provides information to developers on the use of the STREAMS mechanism at user and kernel levels.

STREAMS was incorporated in UNIX® System V Release 3 to augment the character input/output (I/O) mechanism and to support development of communication services.

STREAMS provides developers with integral functions, a set of utility routines, and facilities that expedite software design and implementation.

Audience

The guide is intended for network and systems programmers, who use the STREAMS mechanism at user and kernel levels for UNIX system communication services.

Readers of the guide are expected to possess prior knowledge of the UNIX system, programming, networking, and data communication.

Organization

This guide has several chapters, each discussing a unique topic. Chapters 2, 3, and 4 have introductory information and can be ignored by those already familiar with STREAMS concepts and facilities.

- Chapter 1, "Introduction," describes the organization and purpose of the guide. It also defines an intended audience and an expected background of the users of the guide.

- Chapter 2, "Overview of STREAMS," presents an overview and the benefits of STREAMS.

- Chapter 3, "STREAMS Mechanism," describes the basic operations for constructing, using, and dismantling Streams. These operations are performed using **open**(2), **close**(2), **read**(2), **write**(2), and **ioctl**(2).

- Chapter 4, "STREAMS Processing Routines," gives an overview of the STREAMS **put** and **service** routines.

- Chapter 5, "Messages," discusses STREAMS messages, their structure, linkage, queuing, and interfacing with other STREAMS components.

- Chapter 6, "Polling and Signaling," describes how STREAMS allows user processes to monitor, control, and poll Streams to allow an effective utilization of system resources.

- Chapter 7, "Overview of Modules and Drivers," describes the STREAMS module and driver environment, ioctls, routines, declarations, flush handling, driver–kernel interface, and also provides general design guidelines for modules and drivers.

- Chapter 8, "Modules," provides information on module construction and function.

- Chapter 9, "Drivers," discusses STREAMS drivers, elements of driver flow control, flush handling, cloning, and processing.

- Chapter 10, "Multiplexing," describes the STREAMS multiplexing facility.

- Chapter 11, "STREAMS-based Pipes and FIFOs," provides information on creating, writing, reading, and closing of STREAMS-based pipes and FIFOs and unique connections.

- Chapter 12, "STREAMS-based Terminal Subsystem," discusses STREAMS-based terminal and and pseudo-terminal subsystems.

- Appendix A, "STREAMS Data Structures," summarizes data structures commonly used by STREAMS modules and drivers.

- Appendix B, "Message Types," describes STREAMS messages and their use.

- Appendix C, "STREAMS Utilities," describes STREAMS utility routines and their usage.

- Appendix D, "Debugging," provides debugging aids for developers.

- Appendix E, "Configuration," describes how modules and drivers are configured into the UNIX system, tunable parameters, and the autopush facility.

- Appendix F, "Manual Pages," has STREAMS related manual pages.

- Appendix G, "Hardware Examples," provides information pertaining to certain hardware types, for example the AT&T 3B2, used in the STREAMS environment.

- "Glossary" defines terms unique to STREAMS.

Conventions Used

Throughout this guide, the word "STREAMS" will refer to the mechanism and the word "Stream" will refer to the path between a user application and a driver. In connection with STREAMS-based pipes "Stream" refers to the data transfer path in the kernel between the kernel and one or more user processes.

Examples are given to highlight the most important and common capabilities of STREAMS. They are not exhaustive and, for simplicity, reference fictional drivers and modules.

System calls, STREAMS utility routines, header files, and data structures are given in **bold**, when they are mentioned in the text.

Variable names, pointers, and parameters are in *italics*. Routine, field, and structure names unique to the examples are also in *italics* when they are mentioned in the text.

Declarations and short examples are in constant width.

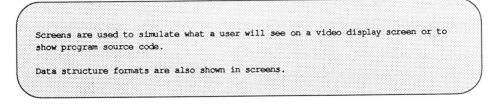

```
Screens are used to simulate what a user will see on a video display screen or to
show program source code.

Data structure formats are also shown in screens.
```

 The caution sign is used to show possible harm or damage to a system, an application, a process, a piece of hardware, etc.

| NOTE | The note sign is used to emphasize points of interest, to present parenthetical information, and to cite references to other documents and commands. |

Other Documentation

Though the *Programmer's Guide: STREAMS* is a principal tool to aid in developing STREAMS applications, readers are encouraged to obtain more information on system calls used by STREAMS (section 2 manual pages), and STREAMS utilities from section 1M manual pages. STREAMS specific input-output control (**ioctl**) calls are provided in **streamio(7)**. STREAMS modules and drivers are described on section 7 manual pages. STREAMS is also described to some extent in the *System V Interface Definition, Third Edition*.

For a complete list of books about AT&T UNIX System V Release 4.0, see the *Product Overview and Master Index* for this release.

2 Overview of STREAMS

What Is STREAMS?   2-1

Basic Streams Operations   2-5

STREAMS Components   2-9
Queues   2-9
Messages   2-9
■ Message Types   2-10
■ Message Queueing Priority   2-11
Modules   2-12
Drivers   2-14

Multiplexing   2-15

Benefits of STREAMS   2-20
Standardized Service Interfaces   2-20
Manipulating Modules   2-20
■ Protocol Portability   2-21
■ Protocol Substitution   2-22
■ Protocol Migration   2-22
■ Module Reusability   2-23

What Is STREAMS?

STREAMS is a general, flexible facility and a set of tools for development of UNIX system communication services. It supports the implementation of services ranging from complete networking protocol suites to individual device drivers. STREAMS defines standard interfaces for character input/output within the kernel, and between the kernel and the rest of the UNIX system. The associated mechanism is simple and open-ended. It consists of a set of system calls, kernel resources, and kernel routines.

The standard interface and mechanism enable modular, portable development and easy integration of high performance network services and their components. STREAMS does not impose any specific network architecture. The STREAMS user interface is upwardly compatible with the character I/O user level functions such as **open**, **close**, **read**, **write**, and **ioctl**. Benefits of STREAMS are discussed in more detail later in this chapter.

A *Stream* is a full-duplex processing and data transfer path between a STREAMS driver in kernel space and a process in user space (see Figure 2-1). In the kernel, a Stream is constructed by linking a Stream head, a driver, and zero or more modules between the Stream head and driver. The *Stream head* is the end of the Stream nearest to the user process. All system calls made by a user level process on a Stream are processed by the Stream head.

Pipes are also STREAMS-based. A STREAMS-based pipe (see Figure 2-2) is a full-duplex (bidirectional) data transfer path in the kernel. It implements a connection between the kernel and one or more user processes and also shares properties of STREAMS-based devices.

A STREAMS *driver* may be a device driver that provides the services of an external I/O device, or a software driver, commonly referred to as a pseudo-device driver. The driver typically handles data transfer between the kernel and the device and does little or no processing of data other than conversion between data structures used by the STREAMS mechanism and data structures that the device understands.

A STREAMS *module* represents processing functions to be performed on data flowing on the Stream. The module is a defined set of kernel-level routines and data structures used to process data, status, and control information. Data processing may involve changing the way the data are represented, adding/deleting header and trailer information to data, and/or packetizing/depacketizing data. Status and control information includes signals and input/output control information. Each module is self-contained and functionally isolated from any other component in the Stream except its two

neighboring components. The module communicates with its neighbors by
passing messages. The module is not a required component in STREAMS,
whereas the driver is, except in a STREAMS-based pipe where only the Stream
head is required.

Figure 2-1: Simple Stream

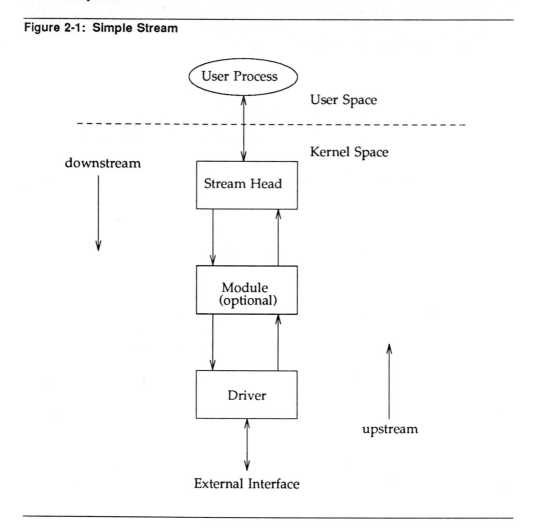

One or more modules may be inserted into a Stream between the Stream head and driver to perform intermediate processing of messages as they pass between the Stream head and driver. STREAMS modules are dynamically interconnected in a Stream by a user process. No kernel programming, assembly, or link editing is required to create the interconnection.

Figure 2-2: STREAMS-based Pipe

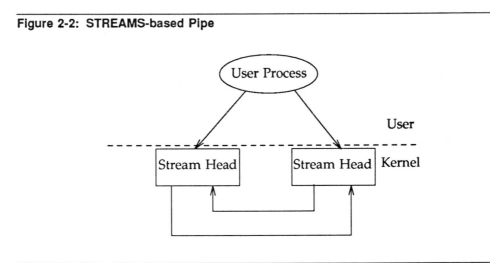

STREAMS uses queue structures to keep information about given instances of a pushed module or opened STREAMS device. A *queue* is a data structure that contains status information, a pointer to routines processing messages, and pointers for administering the Stream. Queues are always allocated in pairs; one queue for the read-side and other for the write-side. There is one queue pair for each driver and module, and the Stream head. The pair of queues is allocated whenever the Stream is opened or the module is pushed (added) onto the Stream.

Data are passed between a driver and the Stream head and between modules in the form of messages. A *message* is a set of data structures used to pass data, status, and control information between user processes, modules, and drivers. Messages that are passed from the Stream head toward the driver or from the process to the device, are said to travel *downstream* (also called *write-side*). Similarly, messages passed in the other direction, from the device to the process or from the driver to the Stream head, travel *upstream* (also called *read-side*).

A STREAMS message is made up of one or more message blocks. Each *block* is a 3-tuple consisting of a header, a data block, and a data buffer. The Stream head transfers data between the data space of a user process and STREAMS kernel data space. Data to be sent to a driver from a user process are packaged into STREAMS messages and passed downstream. When a message containing data arrives at the Stream head from downstream, the message is processed by the Stream head, which copies the data into user buffers.

Within a Stream, messages are distinguished by a type indicator. Certain message types sent upstream may cause the Stream head to perform specific actions, such as sending a signal to a user process. Other message types are intended to carry information within a Stream and are not directly seen by a user process.

Basic Streams Operations

This section describes the basic set of operations for manipulating STREAMS entities.

A STREAMS driver is similar to a traditional character I/O driver in that it has one or more nodes associated with it in the file system and it is accessed using the **open** system call. Typically, each file system node corresponds to a separate minor device for that driver. Opening different minor devices of a driver will cause separate Streams to be connected between a user process and the driver. The file descriptor returned by the **open** call is used for further access to the Stream. If the same minor device is opened more than once, only one Stream will be created; the first **open** call will create the Stream, and subsequent **open** calls will return a file descriptor that references that Stream. Each process that opens the same minor device will share the same Stream to the device driver.

Once a device is opened, a user process can send data to the device using the **write** system call and receive data from the device using the **read** system call. Access to STREAMS drivers using **read** and **write** is compatible with the traditional character I/O mechanism.

The **close** system call will close a device and dismantle the associated Stream when the last open reference to the Stream is given up.

The following example shows how a simple Stream is used. In the example, the user program interacts with a communications device that provides point-to-point data transfer between two computers. Data written to the device are transmitted over the communications line, and data arriving on the line can be retrieved by reading from the device.

```
#include <fcntl.h>

main()
{
    char buf[1024];
    int fd, count;

    if ((fd = open("/dev/comm/01", O_RDWR)) < 0) {
        perror("open failed");
        exit(1);
    }

    while ((count = read(fd, buf, 1024)) > 0) {
        if (write(fd, buf, count) != count) {
            perror("write failed");
            break;
        }
    }
    exit(0);
}
```

In the example, **/dev/comm/01** identifies a minor device of the communications device driver. When this file is opened, the system recognizes the device as a STREAMS device and connects a Stream to the driver. Figure 2-3 shows the state of the Stream following the call to **open**.

Figure 2-3: Stream to Communications Driver

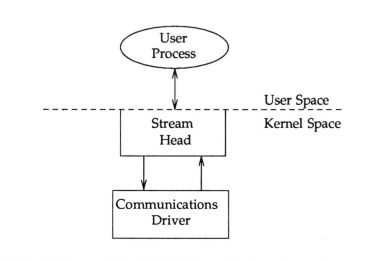

This example illustrates a user reading data from the communications device and then writing the input back out to the same device. In short, this program echoes all input back over the communications line. The example assumes that a user is sending data from the other side of the communications line. The program reads up to 1024 bytes at a time, and then writes the number of bytes just read.

The **read** call returns the available data, which may contain fewer than 1024 bytes. If no data are currently available at the Stream head, the **read** call blocks until data arrive.

Similarly, the **write** call attempts to send *count* bytes to **/dev/comm/01**. However, STREAMS implements a flow control mechanism that prevents a user from exhausting system resources by flooding a device driver with data.

Flow control is a STREAMS mechanism that controls the rate of message transfer among the modules, drivers, Stream head, and processes. Flow control is local to each Stream and advisory (voluntary). It limits the number of characters that can be queued for processing at any queue in a Stream. This mechanism limits buffers and related processing at any queue and in any one Stream, but does not consider buffer pool levels or buffer usage in other Streams. Flow control is not applied to high priority messages (message priority will be discussed later).

If the Stream exerts flow control on the user, the **write** call blocks until flow control has been relieved. The call will not return until it has sent *count* bytes to the device. **exit** is called to terminate the user process. This system call also closes all open files, thereby dismantling the Stream in this example.

STREAMS Components

This section gives an overview of the STREAMS components and discusses how these components interact with each other. A more detailed description of each STREAMS component is given in the later chapters.

Queues

A queue is an interface between a STREAMS driver or module and the rest of the Stream. Queues are always allocated as an adjacent pair. The queue with the lower address in the pair is a read queue, and the queue with the higher address is used for the write queue.

A queue's **service** routine is invoked to process messages on the queue. It usually removes successive messages from the queue, processes them, and calls the **put** routine of the next module in the Stream to give the processed message to the next queue.

A queue's **put** routine is invoked by the preceding queue's **put** and/or **service** routine to add a message to the current queue. If a module does not need to enqueue messages, its **put** routine can call the neighboring queue's **put** routine. (Chapter 4 discusses the **service** and **put** routines in more detail.)

Each queue also has a pointer to an **open** and **close** routine. The **open** routine of a driver is called when the driver is first opened and on every successive open of the Stream. The **open** routine of a module is called when the module is first pushed on the Stream and on every successive open of the Stream. The **close** routine of the module is called when the module is popped (removed) off the Stream. The **close** routine of the driver is called when the last reference to the Stream is given up and the Stream is dismantled.

Messages

All input and output under STREAMS is based on messages. The objects passed between STREAMS modules are pointers to messages. All STREAMS messages use two data structures (**msgb** and **datab**) to refer to the message data. These data structures describe the type of the message and contain pointers to the data of the message, as well as other information. Messages are sent through a Stream by successive calls to the **put** procedure of each module or driver in the Stream.

Message Types

All STREAMS messages are assigned message types to indicate their intended use by modules and drivers and to determine their handling by the Stream head. A driver or module can assign most types to a message it generates, and a module can modify a message type during processing. The Stream head will convert certain system calls to specified message types and send them downstream, and it will respond to other calls by copying the contents of certain message types that were sent upstream.

Most message types are internal to STREAMS and can only be passed from one STREAMS component to another. A few message types, for example M_DATA, M_PROTO, and M_PCPROTO, can also be passed between a Stream and user processes. M_DATA messages carry data within a Stream and between a Stream and a user process. M_PROTO or M_PCPROTO messages carry both data and control information.

As shown in Figure 2-4, a STREAMS message consists of one or more linked message blocks that are attached to the first message block of the same message.

Figure 2-4: A Message

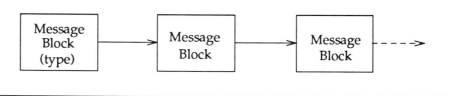

Messages can exist stand-alone, as in Figure 2-4, when the message is being processed by a procedure. Alternately, a message can await processing on a linked list of messages, called a message queue. In Figure 2-5, Message 2 is linked to Message 1.

Figure 2-5: Messages on a Message Queue

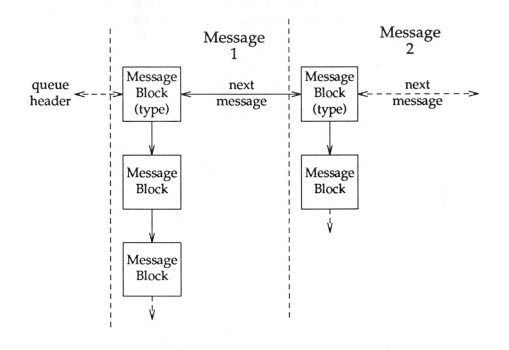

When a message is on a queue, the first block of the message contains links to preceding and succeeding messages on the same message queue, in addition to the link to the second block of the message (if present). The message queue head and tail are contained in the queue.

STREAMS utility routines enable developers to manipulate messages and message queues.

Message Queueing Priority

In certain cases, messages containing urgent information (such as a break or alarm conditions) must pass through the Stream quickly. To accommodate these cases, STREAMS provides multiple classes of message queuing priority. All messages have an associated priority field. Normal (ordinary) messages have a priority of zero. Priority messages have a priority greater than zero. High priority messages are high priority by virtue of their message type. The priority field in high priority messages is unused and should always be set to zero. STREAMS prevents high priority messages from being blocked by flow control and causes a **service** procedure to process them ahead of all ordinary messages on the queue. This results in the high priority message transiting each module with minimal delay.

Non-priority, ordinary messages are placed at the end of the queue following all other messages in the queue. Priority messages can be either high priority or priority band messages. High priority messages are placed at the head of the queue but after any other high priority messages already in the queue. Priority band messages that enable support of urgent, expedited data are placed in the queue after high priority messages but before ordinary messages.

Message priority is defined by the message type; once a message is created, its priority cannot be changed. Certain message types come in equivalent high priority/ordinary pairs (for example, M_PCPROTO and M_PROTO), so that a module or device driver can choose between the two priorities when sending information.

Modules

A module performs intermediate transformations on messages passing between a Stream head and a driver. There may be zero or more modules in a Stream (zero when the driver performs all the required character and device processing).

Each module is constructed from a pair of queue structures (see "Au/Ad" and "Bu/Bd" in Figure 2-6). One queue performs functions on messages passing upstream through the module ("Au" and "Bu" in Figure 2-6). The other set ("Ad" and "Bd") performs another set of functions on downstream messages.

Each of the two queues in a module will generally have distinct functions, that is, unrelated processing procedures and data. The queues operate independently and "Au" will not know if a message passes through "Ad" unless "Ad" is programmed to inform it. Messages and data can be shared only if the developer specifically programs the module functions to perform the sharing.

Each queue can directly access the adjacent queue in the direction of message flow (for example, "Au" to "Bu" or "Bd" to "Ad"). In addition, within a module, a queue can readily locate its mate and access its messages and data.

Figure 2-6: A Stream in More Detail

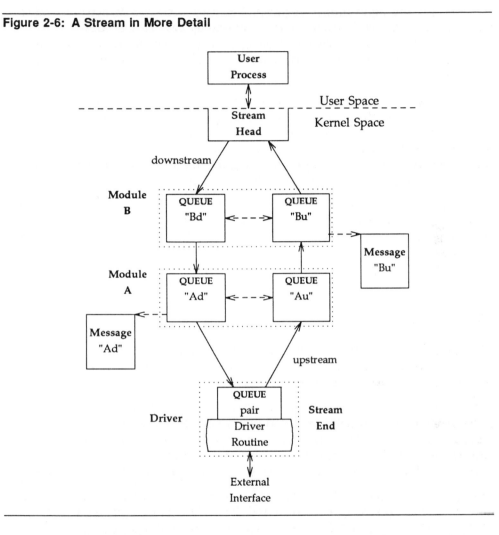

Each queue in a module points to messages, processing procedures, and data:

- Messages – These are dynamically attached to the queue on a linked list ("message queue", see "Ad" and "Bu" in Figure 2-6) as they pass through the module.

- Processing procedures – A **put** procedure processes messages and must be incorporated in each queue. An optional **service** procedure can also be incorporated. According to their function, the procedures can send messages upstream and/or downstream, and they can also modify the private data in their module.

- Data – Developers may use a private field in the queue to reference private data structures (for example, state information and translation tables).

In general, each of the two queues in a module has a distinct set of all of these elements.

Drivers

STREAMS device drivers are an initial part of a Stream. They are structurally similar to STREAMS modules. The call interfaces to driver routines are identical to the interfaces used for modules.

There are three significant differences between modules and drivers. A driver must be able to handle interrupts from the device, a driver can have multiple Streams connected to it, and a driver is initialized/deinitialized via **open** and **close**. A module is initialized/deinitialized via the I_PUSH **ioctl** and I_POP **ioctl**.

Drivers and modules can pass signals, error codes, and return values to processes via message types provided for that purpose.

Multiplexing

Earlier, Streams were described as linear connections of modules, where each invocation of a module is connected to at most one upstream module and one downstream module. While this configuration is suitable for many applications, others require the ability to multiplex Streams in a variety of configurations. Typical examples are terminal window facilities, and internetworking protocols (which might route data over several subnetworks).

An example of a multiplexor is one that multiplexes data from several upper Streams over a single lower Stream, as shown in Figure 2-7. An *upper Stream* is one that is upstream from a multiplexor, and a *lower Stream* is one that is downstream from a multiplexor. A terminal windowing facility might be implemented in this fashion, where each upper Stream is associated with a separate window.

Figure 2-7: Many-to-one Multiplexor

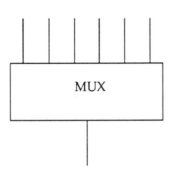

A second type of multiplexor might route data from a single upper Stream to one of several lower Streams, as shown in Figure 2-8. An internetworking protocol could take this form, where each lower Stream links the protocol to a different physical network.

Figure 2-8: One-to-many Multiplexor

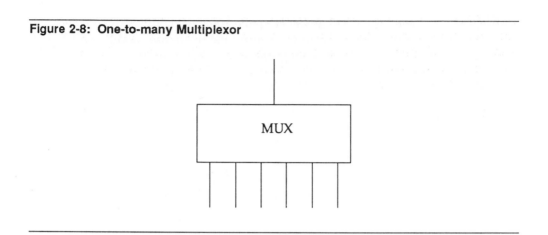

A third type of multiplexor might route data from one of many upper Streams to one of many lower Streams, as shown in Figure 2-9.

Figure 2-9: Many-to-many Multiplexor

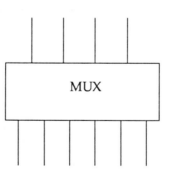

The STREAMS mechanism supports the multiplexing of Streams through special pseudo-device drivers. Using a linking facility, users can dynamically build, maintain, and dismantle multiplexed Stream configurations. Simple configurations like the ones shown in three previous figures can be further combined to form complex, multi-level multiplexed Stream configurations.

STREAMS multiplexing configurations are created in the kernel by interconnecting multiple Streams. Conceptually, there are two kinds of multiplexors: upper and lower multiplexors. *Lower multiplexors* have multiple lower Streams between device drivers and the multiplexor, and *upper multiplexors* have multiple upper Streams between user processes and the multiplexor.

Figure 2-10: Internet Multiplexing Stream

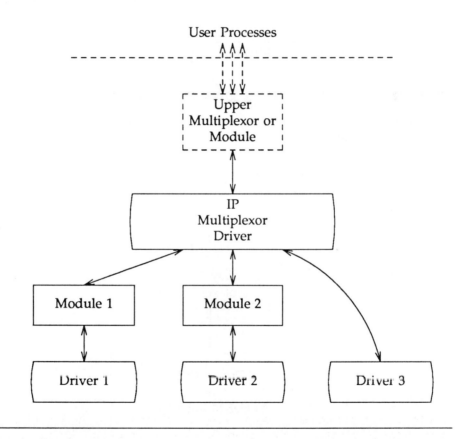

Figure 2-10 is an example of the multiplexor configuration that would typically occur where internetworking functions were included in the system. This configuration contains three hardware device drivers. The IP (Internet Protocol) is a multiplexor.

The IP multiplexor switches messages among the lower Streams or sends them upstream to user processes in the system. In this example, the multiplexor expects to see the same interface downstream to Module 1, Module 2, and Driver 3.

Figure 2-10 depicts the IP multiplexor as part of a larger configuration. The multiplexor configuration, as shown in the dashed rectangle, would generally have an upper multiplexor and additional modules. Multiplexors could also be cascaded below the IP multiplexor driver if the device drivers were replaced by multiplexor drivers.

Figure 2-11: X.25 Multiplexing Stream

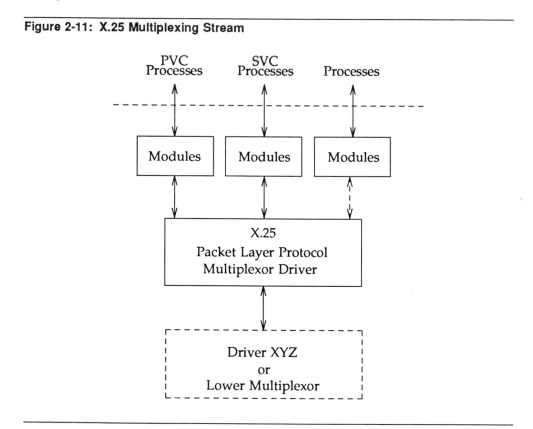

Programmer's Guide: STREAMS

Figure 2-11 shows a multiplexor configuration where the multiplexor (or multiplexing driver) routes messages between the lower Stream and one of the upper Streams. This Stream performs X.25 multiplexing to multiple independent SVC (Switched Virtual Circuit) and PVC (Permanent Virtual Circuit) user processes. Upper multiplexors are a specific application of standard STREAMS facilities that support multiple minor devices in a device driver. This figure also shows that more complex configurations can be built by having one or more multiplexed drivers below and multiple modules above an upper multiplexor.

Developers can choose either upper or lower multiplexing, or both, when designing their applications. For example, a window multiplexor would have a similar configuration to the X.25 configuration of Figure 2-11, with a window driver replacing Packet Layer, a tty driver replacing the driver XYZ, and the child processes of the terminal process replacing the user processes. Although the X.25 and window multiplexing Streams have similar configurations, their multiplexor drivers would differ significantly. The IP multiplexor of Figure 2-10 has a different configuration than the X.25 multiplexor, and the driver would implement its own set of processing and routing requirements in each configuration.

In addition to upper and lower multiplexors, more complex configurations can be created by connecting Streams containing multiplexors to other multiplexor drivers. With such a diversity of needs for multiplexors, it is not possible to provide general purpose multiplexor drivers. Rather, STREAMS provides a general purpose multiplexing facility. The facility allows users to set up the inter-module/driver plumbing to create multiplexor configurations of generally unlimited interconnection.

Benefits of STREAMS

STREAMS provides a flexible, portable, and reusable set of tools for development of UNIX system communication services. STREAMS allows an easy creation of modules that offer standard data communications services and the ability to manipulate those modules on a Stream. From user level, modules can be dynamically selected and interconnected; kernel programming, assembly, and link editing are not required to create the interconnection.

STREAMS also greatly simplifies the user interface for languages that have complex input and output requirements. This is discussed in Chapter 12.

Standardized Service Interfaces

STREAMS simplifies the creation of modules that present a service interface to any neighboring application program, module, or device driver. A service interface is defined at the boundary between two neighbors. In STREAMS, a *service interface* is a specified set of messages and the rules that allow passage of these messages across the boundary. A module that implements a service interface will receive a message from a neighbor and respond with an appropriate action (for example, send back a request to retransmit) based on the specific message received and the preceding sequence of messages.

In general, any two modules can be connected anywhere in a Stream. However, rational sequences are generally constructed by connecting modules with compatible protocol service interfaces. For example, a module that implements an X.25 protocol layer, as shown in Figure 2-12, presents a protocol service interface at its input and output sides. In this case, other modules should only be connected to the input and output side if they have the compatible X.25 service interface.

Manipulating Modules

STREAMS provides the capabilities to manipulate modules from user level, to interchange modules with common service interfaces, and to change the service interface to a STREAMS user process. These capabilities yield further benefits when implementing networking services and protocols, including:

- User level programs can be independent of underlying protocols and physical communication media.

- Network architectures and higher level protocols can be independent of underlying protocols, drivers, and physical communication media.

- Higher level services can be created by selecting and connecting lower level services and protocols.

The following examples show the benefits of STREAMS capabilities for creating service interfaces and manipulating modules. These examples are only illustrations and do not necessarily reflect real situations.

Protocol Portability

Figure 2-12 shows how the same X.25 protocol module can be used with different drivers on different machines by implementing compatible service interfaces. The X.25 protocol module interfaces are Connection Oriented Network Service (CONS) and Link Access Protocol – Balanced (LAPB).

Figure 2-12: Protocol Module Portability

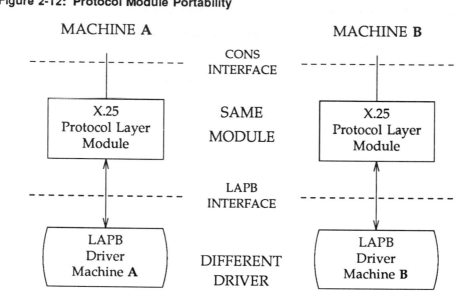

Protocol Substitution

Alternate protocol modules (and device drivers) can be interchanged on the same machine if they are implemented to an equivalent service interface.

Protocol Migration

Figure 2-13 illustrates how STREAMS can move functions between kernel software and front end firmware. A common downstream service interface allows the transport protocol module to be independent of the number or type of modules below. The same transport module will connect without modification to either an X.25 module or X.25 driver that has the same service interface.

By shifting functions between software and firmware, developers can produce cost effective, functionally equivalent systems over a wide range of configurations. They can rapidly incorporate technological advances. The same transport protocol module can be used on a lower capacity machine, where economics may preclude the use of front-end hardware, and also on a larger scale system where a front-end is economically justified.

Figure 2-13: Protocol Migration

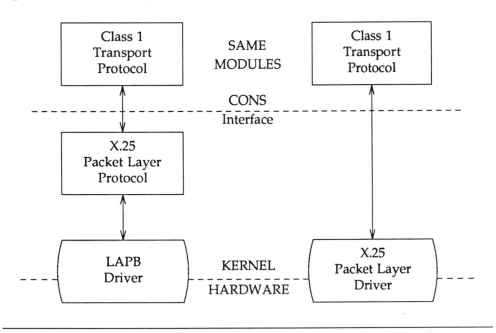

Module Reusability

Figure 2-14 shows the same canonical module (for example, one that provides delete and kill processing on character strings) reused in two different Streams. This module would typically be implemented as a filter, with no downstream service interface. In both cases, a tty interface is presented to the Stream's user process since the module is nearest the Stream head.

Figure 2-14: Module Reusability

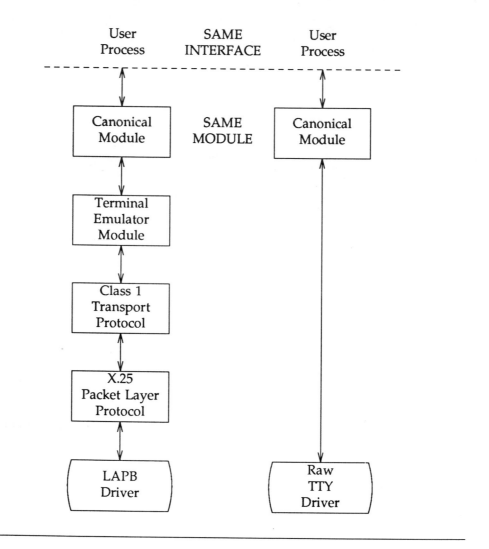

3 STREAMS Mechanism

STREAMS Mechanism Overview — 3-1
STREAMS System Calls — 3-1

Stream Construction — 3-3
Opening a STREAMS Device File — 3-5
Creating a STREAMS-based Pipe — 3-8
Adding and Removing Modules — 3-10
Closing the Stream — 3-11
Stream Construction Example — 3-11
■ Inserting Modules — 3-11
■ Module and Driver Control — 3-14

STREAMS Mechanism Overview

This chapter shows how to construct, use, and dismantle a Stream using STREAMS-related systems calls. General and STREAMS-specific system calls provide the user level facilities required to implement application programs. This system call interface is upwardly compatible with the traditional character I/O facilities. The **open**(2) system call will recognize a STREAMS file and create a Stream to the specified driver. A user process can receive and send data on STREAMS files using **read**(2) and **write**(2) in the same manner as with traditional character files. The **ioctl**(2) system call enables users to perform functions specific to a particular device. STREAMS **ioctl** commands [see **streamio**(7)] support a variety of functions for accessing and controlling Streams. The last **close**(2) in a Stream will dismantle a Stream.

In addition to the traditional **ioctl** commands and system calls, there are other system calls used by STREAMS. The **poll**(2) system call enables a user to poll multiple Streams for various events. The **putmsg**(2) and **getmsg**(2) system calls enable users to send and receive STREAMS messages, and are suitable for interacting with STREAMS modules and drivers through a service interface.

STREAMS provides kernel facilities and utilities to support development of modules and drivers. The Stream head handles most system calls so that the related processing does not have to be incorporated in a module or driver.

STREAMS System Calls

The STREAMS-related system calls are:

open(2)	Open a Stream
close(2)	Close a Stream
read(2)	Read data from a Stream
write(2)	Write data to a Stream
ioctl(2)	Control a Stream
getmsg(2)	Receive a message at the Stream head
putmsg(2)	Send a message downstream

poll(2)   Notify the application program when selected events occur on a Stream

pipe(2)   Create a channel that provides a communication path between multiple processes

Stream Construction

STREAMS constructs a Stream as a linked list of kernel resident data structures. The list is created as a set of linked queue pairs. The first queue pair is the head of the Stream and the second queue pair is the end of the Stream. The end of the Stream represents a device driver, pseudo device driver, or the other end of a STREAMS-based pipe. Kernel routines interface with the Stream head to perform operations on the Stream. Figure 3-1 depicts the upstream (read) and downstream (write) portions of the Stream. Queue H2 is the upstream half of the Stream head and queue H1 is the downstream half of the Stream head. Queue E2 is the upstream half of the Stream end and queue E1 is the downstream half of the Stream end.

Figure 3-1: Upstream and Downstream Stream Construction

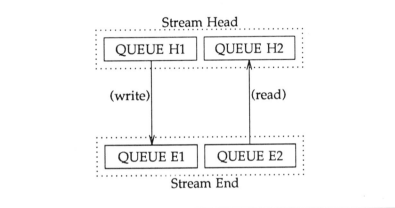

At the same relative location in each queue is the address of the entry point, a procedure to process any message received by that queue. The procedure for queues H1 and H2 process messages sent to the Stream head. The procedure for queues E1 and E2, process messages received by the other end of the Stream, the Stream end (tail). Messages move from one end to the other, from one queue to the next linked queue, as the procedure specified by that queue is executed.

Figure 3-2 shows the data structures forming each queue: **queue, qinit, qband, module_info,** and **module_stat**. The qband structures have information for each priority band in the queue. The **queue** data structure contains various modifiable values for that queue. The **qinit** structure contains a pointer to the processing procedures, the **module_info** structure contains initial limit values, and the **module_stat** structure is used for statistics gathering. Each queue in the queue pair contains a different set of these data structures. There is a **queue, qinit, module_info,** and **module_stat** data structure for the upstream portion of the queue pair and a set of data structures for the downstream portion of the pair. In some situations, a queue pair may share some or all of the data structures. For example, there may be a separate **qinit** structure for each queue in the pair and one **module_stat** structure that represents both queues in the pair. These data structures are described in Appendix A.

Figure 3-2: Stream Queue Relationship

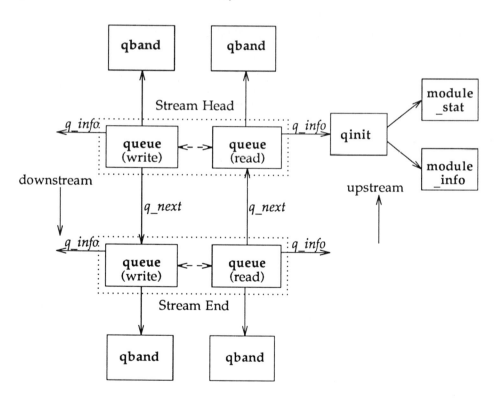

Figure 3-2 shows two neighboring queue pairs with links (solid vertical arrows) in both directions. When a module is pushed onto a Stream, STREAMS creates a queue pair and links each queue in the pair to its neighboring queue in the upstream and downstream direction. The linkage allows each queue to locate its next neighbor. This relation is implemented between adjacent queue pairs by the *q_next* pointer. Within a queue pair, each **queue** locates its mate (see dashed arrows in Figure 3-2) by use of STREAMS macros, since there is no pointer between the two **queues**. The existence of the Stream head and Stream end is known to the queue procedures only as destinations towards which messages are sent.

Opening a STREAMS Device File

One way to construct a Stream is to open [see **open**(2)] a STREAMS-based driver file (see Figure 3-3). All entry points into the driver are defined by the **streamtab** structure for that driver. The **streamtab** structure has a format as follows:

```
struct streamtab {
    struct qinit    *st_rdinit;
    struct qinit    *st_wrinit;
    struct qinit    *st_muxrinit;
    struct qinit    *st_muxwinit;
};
```

The **streamtab** structure defines a module or driver. *st_rdinit* points to the read **qinit** structure for the driver and *st_wdinit* points to the driver's write **qinit** structure. *st_muxrinit* and *st_muxwinit* point to the lower read and write **qinit** structures if the driver is a multiplexor driver.

If the **open** call is the initial file open, a Stream is created. (There is one Stream per major/minor device pair.) First, an entry is allocated in the user's file table and a **vnode** is created to represent the opened file. The file table entry is initialized to point to the allocated **vnode** (see *f_vnode* in Figure 3-3) and the **vnode** is initialized to specify a file of type *character special*.

Second, a Stream header is created from an **stdata** data structure and a Stream head is created from a pair of **queue** structures. The content of **stdata** and **queue** are initialized with predetermined values, including the Stream head processing procedures.

The **snode** contains the file system dependent information. It is associated with the **vnode** representing the device. The *s_commonvp* field of the **snode** points to the *common* device **vnode**. The **vnode** field, *v_data*, contains a pointer to the **snode**. Instead of maintaining a pointer to the **vnode**, the **snode** contains the **vnode** as an element. The *sd_vnode* field of **stdata** is initialized to point to the allocated **vnode**. The *v_stream* field of the **vnode** data structure is initialized to point to the Stream header, thus there is a forward and backward pointer between the Stream header and the **vnode**. There is one Stream header per Stream. The **header** is used by STREAMS while performing operations on the Stream. In the downstream portion of the Stream, the Stream header points to the downstream half of the Stream head queue pair. Similarly, the upstream portion of the Stream terminates at the Stream header, since the upstream half of the Stream head queue pair points to the **header**. As shown in Figure 3-3, from the Stream header onward, a Stream is constructed of linked queue pairs.

Figure 3-3: Opened STREAMS-based Driver

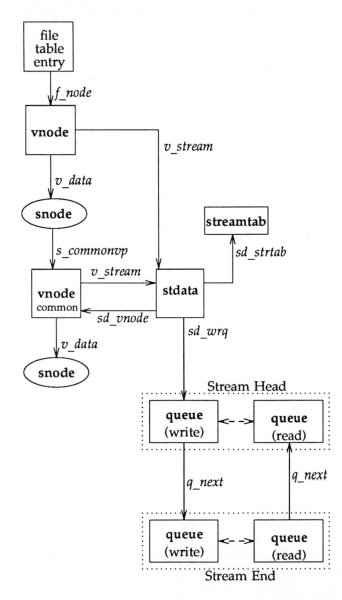

Next, a **queue** structure pair is allocated for the driver. The **queue** limits are initialized to those values specified in the corresponding **module_info** structure. The **queue** processing routines are initialized to those specified by the corresponding **qinit** structure.

Then, the *q_next* values are set so that the Stream head write **queue** points to the driver write **queue** and the driver read **queue** points to the Stream head read **queue**. The *q_next* values at the ends of the Stream are set to null. Finally, the driver open procedure (located via its read **qinit** structure) is called.

If this open is not the initial open of this Stream, the only actions performed are to call the driver open and the open procedures of all pushable modules on the Stream. When a Stream is already open, further opens of the same device will result in the open routines of all modules and the driver on the Stream being called. Note that this is in reverse order from the way a Stream is initially set up. That is, a driver is opened and a module is pushed on a Stream. When a push occurs the module open routine is called. If another open of the same device is made, the open routine of the module will be called followed by the open routine of the driver. This is opposite from the initial order of opens when the Stream is created.

Creating a STREAMS-based Pipe

In addition to opening a STREAMS-based driver, a Stream can be created by creating a pipe [see **pipe**(2)]. Since pipes are not character devices, STREAMS creates and initializes a **streamtab** structure for each end of the pipe. As with modules and drivers, the **streamtab** structure defines the pipe. The *st_rdinit*, however, points to the read **qinit** structure for the Stream head and not for a driver. Similarly, the *st_wdinit* points to the Stream head's write **qinit** structure and not to a driver. The *st_muxrinit* and *st_muxwinit* are initialized to null since a pipe cannot be a multiplexor driver.

When the **pipe** system call is executed, two Streams are created. STREAMS follows the procedures similar to those of opening a driver; however, duplicate data structures are created. That is, two entries are allocated in the user's file table and two **vnodes** are created to represent each end of the pipe, as shown in Figure 3-4. The file table entries are initialized to point to the allocated **vnodes** and each **vnode** is initialized to specify a file of type *FIFO*.

Next, two Stream headers are created from **stdata** data structures and two Stream heads are created from two pairs of **queue** structures. The content of **stdata** and **queue** are initialized with the same values for all pipes.

Each Stream header represents one end of the pipe and it points to the downstream half of each Stream head queue pair. Unlike STREAMS-based devices, however, the downstream portion of the Stream terminates at the upstream portion of the other Stream.

Figure 3-4: Creating STREAMS-based Pipe

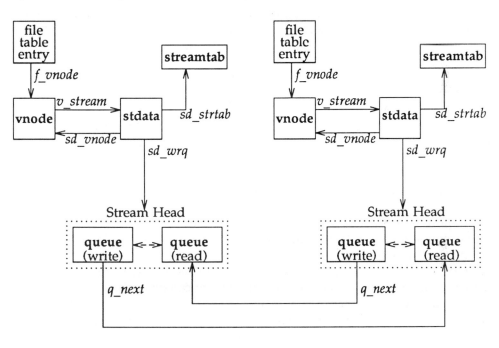

The *q_next* values are set so that the Stream head write **queue** points to the Stream head read **queue** on the other side. The *q_next* values for the Stream head's read **queue** points to null since it terminates the Stream.

Adding and Removing Modules

As part of constructing a Stream, a module can be added (pushed) with an **ioctl** I_PUSH [see **streamio**(7)] system call. The push inserts a module beneath the Stream head. Because of the similarity of STREAMS components, the push operation is similar to the driver open. First, the address of the **qinit** structure for the module is obtained.

Next, STREAMS allocates a pair of **queue** structures and initializes their contents as in the driver open.

Then, *q_next* values are set and modified so that the module is interposed between the Stream head and its neighbor immediately downstream. Finally, the module open procedure (located via **qinit**) is called.

Each push of a module is independent, even in the same Stream. If the same module is pushed more than once on a Stream, there will be multiple occurrences of that module in the Stream. The total number of pushable modules that may be contained on any one Stream is limited by the kernel parameter NSTRPUSH (see Appendix E).

An **ioctl** I_POP [see **streamio**(7)] system call removes (pops) the module immediately below the Stream head. The pop calls the module close procedure. On return from the module close, any messages left on the module's message queues are freed (deallocated). Then, STREAMS connects the Stream head to the component previously below the popped module and deallocates the module's **queue** pair. I_PUSH and I_POP enable a user process to dynamically alter the configuration of a Stream by pushing and popping modules as required. For example, a module may be removed and a new one inserted below the Stream head. Then the original module can be pushed back after the new module has been pushed.

Closing the Stream

The last **close** to a STREAMS file dismantles the Stream. Dismantling consists of popping any modules on the Stream and closing the driver. Before a module is popped, the **close** may delay to allow any messages on the write message queue of the module to be drained by module processing. Similarly, before the driver is closed, the **close** may delay to allow any messages on the write message queue of the driver to be drained by driver processing. If O_NDELAY (or O_NONBLOCK) [see **open**(2)] is clear, **close** will wait up to 15 seconds for each module to drain and up to 15 seconds for the driver to drain. If O_NDELAY (or O_NONBLOCK) is set, the pop is performed immediately and the driver is closed without delay. Messages can remain queued, for example, if flow control is inhibiting execution of the write queue **service** procedure. When all modules are popped and any wait for the driver to drain is completed, the driver close routine is called. On return from the driver close, any messages left on the driver's queues are freed, and the **queue** and **stdata** structures are deallocated.

 NOTE STREAMS frees only the messages contained on a message queue. Any message or data structures used internally by the driver or module must be freed by the driver or module close procedure.

Finally, the user's file table entry and the **vnode** are deallocated and the file is closed.

Stream Construction Example

The following example extends the previous communications device echoing example (see the section "Basic Streams Operations" in Chapter 2) by inserting a module in the Stream. The (hypothetical) module in this example can convert (change case, delete, duplicate) selected alphabetic characters.

Inserting Modules

An advantage of STREAMS over the traditional character I/O mechanism stems from the ability to insert various modules into a Stream to process and manipulate data that pass between a user process and the driver. In the example, the character conversion module is passed a command and a corresponding string of characters by the user. All data passing through the module are inspected for instances of characters in this string; the operation identified by the command is performed on all matching characters. The necessary declarations for this program are shown below:

```
#include <string.h>
#include <fcntl.h>
#include <stropts.h>

#define   BUFLEN    1024

/*
 * These defines would typically be
 * found in a header file for the module
 */
#define   XCASE     1   /* change alphabetic case of char */
#define   DELETE    2   /* delete char */
#define   DUPLICATE 3   /* duplicate char */

main()
{
    char buf[BUFLEN];
    int fd, count;
    struct strioctl strioctl;
```

The first step is to establish a Stream to the communications driver and insert the character conversion module. The following sequence of system calls accomplishes this:

```
    if ((fd = open("/dev/comm/01", O_RDWR)) < 0) {
        perror("open failed");
        exit(1);
    }

    if (ioctl(fd, I_PUSH, "chconv") < 0) {
        perror("ioctl I_PUSH failed");
        exit(2);
    }
```

The I_PUSH **ioctl** call directs the Stream head to insert the character conversion module between the driver and the Stream head, creating the Stream shown in Figure 3-5. As with drivers, this module resides in the kernel and must have been configured into the system before it was booted.

Figure 3-5: Case Converter Module

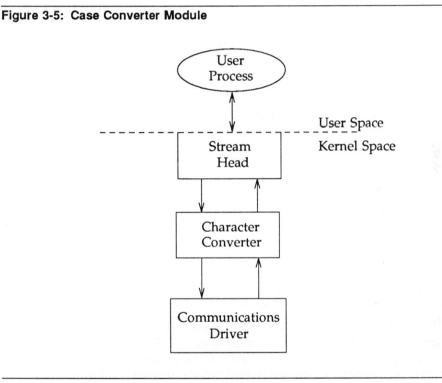

An important difference between STREAMS drivers and modules is illustrated here. Drivers are accessed through a node or nodes in the file system and may be opened just like any other device. Modules, on the other hand, do not occupy a file system node. Instead, they are identified through a separate naming convention, and are inserted into a Stream using I_PUSH. The name of a module is defined by the module developer.

Modules are pushed onto a Stream and removed from a Stream in Last-In-First-Out (LIFO) order. Therefore, if a second module was pushed onto this Stream, it would be inserted between the Stream head and the character conversion module.

Module and Driver Control

The next step in this example is to pass the commands and corresponding strings to the character conversion module. This can be accomplished by issuing **ioctl** calls to the character conversion module as follows:

```
        /* change all uppercase vowels to lowercase */
        strioctl.ic_cmd = XCASE;
        strioctl.ic_timout = 0;                 /* default timeout (15 sec) */
        strioctl.ic_dp = "AEIOU";
        strioctl.ic_len = strlen(strioctl.ic_dp);

        if (ioctl(fd, I_STR, &strioctl) < 0) {
                perror("ioctl I_STR failed");
                exit(3);
        }

        /* delete all instances of the chars 'x' and 'X' */
        strioctl.ic_cmd = DELETE;
        strioctl.ic_dp = "xX";
        strioctl.ic_len = strlen(strioctl.ic_dp);

        if (ioctl(fd, I_STR, &strioctl) < 0) {
                perror("ioctl I_STR failed");
                exit(4);
        }
```

ioctl requests are issued to STREAMS drivers and modules indirectly, using the I_STR **ioctl** call [see **streamio**(7)]. The argument to I_STR must be a pointer to a **strioctl** structure, which specifies the request to be made to a module or driver. This structure is defined in **<stropts.h>** and has the following format:

```
struct strioctl {
    int   ic_cmd;     /* ioctl request */
    int   ic_timout;  /* ACK/NAK timeout */
    int   ic_len;     /* length of data argument */
    char *ic_dp;      /* ptr to data argument */
};
```

where *ic_cmd* identifies the command intended for a module or driver, *ic_timout* specifies the number of seconds an I_STR request should wait for an acknowledgement before timing out, *ic_len* is the number of bytes of data to accompany the request, and *ic_dp* points to that data.

In the example, two separate commands are sent to the character conversion module. The first sets *ic_cmd* to the command XCASE and sends as data the string "AEIOU"; it will convert all uppercase vowels in data passing through the module to lowercase. The second sets *ic_cmd* to the command DELETE and sends as data the string "xX"; it will delete all occurrences of the characters 'x' and 'X' from data passing through the module. For each command, the value of *ic_timout* is set to zero, which specifies the system default timeout value of 15 seconds. The *ic_dp* field points to the beginning of the data for each command; *ic_len* is set to the length of the data.

I_STR is intercepted by the Stream head, which packages it into a message, using information contained in the **strioctl** structure, and sends the message downstream. Any module that does not understand the command in *ic_cmd* will pass the message further downstream. The request will be processed by the module or driver closest to the Stream head that understands the command specified by *ic_cmd*. The **ioctl** call will block up to *ic_timout* seconds, waiting for the target module or driver to respond with either a positive or negative acknowledgement message. If an acknowledgement is not received in *ic_timout* seconds, the **ioctl** call will fail.

 NOTE Only one I_STR request can be active on a Stream at one time. Further requests will block until the active I_STR request is acknowledged and the system call completes.

The **strioctl** structure is also used to retrieve the results, if any, of an I_STR request. If data are returned by the target module or driver, *ic_dp* must point to a buffer large enough to hold that data, and *ic_len* will be set on return to indicate the amount of data returned.

The remainder of this example is identical to the example in Chapter 2:

```
while ((count = read(fd, buf, BUFLEN)) > 0) {
    if (write(fd, buf, count) != count) {
        perror("write failed");
        break;
    }
}
exit(0);
}
```

Notice that the character conversion processing was realized with *no* change to the communications driver.

The **exit** system call will dismantle the Stream before terminating the process. The character conversion module will be removed from the Stream automatically when it is closed. Alternatively, modules may be removed from a Stream using the I_POP **ioctl** call described in **streamio**(7). This call removes the topmost module on the Stream, and enables a user process to alter the configuration of a Stream dynamically, by popping modules as needed.

A few of the important **ioctl** requests supported by STREAMS have been discussed. Several other requests are available to support operations such as determining if a given module exists on the Stream, or flushing the data on a Stream. These requests are described fully in **streamio**(7).

4 STREAMS Processing Routines

Put and Service Procedures
4-1

Put Procedure
4-1

Service Procedure
4-2

An Asynchronous Protocol Stream Example
4-4

Read-Side Processing
4-8

■ Driver Processing
4-8

■ CHARPROC
4-8

■ CANONPROC
4-10

Write-Side Processing
4-10

Analysis
4-11

Put and Service Procedures

The **put** and **service** procedures in the queue are routines that process messages as they transit the queue. The processing is generally performed according to the message type and can result in a modified message, new message(s), or no message. A resultant message, if any, is generally sent in the same direction in which it was received by the queue, but may be sent in either direction. Typically, each **put** procedure places messages on its queue as they arrive, for later processing by the **service** procedure.

A queue will always contain a **put** procedure and may also contain an associated **service** procedure. Having both a **put** and **service** procedure in a queue enables STREAMS to provide the rapid response and the queuing required in multi-user systems.

The **service** and **put** routines pointed at by a queue, and the queues themselves, are not associated with any process. These routines may not sleep if they cannot continue processing, but must instead return. Any information about the current status of the queue must be saved by the routine before returning.

Put Procedure

A **put** procedure is the queue routine that receives messages from the preceding queues in the Stream. Messages are passed between queues by a procedure in one queue calling the **put** procedure contained in the following queue. A call to the **put** procedure in the appropriate direction is generally the only way to pass messages between STREAMS components. There is usually a separate **put** procedure for the read and write queues because of the full-duplex operation of most Streams. However, there can be a single **put** procedure shared between both the read and write queues.

The **put** procedure allows rapid response to certain data and events, such as echoing of input characters. It has higher priority than any scheduled **service** procedure and is associated with immediate, as opposed to deferred, processing of a message. The **put** procedure executes before the scheduled **service** procedure of any queue is executed.

Each STREAMS component accesses the adjacent **put** procedure as a subroutine. For example, consider that *modA*, *modB*, and *modC* are three consecutive components in a Stream, with *modC* connected to the Stream head. If *modA* receives a message to be sent upstream, *modA* processes that message and calls *modB*'s read **put** procedure, which processes it and calls *modC*'s read **put** procedure, which processes it and calls the Stream head's read **put** procedure. Thus, the message will be passed along the Stream in one continuous processing sequence. This sequence has the benefit of completing the entire processing in a short time with low overhead (subroutine calls). On the other hand, if this sequence is lengthy and the processing is implemented on a multi-user system, then this manner of processing may be good for this Stream but may be detrimental for others. Streams may have to wait too long to get their turn, since each **put** procedure is called from the preceding one, and the kernel stack (or interrupt stack) grows with each function call. The possibility of running off the stack exists, thus panicking the system or producing undeterminate results.

Service Procedure

In addition to the **put** procedure, a **service** procedure may be contained in each queue to allow deferred processing of messages. If a queue has both a **put** and **service** procedure, message processing will generally be divided between the procedures. The **put** procedure is always called first, from a preceding queue. After completing its part of the message processing, it arranges for the **service** procedure to be called by passing the message to the putq() routine. putq() does two things: it places the message on the message queue of the queue (see Figure 2-5) and links the queue to the end of the STREAMS scheduling queue. When **putq()** returns to the **put** procedure, the procedure can return or continue to process the message. Some time later, the **service** procedure will be automatically called by the STREAMS scheduler.

The STREAMS scheduler is separate and distinct from the UNIX system process scheduler. It is concerned only with queues linked on the STREAMS scheduling queue. The scheduler calls each **service** procedure of the scheduled queues one at a time in a First-In-First-Out (FIFO) manner.

NOTE   The scheduling of queue **service** routines is machine dependent. However, they are guaranteed to run before returning to user level.

STREAMS utilities deliver the messages to the processing **service** routine in the FIFO manner within each priority class (high priority, priority band, ordinary), because the **service** procedure is unaware of the message priority and simply receives the next message. The **service** routine receives control in the order it was scheduled. When the **service** routine receives control, it may encounter multiple messages on its message queue. This buildup can occur if there is a long interval between the time a message is queued by a **put** procedure and the time that the STREAMS scheduler calls the associated **service** routine. In this interval, there can be multiple calls to the **put** procedure causing multiple messages to build up. The **service** procedure always processes all messages on its message queue unless prevented by flow control.

Terminal output and input erase and kill processing, for example, would typically be performed in a **service** procedure because this type of processing does not have to be as timely as echoing. Use of a **service** procedure also allows processing time to be more evenly spread among multiple Streams. As with the **put** procedure there can be a separate **service** procedure for each queue in a STREAMS component or a single procedure used by both the read and write queues.

Rules that should be observed in **put** and **service** procedures are listed in Chapter 7.

An Asynchronous Protocol Stream Example

In the following example, our computer runs the UNIX system and supports different kinds of asynchronous terminals, each logging in on its own port. The port hardware is limited in function; for example, it detects and reports line and modem status, but does not check parity.

Communications software support for these terminals is provided via a STREAMS based asynchronous protocol. The protocol includes a variety of options that are set when a terminal operator dials in to log on. The options are determined by a STREAMS user process, *getstrm*, which analyzes data sent to it through a series of dialogs (prompts and responses) between the process and terminal operator.

The process sets the terminal options for the duration of the connection by pushing modules onto the Stream or by sending control messages to cause changes in modules (or in the device driver) already on the Stream. The options supported include:

- ASCII or EBCDIC character codes

- For ASCII code, the parity (odd, even or none)

- Echo or not echo input characters

- Canonical input and output processing or transparent (raw) character handling

These options are set with the following modules:

CHARPROC   Provides input character processing functions, including dynamically settable (via control messages passed to the module) character echo and parity checking. The module's default settings are to echo characters and not check character parity.

CANONPROC   Performs canonical processing on ASCII characters upstream and downstream (note that this performs some processing in a different manner from the standard UNIX system character I/O tty subsystem).

ASCEBC   Translates EBCDIC code to ASCII upstream and ASCII to EBCDIC downstream.

At system initialization a user process, *getstrm*, is created for each tty port. *getstrm* opens a Stream to its port and pushes the CHARPROC module onto the Stream by use of an **ioctl** I_PUSH command. Then, the process issues a **getmsg** system call to the Stream and sleeps until a message reaches the Stream head. The Stream is now in its idle state.

The initial idle Stream, shown in Figure 4-1, contains only one pushable module, CHARPROC. The device driver is a limited function raw tty driver connected to a limited-function communication port. The driver and port transparently transmit and receive one unbuffered character at a time.

Figure 4-1: Idle Stream Configuration for Example

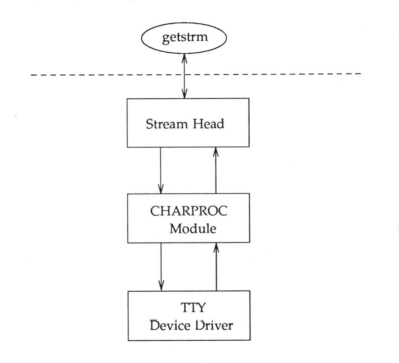

Upon receipt of initial input from a tty port, *getstrm* establishes a connection with the terminal, analyzes the option requests, verifies them, and issues STREAMS system calls to set the options. After setting up the options, *getstrm* creates a user application process. Later, when the user terminates that application, *getstrm* restores the Stream to its idle state by use of similar system calls.

The following figure continues the example and associates kernel operations with user-level system calls. As a result of initializing operations and pushing a module, the Stream for port one has the following configuration:

Figure 4-2: Operational Stream for Example

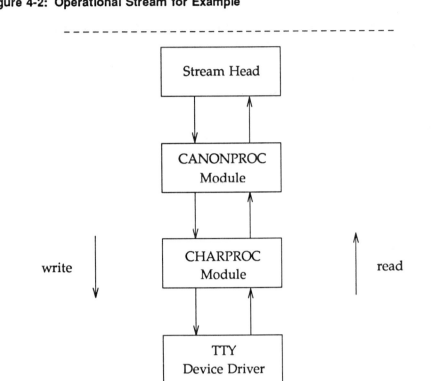

As mentioned before, the upstream queue is also referred to as the read queue reflecting the message flow direction. Correspondingly, downstream is referred to as the write queue.

Read-Side Processing

In our example, read-side processing consists of driver processing, CHARPROC processing, and CANONPROC processing.

Driver Processing

The user process has been blocked on the **getmsg**(2) system call while waiting for a message to reach the Stream head, and the device driver independently waits for input of a character from the port hardware or for a message from upstream. Upon receipt of an input character interrupt from the port, the driver places the associated character in an M_DATA message, allocated previously. Then, the driver sends the message to the CHARPROC module by calling CHARPROC's upstream **put** procedure. On return from CHARPROC, the driver calls the **allocb**() utility routine to get another message for the next character.

CHARPROC

CHARPROC has both **put** and **service** procedures on its read-side. In the example, the other queues in the modules also have both procedures:

Figure 4-3: Module Put and Service Procedures

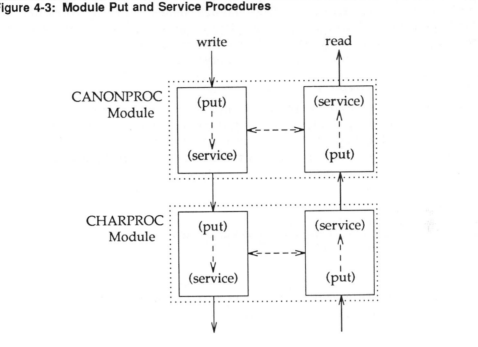

When the driver calls CHARPROC's read queue **put** procedure, the procedure checks private data flags in the queue. In this case, the flags indicate that echoing is to be performed (recall that echoing is optional and that we are working with port hardware which can not automatically echo). CHARPROC causes the echo to be transmitted back to the terminal by first making a copy of the message with a STREAMS utility routine. Then, CHARPROC uses another utility routine to obtain the address of its own write queue. Finally, the CHARPROC read **put** procedure calls its write **put** procedure and passes it the message copy. The write procedure sends the message to the driver to effect the echo and then returns to the read procedure.

This part of read-side processing is implemented with **put** procedures so that the entire processing sequence occurs as an extension of the driver input character interrupt. The CHARPROC read and write **put** procedures appear as subroutines (nested in the case of the write procedure) to the driver. This manner of processing is intended to produce the character echo in a minimal time frame.

After returning from echo processing, the CHARPROC read **put** procedure checks another of its private data flags and determines that parity checking should be performed on the input character. Parity should most reasonably be checked as part of echo processing. However, for this example, parity is checked only when the characters are sent upstream. This relaxes the timing in which the checking must occur, that is, it can be deferred along with the canonical processing. CHARPROC uses **putq()** to schedule the (original) message for parity check processing by its read **service** procedure. When the CHARPROC read **service** procedure is complete, it forwards the message to the read **put** procedure of CANONPROC. Note that if parity checking was not required, the CHARPROC **put** procedure would call the CANONPROC **put** procedure directly.

CANONPROC

CANONPROC performs canonical processing. As implemented, all read queue processing is performed in its **service** procedure so that CANONPROC's **put** procedure simply calls **putq()** to schedule the message for its read **service** procedure and then exits. The **service** procedure extracts the character from the message buffer and places it in the "line buffer" contained in another M_DATA message it is constructing. Then, the message which contained the single character is returned to the buffer pool. If the character received was not an end-of-line, CANONPROC exits. Otherwise, a complete line has been assembled and CANONPROC sends the message upstream to the Stream head which unblocks the user process from the **getmsg(2)** call and passes it the contents of the message.

Write-Side Processing

The write-side of this Stream carries two kinds of messages from the user process: **ioctl** messages for CHARPROC, and M_DATA messages to be output to the terminal.

ioctl messages are sent downstream as a result of an **ioctl(2)** system call. When CHARPROC receives an **ioctl** message type, it processes the message contents to modify internal flags and then uses a utility routine to send an acknowledgement message upstream to the Stream head. The Stream head acts on the acknowledgement message by unblocking the user from the **ioctl**.

For terminal output, it is presumed that M_DATA messages, sent by **write**(2) system calls, contain multiple characters. In general, STREAMS returns to the user process immediately after processing the **write** call so that the process may send additional messages. Flow control will eventually block the sending process. The messages can queue on the write-side of the driver because of character transmission timing. When a message is received by the driver's write **put** procedure, the procedure will use **putq**() to place the message on its write-side **service** message queue if the driver is currently transmitting a previous message buffer. However, there is generally no write queue **service** procedure in a device driver. Driver output interrupt processing takes the place of scheduling and performs the **service** procedure functions, removing messages from the queue.

Analysis

For reasons of efficiency, a module implementation would generally avoid placing one character per message and using separate routines to echo and parity check each character, as was done in this example. Nevertheless, even this design yields potential benefits. Consider a case where alternate, more intelligent, port hardware was substituted. If the hardware processed multiple input characters and performed the echo and parity checking functions of CHARPROC, then the new driver could be implemented to present the same interface as CHARPROC. Other modules such as CANONPROC could continue to be used without modification.

5 Messages

Messages   5-1
Message Types   5-1
Expedited Data   5-3

Message Structure   5-4
Message Linkage   5-6
Sending/Receiving Messages   5-8
Control of Stream Head Processing   5-12
  ■ Read Options   5-13
  ■ Write Offset   5-14

Message Queues and Message Priority   5-15
The queue Structure   5-19
  ■ Using queue Information   5-21
  ■ Queue Flags   5-21
  ■ The equeue Structure   5-22
  ■ The qband Structure   5-22
  ■ Using equeue and qband Information   5-24
Message Processing   5-26
  ■ Flow Control   5-28

Service Interfaces   5-34
Service Interface Benefits   5-35
Service Interface Library Example   5-38
  ■ Accessing the Service Provider   5-40
  ■ Closing the Service Provider   5-43
  ■ Sending Data to Service Provider   5-44

- Receiving Data   5-45
- Module Service Interface Example   5-47

Message Allocation and Freeing   5-54
Recovering From No Buffers   5-57

Extended STREAMS Buffers   5-60

Messages

Messages are the means of communication within a Stream. All input and output under STREAMS is based on messages. The objects passed between Streams components are pointers to messages. All messages in STREAMS use two data structures to refer to the data in the message. These data structures describe the type of the message and contain pointers to the data of the message, as well as other information. Messages are sent through a Stream by successive calls to the **put** routine of each queue in the Stream. Messages may be generated by a driver, a module, or by the Stream head.

Message Types

There are several different STREAMS messages (see Appendix B) and they are defined in **sys/stream.h**. The messages differ in their intended purpose and their queueing priority. The contents of certain message types can be transferred between a process and a Stream by use of system calls.

Below, the message types are briefly described and classified according to their queueing priority.

Ordinary Messages (also called **normal messages**):

- M_BREAK   Request to a Stream driver to send a "break"
- M_CTL   Control/status request used for inter-module communication
- M_DATA   User data message for I/O system calls
- M_DELAY   Request a real-time delay on output
- M_IOCTL   Control/status request generated by a Stream head
- M_PASSFP   File pointer passing message
- M_PROTO   Protocol control information
- M_RSE   Reserved for internal use
- M_SETOPTS   Set options at the Stream head, sent upstream
- M_SIG   Signal sent from a module/driver to a user

High Priority Messages:

- M_COPYIN   Copy in data for transparent **ioctls**, sent upstream
- M_COPYOUT   Copy out data for transparent **ioctls**, sent upstream
- M_ERROR   Report downstream error condition, sent upstream
- M_FLUSH   Flush module queue
- M_HANGUP   Set a Stream head hangup condition, sent upstream
- M_IOCACK   Positive **ioctl**(2) acknowledgement
- M_IOCDATA   Data for transparent **ioctls**, sent downstream
- M_IOCNAK   Negative **ioctl**(2) acknowledgement
- M_PCPROTO   Protocol control information
- M_PCRSE   Reserved for internal use
- M_PCSIG   Signal sent from a module/driver to a user
- M_READ   Read notification, sent downstream
- M_START   Restart stopped device output
- M_STARTI   Restart stopped device input
- M_STOP   Suspend output
- M_STOPI   Suspend input

 Transparent **ioctls** support applications developed prior to the introduction of STREAMS.

Expedited Data

The Open Systems Interconnection (OSI) Reference Model developed by the International Standards Organization (ISO) and International Telegraph and Telephone Consultative Committee (CCITT) provides an international standard seven-layer architecture for the development of communication protocols. AT&T adheres to this standard and also supports the Transmission Control Protocol and Internet Protocol (TCP/IP).

OSI and TCP/IP support the transport of expedited data (see note below) for transmission of high priority, emergency data. This is useful for flow control, congestion control, routing, and various applications where immediate delivery of data is necessary.

Expedited data are mainly for exceptional cases and transmission of control signals. These are emergency data that are processed immediately, ahead of normal data. These messages are placed ahead of normal data on the queue, but after STREAMS high priority messages and after any expedited data already on the queue.

Expedited data flow control is unaffected by the flow control constraints of normal data transfer. Expedited data have their own flow control because they can easily run the system out of buffers if their flow is unrestricted.

Drivers and modules define separate high and low water marks for priority band data flow. (Water marks are defined for each queue and they indicate the upper and lower limit of bytes that can be contained on the queue; see M_SETOPTS in Appendix B). The default water marks for priority band data and normal data are the same. The Stream head also ensures that incoming priority band data are not blocked by normal data already on the queue. This is accomplished by associating a priority with the messages. This priority implies a certain ordering of the messages in the queue. (Message queues and priorities are discussed later in this chapter.)

 NOTE Within the STREAMS mechanism and in this guide expedited data are also referred to as priority band data.

Message Structure

All messages are composed of one or more message blocks. A message block is a linked triplet of two structures and a variable length data buffer. The structures are a message block (**msgb**) and a data block (**datab**). The data buffer is a location in memory where the data of a message are stored.

```
#ifdef _STYPES
struct    msgb {
          struct    msgb     *b_next;  /* next message on queue */
          struct    msgb     *b_prev;  /* previous message on queue */
          struct    msgb     *b_cont;  /* next message block of message */
          unsigned  char     *b_rptr;  /* first unread data byte in buffer */
          unsigned  char     *b_wptr;  /* first unwritten data byte in buffer  */
          struct    datab    *b_datap; /* data block */
};
#define b_band    b_datap->db_band
#define b_flag    b_datap->db_flag

#else
struct    msgb {
          struct    msgb     *b_next;  /* next message on queue */
          struct    msgb     *b_prev;  /* previous message on queue */
          struct    msgb     *b_cont;  /* next message block of message */
          unsigned  char     *b_rptr;  /* first unread data byte in buffer */
          unsigned  char     *b_wptr;  /* first unwritten data byte in buffer  */
          struct    datab    *b_datap; /* data block */
          unsigned  char     b_band;   /* message priority */
          unsigned  char     b_pad1;
          unsigned  short    b_flag;   /* see below - Message flags */
          long               b_pad2;
};
#endif    /* _STYPES */
typedef struct msgb mblk_t;

/* Message flags. These are interpreted by the Stream head. */
#define MSGMARK      0x01                /* last byte of message is "marked" */
#define MSGNOLOOP    0x02                /* don't loop message around to */
                                        /* write-side of Stream */
#define MSGDELIM     0x04                /* message is delimited */
```

```
#ifdef _STYPES

struct datab {
    union {
        struct datab     *freep;
        struct free_rtn *frtnp;
    } db_f;                             /* used internally */
        unsigned char      *db_base;  /* first byte of buffer */
        unsigned char      *db_lim;   /* last byte+1 of buffer */
        unsigned char       db_ref;   /* message count pointing to this block */
        unsigned char       db_type;  /* message type */
        unsigned char       db_band;  /* message priority, determines where a
                                         message is placed when enqueued */
        unsigned char       db_iswhat;/* status of message/data/buffer triplet */
        unsigned int        db_size;  /* used internally */
        unsigned short      db_flag;  /* data block flag */
        unsigned short      db_pad;
        caddr_t             db_msgaddr;/* triplet message header pointing to datab */
};

#else

struct datab {
    union {
        struct datab     *freep;
        struct free_rtn *frtnp;
    } db_f;                             /* used internally */
        unsigned char      *db_base;  /* first byte of buffer */
        unsigned char      *db_lim;   /* last byte+1 of buffer */
        unsigned char       db_ref;   /* message count pointing to this block */
        unsigned char       db_type;  /* message type */
        unsigned char       db_iswhat;/* status of message/dat buffer triplet */
        unsigned int        db_size;  /* used internally */
        caddr_t             db_msgaddr;/* triplet message header pointing to datab */
        long                db_filler; /* reserved for future use */
};

#endif   /* _STYPES */

#define db_freep db_f.freep
#define db_frtnp db_f.frtnp

typedef struct datab dblk_t;
typedef struct free_rtn frtn_t;
```

UNIX System V Release 4.0 includes a feature called Expanded Fundamental Types (EFT) that does not support previously designed modules and drivers. If the system supports EFT, a variable _STYPES is defined and different data structure definitions are used. If the system must maintain binary compatibility with existing modules and drivers _STYPES should not be defined. (Appendix A includes several STREAMS data structures.)

If the system does not support the Expanded Fundamental Types (non-EFT) feature, the message priority band is stored in the data block. Conceptually the band belongs in the message block since it is associated with the message and not just with the data. However, the size of a message block is visible to modules and drivers, so the band is placed in the data block instead. Modules and drivers should have no knowledge of the size of the data block.

If the system supports the Expanded Fundamental Types feature, the message priority is stored in the message block. To increase the portability of modules and drivers between EFT and non-EFT systems, the field *b_band* is defined. This field is the priority band. It is defined as b_datap->db_band on non-EFT systems.

The field *b_band* determines where the message is placed when it is enqueued using the STREAMS utility routines. This field has no meaning for high priority messages and is set to zero for these messages. When a message is allocated via **allocb**(), the *b_band* field will be initially set to zero. Modules and drivers may set this field if so desired.

Message Linkage

The message block is used to link messages on a message queue, link message blocks to form a message, and manage the reading and writing of the associated data buffer. The *b_rptr* and *b_wptr* fields in the **msgb** structure are used to locate the data currently contained in the buffer. As shown in Figure 5-1, the message block (**mblk_t**) points to the data block of the triplet. The data block contains the message type, buffer limits, and control variables. STREAMS allocates message buffer blocks of varying sizes. *db_base* and *db_lim* are the fixed beginning and end (+1) of the buffer.

A message consists of one or more linked message blocks. Multiple message blocks in a message can occur, for example, because of buffer size limitations, or as the result of processing that expands the message. When a message is composed of multiple message blocks, the type associated with the first message block determines the message type, regardless of the types of the attached message blocks.

Figure 5-1: Message Form and Linkage

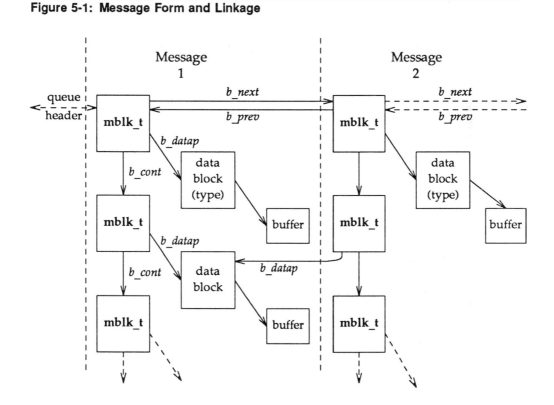

A message may occur singly, as when it is processed by a **put** procedure, or it may be linked on the message queue in a queue, generally waiting to be processed by the **service** procedure. Message 2, as shown in Figure 5-1, links to message 1.

Note that a data block in message 1 is shared between message 1 and another message. Multiple message blocks can point to the same data block to conserve storage and to avoid copying overhead. For example, the same data block, with associated buffer, may be referenced in two messages, from separate modules that implement separate protocol levels. (Figure 5-1 illustrates the concept, but data blocks would not typically be shared by messages on the same queue). The buffer can be retransmitted, if required because of errors or timeouts, from either protocol level without replicating the data. Data block sharing is accomplished by means of a utility routine [see **dupmsg**() in Appendix C]. STREAMS maintains a count of the message blocks sharing a data block in the *db_ref* field.

STREAMS provides utility routines and macros, specified in Appendix C, to assist in managing messages and message queues, and to assist in other areas of module and driver development. A utility routine should always be used when operating on a message queue or accessing the message storage pool. If messages are manipulated on the queue without using the STREAMS utilities, the message ordering may become confused and lead to inconsistent results.

Sending/Receiving Messages

Most message types can be generated by modules and drivers. A few are reserved for the Stream head. The most commonly used messages are M_DATA, M_PROTO, and M_PCPROTO. These messages can also be passed between a process and the topmost module in a Stream, with the same message boundary alignment maintained on both sides of the kernel. This allows a user process to function, to some degree, as a module above the Stream and maintain a service interface. M_PROTO and M_PCPROTO messages are intended to carry service interface information among modules, drivers, and user processes. Some message types can only be used within a Stream and cannot be sent or received from user level.

Modules and drivers do not interact directly with any system calls except **open**(2) and **close**(2). The Stream head handles all message translation and passing between user processes and STREAMS components. Message transfer between processes and the Stream head can occur in different forms. For

example, M_DATA and M_PROTO messages can be transferred in their direct
form by the **getmsg**(2) and **putmsg**(2) system calls. Alternatively, **write**(2)
causes one or more M_DATA messages to be created from the data buffer supplied in the call. M_DATA messages received at the Stream head will be consumed by **read**(2) and copied into the user buffer. As another example, M_SIG
causes the Stream head to send a signal to a process.

Any module or driver can send any message in either direction on a Stream.
However, based on their intended use in STREAMS and their treatment by the
Stream head, certain messages can be categorized as upstream, downstream, or
bidirectional. M_DATA, M_PROTO, or M_PCPROTO messages, for example,
can be sent in both directions. Other message types are intended to be sent
upstream to be processed only by the Stream head. Messages intended to be
sent downstream are silently discarded if received by the Stream head.

STREAMS enables modules to create messages and pass them to neighboring
modules. However, the **read**(2) and **write**(2) system calls are not sufficient to
enable a user process to generate and receive all such messages. First, **read** and
write are byte-stream oriented with no concept of message boundaries. To support service interfaces, the message boundary of each service primitive must be
preserved so that the beginning and end of each primitive can be located. Also,
read and **write** offer only one buffer to the user for transmitting and receiving
STREAMS messages. If control information and data were placed in a single
buffer, the user would have to parse the contents of the buffer to separate the
data from the control information.

The **putmsg** system call enables a user to create messages and send them downstream. The user supplies the contents of the control and data parts of the message in two separate buffers. The **getmsg** system call retrieves M_DATA or
M_PROTO messages from a Stream and places the contents into two user
buffers.

The format of **putmsg** is as follows:

```
int putmsg(
        int fd,
        struct strbuf *ctlptr,
        struct strbuf *dataptr,
        int flags);
```

fd identifies the Stream to which the message will be passed, *ctlptr* and *dataptr* identify the control and data parts of the message, and *flags* may be used to specify that a high priority message (M_PCPROTO) should be sent. When a control part is present, setting *flags* to 0 generates an M_PROTO message. If *flags* is set to RS_HIPRI, an M_PCPROTO message is generated.

 NOTE The Stream head guarantees that the control part of a message generated by **putmsg**(2) is at least 64 bytes in length. This promotes reusability of the buffer. When the buffer is a reasonable size, modules and drivers may reuse the buffer for other headers.

The **strbuf** structure is used to describe the control and data parts of a message, and has the following format:

```
struct strbuf {
    int   maxlen;    /* maximum buffer length */
    int   len;       /* length of data */
    char  *buf;      /* pointer to buffer */
}
```

buf points to a buffer containing the data and *len* specifies the number of bytes of data in the buffer. *maxlen* specifies the maximum number of bytes the given buffer can hold, and is only meaningful when retrieving information into the buffer using **getmsg**.

The **getmsg** system call retrieves M_DATA, M_PROTO, or M_PCPROTO messages available at the Stream head, and has the following format:

```
int getmsg(
        int fd,
        struct strbuf *ctlptr,
        struct strbuf *dataptr,
        int *flagsp);
```

The arguments to **getmsg** are the same as those of **putmsg** except that the *flagsp* parameter is a pointer to an *int*.

putpmsg() and **getpmsg**() [see **putmsg**(2) and **getmsg**(2)] support multiple bands of data flow. They are analogous to the system calls **putmsg** and **getmsg**. The extra parameter is the priority band of the message.

putpmsg() has the following interface:

```
int putpmsg(
        int fd,
        struct strbuf *ctlptr,
        struct strbuf *dataptr,
        int band,
        int flags);
```

The parameter *band* is the priority band of the message to put downstream. The valid values for *flags* are MSG_HIPRI and MSG_BAND. MSG_BAND and MSG_HIPRI are mutually exclusive. MSG_HIPRI generates a high priority message (M_PCPROTO) and *band* is ignored. MSG_BAND causes an M_PROTO or M_DATA message to be generated and sent down the priority band specified by *band*. The valid range for *band* is from 0 to 255 inclusive.

The call

```
    putpmsg(fd, ctlptr, dataptr, 0, MSG_BAND);
```

is equivalent to the the system call

```
    putmsg(fd, ctlptr, dataptr, 0);
```

and the call

```
    putpmsg(fd, ctlptr, dataptr, 0, MSG_HIPRI);
```

is equivalent to the system call

```
    putmsg(fd, ctlptr, dataptr, RS_HIPRI);
```

If MSG_HIPRI is set and *band* is non-zero, **putpmsg**() fails with EINVAL.

getpmsg() has the following format:

```
int getpmsg(
      int fd,
      struct strbuf *ctlptr,
      struct strbuf *dataptr,
      int *bandp,
      int *flagsp);
```

bandp is the priority band of the message. This system call retrieves a message from the Stream. If *flagsp* is set to MSG_HIPRI, **getpmsg**() attempts to retrieve a high priority message. If MSG_BAND is set, **getpmsg**() tries to retrieve a message from priority band *bandp* or higher. If MSG_ANY is set, the first message on the Stream head read queue is retrieved. These three flags (MSG_HIPRI, MSG_BAND, and MSG_ANY) are mutually exclusive. On return, if a high priority message was retrieved, *flagsp* is set to MSG_HIPRI and *bandp* is set to 0. Otherwise, *flagsp* is set to MSG_BAND and *bandp* is set to the band of the message retrieved.

The call

```
int band = 0;
int flags = MSG_ANY;
getpmsg(fd, ctlptr, dataptr, &band, &flags);
```

is equivalent to

```
int flags = 0;
getmsg(fd, ctlptr, dataptr, &flags);
```

If MSG_HIPRI is set and *bandp* is non-zero, **getpmsg**() fails with EINVAL.

Control of Stream Head Processing

The M_SETOPTS message allows a driver or module to exercise control over certain Stream head processing. An M_SETOPTS can be sent upstream at any time. The Stream head responds to the message by altering the processing associated with certain system calls. The options to be modified are specified by the contents of the **stroptions** structure (see Appendix A) contained in the message.

Six Stream head characteristics can be modified. Four characteristics correspond to fields contained in **queue** (min/max packet sizes and high/low water marks). The other two are discussed here.

Read Options

The value for read options (*so_readopt*) corresponds to two sets of three modes a user can set via the I_SRDOPT **ioctl** [see **streamio**(7)] call. The first set deals with data and message boundaries:

byte-stream (RNORM)

> The **read**(2) call completes when the byte count is satisfied, the Stream head read queue becomes empty, or a zero length message is encountered. In the last case, the zero length message is put back on the queue. A subsequent **read** will return 0 bytes.

message non-discard (RMSGN)

> The **read**(2) call completes when the byte count is satisfied or at a message boundary, whichever comes first. Any data remaining in the message are put back on the Stream head read queue.

message discard (RMSGD)

> The **read**(2) call completes when the byte count is satisfied or at a message boundary. Any data remaining in the message are discarded.

Byte-stream mode approximately models pipe data transfer. Message non-discard mode approximately models a TTY in canonical mode.

The second set deals with the treatment of protocol messages by the **read**(2) system call:

normal protocol (RPROTNORM)

> The **read**(2) call fails with EBADMSG if an M_PROTO or M_PCPROTO message is at the front of the Stream head read queue. This is the default operation protocol.

protocol discard (RPROTDIS)

> The **read**(2) call will discard any M_PROTO or M_PCPROTO blocks in a message, delivering the M_DATA blocks to the user.

protocol data (RPROTDAT)

> The **read**(2) call converts the M_PROTO and M_PCPROTO message blocks to M_DATA blocks, treating the entire message as data.

Write Offset

The value for write offset (*so_wroff*) is a hook to allow more efficient data handling. It works as follows: In every data message generated by a **write**(2) system call and in the first M_DATA block of the data portion of every message generated by a **putmsg**(2) call, the Stream head will leave *so_wroff* bytes of space at the beginning of the message block. Expressed as a C language construct:

$$bp\text{->}b\_rptr = bp\text{->}b\_datap\text{->}db\_base + \text{write offset.}$$

The write offset value must be smaller than the maximum STREAMS message size, STRMSGSZ (see the section titled "Tunable Parameters" in Appendix E). In certain cases (e.g., if a buffer large enough to hold the offset+data is not currently available), the write offset might not be included in the block. To handle all possibilities, modules and drivers should not assume that the offset exists in a message, but should always check the message.

The intended use of write offset is to leave room for a module or a driver to place a protocol header before user data in the message rather than by allocating and prepending a separate message.

Message Queues and Message Priority

Message queues grow when the STREAMS scheduler is delayed from calling a **service** procedure because of system activity, or when the procedure is blocked by flow control. When called by the scheduler the **service** procedure processes enqueued messages in a First-In-First-Out (FIFO) manner. However, expedited data support and certain conditions require that associated messages (e.g., an M_ERROR) reach their Stream destination as rapidly as possible. This is accomplished by associating priorities to the messages. These priorities imply a certain ordering of messages on the queue as shown in Figure 5-2. Each message has a priority band associated with it. Ordinary messages have a priority of zero. High priority messages are high priority by nature of their message type. Their priority band is ignored. By convention, they are not affected by flow control. The **putq()** utility routine places high priority messages at the head of the message queue followed by priority band messages (expedited data) and ordinary messages.

Figure 5-2: Message Ordering on a Queue

normal band 0 messages	priority band 1 messages	priority band 2 messages	. . . .	priority band n messages	high priority messages

tail   head

When a message is queued, it is placed after the messages of the same priority already on the queue (i.e., FIFO within their order of queueing). This affects the flow control parameters associated with the band of the same priority. Message priorities range from 0 (normal) to 255 (highest). This provides up to 256 bands of message flow within a Stream. Expedited data can be implemented with one extra band of flow (priority band 1) of data. This is shown in Figure 5-3.

Figure 5-3: Message Ordering with One Priority Band

	normal (band 0) messages	expedited (band 1) messages	high priority messages	
tail				head

High priority messages are not subject to flow control. When they are queued by **putq()**, the associated queue is always scheduled (in the same manner as any queue; following all other queues currently scheduled). When the **service** procedure is called by the scheduler, the procedure uses **getq()** to retrieve the first message on queue, which will be a high priority message, if present. **Service** procedures must be implemented to act on high priority messages immediately. The above mechanisms—priority message queueing, absence of flow control, and immediate processing by a procedure—result in rapid transport of high priority messages between the originating and destination components in the Stream.

Since the priority band information is contained in the data block on non-EFT systems, care must be taken if a message is duplicated via **dupb()** or **dupmsg()**. This could lead to the possibility that a message may be out of order on the queue. For example, a module may want take a message off its queue, duplicate it, and put the original message back on its queue. It may then pass the new message on to the next module. If the priority band of the new message is changed somewhere else on the Stream, the original message will be out of order on the queue. Therefore, if the reference count of the message is greater than one, it is recommended that the module copy the message via **copymsg()**, free the duplicated message, and then change the priority of the copied message.

Several routines are provided to aid users in controlling each priority band of data flow. These routines are flushband(), bcanput(), strqget(), and strqset(). The **flushband()** routine is discussed in the section titled "Flush Handling" in Chapter 7, the **bcanput()** routine is discussed under "Flow Control" later in this chapter, and the other two routines are described next. Appendix C also has a description of these routines.

The **strqget()** routine allows modules and drivers to obtain information about a queue or particular band of the queue. This provides a way to insulate the STREAMS data structures from the modules and drivers. The format of the routine is:

```
int strqget (q, what, pri, valp)
     register queue_t    *q;
     qfields_t   what;
     register unsigned char   pri;
     long    *valp;
```

The information is returned in the *long* referenced by *valp*. The fields that can be obtained are defined by the following:

```
typedef enum qfields {
        QHIWAT  = 0, /* q_hiwat or qb_hiwat */
        QLOWAT  = 1, /* q_lowat or qb_lowat */
        QMAXPSZ = 2, /* q_maxpsz */
        QMINPSZ = 3, /* q_minpsz */
        QCOUNT  = 4, /* q_count or qb_count */
        QFIRST  = 5, /* q_first or qb_first */
        QLAST   = 6, /* q_last or qb_last */
        QFLAG   = 7, /* q_flag or qb_flag */
        QBAD    = 8
} qfields_t;
```

This routine returns 0 on success and an error number on failure.

The routine **strqset()** allows modules and drivers to change information about a queue or particular band of the queue. This also insulates the STREAMS data structures from the modules and drivers. Its format is:

```
int strqset (q, what, pri, val)
     register queue_t    *q;
     qfields_t   what;
     register unsigned char   pri;
     long    val;
```

The updated information is provided by *val*. **strqset()** returns 0 on success and an error number on failure. If the field is intended to be read-only, then the error EPERM is returned and the field is left unchanged. The following fields are currently read-only: QCOUNT, QFIRST, QLAST, and QFLAG.

The **ioctls** I_FLUSHBAND, I_CKBAND, I_GETBAND, I_CANPUT, and I_ATMARK support multiple bands of data flow. The **ioctl** I_FLUSHBAND allows a user to flush a particular band of messages. It is discussed in more detail in the section titled "Flush Handling" in Chapter 7.

The **ioctl** I_CKBAND allows a user to check if a message of a given priority exists on the Stream head read queue. Its interface is:

```
ioctl(fd, I_CKBAND, pri);
```

This returns 1 if a message of priority *pri* exists on the Stream head read queue and 0 if no message of priority *pri* exists. If an error occurs, -1 is returned. Note that *pri* should be of type *int*.

The **ioctl** I_GETBAND allows a user to check the priority of the first message on the Stream head read queue. The interface is:

```
ioctl(fd, I_GETBAND, prip);
```

This results in the integer referenced by *prip* being set to the priority band of the message on the front of the Stream head read queue.

The **ioctl** I_CANPUT allows a user to check if a certain band is writable. Its interface is:

```
ioctl(fd, I_CANPUT, pri);
```

The return value is 0 if the priority band *pri* is flow controlled, 1 if the band is writable, and -1 on error.

The field *b_flag* of the **msgb** structure can have a flag MSGMARK that allows a module or driver to *mark* a message. This is used to support TCP's (Transport Control Protocol) ability to indicate to the user the last byte of out-of-band data. Once *marked*, a message sent to the Stream head causes the Stream head to remember the message. A user may check to see if the message on the front of its Stream head read queue is *marked* or not with the I_ATMARK **ioctl**. If a user is reading data from the Stream head and there are multiple messages on the read queue, and one of those messages is *marked*, the **read**(2) terminates when it reaches the *marked* message and returns the data only up to that *marked* message. The rest of the data may be obtained with successive reads.

The **ioctl** I_ATMARK has the following format:

```
ioctl(fd, I_ATMARK, flag);
```

where *flag* may be either ANYMARK or LASTMARK. ANYMARK indicates that the user merely wants to check if the message is *marked*. LASTMARK indicates that the user wants to see if the message is the only one *marked* on the queue. If the test succeeds, 1 is returned. On failure, 0 is returned. If an error occurs, -1 is returned.

The queue Structure

Service procedures, message queues, message priority, and basic flow control are all intertwined in STREAMS. A queue will generally not use its message queue if there is no **service** procedure in the queue. The function of a **service** procedure is to process messages on its queue. Message priority and flow control are associated with message queues.

The operation of a queue revolves around the **queue** structure:

```
#ifdef   _STYPES

struct queue {
    struct qinit     *q_qinfo;     /* procedures and limits for queue */
    struct msgb      *q_first;     /* head of message queue for this queue */
    struct msgb      *q_last;      /* tail of message queue for this queue */
    struct queue     *q_next;      /* next queue in Stream*/
    struct equeue    *q_eq;        /* pointer to an extended queue structure */
    _VOID            *q_ptr;       /* to private data structure */
    ushort           q_count;      /* number of bytes in queue */
    ushort           q_flag;       /* queue state */
    short            q_minpsz;     /* min packet size accepted by this module */
    short            q_maxpsz;     /* max packet size accepted by this module */
    ushort           q_hiwat;      /* queue high water mark for flow control */
    ushort           q_lowat;      /* queue low water mark for flow control */
};

#else

struct queue {
    struct qinit     *q_qinfo;     /* procedures and limits for queue */
    struct msgb      *q_first;     /* head of message queue for this queue */
    struct msgb      *q_last;      /* tail of message queue for this queue */
    struct queue     *q_next;      /* next queue in Stream*/
    struct queue     *q_link;      /* to next queue for scheduling */
    _VOID            *q_ptr;       /* to private data structure */
    ulong            q_count;      /* number of bytes in queue */
    ulong            q_flag;       /* queue state */
    long             q_minpsz;     /* min packet size accepted by this module */
    long             q_maxpsz;     /* max packet size accepted by this module */
    ulong            q_hiwat;      /* queue high water mark for flow control */
    ulong            q_lowat;      /* queue low water mark for flow control */
    struct qband     *q_bandp;     /* separate flow information */
    unsigned char    q_nband;      /* number of priority bands */
    unsigned char    q_pad1[3];    /* reserved for future use */
    long             q_pad2[2];    /* reserved for future use */
};

#endif   /* _STYPES */

typedef struct queue queue_t;
```

Queues are always allocated in pairs (read and write); one queue pair per a
module, a driver, or a Stream head. A queue contains a linked list of messages.
When a **queue** pair is allocated, the following fields are initialized by
STREAMS:

- *q_qinfo* - from **streamtab**

- *q_minpsz, q_maxpsz, q_hiwat, q_lowat* - from **module_info**

Copying values from **module_info** allows them to be changed in the **queue** without modifying the **streamtab** and **module_info** values.

q_count is used in flow control calculations and is the number of bytes in messages on the queue.

Using queue Information

Modules and drivers should use STREAMS utility routines (see Appendix C) to alter *q_first, q_last, q_count*, and *q_flag*.

Modules and drivers can change *q_ptr, q_minpsz, q_maxpsz, q_hiwat*, and *q_lowat*.

Modules and drivers can read but should not change *q_qinfo, q_next, q_bandp,* and *q_nband*.

Modules and drivers should not touch *q_link, q_pad1*, and *q_pad2*.

Modules and drivers should not change any fields in the **equeue** structure. They can only reference *eq_bandp*.

Queue Flags

Programmers using the STREAMS mechanism should be aware of the following queue flags:

- QENAB - queue is enabled to run the **service** procedure (it is on the run queue)

- QWANTR - someone wants to read from the queue

- QWANTW - someone wants to write to the queue

- QFULL - queue is full

- QREADR - set for read queues

- QUSE - queue has been allocated

- QNOENB - do not enable the queue when data are placed on it

- QBACK - queue has been back-enabled
- QOLD - queue supports module/driver interface to open/close developed prior to UNIX System V Release 4.0
- QHLIST - the Stream head write queue is scanned

The equeue Structure

The extended queue structure **equeue** is only present for non-EFT systems. It contains the field *eq_link* that is a pointer to the next queue for scheduling (i.e., when the queue is on the run queue). *eq_bandp* is a pointer to the flow control information for the bands. The **equeue** structure is defined as follows:

```
#ifdef _STYPES

struct equeue {
    struct queue      *eq_link;      /* to next queue for scheduling */
    struct qband      *eq_bandp;     /* separate flow information */
    unsigned char     eq_nband;      /* number of priority bands > 0 */
};

#define q_link    q_eq->eq_link
#define q_bandp   q_eq->eq_bandp
#define q_nband   q_eq->eq_nband

#endif
```

The qband Structure

The queue flow information for each band is contained in a **qband** structure. It is defined as follows:

Programmer's Guide: STREAMS

```
struct qband {
        struct qband    *qb_next;     /* next band's info */
        ulong           qb_count;     /* number of bytes in band */
        struct msgb     *qb_first;    /* beginning of band's data */
        struct msgb     *qb_last;     /* end of band's data */
        ulong           qb_hiwat;     /* high water mark for band */
        ulong           qb_lowat;     /* low water mark for band */
        ulong           qb_flag;      /* flag, QB_FULL, denotes that a band of
                                         data flow is flow controlled */

        long            qb_pad1;      /* reserved for future use */
};

typedef struct qband qband_t;


/*
 * qband flags
 */
#define QB_FULL     0x01        /* band is considered full */
#define QB_WANTW    0x02        /* someone wants to write to band */
#define QB_BACK     0x04        /* queue has been back-enabled */
```

This structure contains pointers to the linked list of messages on the queue.
These pointers, *qb_first* and *qb_last*, denote the beginning and end of messages
for the particular band. The *qb_count* field is analogous to the **queue**'s *q_count*
field. However, *qb_count* only applies to the messages on the queue in the band
of data flow represented by the corresponding **qband** structure. In contrast,
q_count only contains information regarding normal and high priority messages.

Each band has a separate high and low water mark, *qb_hiwat* and *qb_lowat*.
These are initially set to the **queue**'s *q_hiwat* and *q_lowat* respectively. Modules
and drivers may change these values if desired through the **strqset**() function.
Three flags, QB_FULL, QB_WANTW, and QB_BACK, are defined for *qb_flag*.
QB FULL denotes that the particular band is full. QB_WANTW indicates that
someone tried to write to the band that was flow controlled. QB_BACK is set
when the **service** procedure runs as a result of being back-enabled because the
queue is no longer flow-controlled.

The **qband** structures are not preallocated per queue. Rather, they are allocated
when a message with a priority greater than zero is placed on the queue via
putq(), **putbq**(), or **insq**(). Since band allocation can fail, these routines return 0
on failure and 1 on success. Once a **qband** structure is allocated, it remains

associated with the queue until the queue is freed. **strqset**() and **strqget**() will cause **qband** allocation to occur.

Using equeue and qband Information

The STREAMS utility routines should be used when manipulating the fields in the **equeue** and **qband** structures. The routines **strqset**() and **strqget**() should be used to access band information.

Drivers and modules should not change any fields in the **equeue** structure. They are only allowed to reference *eq_bandp*.

Drivers and modules are allowed to change the *qp_hiwat* and *qp_lowat* fields of the **qband** structure.

Drivers and modules may only read the *qb_count, qb_first, qb_last,* and *qb_flag* fields of the **qband** structure.

The *pad* fields should not be used in the **qband** structure; they are intended for future use.

The following figure depicts a queue with two extra bands of flow.

Figure 5-4: Data Structure Linkage on non-EFT Systems

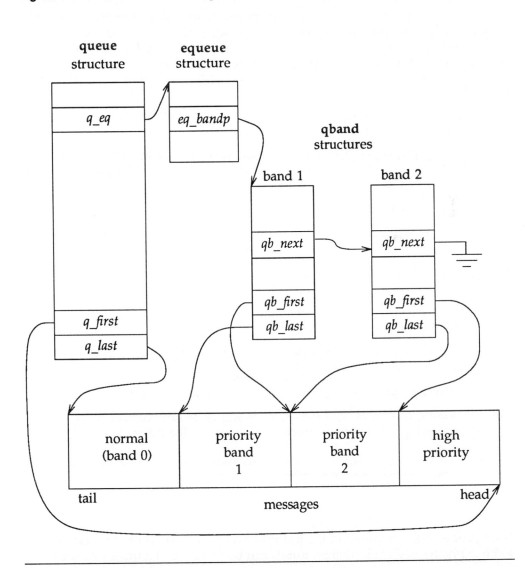

Message Processing

Put procedures are generally required in pushable modules. **Service** procedures are optional. If the **put** routine enqueues messages, there must exist a corresponding **service** routine that handles the enqueued messages. If the **put** routine does not enqueue messages, the **service** routine need not exist.

The general processing flow when both procedures are present is as follows:

1. A message is received by the **put** procedure in a queue, where some processing may be performed on the message.

2. The **put** procedure places the message on the queue by use of the **putq()** utility routine for the **service** procedure to perform further processing at some later time.

3. **putq()** places the message on the queue based on its priority.

4. Then, **putq()** makes the queue ready for execution by the STREAMS scheduler following all other queues currently scheduled.

5. After some indeterminate delay (intended to be short), the STREAMS scheduler calls the **service** procedure.

6. The **service** procedure gets the first message (*q_first*) from the message queue with the **getq()** utility.

7. The **service** procedure processes the message and passes it to the **put** procedure of the next queue with **putnext()**.

8. The **service** procedure gets the next message and processes it.

This processing continues until the queue is empty or flow control blocks further processing. The **service** procedure returns to the caller.

> ⚠ **CAUTION** A **service** procedure must never sleep since it has no user context. It must always return to its caller.

If no processing is required in the **put** procedure, the procedure does not have to be explicitly declared. Rather, **putq()** can be placed in the **qinit** structure declaration for the appropriate queue side to queue the message for the **service** procedure, e.g.,

```
static struct qinit winit = { putq, modwsrv, ...... };
```

More typically, **put** procedures will, at a minimum, process high priority messages to avoid queueing them.

The key attribute of a **service** procedure in the STREAMS architecture is delayed processing. When a **service** procedure is used in a module, the module developer is implying that there are other, more time-sensitive activities to be performed elsewhere in this Stream, in other Streams, or in the system in general. The presence of a **service** procedure is mandatory if the flow control mechanism is to be utilized by the queue.

The delay for STREAMS to call a **service** procedure will vary with implementation and system activity. However, once the **service** procedure is scheduled, it is guaranteed to be called before user level activity is resumed.

If a module or driver wishes to recognize priority bands, the **service** procedure is written to the following algorithm:

```
        .
        .
        .
while ((bp = getq(q)) != NULL) {
        if (bp->b_datap->db_type >= QPCTL) {
            putnext(q, bp);
        } else if (bcanput(q, bp->b_band)) {
            putnext(q, bp);
        } else {
            putbq(q, bp);
            return;
        }
}
        .
        .
```

Flow Control

The STREAMS flow control mechanism is voluntary and operates between the two nearest queues in a Stream containing **service** procedures (see Figure 5-5). Messages are generally held on a queue only if a **service** procedure is present in the associated queue.

Messages accumulate on a queue when the queue's **service** procedure processing does not keep pace with the message arrival rate, or when the procedure is blocked from placing its messages on the following Stream component by the flow control mechanism. Pushable modules contain independent upstream and downstream limits. The Stream head contains a preset upstream limit (which can be modified by a special message sent from downstream) and a driver may contain a downstream limit.

Flow control operates as follows:

1. Each time a STREAMS message handling routine (for example, **putq**) adds or removes a message from a message queue, the limits are checked. STREAMS calculates the total size of all message blocks (bp->b_wptr − bp->b_rptr) on the message queue.

2. The total is compared to the queue high water and low water values. If the total exceeds the high water value, an internal full indicator is set for the queue. The operation of the **service** procedure in this queue is not affected if the indicator is set, and the **service** procedure continues to be scheduled.

3. The next part of flow control processing occurs in the nearest preceding queue that contains a **service** procedure. In Figure 5-5, if D is full and C has no **service** procedure, then B is the nearest preceding queue.

Figure 5-5: Flow Control

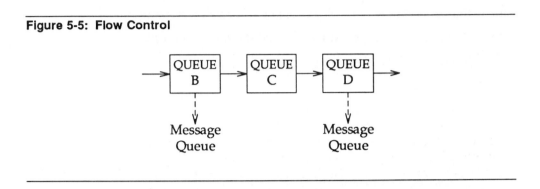

4. The **service** procedure in B uses a STREAMS utility routine to see if a queue ahead is marked full. If messages cannot be sent, the scheduler blocks the **service** procedure in B from further execution. B remains blocked until the low water mark of the full queue, D, is reached.

5. While B is blocked, any messages except high priority messages arriving at B will accumulate on its message queue (recall that high priority messages are not subject to flow control). Eventually, B may reach a full state and the full condition will propagate back to the module in the Stream.

6. When the **service** procedure processing on D causes the message block total to fall below the low water mark, the full indicator is turned off. Then, STREAMS automatically schedules the nearest preceding blocked queue (B in this case), getting things moving again. This automatic scheduling is known as back-enabling a queue.

Modules and drivers need to observe the message priority. High priority messages, determined by the type of the first block in the message,

> (mp->b_datap->db_type >= QPCTL),

are not subject to flow control. They are processed immediately and forwarded, as appropriate.

For ordinary messages, flow control must be tested before any processing is performed. The **canput()** utility determines if the forward path from the queue is blocked by flow control.

This is the general flow control processing of ordinary messages:

1. Retrieve the message at the head of the queue with **getq()**.

2. Determine if the message type is high priority and not to be processed here.

3. If so, pass the message to the **put** procedure of the following queue with **putnext()**.

4. Use **canput()** to determine if messages can be sent onward.

5. If messages should not be forwarded, put the message back on the queue with **putbq()** and return from the procedure.

6. Otherwise, process the message.

The canonical representation of this processing within a **service** procedure is as follows:

```
while (getq != NULL)
        if (high priority message || canput)
                process message
                putnext
        else
                putbq
                return
```

Expedited data have their own flow control with the same general processing as that of ordinary messages. **bcanput()** is used to provide modules and drivers with a way to test flow control in the given priority band. It returns 1 if a message of the given priority can be placed on the queue. It returns 0 if the priority band is flow controlled. If the band does not yet exist on the queue in question, the routine returns 1.

If the band is flow controlled, the higher bands are not affected. However, the same is not true for lower bands. The lower bands are also stopped from sending messages. If this didn't take place, the possibility would exist where lower priority messages would be passed along ahead of the flow controlled higher priority ones.

The call bcanput (q, 0) ; is equivalent to the call canput (q) ;.

A **service** procedure must process all messages on its queue unless flow control prevents this.

A **service** procedure continues processing messages form its queue until **getq()** returns NULL. When an ordinary message is enqueued by **putq()**, **putq()** will cause the **service** procedure to be scheduled only if the queue was previously empty, and a previous **getq()** call returns NULL (that is, the QWANTR flag is set). If there are messages on the queue, **putq()** presumes the **service** procedure is blocked by flow control and the procedure will be automatically rescheduled by STREAMS when the block is removed. If the **service** procedure cannot complete processing as a result of conditions other than flow control (e.g., no buffers), it must ensure it will return later [e.g., by use of **bufcall()** utility routine] or it must discard all messages on the queue. If this is not done, STREAMS will never schedule the **service** procedure to be run unless the queue's **put** procedure enqueues a priority message with **putq()**.

High priority messages are discarded only if there is already a high priority message on the Stream head read queue. That is, there can be only one high priority message present on the Stream head read queue at any time.

putbq() replaces messages at the beginning of the appropriate section of the message queue in accordance with their priority. This might not be the same position at which the message was retrieved by the preceding **getq()**. A subsequent **getq()** might return a different message.

putq() only looks at the priority band in the first message. If a high priority message is passed to **putq()** with a non-zero *b_band* value, *b_band* is reset to 0 before placing the message on the queue. If the message is passed to **putq()** with a *b_band* value that is greater than the number of **qband** structures associated with the queue, **putq()** tries to allocate a new **qband** structure for each band up to and including the band of the message.

The above also applies to **putbq()** and **insq()**. If an attempt is made to insert a message out of order in a queue via **insq()**, the message is not inserted and the routine fails.

putq() will not schedule a queue if **noenable**(q) had been previously called for this queue. **noenable**() instructs **putq**() to enqueue the message when called by this queue, but not to schedule the **service** procedure. **noenable**() does not prevent the queue from being scheduled by a flow control back-enable. The inverse of **noenable**() is **enableok**(q).

Driver upstream flow control is explained next as an example. Although device drivers typically discard input when unable to send it to a user process, STREAMS allows driver read-side flow control, possibly for handling temporary upstream blockages. This is done through a driver read **service** procedure which is disabled during the driver open with **noenable**(). If the driver input interrupt routine determines messages can be sent upstream (from **canput**), it sends the message with **putnext**(). Otherwise, it calls **putq**() to queue the message. The message waits on the message queue (possibly with queue length checked when new messages are enqueued by the interrupt routine) until the upstream queue becomes unblocked. When the blockage abates, STREAMS back-enables the driver read **service** procedure. The **service** procedure sends the messages upstream using **getq**() and **canput**(), as described previously. This is similar to *looprsrv*() (see "Loop-Around Driver" in Chapter 9) where the **service** procedure is present only for flow control.

qenable(), another flow control utility, allows a module or driver to cause one of its queues, or another module's queues, to be scheduled. **qenable**() might also be used when a module or driver wants to delay message processing for some reason. An example of this is a buffer module that gathers messages in its message queue and forwards them as a single, larger message. This module uses **noenable**() to inhibit its **service** procedure and queues messages with its **put** procedure until a certain byte count or "in queue" time has been reached. When either of these conditions is met, the module calls **qenable**() to cause its **service** procedure to run.

Another example is a communication line discipline module that implements end-to-end (i.e., to a remote system) flow control. Outbound data are held on the write-side message queue until the read-side receives a transmit window from the remote end of the network.

> **NOTE** STREAMS routines are called at different priority levels. Interrupt routines are called at the interrupt priority of the interrupting device. **Service** routines are called with interrupts enabled (hence **service** routines for STREAMS drivers can be interrupted by their own interrupt routines). **Put** routines are generally called at *str* priority.

Service Interfaces

STREAMS provides the means to implement a service interface between any two components in a Stream, and between a user process and the topmost module in the Stream. A service interface is defined at the boundary between a service user and a service provider (see Figure 5-7). A *service interface* is a set of primitives and the rules that define a service and the allowable state transitions that result as these primitives are passed between the user and the provider. These rules are typically represented by a state machine. In STREAMS, the service user and provider are implemented in a module, driver, or user process. The primitives are carried bidirectionally between a service user and provider in M_PROTO and M_PCPROTO messages.

PROTO messages (M_PROTO and M_PCPROTO) can be multi-block, with the second through last blocks of type M_DATA. The first block in a PROTO message contains the control part of the primitive in a form agreed upon by the user and provider. The block is not intended to carry protocol headers. (Although its use is not recommended, upstream PROTO messages can have multiple PROTO blocks at the start of the message. getmsg(2) will compact the blocks into a single control part when sending to a user process.) The M_DATA block(s) contains any data part associated with the primitive. The data part may be processed in a module that receives it, or it may be sent to the next Stream component, along with any data generated by the module. The contents of PROTO messages and their allowable sequences are determined by the service interface specification.

PROTO messages can be sent bidirectionally (upstream and downstream) on a Stream and between a Stream and a user process. **putmsg**(2) and **getmsg**(2) system calls are analogous, respectively, to **write**(2) and **read**(2) except that the former allow both data and control parts to be (separately) passed, and they retain the message boundaries across the user-Stream interface. **putmsg**(2) and **getmsg**(2) separately copy the control part (M_PROTO or M_PCPROTO block) and data part (M_DATA blocks) between the Stream and user process.

An M_PCPROTO message is normally used to acknowledge primitives composed of other messages. M_PCPROTO insures that the acknowledgement reaches the service user before any other message. If the service user is a user process, the Stream head will only store a single M_PCPROTO message, and discard subsequent M_PCPROTO messages until the first one is read with getmsg(2).

A STREAMS message format has been defined to simplify the design of service interfaces. System calls, **getmsg**(2) and **putmsg**(2) are available for sending messages downstream and receiving messages that are available at the Stream head.

This section describes the system calls **getmsg** and **putmsg** in the context of a service interface example. First, a brief overview of STREAMS service interfaces is presented.

Service Interface Benefits

A principal advantage of the STREAMS mechanism is its modularity. From user level, kernel-resident modules can be dynamically interconnected to implement any reasonable processing sequence. This modularity reflects the layering characteristics of contemporary network architectures.

One benefit of modularity is the ability to interchange modules of like functions. For example, two distinct transport protocols, implemented as STREAMS modules, may provide a common set of services. An application or higher layer protocol that requires those services can use either module. This ability to substitute modules enables user programs and higher level protocols to be independent of the underlying protocols and physical communication media.

Each STREAMS module provides a set of processing functions, or services, and an interface to those services. The service interface of a module defines the interaction between that module and any neighboring modules, and is a necessary component for providing module substitution. By creating a well-defined service interface, applications and STREAMS modules can interact with any module that supports that interface. Figure 5-6 demonstrates this.

Figure 5-6: Protocol Substitution

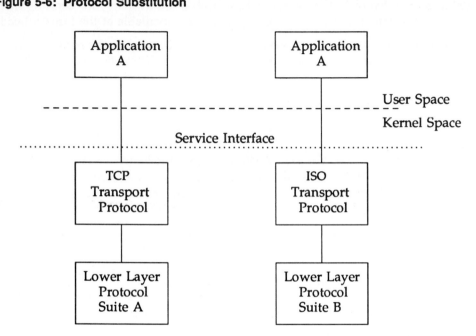

By defining a service interface through which applications interact with a transport protocol, it is possible to substitute a different protocol below that service interface in a manner completely transparent to the application. In this example, the same application can run over the Transmission Control Protocol (TCP) and the ISO transport protocol. Of course, the service interface must define a set of services common to both protocols.

The three components of any service interface are the service user, the service provider, and the service interface itself, as seen in the following figure.

Figure 5-7: Service Interface

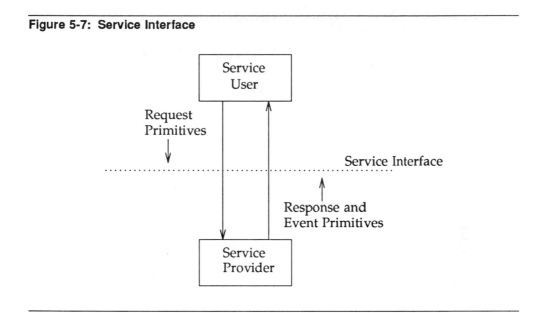

Typically, a user makes a request of a service provider using some well-defined service primitive. Responses and event indications are also passed from the provider to the user using service primitives.

Each service interface primitive is a distinct STREAMS message that has two parts; a control part and a data part. The control part contains information that identifies the primitive and includes all necessary parameters. The data part contains user data associated with that primitive.

An example of a service interface primitive is a transport protocol connect request. This primitive requests the transport protocol service provider to establish a connection with another transport user. The parameters associated with this primitive may include a destination protocol address and specific protocol options to be associated with that connection. Some transport protocols also allow a user to send data with the connect request. A STREAMS message would be used to define this primitive. The control part would identify the primitive as a connect request and would include the protocol address and options. The data part would contain the associated user data.

Service Interface Library Example

The service interface library example presented here includes four functions that enable a user to do the following:

- establish a Stream to the service provider and bind a protocol address to the Stream,

- send data to a remote user,

- receive data from a remote user, and

- close the Stream connected to the provider

First, the structure and constant definitions required by the library are shown. These typically will reside in a header file associated with the service interface.

```
/*
 * Primitives initiated by the service user.
 */
#define BIND_REQ      1   /* bind request */
#define UNITDATA_REQ 2    /* unitdata request */


/*
 * Primitives initiated by the service provider.
 */
#define OK_ACK        3   /* bind acknowledgment */
#define ERROR_ACK     4   /* error acknowledgment */
#define UNITDATA_IND  5   /* unitdata indication */


/*
 * The following structure definitions define the format of the
 * control part of the service interface message of the above
 * primitives.
 */

struct bind_req {         /* bind request */
    long PRIM_type;       /* always BIND_REQ */
    long BIND_addr;       /* addr to bind */
};
struct unitdata_req {     /* unitdata request */
    long PRIM_type;       /* always UNITDATA_REQ */
    long DEST_addr;       /* destination addr */
```

(continued on next page)

```
};
struct ok_ack {              /* positive acknowledgment */
   long PRIM_type;           /* always OK_ACK */
};
struct error_ack {           /* error acknowledgment */
   long PRIM_type;           /* always ERROR_ACK */
   long UNIX_error;          /* UNIX system error code  */
};
struct unitdata_ind {        /* unitdata indication */
   long PRIM_type;           /* always UNITDATA_IND */
   long SRC_addr;            /* source addr */
};
/* union of all primitives */
union primitives {
   long                  type;
   struct bind_req       bind_req;
   struct unitdata_req   unitdata_req;
   struct ok_ack         ok_ack;
   struct error_ack      error_ack;
   struct unitdata_ind   unitdata_ind;
};
/* header files needed by library */
#include <stropts.h>
#include <stdio.h>
#include <errno.h>
```

Five primitives have been defined. The first two represent requests from the service user to the service provider. These are:

BIND_REQ   This request asks the provider to bind a specified proto-col address. It requires an acknowledgement from the provider to verify that the contents of the request were syntactically correct.

UNITDATA_REQ

This request asks the provider to send data to the specified destination address. It does not require an acknowledgement from the provider.

The three other primitives represent acknowledgements of requests, or indications of incoming events, and are passed from the service provider to the service user. These are:

OK_ACK   This primitive informs the user that a previous bind request was received successfully by the service provider.

ERROR_ACK   This primitive informs the user that a non-fatal error was found in the previous bind request. It indicates that no action was taken with the primitive that caused the error.

UNITDATA_IND   This primitive indicates that data destined for the user have arrived.

The defined structures describe the contents of the control part of each service interface message passed between the service user and service provider. The first field of each control part defines the type of primitive being passed.

Accessing the Service Provider

The first routine presented, *inter_open*, opens the protocol driver device file specified by *path* and binds the protocol address contained in *addr* so that it may receive data. On success, the routine returns the file descriptor associated with the open Stream; on failure, it returns -1 and sets *errno* to indicate the appropriate UNIX system error value.

```
inter_open(path, oflags, addr)
    char *path;
    {
    int fd;
    struct bind_req bind_req;
    struct strbuf ctlbuf;
    union primitives rcvbuf;
    struct error_ack *error_ack;
    int flags;

    if ((fd = open(path, oflags)) < 0)
        return(-1);

    /* send bind request msg down stream */

    bind_req.PRIM_type = BIND_REQ;
    bind_req.BIND_addr = addr;
    ctlbuf.len = sizeof(struct bind_req);
    ctlbuf.buf = (char *)&bind_req;

    if (putmsg(fd, &ctlbuf, NULL, 0) < 0) {
        close(fd);
        return(-1);
    }
```

After opening the protocol driver, *inter_open* packages a bind request message to send downstream. **putmsg** is called to send the request to the service provider. The bind request message contains a control part that holds a *bind_req* structure, but it has no data part. *ctlbuf* is a structure of type **strbuf**, and it is initialized with the primitive type and address. Notice that the *maxlen* field of *ctlbuf* is not set before calling **putmsg**. That is because **putmsg** ignores this field. The *dataptr* argument to **putmsg** is set to NULL to indicate that the message contains no data part. Also, the *flags* argument is 0, which specifies that the message is not a high priority message.

After *inter_open* sends the bind request, it must wait for an acknowledgement from the service provider, as follows:

```
/* wait for ack of request */
ctlbuf.maxlen = sizeof(union primitives);
ctlbuf.len = 0;
ctlbuf.buf = (char *)&rcvbuf;
flags = RS_HIPRI;
if (getmsg(fd, &ctlbuf, NULL, &flags) < 0) {
    close(fd);
    return(-1);
}
/* did we get enough to determine type */
if (ctlbuf.len < sizeof(long)) {
    close(fd);
    errno = EPROTO;
    return(-1);
}
/* switch on type (first long in rcvbuf) */
switch(rcvbuf.type) {
    default:
        close(fd);
        errno = EPROTO;
        return(-1);

    case OK_ACK:
        return(fd);

    case ERROR_ACK:
        if (ctlbuf.len < sizeof(struct error_ack)) {
            close(fd);
            errno = EPROTO;
            return(-1);
        }
        error_ack = (struct error_ack *)&rcvbuf;
        close(fd);
        errno = error_ack->UNIX_error;
        return(-1);
}
}
```

getmsg is called to retrieve the acknowledgement of the bind request. The acknowledgement message consists of a control part that contains either an *ok_ack* or *error_ack* structure, and no data part.

The acknowledgement primitives are defined as priority messages. Messages are queued in a first-in-first-out manner within their priority at the Stream head; high priority messages are placed at the front of the Stream head queue followed by priority band messages and ordinary messages. The STREAMS mechanism allows only one high priority message per Stream at the Stream head at one time; any further high priority messages are queued until the message at the Stream head is processed. (There can be only one high priority message present on the Stream head read queue at any time.) High priority messages are particularly suitable for acknowledging service requests when the acknowledgement should be placed ahead of any other messages at the Stream head.

Before calling **getmsg,** this routine must initialize the **strbuf** structure for the control part. *buf* should point to a buffer large enough to hold the expected control part, and *maxlen* must be set to indicate the maximum number of bytes this buffer can hold.

Because neither acknowledgement primitive contains a data part, the *dataptr* argument to **getmsg** is set to NULL. The *flagsp* argument points to an integer containing the value RS_HIPRI. This flag indicates that **getmsg** should wait for a STREAMS high priority message before returning. It is set because we want to catch the acknowledgement primitives that are priority messages. Otherwise if the flag is zero the first message is taken. With RS_HIPRI set, even if a normal message is available, **getmsg** will block until a high priority message arrives.

On return from **getmsg,** the *len* field is checked to ensure that the control part of the retrieved message is an appropriate size. The example then checks the primitive type and takes appropriate actions. An OK_ACK indicates a successful bind operation, and *inter_open* returns the file descriptor of the open Stream. An ERROR_ACK indicates a bind failure, and *errno* is set to identify the problem with the request.

Closing the Service Provider

The next routine in the service interface library example is *inter_close*, which closes the Stream to the service provider.

```
inter_close(fd)
{
    close(fd);
}
```

The routine simply closes the given file descriptor. This will cause the protocol driver to free any resources associated with that Stream. For example, the driver may unbind the protocol address that had previously been bound to that Stream, thereby freeing that address for use by some other service user.

Sending Data to Service Provider

The third routine, *inter_snd*, passes data to the service provider for transmission to the user at the address specified in *addr*. The data to be transmitted are contained in the buffer pointed to by *buf* and contains *len* bytes. On successful completion, this routine returns the number of bytes of data passed to the service provider; on failure, it returns -1 and sets *errno* to an appropriate UNIX system error value.

```
inter_snd(fd, buf, len, addr)
    char  *buf;
    long  addr;
    {
    struct strbuf ctlbuf;
    struct strbuf databuf;
    struct unitdata_req unitdata_req;

    unitdata_req.PRIM_type = UNITDATA_REQ;
    unitdata_req.DEST_addr = addr;
    ctlbuf.len = sizeof(struct unitdata_req);
    ctlbuf.buf = (char *)&unitdata_req;
    databuf.len = len;
    databuf.buf = buf;

    if (putmsg(fd, &ctlbuf, &databuf, 0) < 0)
        return(-1);

    return(len);
}
```

In this example, the data request primitive is packaged with both a control part and a data part. The control part contains a *unitdata_req* structure that identifies the primitive type and the destination address of the data. The data to be transmitted are placed in the data part of the request message.

Unlike the bind request, the data request primitive requires no acknowledgement from the service provider. In the example, this choice was made to minimize the overhead during data transfer. If the **putmsg** call succeeds, this routine assumes all is well and returns the number of bytes passed to the service provider.

Receiving Data

The final routine in this example, *inter_rcv*, retrieves the next available data. *buf* points to a buffer where the data should be stored, *len* indicates the size of that buffer, and *addr* points to a long integer where the source address of the data will be placed. On successful completion, *inter_rcv* returns the number of bytes in the retrieved data; on failure, it returns -1 and sets the appropriate UNIX system error value.

```
inter_rcv(fd, buf, len, addr)
    char   *buf;
    long   *addr;
    {
    struct strbuf ctlbuf;
    struct strbuf databuf;
    struct unitdata_ind unitdata_ind;
    int retval;
    int flagsp;

    ctlbuf.maxlen = sizeof(struct unitdata_ind);
    ctlbuf.len = 0;
    ctlbuf.buf = (char *)&unitdata_ind;
    databuf.maxlen = len;
    databuf.len = 0;
    databuf.buf = buf;
    flagsp = 0;

    if ((retval = getmsg(fd, &ctlbuf, &databuf, &flagsp)) < 0)
        return(-1);
    if (unitdata_ind.PRIM_type != UNITDATA_IND) {
        errno = EPROTO;
        return(-1);
    }
    if (retval) {
        errno = EIO;
        return(-1);
    }
    *addr = unitdata_ind.SRC_addr;
    return(databuf.len);
}
```

getmsg is called to retrieve the data indication primitive, where that primitive contains both a control and data part. The control part consists of a *unitdata_ind* structure that identifies the primitive type and the source address of the data sender. The data part contains the data itself.

In *ctlbuf*, *buf* must point to a buffer where the control information will be stored, and *maxlen* must be set to indicate the maximum size of that buffer. Similar initialization is done for *databuf*.

The integer pointed at by *flagsp* in the **getmsg** call is set to zero, indicating that the next message should be retrieved from the Stream head, regardless of its priority. Data will arrive in normal priority messages. If no message currently exists at the Stream head, **getmsg** will block until a message arrives.

The user's control and data buffers should be large enough to hold any incoming data. If both buffers are large enough, **getmsg** will process the data indication and return 0, indicating that a full message was retrieved successfully. However, if either buffer is not large enough, **getmsg** will only retrieve the part of the message that fits into each user buffer. The remainder of the message is saved for subsequent retrieval (if in message non-discard mode), and a positive, non-zero value is returned to the user. A return value of MORECTL indicates that more control information is waiting for retrieval. A return value of MOREDATA indicates that more data are waiting for retrieval. A return value of (MORECTL | MOREDATA) indicates that data from both parts of the message remain. In the example, if the user buffers are not large enough (that is, **getmsg** returns a positive, non-zero value), the function will set *errno* to EIO and fail.

The type of the primitive returned by **getmsg** is checked to make sure it is a data indication (UNITDATA_IND in the example). The source address is then set and the number of bytes of data is returned.

The example presented is a simplified service interface. The state transition rules for such an interface were not presented for the sake of brevity. The intent was to show typical uses of the **putmsg** and **getmsg** system calls. See **putmsg**(2) and **getmsg**(2) for further details. For simplicity, this example did not also consider expedited data.

Module Service Interface Example

The following example is part of a module which illustrates the concept of a service interface. The module implements a simple service interface and mirrors the service interface library example given earlier. The following rules pertain to service interfaces:

- Modules and drivers that support a service interface must act upon all PROTO messages and not pass them through.

- Modules may be inserted between a service user and a service provider to manipulate the data part as it passes between them. However, these modules may not alter the contents of the control part (PROTO block, first message block) nor alter the boundaries of the control or data parts. That is, the message blocks comprising the data part may be changed, but the message may not be split into separate messages nor combined with other messages.

In addition, modules and drivers must observe the rule that high priority messages are not subject to flow control and forward them accordingly.

Declarations

The service interface primitives are defined in the declarations:

```
#include "sys/types.h"
#include "sys/param.h"
#include "sys/stream.h"
#include "sys/errno.h"

/* Primitives initiated by the service user */

#define BIND_REQ      1   /* bind request */
#define UNITDATA_REQ  2   /* unitdata request */

/* Primitives initiated by the service provider */

#define OK_ACK        3   /* bind acknowledgment */
#define ERROR_ACK     4   /* error acknowledgment */
#define UNITDATA_IND  5   /* unitdata indication */
/*
 * The following structures define the format of the
 * stream message block of the above primitives.
 */
struct bind_req {         /* bind request */
  long PRIM_type;         /* always BIND_REQ */
  long BIND_addr;         /* addr to bind   */
};
struct unitdata_req {     /* unitdata request */
  long PRIM_type;         /* always UNITDATA_REQ */
  long DEST_addr;         /* dest addr */
};
struct ok_ack {           /* ok acknowledgment */
  long PRIM_type;         /* always OK_ACK */
};
struct error_ack {        /* error acknowledgment */
  long PRIM_type;         /* always ERROR_ACK */
  long UNIX_error;        /* UNIX system error code */
};
struct unitdata_ind {     /* unitdata indication */
  long PRIM_type;         /* always UNITDATA_IND */
  long SRC_addr;          /* source addr */
};
union primitives {        /* union of all primitives */
  long type;
  struct bind_req       bind_req;
  struct unitdata_req   unitdata_req;
  struct ok_ack         ok_ack;
  struct error_ack      error_ack;
  struct unitdata_ind   unitdata_ind;
};
```

(continued on next page)

```
struct dgproto {  /* structure per minor device */
    short state;   /* current provider state */
    long addr;     /* net address */
};
/* Provider states */

#define IDLE    0
#define BOUND   1
```

In general, the M_PROTO or M_PCPROTO block is described by a data structure containing the service interface information. In this example, *union primitives* is that structure.

Two commands are recognized by the module:

BIND_REQ   Give this Stream a protocol address (i.e., give it a name on the network). After a BIND_REQ is completed, data from other senders will find their way through the network to this particular Stream.

UNITDATA_REQ   Send data to the specified address.

Three messages are generated:

OK_ACK   A positive acknowledgement (ack) of BIND_REQ.

ERROR_ACK   A negative acknowledgement (nak) of BIND_REQ.

UNITDATA_IND   Data from the network have been received (this code is not shown).

The acknowledgement of a BIND_REQ informs the user that the request was syntactically correct (or incorrect if ERROR_ACK). The receipt of a BIND_REQ is acknowledged with an M_PCPROTO to insure that the acknowledgement reaches the user before any other message. For example, a UNITDATA_IND could come through before the bind has completed, and the user would get confused.

The driver uses a per-minor device data structure, *dgproto*, which contains the following:

state   current state of the service provider IDLE or BOUND

addr   network address that has been bound to this Stream

It is assumed (though not shown) that the module open procedure sets the write queue *q_ptr* to point at the appropriate private data structure.

Service Interface Procedure

The write **put** procedure is:

```
static int protowput(q, mp)
   queue_t   *q;
   mblk_t   *mp;
   {
   union primitives *proto;
   struct dgproto *dgproto;
   int err;

   dgproto = (struct dgproto *) q->q_ptr;

   switch (mp->b_datap->db_type) {

   default:
       /* don't understand it */
       mp->b_datap->db_type = M_ERROR;
       mp->b_rptr = mp->b_wptr = mp->b_datap->db_base;
       *mp->b_wptr++ = EPROTO;
       qreply(q, mp);
       break;

   case M_FLUSH:
       /* standard flush handling goes here ... */
       break;

   case M_PROTO:
       /* Protocol message -> user request */

       proto = (union primitives *) mp->b_rptr;

       switch (proto->type) {
       default:
```

(continued on next page)

```
        mp->b_datap->db_type = M_ERROR;
        mp->b_rptr = mp->b_wptr = mp->b_datap->db_base;
        *mp->b_wptr++ = EPROTO;
        qreply(q, mp);
        return;

case BIND_REQ:
        if (dgproto->state != IDLE) {
            err = EINVAL;
            goto error_ack;
        }
        if (mp->b_wptr - mp->b_rptr != sizeof(struct bind_req)) {
            err = EINVAL;
            goto error_ack;
        }
        if (err = chkaddr(proto->bind_req.BIND_addr))
            goto error_ack;

        dgproto->state = BOUND;
        dgproto->addr = proto->bind_req.BIND_addr;
        mp->b_datap->db_type = M_PCPROTO;
        proto->type = OK_ACK;
        mp->b_wptr = mp->b_rptr + sizeof(struct ok_ack);
        qreply(q, mp);
        break;

error_ack:
        mp->b_datap->db_type = M_PCPROTO;
        proto->type = ERROR_ACK;
        proto->error_ack.UNIX_error = err;
        mp->b_wptr = mp->b_rptr + sizeof(struct error_ack);
        qreply(q, mp);
        break;

case UNITDATA_REQ:
        if (dgproto->state != BOUND)
            goto bad;
        if (mp->b_wptr - mp->b_rptr != sizeof(struct unitdata_req))
            goto bad;
        if (err = chkaddr(proto->unitdata_req.DEST_addr))
            goto bad;
            putq(q, mp);
            /* start device or mux output ... */
        }
        break;
```

(continued on next page)

Programmer's Guide: STREAMS

```
        bad:
                freemsg (mp);
                break;
        }
    }
```

The write **put** procedure switches on the message type. The only types accepted are M_FLUSH and M_PROTO. For M_FLUSH messages, the driver will perform the canonical flush handling (not shown). For M_PROTO messages, the driver assumes the message block contains a *union primitive* and switches on the *type* field. Two types are understood: BIND_REQ and UNITDATA_REQ.

For a BIND_REQ, the current state is checked; it must be IDLE. Next, the message size is checked. If it is the correct size, the passed-in address is verified for legality by calling *chkaddr*. If everything checks, the incoming message is converted into an OK_ACK and sent upstream. If there was any error, the incoming message is converted into an ERROR_ACK and sent upstream.

For UNITDATA_REQ, the state is also checked; it must be BOUND. As above, the message size and destination address are checked. If there is any error, the message is simply discarded. If all is well, the message is put on the queue, and the lower half of the driver is started.

If the write **put** procedure receives a message type that it does not understand, either a bad b_datap->db_type or bad proto->type, the message is converted into an M_ERROR message and sent upstream.

The generation of UNITDATA_IND messages (not shown in the example) would normally occur in the device interrupt if this is a hardware driver or in the lower read **put** procedure if this is a multiplexor. The algorithm is simple: The data part of the message is prepended by an M_PROTO message block that contains a *unitdata_ind* structure and sent upstream.

Message Allocation and Freeing

The **allocb()** utility routine is used to allocate a message and the space to hold the data for the message. **allocb()** returns a pointer to a message block containing a data buffer of at least the size requested, providing there is enough memory available. It returns null on failure. Note that **allocb()** always returns a message of type M_DATA. The type may then be changed if required. *b_rptr* and *b_wptr* are set to *db_base* (see **msgb** and **datab**) which is the start of the memory location for the data.

allocb() may return a buffer larger than the size requested. If **allocb()** indicates buffers are not available [**allocb()** fails], the **put/service** procedure may not call **sleep()** to wait for a buffer to become available. Instead, the **bufcall()** utility can be used to defer processing in the module or the driver until a buffer becomes available.

If message space allocation is done by the **put** procedure and **allocb()** fails, the message is usually discarded. If the allocation fails in the **service** routine, the message is returned to the queue. **bufcall()** is called to enable to the **service** routine when a message buffer becomes available, and the **service** routine returns.

The **freeb()** utility routine releases (de-allocates) the message block descriptor and the corresponding data block, if the reference count (see **datab** structure) is equal to 1. If the reference counter exceeds 1, the data block is not released.

The **freemsg()** utility routine releases all message blocks in a message. It uses **freeb()** to free all message blocks and corresponding data blocks.

In the following example, **allocb()** is used by the *bappend* subroutine that appends a character to a message block:

```
/*
 * Append a character to a message block.
 * If (*bpp) is null, it will allocate a new block
 * Returns 0 when the message block is full, 1 otherwise
 */

#define MODBLKSZ 128     /* size of message blocks */

static bappend(bpp, ch)
    mblk_t  **bpp;
    int   ch;
    {
    mblk_t *bp;

    if ((bp = *bpp) != NULL) {
            if (bp->b_wptr >= bp->b_datap->db_lim)
                return 0;
    } else if ((*bpp = bp = allocb(MODBLKSZ, BPRI_MED)) == NULL)
            return 1;
    *bp->b_wptr++ = ch;
    return 1;
    }
```

bappend receives a pointer to a message block pointer and a character as arguments. If a message block is supplied (*bpp != NULL), *bappend* checks if there is room for more data in the block. If not, it fails. If there is no message block, a block of at least MODBLKSZ is allocated through **allocb()**.

If the **allocb()** fails, *bappend* returns success, silently discarding the character. This may or may not be acceptable. For TTY-type devices, it is generally accepted. If the original message block is not full or the **allocb()** is successful, *bappend* stores the character in the block.

The next example, subroutine *modwput* processes all the message blocks in any downstream data (type M_DATA) messages. **freemsg()** deallocates messages.

```
/* Write side put procedure */
static modwput(q, mp)
  queue_t *q;
  mblk_t *mp;
  {
  switch (mp->b_datap->db_type) {
  default:
        putnext(q, mp);  /* Don't do these, pass them along */
        break;

  case M_DATA: {
        register mblk_t *bp;
        struct mblk_t *nmp = NULL, *nbp = NULL;

        for (bp = mp; bp != NULL; bp = bp->b_cont) {
              while (bp->b_rptr < bp->b_wptr) {
                    if (*bp->b_rptr == '\n')
                          if (!bappend(&nbp, '\r'))
                                goto newblk;
                    if (!bappend(&nbp, *bp->b_rptr))
                          goto newblk;

                    bp->b_rptr++;
                    continue;

              newblk:
                    if (nmp == NULL)
                          nmp = nbp;
                    else linkb(nmp, nbp); /* link message block to tail of nmp */
                    nbp = NULL;
              }
        }

        if (nmp == NULL)
              nmp = nbp;
        else linkb(nmp, nbp);
        freemsg(mp); /* de-allocate message */
        if (nmp)
              putnext(q, nmp);
        break;
  }
  }
  }
```

Data messages are scanned and filtered. *modwput* copies the original message into a new block(s), modifying as it copies. *nbp* points to the current new message block. *nmp* points to the new message being formed as multiple M_DATA message blocks. The outer for () loop goes through each message block of the original message. The inner `while()` loop goes through each byte. *bappend* is used to add characters to the current or new block. If *bappend* fails, the current new block is full. If *nmp* is NULL, *nmp* is pointed at the new block. If *nmp* is not NULL, the new block is linked to the end of *nmp* by use of the **linkb()** utility.

At the end of the loops, the final new block is linked to *nmp*. The original message (all message blocks) is returned to the pool by **freemsg()**. If a new message exists, it is sent downstream.

Recovering From No Buffers

The **bufcall()** utility can be used to recover from an **allocb()** failure. The call syntax is as follows:

```
bufcall(size, pri, func, arg);
int size, pri, (*func)();
long arg;
```

bufcall() calls (**func*)(*arg*) when a buffer of *size* bytes is available. When *func* is called, it has no user context and must return without sleeping. Also, because of interrupt processing, there is no guarantee that when *func* is called, a buffer will actually be available (someone else may steal it).

On success, **bufcall()** returns a nonzero identifier that can be used as a parameter to **unbufcall()** to cancel the request later. On failure, 0 is returned and the requested function will never be called.

 Care must be taken to avoid deadlock when holding resources while waiting for **bufcall()** to call (**func*)(*arg*). **bufcall()** should be used sparingly.

Two examples are provided. The first example is a device receive interrupt handler:

```
#include "sys/types.h"
#include "sys/param.h"
#include "sys/stream.h"

dev_rintr(dev)
{
    /* process incoming message ... */

    /* allocate new buffer for device */
    dev_re_load(dev);
}
/*
 * Reload device with a new receive buffer
 */
dev_re_load(dev)
{
    mblk_t *bp;

    if ((bp = allocb(DEVBLKSZ, BPRI_MED)) == NULL) {
        cmn_err(CE_WARN, "dev: allocb failure (size %d)\n", DEVBLKSZ);
        /*
         * Allocation failed.  Use bufcall to
         * schedule a call to ourselves.
         */
        (void) bufcall(DEVBLKSZ, BPRI_MED, dev_re_load, dev);
        return;
    }

    /* pass buffer to device ... */
}
```

dev_rintr is called when the device has posted a receive interrupt. The code
retrieves the data from the device (not shown). *dev_rintr* must then give the
device another buffer to fill by a call to *dev_re_load*, which calls **allocb()**. If
allocb() fails, *dev_re_load* uses **bufcall()** to call itself when STREAMS determines
a buffer is available.

NOTE Since **bufcall()** may fail, there is still a chance that the device may hang. A better strategy, in the event **bufcall()** fails, would be to discard the current input message and resubmit that buffer to the device. Losing input data is generally better than hanging.

The second example is a write **service** procedure, *mod_wsrv*, which needs to prepend each output message with a header. *mod_wsrv* illustrates a case for potential deadlock:

```
static int mod_wsrv(q)
    queue_t  *q;
    {
    int qenable();
    mblk_t *mp, *bp;

    while (mp = getq(q)) {
        /* check for priority messages and canput ... */

        /* Allocate a header to prepend to the message.  If
         * the allocb fails, use bufcall to reschedule.
         */
        if ((bp = allocb(HDRSZ, BPRI_MED)) == NULL) {
            if (!bufcall(HDRSZ, BPRI_MED, qenable, q)) {
                timeout(qenable, q, HZ*2);
            }
            /* Put the message back and exit, we will be re-enabled later */
            putbq(q, mp);
            return;
        }
        /* process message .... */
    }
}
```

However, if **allocb()** fails, *mod_wsrv* wants to recover without loss of data and calls **bufcall()**. In this case, the routine passed to **bufcall()** is **qenable()**. When a buffer is available, the **service** procedure will be automatically re-enabled. Before exiting, the current message is put back on the queue. This example deals with **bufcall()** failure by resorting to the **timeout()** operating system utility routine. **timeout()** will schedule the given function to be run with the given argument in the given number of clock ticks (there are HZ ticks per second). In this example, if **bufcall()** fails, the system will run **qenable()** after two seconds have passed.

Extended STREAMS Buffers

Some hardware using the STREAMS mechanism supports memory-mapped I/O that allows the sharing of buffers between users, kernel, and the I/O card.

If the hardware supports memory-mapped I/O, data received from the network are placed in the DARAM (dual access RAM) section of the I/O card. Since DARAM is a shared memory between the kernel and the I/O card, data transfer between the kernel and the I/O card is eliminated. Once in kernel space, the data buffer can be manipulated as if it were a kernel resident buffer. Similarly, data being sent downstream are placed in DARAM and then forwarded to the network.

In a typical network arrangement, data are received from the network by the I/O card. The disk controller reads the block of data into the card's internal buffer. It interrupts the host computer to denote that data have arrived. The STREAMS driver gives the controller the kernel address where the data block is to go and the number of bytes to transfer. After the disk controller has read the data into its buffer and verified the checksum, it copies the data into main memory to the address specified by the the DMA (direct memory access) memory address. Once in the kernel space, the data are packaged into message blocks and processed on the usual manner.

When data are transmitted from user process to the network, data are copied from the user space to the kernel space, and packaged as a message block and sent to the downstream driver. The driver interrupts the I/O card signaling that data are ready to be transmitted to the network. The controller copies the data from the kernel space to the internal buffer on the I/O card, and from there data are placed on the network.

The STREAMS buffer allocation mechanism enables the allocation of message and data blocks to point directly to a client-supplied (non-STREAMS) buffer. Message and data blocks allocated this way are indistinguishable (for the most part) from the normal data blocks. The client-supplied buffers are processed as if they were normal STREAMS data buffers.

Drivers may not only attach non-STREAMS data buffers but also free them. This is accomplished as follows:

- **Allocation** - If the drivers are to use DARAM without wasting STREAMS resources and without being dependent on upstream modules, a data and message block can be allocated without an attached data buffer. The routine to use is called **esballoc()**. This returns a message block and data block without an associated STREAMS buffer. Rather, the buffer used is the one supplied by the caller.

■ **Freeing** - Each driver using non-STREAMS resources in a STREAMS environment must fully manage those resources, including freeing them. However, to make this as transparent as possible, a driver-dependent routine is executed in the event **freeb()** is called to free a message and data block with an attached non-STREAMS buffer.

freeb() detects if a buffer is a client supplied, non-STREAMS buffer. If it is, **freeb()** finds the **free_rtn** structure associated with that buffer. After calling the driver-dependent routine (defined in **free_rtn**) to free the buffer, the **freeb()** routine frees the message and data block.

The format of the **free_rtn** structure is as follows:

```
struct free_rtn {
        void (*free_func)();            /* driver dependent free routine */
        char *free_arg;                 /* argument for free_rtn */
};
typedef struct free_rtn frtn_t;
```

The structure has two fields: a pointer to a function and a location for any argument passed to the function. Instead of defining a specific number of arguments, *free_arg* is defined as a *char **. This way, drivers can pass pointers to structures in the event more than one argument is needed.

The STREAMS utility routine, **esballoc()**, provides a common interface for allocating and initializing data blocks. It makes the allocation as transparent to the driver as possible and provides a way to modify the fields of the data block, since modification should only be performed by STREAMS. The driver calls this routine when it wants to attach its own data buffer to a newly allocated message and data block. If the routine successfully completes the allocation and assigns the buffer, it returns a pointer to the message block. The driver is responsible for supplying the arguments to **esballoc()**, namely, a pointer to its data buffer, the size of the buffer, the priority of the data block, and a pointer to the **free_rtn** structure. All arguments should be non-NULL. See Appendix C for a detailed description of **esballoc**. Appendix G has examples of extended STREAMS buffers implemented in different hardware.

6 Polling and Signaling

Input/Output Polling   6-1
Synchronous Input/Output   6-1
Asynchronous Input/Output   6-6
Signals   6-7
■ Extended Signals   6-8

Stream as a Controlling Terminal   6-9
Job Control   6-9
Allocation and Deallocation   6-12
Hung-up Streams   6-12
Hangup Signals   6-13
Accessing the Controlling Terminal   6-13

Input/Output Polling

This chapter describes the synchronous polling mechanism and asynchronous event notification within STREAMS. Also discussed is how a Stream can be a controlling terminal.

User processes can efficiently monitor and control multiple Streams with two system calls: poll(2) and the I_SETSIG ioctl(2) command. These calls allow a user process to detect events that occur at the Stream head on one or more Streams, including receipt of data or messages on the read queue and cessation of flow control.

To monitor Streams with poll(2), a user process issues that system call and specifies the Streams to be monitored, the events to look for, and the amount of time to wait for an event. The poll(2) system call will block the process until the time expires or until an event occurs. If an event occurs, it will return the type of event and the Stream on which the event occurred.

Instead of waiting for an event to occur, a user process may want to monitor one or more Streams while processing other data. It can do so by issuing the I_SETSIG ioctl(2) command, specifying one or more Streams and events [as with poll(2)]. This ioctl does not block the process and force the user process to wait for the event but returns immediately and issues a signal when an event occurs. The process must request signal(2) to catch the resultant SIGPOLL signal.

If any selected event occurs on any of the selected Streams, STREAMS will cause the SIGPOLL catching function to be executed in all associated requesting processes. However, the process(es) will not know which event occurred, nor on what Stream the event occurred. A process that issues the I_SETSIG can get more detailed information by issuing a poll after it detects the event.

Synchronous Input/Output

The poll(2) system call provides a mechanism to identify those Streams over which a user can send or receive data. For each Stream of interest users can specify one or more events about which they should be notified. The types of events that can be polled are POLLIN, POLLRDNORM, POLLRDBAND, POLLPRI, POLLOUT, POLLWRNORM, POLLWRBAND, POLLMSG:

    POLLIN   A message other than an M_PCPROTO is at the front of the Stream head read queue. This event is maintained for compatibility with the previous releases of the UNIX System V.

POLLRDNORM	A normal (non-priority) message is at the front of the Stream head read queue.
POLLRDBAND	A priority message (band > 0) is at the front of the Stream head queue.
POLLPRI	A high priority message (M_PCPROTO) is at the front of the Stream head read queue.
POLLOUT	The normal priority band of the queue is writable (not flow controlled).
POLLWRNORM	The same as POLLOUT.
POLLWRBAND	A priority band greater than 0 of a queue down-stream exists and is writable.
POLLMSG	An M_SIG or M_PCSIG message containing the SIG-POLL signal has reached the front of the Stream head read queue.

Some of the events may not be applicable to all file types. For example, it is not expected that the POLLPRI event will be generated when polling a regular file. POLLIN, POLLRDNORM, POLLRDBAND, and POLLPRI are set even if the message is of zero length.

The **poll** system call will examine each file descriptor for the requested events and, on return, will indicate which events have occurred for each file descriptor. If no event has occurred on any polled file descriptor, **poll** blocks until a requested event or timeout occurs. **poll**(2) takes the following arguments:

■ an array of file descriptors and events to be polled

■ the number of file descriptors to be polled

■ the number of milliseconds **poll** should wait for an event if no events are pending (-1 specifies wait forever)

The following example shows the use of **poll**. Two separate minor devices of the communications driver are opened, thereby establishing two separate Streams to the driver. The *pollfd* entry is initialized for each device. Each Stream is polled for incoming data. If data arrive on either Stream, data are read and then written back to the other Stream.

```
#include <fcntl.h>
#include <poll.h>

#define NPOLL 2       /* number of file descriptors to poll */

main()
{
    struct pollfd pollfds[NPOLL];
    char buf[1024];
    int count, i;

    if ((pollfds[0].fd = open("/dev/comm/01", O_RDWR|O_NDELAY)) < 0) {
        perror("open failed for /dev/comm/01");
        exit(1);
    }

    if ((pollfds[1].fd = open("/dev/comm/02", O_RDWR|O_NDELAY)) < 0) {
        perror("open failed for /dev/comm/02");
        exit(2);
    }
```

The variable *pollfds* is declared as an array of the **pollfd** structure that is defined in <**poll.h**> and has the following format:

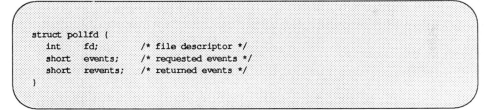

```
struct pollfd {
    int     fd;        /* file descriptor */
    short   events;    /* requested events */
    short   revents;   /* returned events */
}
```

For each entry in the array, *fd* specifies the file descriptor to be polled and *events* is a bitmask that contains the bitwise inclusive OR of events to be polled on that file descriptor. On return, the *revents* bitmask will indicate which of the requested events has occurred.

The example continues to process incoming data as follows:

```
    pollfds[0].events = POLLIN;   /* set events to poll
    pollfds[1].events = POLLIN;    * for incoming data
                             */
    while (1) {
        /* poll and use -1 timeout (infinite) */
        if (poll(pollfds, NPOLL, -1) < 0) {
            perror("poll failed");
            exit(3);
        }
        for (i = 0; i < NPOLL; i++) {
            switch (pollfds[i].revents) {

            default:                         /* default error case */
                perror("error event");
                exit(4);

            case 0:                          /* no events */
                break;

            case POLLIN:
                /* echo incoming data on "other" Stream */
                while ((count = read(pollfds[i].fd, buf, 1024)) > 0)
                    /*
                     * the write loses data if flow control
                     * prevents the transmit at this time.
                     */
                    if (write(pollfds[(i+1)%2].fd, buf, count) != count)
                        fprintf(stderr,"writer lost data\n");
                break;
            }
        }
    }
}
```

The user specifies the polled events by setting the *events* field of the **pollfd** structure to **POLLIN**. This requested event directs **poll** to notify the user of any incoming data on each Stream. The bulk of the example is an infinite loop, where each iteration will poll both Streams for incoming data.

The second argument to the **poll** system call specifies the number of entries in the *pollfds* array (2 in this example). The third argument is a timeout value indicating the number of milliseconds **poll** should wait for an event if none has occurred. On a system where millisecond accuracy is not available, *timeout* is rounded up to the nearest value available on that system. If the value of *timeout* is 0, **poll** returns immediately. Here, the value of *timeout* is -1, specifying that **poll** should block until a requested event occurs or until the call is interrupted.

If the **poll** call succeeds, the program looks at each entry in the *pollfds* array. If *revents* is set to 0, no event has occurred on that file descriptor. If *revents* is set to **POLLIN**, incoming data are available. In this case, all available data are read from the polled minor device and written to the other minor device.

If *revents* is set to a value other than 0 or **POLLIN**, an error event must have occurred on that Stream, because **POLLIN** was the only requested event. The following are **poll** error events:

POLLERR   A fatal error has occurred in some module or driver on the Stream associated with the specified file descriptor. Further system calls will fail.

POLLHUP   A hangup condition exists on the Stream associated with the specified file descriptor. This event and POLLOUT are mutually exclusive; a Stream can't be writable if a hangup has occurred.

POLLNVAL   The specified file descriptor is not associated with an open Stream.

These events may not be polled for by the user, but will be reported in *revents* whenever they occur. As such, they are only valid in the *revents* bitmask.

The example attempts to process incoming data as quickly as possible. However, when writing data to a Stream, the **write** call may block if the Stream is exerting flow control. To prevent the process from blocking, the minor devices of the communications driver were opened with the O_NDELAY (or O_NONBLOCK, see note) flag set. The **write** will not be able to send all the data if flow control is exerted and O_NDELAY (O_NONBLOCK) is set. This can occur if the communications driver is unable to keep up with the user's rate of data transmission. If the Stream becomes full, the number of bytes the **write** sends will be less than the requested *count*. For simplicity, the example ignores the data if the Stream becomes full, and a warning is printed to **stderr**.

 NOTE   For conformance with the IEEE operating system interface standard, POSIX, it is recommended that new applications use the O_NONBLOCK flag, whose behavior is the same as that of O_NDELAY unless otherwise noted.

This program continues until an error occurs on a Stream, or until the process is interrupted.

Asynchronous Input/Output

The **poll** system call described before enables a user to monitor multiple Streams in a synchronous fashion. The **poll**(2) call normally blocks until an event occurs on any of the polled file descriptors. In some applications, however, it is desirable to process incoming data asynchronously. For example, an application may wish to do some local processing and be interrupted when a pending event occurs. Some time-critical applications cannot afford to block, but must have immediate indication of success or failure.

The I_SETSIG **ioctl** call [see **streamio**(7)] is used to request that a SIGPOLL signal be sent to a user process when a specific event occurs. Listed below are events for the **ioctl** I_SETSIG. These are similar to those described for **poll**(2).

S_INPUT	A message other than an M_PCPROTO is at the front of the Stream head read queue. This event is maintained for compatibility with the previous releases of the UNIX System V.
S_RDNORM	A normal (non-priority) message is at the front of the Stream head read queue.
S_RDBAND	A priority message (band > 0) is at the front of the Stream head read queue.
S_HIPRI	A high priority message (M_PCPROTO) is present at the front of the Stream head read queue.
S_OUTPUT	A write queue for normal data (priority band = 0) is no longer full (not flow controlled). This notifies a user that there is room on the queue for sending or writing normal data downstream.
S_WRNORM	The same as S_OUTPUT.
S_WRBAND	A priority band greater than 0 of a queue downstream exists and is writable. This notifies a user that there is room on the queue for sending or writing priority data downstream.

S_MSG	An M_SIG or M_PCSIG message containing the SIGPOLL flag has reached the front of Stream head read queue.
S_ERROR	An M_ERROR message reaches the Stream head.
S_HANGUP	An M_HANGUP message reaches the Stream head.
S_BANDURG	When used in conjunction with S_RDBAND, SIGURG is generated instead SIGPOLL when a priority message reaches the front of the Stream head read queue.

S_INPUT, S_RDNORM, S_RDBAND, and S_HIPRI are set even if the message is of zero length. A user process may choose to handle only high priority messages by setting the *arg* to S_HIPRI.

Signals

STREAMS allows modules and drivers to cause a signal to be sent to user process(es) through an M_SIG or M_PCSIG message. The first byte of the message specifies the signal for the Stream head to generate. If the signal is not SIGPOLL [see **signal**(2)], the signal is sent to the process group associated with the Stream. If the signal is SIGPOLL, the signal is only sent to processes that have registered for the signal by using the I_SETSIG **ioctl**(2).

An M_SIG message can be used by modules or drivers that wish to insert an explicit inband signal into a message Stream. For example, this message can be sent to the user process immediately before a particular service interface message to gain the immediate attention of the user process. When the M_SIG message reaches the head of the Stream head read queue, a signal is generated and the M_SIG message is removed. This leaves the service interface message as the next message to be processed by the user. Use of the M_SIG message is typically defined as part of the service interface of the driver or module.

Extended Signals

To enable a process to obtain the band and event associated with SIGPOLL
more readily, STREAMS supports extended signals. For the given events, a
special code is defined in <siginfo.h> that describes the reason SIGPOLL was
generated. The following table describes the data available in the siginfo_t
structure passed to the signal handler.

event	si_signo	si_code	si_band	si_errno
S_INPUT	SIGPOLL	POLL_IN	band readable	unused
S_OUTPUT	SIGPOLL	POLL_OUT	band writable	unused
S_MSG	SIGPOLL	POLL_MSG	band signaled	unused
S_ERROR	SIGPOLL	POLL_ERR	unused	Stream error
S_HANGUP	SIGPOLL	POLL_HUP	unused	unused
S_HIPRI	SIGPOLL	POLL_PRI	unused	unused

Stream as a Controlling Terminal

Job Control

An overview of Job Control is provided here for completeness and because it interacts with the STREAMS-based terminal subsystem. More information on Job Control may be obtained from the following manual pages: **exit**(2), **getpgid**(2), **getpgrp**(2), **getsid**(2), **kill**(2), **setpgid**(2), **setpgrp**(2), **setsid**(2), **sigaction**(2), **signal**(2), **sigsend**(2), **termios**(2), **waitid**(2), **waitpid**(3C), **signal**(5), and **termio**(7).

Job Control is a feature supported by the BSD UNIX operating system. It is also an optional part of the IEEE P1003.1 POSIX standard. Job Control breaks a login session into smaller units called *jobs*. Each job consists of one or more related and cooperating processes. One job, the *foreground job*, is given complete access to the controlling terminal. The other jobs, *background jobs*, are denied read access to the controlling terminal and given conditional write and **ioctl** access to it. The user may stop an executing job and resume the stopped job either in the foreground or in the background.

Under Job Control, background jobs do not receive events generated by the terminal and are not informed with a hangup indication when the controlling process exits. Background jobs that linger after the login session has been dissolved are prevented from further access to the controlling terminal, and do not interfere with the creation of new login sessions.

The following defines terms associated with Job Control:

- **Background Process group** - A process group that is a member of a session that established a connection with a controlling terminal and is not the foreground process group.

- **Controlling Process** - A session leader that established a connection to a controlling terminal.

- **Controlling Terminal** - A terminal that is associated with a session. Each session may have at most one controlling terminal associated with it and a controlling terminal may be associated with at most one session. Certain input sequences from the controlling terminal cause signals to be sent to the process groups in the session associated with the controlling terminal.

- **Foreground Process Group** - Each session that establishes a connection with a controlling terminal distinguishes one process group of the session as a foreground process group. The foreground process group has certain privileges that are denied to background process groups when accessing its controlling terminal.

- **Orphaned Process Group** - A process group in which the parent of every member in the group is either a member of the group, or is not a member of the process group's session.

- **Process Group** - Each process in the system is a member of a process group that is identified by a process group ID. Any process that is not a process group leader may create a new process group and become its leader. Any process that is not a process group leader may join an existing process group that shares the same session as the process. A newly created process joins the process group of its creator.

- **Process Group Leader** - A process whose process ID is the same as its process group ID.

- **Process Group Lifetime** - A time period that begins when a process group is created by its process group leader and ends when the last process that is a member in the group leaves the group.

- **Process ID** - A positive integer that uniquely identifies each process in the system. A process ID may not be reused by the system until the process lifetime, process group lifetime, and session lifetime ends for any process ID, process group ID, and session ID sharing that value.

- **Process Lifetime** - A time period that begins when the process is forked and ends after the process exits, when its termination has been acknowledged by its parent process.

- **Session** - Each process group is a member of a session that is identified by a session ID.

- **Session ID** - A positive integer that uniquely identifies each session in the system. It is the same as the process ID of its session leader.

- **Session Leader** - A process whose session ID is the same as its process and process group ID.

- **Session Lifetime** - A time period that begins when the session is created by its session leader and ends when the lifetime of the last process group that is a member of the session ends.

The following signals manage Job Control: [see also **signal**(5)]

SIGCONT   Sent to a stopped process to continue it.

SIGSTOP   Sent to a process to stop it. This signal cannot be
                        caught or ignored.

SIGTSTP   Sent to a process to stop it. It is typically used when
                        a user requests to stop the foreground process.

SIGTTIN   Sent to a background process to stop it when it
                        attempts to read from the controlling terminal.

SIGTTOU   Sent to a background process to stop it when one
                        attempts to write to or modify the controlling termi-
                        nal.

A session may be allocated a controlling terminal. For every allocated controlling terminal, Job Control elevates one process group in the controlling process's
session to the status of foreground process group. The remaining process
groups in the controlling process's session are background process groups. A
controlling terminal gives a user the ability to control execution of jobs within
the session. Controlling terminals play a central role in Job Control. A user
may cause the foreground job to stop by typing a predefined key on the controlling terminal. A user may inhibit access to the controlling terminal by background jobs. Background jobs that attempt to access a terminal that has been so
restricted will be sent a signal that typically will cause the job to stop. (See
"Accessing the Controlling Terminal" later in this chapter.)

Job Control requires support from a line discipline module on the controlling
terminal's Stream. The TCSETA, TCSETAW, and TCSETAF commands of **termio**(7) allow a process to set the following line discipline values relevant to Job
Control:

SUSP   A user defined character that, when typed, causes the
                        line discipline module to request that the Stream
                        head sends a SIGTSTP signal to the foreground pro-
                        cess with an M_PCSIG message, which by default
                        stops the members of that group. If the value of
                        SUSP is zero, the SIGTSTP signal is not sent, and the
                        SUSP character is disabled.

TOSTOP   If TOSTOP is set, background processes are inhibited
                                from writing to their controlling terminal.

A line discipline module must record the SUSP suspend character and notify the
Stream head when the user has typed it, and record the state of the TOSTOP bit
and notify the Stream head when the user has changed it.

Allocation and Deallocation

A Stream is allocated as a controlling terminal for a session if:

- The Stream is acting as a terminal,

- The Stream is not already allocated as a controlling terminal, and

- The Stream is opened by a session leader that does not have a controlling
  terminal.

Drivers and modules can inform the Stream head to act as a terminal Stream by
sending an M_SETOPTS message with the SO_ISTTY flag set upstream. This
state may be changed by sending an M_SETOPTS message with the SO_ISNTTY
flag set upstream.

Controlling terminals are allocated with the **open**(2) system call. A Stream head
must be informed that it is acting as a terminal by an M_SETOPTS message sent
upstream before or while the Stream is being opened by a potential controlling
process. If the Stream head is opened before receiving this message, the Stream
is not allocated as a controlling terminal.

Hung-up Streams

When a Stream head receives an M_HANGUP message, it is marked as hung-
up. Streams that are marked as hung-up are allowed to be reopened by their
session leader if they are allocated as a controlling terminal, and by any process
if they are not allocated as a controlling terminal. This way, the hangup error
can be cleared without forcing all file descriptors to be closed first.

If the reopen is successful, the hung-up condition is cleared.

Hangup Signals

When the SIGHUP signal is generated via an M_HANGUP message (instead of an M_SIG or M_PCSIG message), the signal is sent to the controlling process instead of the foreground process group, since the allocation and deallocation of controlling terminals to a session is the responsibility of that process group.

Accessing the Controlling Terminal

If a process attempts to access its controlling terminal after it has been deallocated, access will be denied. If the process is not holding or ignoring SIGHUP, it is sent a SIGHUP signal. Otherwise, the access will fail with an EIO error.

Members of background process groups have limited access to their controlling terminals:

- If the background process is ignoring or holding the SIGTTIN signal or is a member of an orphaned process group, an attempt to read from the controlling terminal will fail with an EIO error. Otherwise, the process is sent a SIGTTIN signal, which by default stops the process.

- If the process is attempting to write to the terminal and if the terminal's TOSTOP flag is clear, the process is allowed access.

  The TOSTOP flag is set upon reception of an M_SETOPTS message with the SO_TOSTOP flag set in the *so_flags* field. It is cleared upon reception of an M_SETOPTS message with the SO_TONSTOP flag set.

- If the terminal's TOSTOP flag is set and a background process is attempting to write to the terminal, the write will succeed if the process is ignoring or holding SIGTTOU. Otherwise, the process will stop except when it is a member of an orphaned process group, in which case it is denied access to the terminal and it is returned an EIO error.

■ If a background process is attempting to perform a destructive **ioctl** (an **ioctl** that modifies terminal parameters), the **ioctl** call will succeed if the process is ignoring or holding SIGTTOU. Otherwise, the process will stop except when the process is a member of the orphaned process group. In that case the access to the terminal is denied and an EIO error is returned.

7 Overview of Modules and Drivers

Module and Driver Environment   7-1
Module and Driver Declarations   7-2
   ■ Null Module Example   7-6

Module and Driver ioctls   7-9
General ioctl Processing   7-10
I_STR ioctl Processing   7-12
Transparent ioctl Processing   7-14
Transparent ioctl Messages   7-17
Transparent ioctl Examples   7-17
   ■ M_COPYIN Example   7-18
   ■ M_COPYOUT Example   7-22
   ■ Bidirectional Transfer Example   7-24
I_LIST ioctl   7-29

Flush Handling   7-31

Driver–Kernel Interface   7-37
Device Driver Interface and Driver–Kernel Interface 7-39
STREAMS Interface   7-40

Design Guidelines   7-42
Modules and Drivers   7-42
   ■ Rules for Open/Close Routines   7-43
   ■ Rules for ioctls   7-43
   ■ Rules for Put and Service Procedures 7-44

Data Structures   7-47
  ■ Dynamic Allocation of STREAMS Data Structures   7-47
Header Files   7-48
Accessible Symbols and Functions   7-49

Module and Driver Environment

Modules and drivers are processing elements in STREAMS. A Stream device driver is similar to a conventional UNIX® system driver. It is opened like a conventional driver and is responsible for the system interface to the device.

STREAMS modules and drivers are structurally similar. The call interfaces to driver routines are identical to interfaces used for modules. Drivers and modules must declare **streamtab**, **qinit**, and **module_info** structures. Within the STREAMS mechanism drivers are required elements, but modules are optional. However, in the STREAMS-based pipe mechanism and the pseudo-terminal subsystem only the Stream head is required.

There are three significant differences between modules and drivers. A driver must be able to handle interrupts from a device, so the driver will typically include an interrupt handler routine. Another difference is that a driver may have multiple Streams connected to it. The third difference is the initialization/deinitialization process that happens via **open/close** with a driver and via the **ioctls** I_PUSH/I_POP with a module. (I_PUSH/I_POP results in calls to **open/close**.)

User context is not generally available to STREAMS module procedures and drivers. The exception is during execution of the **open** and **close** routines. Driver and module **open** and **close** routines have user context and may access the **u_area** structure (defined in **user.h**, see "Accessible Symbols and Functions" later in this chapter) although this is discouraged. These routines are allowed to sleep, but must always return to the caller. That is, if they sleep, it must be at priority numerically <= PZERO, or with PCATCH set in the sleep priority. Priorities are higher as they decrease in numerical value. The process will never return from the sleep call and the system call will be aborted if:

- A process is sleeping at priority > PZERO,

- PCATCH is not set, and

- A process is sent signal via **kill**(2).

CAUTION STREAMS driver and module **put** procedures and **service** procedures have no user context. They cannot access the **u_area** structure of a process and must not sleep.

NOTE The module and driver **open/close** interface has been modified for UNIX System V Release 4.0. However, the system defaults to UNIX System V Release 3.0 interface unless *prefixflag* is defined. This is discussed in the section titled "Driver–Kernel Interface" later in this chapter. Examples and descriptions in this chapter reflect Release 4.0 interface.

Module and Driver Declarations

A module and driver will contain, at a minimum, declarations of the following form:

```
#include "sys/types.h"     /* required in all modules and drivers */
#include "sys/stream.h"     /* required in all modules and drivers */
#include "sys/param.h"

static struct module_info rminfo = { 0x08, "mod", 0, INFPSZ, 0, 0 };
static struct module_info wminfo = { 0x08, "mod", 0, INFPSZ, 0, 0 };
static int modopen(), modput(), modclose();

static struct qinit rinit = {
        modput, NULL, modopen, modclose, NULL, &rminfo, NULL };

static struct qinit winit = {
        modput, NULL, NULL, NULL, NULL, &wminfo, NULL };

struct streamtab modinfo = { &rinit, &winit, NULL, NULL };

extern int moddevflag = 0;
```

The contents of these declarations are constructed for the null module example in this section. This module performs no processing. Its only purpose is to show linkage of a module into the system. The descriptions in this section are general to all STREAMS modules and drivers unless they specifically reference the example.

The declarations shown are: the header set; the read and write queue (*rminfo* and *wminfo*) **module_info** structures; the module open, read-put, write-put, and close procedures; the read and write (*rinit*, and *winit*) **qinit** structures; and the **streamtab** structure.

The header files, **types.h** and **stream.h**, are always required for modules and drivers. The header file, **param.h**, contains definitions for NULL and other values for STREAMS modules and drivers as shown in the section titled "Accessible Symbols and Functions" later in this chapter.

When configuring a STREAMS module or driver (see Appendix E) the **streamtab** structure must be externally accessible. The **streamtab** structure name must be the prefix appended with "info." Also, the driver flag must be externally accessible. The flag name must be the prefix appended with "devflag."

The **streamtab** contains **qinit** values for the read and write queues. The **qinit** structures in turn point to a **module_info** and an optional **module_stat** structure. The two required structures are:

```
struct qinit {
        int       (*qi_putp)();      /* put procedure */
        int       (*qi_srvp)();      /* service procedure */
        int       (*qi_qopen)();     /* called on each open or a push */
        int       (*qi_qclose)();    /* called on last close or a pop */
        int       (*qi_qadmin)();    /* reserved for future use */
struct module_info  *qi_minfo;       /* information structure */
struct module_stat  *qi_mstat;       /* statistics structure - optional */
};
#ifdef _STYPES

struct module_info {
        ushort    mi_idnum;          /* module ID number */
        char      *mi_idname;        /* module name */
        short     mi_minpsz;         /* min packet size, for developer use */
        short     mi_maxpsz;         /* max packet size, for developer use */
        ushort    mi_hiwat;          /* hi-water mark */
        ushort    mi_lowat;          /* lo-water mark */
};
#else

struct module_info {
        ushort    mi_idnum;          /* module ID number */
        char      *mi_idname;        /* module name */
        long      mi_minpsz;         /* min packet size, for developer use */
        long      mi_maxpsz;         /* max packet size, for developer use */
        ulong     mi_hiwat;          /* hi-water mark */
        ulong     mi_lowat;          /* lo-water mark */
};
#endif
```

The **qinit** contains the queue procedures: **put, service, open,** and **close.** All modules and drivers with the same **streamtab** (i.e., the same **fmodsw** or **cdevsw** entry) point to the same upstream and downstream **qinit** structure(s). The structure is meant to be software read-only, as any changes to it affect all instantiations of that module in all Streams. Pointers to the open and close procedures must be contained in the read **qinit** structure. These fields are ignored on the write-side. Our example has no **service** procedure on the read-side or write-side.

The **module_info** contains identification and limit values. All queues associated with a certain driver/module share the same **module_info** structures. The **module_info** structures define the characteristics of that driver/module's queues. As with the **qinit**, this structure is intended to be software read-only.

However, the four limit values (*q_minpsz, q_maxpsz, q_hiwat, q_lowat*) are copied to a **queue** structure where they are modifiable. In the example, the flow control high and low water marks are zero since there is no **service** procedure and messages are not queued in the module.

Three names are associated with a module: the character string in **fmodsw**, obtained from the name of the **master.d** file used to configure the module; the prefix for **streamtab**, used in configuring the module; and the module name field in the **module_info** structure. The module name must be the same as that of **master.d** for autoconfiguration. Each module ID and module name should be unique in the system. The module ID is currently used only in logging and tracing. It is 0x08 in the example.

Minimum and maximum packet sizes are intended to limit the total number of characters contained in M_DATA messages passed to this queue. These limits are advisory except for the Stream head. For certain system calls that write to a Stream, the Stream head will observe the packet sizes set in the write queue of the module immediately below it. Otherwise, the use of packet size is developer dependent. In the example, INFPSZ indicates unlimited size on the read-side.

The **module_stat** is optional. Currently, there is no STREAMS support for statistical information gathering.

Null Module Example

The null module procedures are as follows:

```
static int modopen(q, devp, flag, sflag, credp)
    queue_t *q;        /* pointer to the read queue */
    dev_t   *devp;     /* pointer to major/minor device number */
    int     flag;      /* file flags */
    int     sflag;     /* stream open flags */
    cred_t  *credp;    /* pointer to a credentials structure */
{
    /* return success */
    return 0;
}

static int modput(q, mp)   /* put procedure */
    queue_t *q;        /* pointer to the queue */
    mblk_t  *mp;       /* message pointer */
{
    putnext(q, mp);    /* pass message through */
}
/* Note: we only need one put procedure that can be used for both
 * read-side and write-side.
 */

static int modclose(q, flag, credp)
    queue_t *q;        /* pointer to the read queue */
    int     flag;      /* file flags */
    cred_t  *credp;    /* pointer to a credentials structure */
{
    return 0;
}
```

The form and arguments of these procedures are the same in all modules and
all drivers. Modules and drivers can be used in multiple Streams and their procedures must be reentrant.

NOTE If a module or driver uses the definition `l_dev_t   *devp` instead of
`dev_t   *devp`, then that module or driver will only work on a system
where _STYPES is not defined (that is, types have been expanded). If a
driver or module is being used in environments where _STYPES may or may
not be defined, then a driver should use `dev_t   *devp`, because *dev_t*
changes depending on whether _STYPES is defined.

modopen illustrates the open call arguments and return value. The arguments are the read queue pointer (*q*), the pointer (*devp*) to the major/minor device number, the file flags (*flag*, defined in **sys/file.h**), the Stream open flag (*sflag*), and a pointer to a credentials structure (*credp*). The Stream open flag can take on the following values:

MODOPEN	normal module open
0	normal driver open
CLONEOPEN	clone driver open

The return value from open is 0 for success and an error number for failure. If a driver is called with the CLONEOPEN flag, the device number pointed to by the *devp* should be set by the driver to an unused device number accessible to that driver. This should be an entire device number (major and minor device number). The open procedure for a module is called on the first I_PUSH and on all subsequent **open** calls to the same Stream. During a push, a nonzero return value causes the I_PUSH to fail and the module to be removed from the Stream. If an error is returned by a module during an **open** call, the **open** fails, but the Stream remains intact.

The module open fails if not opened by the super-user (also referred to as a privileged user) that in future releases will be a user with "driver/special" permissions. Permission checks in module and driver open routines should be done with the **drv_priv()** routine. For UNIX System V Release 4.0, there is no need to check if `u.u_uid == 0`. This and the **suser()** routine are replaced with:

```
error = drv_priv(credp);
if (error)        /* not super-user */
return errno;
```

In the null module example, *modopen* simply returns successfully. *modput* illustrates the common interface to **put** procedures. The arguments are the read or write **queue** pointer, as appropriate, and the message pointer. The **put** procedure in the appropriate side of the queue is called when a message is passed from upstream or downstream. The **put** procedure has no return value. In the example, no message processing is performed. All messages are forwarded using the **putnext** macro (see Appendix C). **putnext** calls the **put** procedure of the next queue in the proper direction.

The close routine is only called on an I_POP **ioctl** or on the last **close** call of the Stream. The arguments are the read queue pointer, the file flags as in *modopen*, and a pointer to a credentials structure. The return value is 0 on success and *errno* on failure.

Module and Driver ioctls

STREAMS is an addition to the UNIX system traditional character input/output (I/O) mechanism. In this section, the phrases "character I/O mechanism" and "I/O mechanism" refer only to that part of the mechanism that pre-existed STREAMS.

The character I/O mechanism handles all **ioctl**(2) system calls in a transparent manner. That is, the kernel expects all **ioctls** to be handled by the device driver associated with the character special file on which the call is sent. All **ioctl** calls are sent to the driver, which is expected to perform all validation and processing other than file descriptor validity checking. The operation of any specific **ioctl** is dependent on the device driver. If the driver requires data to be transferred in from user space, it will use the kernel **copyin**() function. It may also use **copyout**() to transfer out any data results back to user space.

With STREAMS, there are a number of differences from the character I/O mechanism that impact **ioctl** processing.

First, there are a set of generic STREAMS **ioctl** command values [see **ioctl**(2)] recognized and processed by the Stream head. These are described in **streamio**(7). The operation of the generic STREAMS **ioctls** are generally independent of the presence of any specific module or driver on the Stream.

The second difference is the absence of user context in a module and driver when the information associated with the **ioctl** is received. This prevents use of **copyin**() or **copyout**() by the module. This also prevents the module and driver from associating any kernel data with the currently running process. (It is likely that by the time the module or driver receives the **ioctl**, the process generating it may no longer be running.)

A third difference is that for the character I/O mechanism, all **ioctls** are handled by the single driver associated with the file. In STREAMS, there can be multiple modules on a Stream and each one can have its own set of **ioctls**. That is, the **ioctls** that can be used on a Stream can change as modules are pushed and popped.

STREAMS provides the capability for user processes to perform control functions on specific modules and drivers in a Stream with **ioctl** calls. Most **streamio**(7) **ioctl** commands go no further than the Stream head. They are fully processed there and no related messages are sent downstream. However, certain commands and all unrecognized commands cause the Stream head to create an M_IOCTL message which includes the **ioctl** arguments and send the message downstream to be received and processed by a specific module or driver. The

M_IOCTL message is the initial message type which carries **ioctl** information to modules. Other message types are used to complete the **ioctl** processing in the Stream. In general, each module must uniquely recognize and take action on specific M_IOCTL messages.

STREAMS **ioctl** handling is equivalent to the transparent processing of the character I/O mechanism. STREAMS modules and drivers can process **ioctls** generated by applications that are implemented for a non-STREAMS environment.

General ioctl Processing

STREAMS blocks a user process which issues an **ioctl** and causes the Stream head to generate an M_IOCTL message. The process remains blocked until either:

- a module or a driver responds with an M_IOCACK (ack, positive acknowledgement) message or an M_IOCNAK (nak, negative acknowledgement) message, or

- no message is received and the request "times out," or

- the **ioctl** is interrupted by the user process, or

- an error condition occurs.

For the **ioctl** I_STR the timeout period can be a user specified interval or a default. For the other M_IOCTL **ioctls**, the default value (infinite) is used.

For an I_STR, the STREAMS module or driver that generates a positive acknowledgement message can also return data to the process in that message. An alternate means to return data is provided with transparent **ioctls**. If the Stream head does not receive a positive or negative acknowledgement message in the specified time, the **ioctl** call fails.

A module that receives an unrecognized M_IOCTL message should pass it on unchanged. A driver that receives an unrecognized M_IOCTL should produce a negative acknowledgement.

The form of an M_IOCTL message is a single M_IOCTL message block followed by (see Figure B-1 in Appendix B) zero or more M_DATA blocks. The M_IOCTL message block contains an **iocblk** structure, defined in **<sys/stream.h>**:

```
#ifdef _STYPES

struct iocblk {
    int        ioc_cmd;         /* ioctl command type */
    o_uid_t    ioc_uid;         /* effective uid of user */
    o_gid_t    ioc_gid;         /* effective gid of user */
    uint       ioc_id;          /* ioctl id */
    uint       ioc_count;       /* count of bytes in data block(s) */
    int        ioc_error;       /* error code */
    int        ioc_rval;        /* return value */
};
#else

struct iocblk {
    int        ioc_cmd;         /* ioctls command type */
    cred_t     *ioc_cr;         /* full credentials */
    uint       ioc_id;          /* ioctl id */
    uint       ioc_count;       /* count of bytes in data field */
    int        ioc_error;       /* error code */
    int        ioc_rval;        /* return value */
    long       ioc_filler[4];   /* reserved for future use */
};
#define ioc_uid ioc_cr->cr_uid
#define ioc_gid ioc_cr->cr_gid

#endif
```

For an I_STR **ioctl**, *ioc_cmd* contains the command supplied by the user in the **strioctl** structure defined in **streamio**(7).

If a module or driver determines an M_IOCTL message is in error for any reason, it must produce the negative acknowledgement message. This is typically done by setting the message type to M_IOCNAK and sending the message upstream. No data or a return value can be sent to a user in this case. If *ioc_error* is set to 0, the Stream head will cause the **ioctl** call to fail with EINVAL. The driver has the option of setting *ioc_error* to an alternate error number if desired.

NOTE   *ioc_error* can be set to a nonzero value in both M_IOCACK and M_IOCNAK. This will cause that value to be returned as an error number to the process that sent the **ioctl**.

If a module wants to look at what **ioctls** of other modules are doing, the module should not look for a specific M_IOCTL on the write-side but look for M_IOCACK or M_IOCNAK on the read-side. For example, the module sees TCSETA [see **termio**(7)] going down and wants to know what is being set. The module should look at it and save away the answer but not use it. The read-side processing knows that the module is waiting for an answer for the ioctl. When the read-side processing sees an "ack" or "nak" next time, it checks if it is the same **ioctl** (here TCSETA) and if it is, the module may use the answer previously saved.

The two STREAMS **ioctl** mechanisms, I_STR and transparent, are described next. [Here, I_STR means the **streamio**(7) I_STR command and implies the related STREAMS processing unless noted otherwise.] I_STR has a restricted format and restricted addressing for transferring **ioctl**-related data between user and kernel space. It requires only a single pair of messages to complete **ioctl** processing. The transparent mechanism is more general and has almost no restrictions on **ioctl** data format and addressing. The transparent mechanism generally requires that multiple pairs of messages be exchanged between the Stream head and module to complete the processing.

I_STR ioctl Processing

The I_STR **ioctl** provides a capability for user applications to perform module and driver control functions on STREAMS files. I_STR allows an application to specify the **ioctl** timeout. It requires that all user **ioctl** data (to be received by the destination module) be placed in a single block which is pointed to from the user **strioctl** structure. The module can also return data to this block.

If the module is looking at for example the TCSETA/TCGETA group of **ioctl** calls as they pass up or down a Stream, it must never assume that because TCSETA comes down that it actually has a data buffer attached to it. The user may have formed TCSETA as an I_STR call and accidentally given a null data buffer pointer. One must always check *b_cont* to see if it is NULL before using it as an index to the data block that goes with M_IOCTL messages.

The TCGETA call, if formed as an I_STR call with a data buffer pointer set to a value by the user, will always have a data buffer attached to *b_cont* from the main message block. If one assumes that the data block is not there and allocates a new buffer and assigns *b_cont* to point at it, the original buffer will be lost. Thus, before assuming that the **ioctl** message does not have a buffer attached, one should check first.

The following example illustrates processing associated with an I_STR **ioctl**. *lpdoioctl* is called to process trapped M_IOCTL messages:

```
lpdoioctl(lp, mp)
    struct lp *lp;
    mblk_t *mp;
{
    struct iocblk *iocp;
    queue_t *q;

    q = lp->qptr;

    /* 1st block contains iocblk structure */
    iocp = (struct iocblk *)mp->b_rptr;

    switch (iocp->ioc_cmd) {
    case SET_OPTIONS:
        /* Count should be exactly one short's worth (for this example) */
        if (iocp->ioc_count != sizeof(short))
            goto iocnak;
        if (mp->b_cont == NULL)
            goto lognak; /* not shown in this example */
        /* Actual data is in 2nd message block */
        lpsetopt(lp, *(short *)mp->b_cont->b_rptr);

        /* ACK the ioctl */
        mp->b_datap->db_type = M_IOCACK;
        iocp->ioc_count = 0;
        qreply(q, mp);
        break;
    default:
    iocnak:
        /* NAK the ioctl */
        mp->b_datap->db_type = M_IOCNAK;
        qreply(q, mp);
    }
}
```

lpdoioctl illustrates driver M_IOCTL processing which also applies to modules. However, at case *default*, a module would not "nak" an unrecognized command, but would pass the message on. In this example, only one command is recognized, *SET_OPTIONS*. *ioc_count* contains the number of user supplied data bytes. For this example, it must equal the size of a short. The user data are sent directly to the printer interface using *lpsetopt*. Next, the M_IOCTL message is changed to type M_IOCACK and the *ioc_count* field is set to zero to indicate that no data are to be returned to the user. Finally, the message is sent upstream using **qreply()**. If *ioc_count* was left nonzero, the Stream head would copy that many bytes from the 2nd - Nth message blocks into the user buffer.

Transparent ioctl Processing

The transparent STREAMS **ioctl** mechanism allows application programs to perform module and driver control functions with **ioctls** other than I_STR. It is intended to transparently support applications developed prior to the introduction of STREAMS. It alleviates the need to recode and recompile the user level software to run over STREAMS files.

The mechanism extends the data transfer capability for STREAMS **ioctl** calls beyond that provided in the I_STR form. Modules and drivers can transfer data between their kernel space and user space in any **ioctl** which has a value of the *command* argument not defined in **streamio**(7). These **ioctls** are known as transparent **ioctls** to differentiate them from the I_STR form. Transparent processing support is necessary when existing user level applications perform **ioctls** on a non-STREAMS character device and the device driver is converted to STREAMS. The **ioctl** data can be in any format mutually understood by the user application and module.

The transparent mechanism also supports STREAMS applications that want to send **ioctl** data to a driver or module in a single call, where the data may not be in a form readily embedded in a single user block. For example, the data may be contained in nested structures, different user space buffers, etc.

This mechanism is needed because user context does not exist in modules and drivers when **ioctl** processing occurs. This prevents them from using the kernel **copyin()**/**copyout()** functions. For example, consider the following **ioctl** call:

```
ioctl (stream_fildes, user_command, &ioctl_struct);
```

where *ioctl_struct* is a structure containing the members:

```
int stringlen;  /* string length */
char *string;
struct other_struct *other1;
```

To read (or write) the elements of *ioctl_struct*, a module would have to perform a series of **copyin()**/**copyout()** calls using pointer information from a prior **copyin()** to transfer additional data. A non-STREAMS character driver could directly execute these copy functions because user context exists during all UNIX system calls to the driver. However, in STREAMS, user context is only available to modules and drivers in their open and close routines.

The transparent mechanism enables modules and drivers to request that the Stream head perform a **copyin()** or **copyout()** on their behalf to transfer **ioctl** data between their kernel space and various user space locations. The related data are sent in message pairs exchanged between the Stream head and the module. A pair of messages is required so that each transfer can be acknowledged. In addition to M_IOCTL, M_IOCACK, and M_IOCNAK messages, the transparent mechanism also uses M_COPYIN, M_COPYOUT, and M_IOCDATA messages.

The general processing by which a module or a driver reads data from user space for the transparent case involves pairs of request/response messages, as follows:

1. The Stream head does not recognize the *command* argument of an **ioctl** call and creates a transparent M_IOCTL message (the **iocblk** structure has a TRANSPARENT indicator, see "Transparent ioctl Messages") containing the value of the *arg* argument in the call. It sends the M_IOCTL message downstream.

2. A module receives the M_IOCTL message, recognizes the *ioc_cmd*, and determines that it is TRANSPARENT.

3. If the module requires user data, it creates an M_COPYIN message to request a **copyin**() of user data. The message will contain the address of user data to copy in and how much data to transfer. It sends the message upstream.

4. The Stream head receives the M_COPYIN message and uses the contents to **copyin**() the data from user space into an M_IOCDATA response message which it sends downstream. The message also contains an indicator of whether the data transfer succeeded (the **copyin**() might fail, for instance, because of an EFAULT [see **intro**(2)] condition).

5. The module receives the M_IOCDATA message and processes its contents.

   The module may use the message contents to generate another M_COPYIN. Steps 3 through 5 may be repeated until the module has requested and received all the user data to be transferred.

6. When the module completes its data transfer, it performs the **ioctl** processing and sends an M_IOCACK message upstream to notify the Stream head that **ioctl** processing has successfully completed.

Writing data from a module to user space is similar except that the module uses an M_COPYOUT message to request the Stream head to write data into user space. In addition to length and user address, the message includes the data to be copied out. In this case, the M_IOCDATA response will not contain user data, only an indication of success or failure.

The module may intermix M_COPYIN and M_COPYOUT messages in any order. However, each message must be sent one at a time; the module must receive the associated M_IOCDATA response before any subsequent M_COPYIN/M_COPYOUT request or "ack/nak" message is sent upstream. After the last M_COPYIN/M_COPYOUT message, the module must send an M_IOCACK message (or M_IOCNAK in the event of a detected error condition).

For a transparent M_IOCTL, user data can not be returned with an M_IOCACK message. The data must have been sent with a preceding M_COPYOUT message.

Transparent ioctl Messages

The form of the M_IOCTL message generated by the Stream head for a transparent **ioctl** is a single M_IOCTL message block followed by one M_DATA block. The form of the **iocblk** structure in the M_IOCTL block is the same as described under "General ioctl Processing." However, *ioc_cmd* is set to the value of the *command* argument in the **ioctl** system call and *ioc_count* is set to TRANSPARENT, defined in <sys/stream.h>. TRANSPARENT distinguishes the case where an I_STR **ioctl** may specify a value of *ioc_cmd* equivalent to the *command* argument of a transparent **ioctl**. The M_DATA block of the message contains the value of the *arg* parameter in the call.

Modules that process a specific *ioc_cmd* which did not validate the *ioc_count* field of the M_IOCTL message will break if transparent **ioctls** with the same *command* are performed from user space.

M_COPYIN, M_COPYOUT, and M_IOCDATA messages and their use are described in more detail in Appendix B.

Transparent ioctl Examples

Following are three examples of transparent **ioctl** processing. The first illustrates M_COPYIN. The second illustrates M_COPYOUT. The third is a more complex example showing state transitions combining both M_COPYIN and M_COPYOUT.

M_COPYIN Example

In this example, the contents of a user buffer are to be transferred into the kernel as part of an **ioctl** call of the form

```
ioctl(fd, SET_ADDR, &bufadd)
```

where *bufadd* is a structure declared as

```
struct address {
    int ad_len;          /* buffer length in bytes */
    caddr_t ad_addr;     /* buffer address */
};
```

This requires two pairs of messages (request/response) following receipt of the M_IOCTL message. The first will **copyin** the structure and the second will **copyin** the buffer. This example illustrates processing that supports only the transparent form of **ioctl**. *xxxwput* is the write-side **put** procedure for module or driver *xxx*:

```
struct address {      /* same members as in user space */
    int ad_len;       /* length in bytes */
    caddr_t ad_addr;  /* buffer address */
};
/* state values (overloaded in private field) */
#define GETSTRUCT    0       /* address structure */
#define GETADDR      1       /* byte string from ad_addr */
xxxwput(q, mp)
    queue_t *q;     /* write queue */
    mblk_t *mp;
{
    struct iocblk *iocbp;
    struct copyreq *cqp;

    switch (mp->b_datap->db_type) {
          .
          .
          .
    case M_IOCTL:
        iocbp = (struct iocblk *)mp->b_rptr;
        switch (iocbp->ioc_cmd) {
        case SET_ADDR:
            if (iocbp->ioc_count != TRANSPARENT) {/* fail if I_STR */
```

(continued on next page)

```
                    if (mp->b_cont) {          /* return buffer to pool ASAP */
                        freemsg(mp->b_cont);
                        mp->b_cont = NULL;
                    }
                    mp->b_datap->db_type = M_IOCNAK;  /* EINVAL */
                    qreply(q, mp);
                    break;
                }
                /* Reuse M_IOCTL block for M_COPYIN request */
                cqp = (struct copyreq *)mp->b_rptr;
                /* Get user space structure address from linked M_DATA block */
                cqp->cq_addr = (caddr_t) *(long *)mp->b_cont->b_rptr;
                freemsg(mp->b_cont);         /* MUST free linked blocks */
                mp->b_cont = NULL;
                cqp->cq_private = (mblk_t *)GETSTRUCT;   /* to identify response */
                /* Finish describing M_COPYIN message */
                cqp->cq_size = sizeof(struct address);
                cqp->cq_flag = 0;
                mp->b_datap->db_type = M_COPYIN;
                mp->b_wptr = mp->b_rptr + sizeof(struct copyreq);
                qreply(q, mp);
                break;
            default:        /* M_IOCTL not for us */
                /* if module, pass on */
                /* if driver, nak ioctl */
                break;
            }  /* switch (iocbp->ioc_cmd) */
        break;
    case M_IOCDATA:
        xxxioc(q, mp); /* all M_IOCDATA processing done here */
        break;
        .
        .
        .
    }    /* switch (mp->b_datap->db_type) */
}
```

xxxwput verifies that the *SET_ADDR* is TRANSPARENT to avoid confusion with
an I_STR **ioctl** which uses a value of *ioc_cmd* equivalent to the *command* argument of a transparent **ioctl**. When sending an M_IOCNAK, freeing the linked
M_DATA block is not mandatory as the Stream head will free it. However, this
returns the block to the buffer pool more quickly.

In this and all following examples in this section, the message blocks are reused to avoid the overhead of deallocating and allocating.

 NOTE The Stream head will guarantee that the size of the message block containing an **iocblk** structure will be large enough also to hold the **copyreq** and **copyresp** structures.

cq_private is set to contain state information for **ioctl** processing (tells us what the subsequent M_IOCDATA response message contains). Keeping the state in the message makes the message self-describing and simplifies the **ioctl** processing. M_IOCDATA processing is done in *xxxioc*. Two M_IOCDATA types are processed, *GETSTRUCT* and *GETADDR*:

```
xxxioc(q, mp)       /* M_IOCDATA processing */
    queue_t *q;
    mblk_t *mp;
{
    struct iocblk *iocbp;
    struct copyreq *cqp;
    struct copyresp *csp;
    struct address *ap;
    csp = (struct copyresp *)mp->b_rptr;
    iocbp = (struct iocblk *)mp->b_rptr;
    switch (csp->cp_cmd) {    /* validate this M_IOCDATA is for this module */
    case SET_ADDR:
        if (csp->cp_rval) {        /* GETSTRUCT or GETADDR failed */
            freemsg(mp);
            return;
        }
        switch ((int)csp->cp_private) {      /* determine state */
        case GETSTRUCT:          /* user structure has arrived */
            mp->b_datap->db_type = M_COPYIN;   /* reuse M_IOCDATA block */
            cqp = (struct copyreq *)mp->b_rptr;
            ap = (struct address *)mp->b_cont->b_rptr;/* user structure */
            cqp->cq_size = ap->ad_len;        /* buffer length */
            cqp->cq_addr = ap->ad_addr;       /* user space buffer address */
            freemsg(mp->b_cont);
            mp->b_cont = NULL;
            cqp->cq_flag = 0;
            csp->cp_private = (mblk_t *)GETADDR; /* next state */
            qreply(q, mp);
```

(continued on next page)

```
            break;
        case GETADDR:   /* user address is here */
            if (xxx_set_addr(mp->b_cont) == FAILURE) { /* hypothetical routine */
                mp->b_datap->db_type = M_IOCNAK;
                iocbp->ioc_error = EIO;
            } else {
                mp->b_datap->db_type = M_IOCACK; /* success */
                iocbp->ioc_error = 0;        /* may have been overwritten */
                iocbp->ioc_count = 0;        /* may have been overwritten */
                iocbp->ioc_rval = 0;         /* may have been overwritten */
            }
            mp->b_wptr = mp->b_rptr + sizeof(struct ioclk);
            freemsg(mp->b_cont);
            mp->b_cont = NULL;
            qreply(q, mp);
            break;
        default:         /* invalid state: can't happen */
            freemsg(mp->b_cont);
            mp->b_cont = NULL;
            mp->b_datap->db_type = M_IOCNAK;
            mp->b_wptr = mp->rptr + sizeof(struct iocblk);
            iocbp->ioc_error = EINVAL;         /* may have been overwritten */
            qreply(q, mp);
            ASSERT(0);   /* panic if debugging mode */
            break;
        }
        break; /* switch (cp_private) */
    default:         /* M_IOCDATA not for us */
        /* if module, pass message on */
        /* if driver, free message */
        break;
    }   /* switch (cp_cmd) */
}
```

xxx_set_addr is a routine (not shown in the example) that processes the user
address from the **ioctl**. Since the message block has been reused, the fields that
the Stream head will examine (denoted by "may have been overwritten") must
be cleared before sending an M_IOCNAK.

M_COPYOUT Example

In this example, the user wants option values for this Stream device to be placed into the user's *options* structure (see beginning of example code, below). This can be accomplished by use of a transparent **ioctl** call of the form

        ioctl(fd, GET_OPTIONS, &optadd)

or, alternately, by use of a **streamio** call

        ioctl(fd, I_STR, &opts_strioctl) call

In the first case, *optadd* is declared *struct options*. In the I_STR case, *opts_strioctl* is declared *struct strioctl* where *opts_strioctl.ic_dp* points to the user *options* structure.

This example illustrates support of both the I_STR and transparent forms of an **ioctl**. The transparent form requires a single M_COPYOUT message following receipt of the M_IOCTL to **copyout** the contents of the structure. *xxxwput* is the write-side **put** procedure for module or driver *xxx*:

```
struct options {      /* same members as in user space */
    int op_one;
    int op_two;
    short   op_three;
    long    op_four;
};

xxxwput(q, mp)
    queue_t *q;     /* write queue */
    mblk_t *mp;
{
    struct iocblk *iocbp;
    struct copyreq *cqp;
    struct copyresp *csp;
    int transparent = 0;
    switch (mp->b_datap->db_type) {
        .
        .
        .
    case M_IOCTL:
        iocbp = (struct iocblk *)mp->b_rptr;
```

(continued on next page)

Programmer's Guide: STREAMS

```
    switch (iocbp->ioc_cmd) {
    case GET_OPTIONS:
        if (iocbp->ioc_count == TRANSPARENT) {
            transparent = 1;
            cqp = (struct copyreq *)mp->b_rptr;
            cqp->cq_size = sizeof(struct options);
            /* Get structure address from linked M_DATA block */
            cqp->cq_addr = (caddr_t) *(long *)mp->b_cont->b_rptr;
            cqp->cq_flag = 0;

            /* No state necessary - we will only ever get one M_IOCDATA from
             * the Stream head indicating success or failure for the copyout */
        }
        if (mp->b_cont)
            freemsg(mp->b_cont);        /* overwritten below */
        if ((mp->b_cont = allocb(sizeof(struct options), BPRI_MED)) == NULL) {
            mp->b_datap->db_type = M_IOCNAK;
            iocbp->ioc_error = EAGAIN;
            qreply(q, mp);
            break;
        }
        xxx_get_options(mp->b_cont);    /* hypothetical routine */
        if (transparent) {
            mp->b_datap->db_type = M_COPYOUT;
            mp->b_wptr = mp->b_rptr + sizeof(struct copyreq);
        } else {
            mp->b_datap->db_type = M_IOCACK;
            iocbp->ioc_count = sizeof(struct options);
        }
        qreply(q, mp);
        break;
    default:        /* M_IOCTL not for us */
        /* if module, pass on; if driver, nak ioctl */
        break;
    } /* switch (iocbp->ioc_cmd) */
    break;
case M_IOCDATA:
    csp = (struct copyresp *)mp->b_rptr;
    if (csp->cmd != GET_OPTIONS) {     /* M_IOCDATA not for us */
        /* if module, pass on; if driver, free message */
        break;
    }
    if ( csp->cp_rval ) {
        freemsg(mp);        /* failure */
        return;
```

(continued on next page)

```
        }
        /* Data successfully copied out, ack */
        mp->b_datap->db_type = M_IOCACK; /* reuse M_IOCDATA for ack */
        mp->b_wptr = mp->b_rptr + sizeof(struct iocblk);
        iocbp->ioc_error = 0;       /* may have been overwritten */
        iocbp->ioc_count = 0;       /* may have been overwritten */
        iocbp->ioc_rval = 0;        /* may have been overwritten */
        qreply(q, mp);
        break;
        .
        .
        .
    } /* switch (mp->b_datap->db_type) */
}
```

Bidirectional Transfer Example

This example illustrates bidirectional data transfer between the kernel and user space during transparent **ioctl** processing. It also shows how more complex state information can be used.

The user wants to send and receive data from user buffers as part of a transparent **ioctl** call of the form

```
        ioctl(fd, XXX_IOCTL, &addr_xxxdata)
```

The user *addr_xxxdata* structure defining the buffers is declared as *struct xxxdata*, shown below. This requires three pairs of messages following receipt of the M_IOCTL message: the first to **copyin** the structure; the second to **copyin** one user buffer; and the last to **copyout** the second user buffer. *xxxwput* is the write-side **put** procedure for module or driver *xxx*:

```
struct xxxdata {           /* same members in user space */
   int x_inlen;            /* number of bytes copied in */
   caddr_t x_inaddr;      /* buffer address of data copied in */
   int x_outlen;           /* number of bytes copied out */
   caddr_t x_outaddr;     /* buffer address of data copied out */
};
/*  State information for ioctl processing */
struct state {
   int     st_state;       /* see below */
   struct xxxdata st_data;   /* see above */
};
/* state values */
#define GETSTRUCT         0      /* get xxxdata structure */
#define GETINDATA         1      /* get data from x_inaddr */
#define PUTOUTDATA        2      /* get response from M_COPYOUT */

xxxwput(q, mp)
   queue_t *q;    /* write queue */
   mblk_t *mp;
{
   struct iocblk *iocbp;
   struct copyreq *cqp;
   struct state *stp;
   mblk_t *tmp;

   switch (mp->b_datap->db_type) {
      .
      .
      .
   case M_IOCTL:
      iocbp = (struct iocblk *)mp->b_rptr;
      switch (iocbp->ioc_cmd) {
      case XXX_IOCTL:
         if (iocbp->ioc_count != TRANSPARENT) {/* fail if I_STR */
            if (mp->b_cont) {          /* return buffer to pool ASAP */
               freemsg(mp->b_cont);
               mp->b_cont = NULL;
            }
            mp->b_datap->db_type = M_IOCNAK; /* EINVAL */
            qreply(q, mp);
            break;
         }
         /* Reuse M_IOCTL block for M_COPYIN request */
         cqp = (struct copyreq *)mp->b_rptr;
         /* Get structure's user address from linked M_DATA block */
```

(continued on next page)

```
            cqp->cq_addr = (caddr_t) *(long *)mp->b_cont->b_rptr;
            freemsg(mp->b_cont);
            mp->b_cont = NULL;

            /* Allocate state buffer */

            if ((tmp = allocb(sizeof(struct state), BPRI_MED)) == NULL) {
                mp->b_datap->db_type = M_IOCNAK;
                iocbp->ioc_error = EAGAIN;
                qreply(q, mp);
                break;
            }
            tmp->b_wptr += sizeof(struct state);
            stp = (struct state *)tmp->b_rptr;
            stp->st_state = GETSTRUCT;
            cqp->cq_private = tmp;

            /* Finish describing M_COPYIN message */

            cqp->cq_size = sizeof(struct xxxdata);
            cqp->cq_flag = 0;
            mp->b_datap->db_type = M_COPYIN;
            mp->b_wptr = mp->b_rptr + sizeof(struct copyreq);
            qreply(q, mp);
            break;
        default:        /* M_IOCTL not for us */
            /* if module, pass on */
            /* if driver, nak ioctl */
            break;
        } /* switch (iocbp->ioc_cmd) */
        break;
    case M_IOCDATA:
        xxxioc(q, mp); /* all M_IOCDATA processing done here */
        break;
        .
        .
        .
    } /* switch (mp->b_datap->db_type) */
}
```

xxxwput allocates a message block to contain the state structure and reuses the M_IOCTL to create an M_COPYIN message to read in the *xxxdata* structure.

M_IOCDATA processing is done in *xxxioc*:

```
xxxioc(q, mp)      /* M_IOCDATA processing */
  queue_t *q;
  mblk_t *mp;
{
  struct iocblk *iocbp;
  struct copyreq *cqp;
  struct copyresp *csp;
  struct state *stp;
  mblk_t *xxx_indata();

  csp = (struct copyresp *)mp->b_rptr;
  iocbp = (struct iocblk *)mp->b_rptr;
  switch (csp->cp_cmd) {
  case XXX_IOCTL:
      if (csp->cp_rval) {        /* failure */
          if (csp->cp_private)       /* state structure */
              freemsg(csp->cp_private);
          freemsg(mp);
          return;
      }
      stp = (struct state *)csp->cp_private->b_rptr;
      switch (stp->st_state) {
      case GETSTRUCT:            /* xxxdata structure copied in */
          /* save structure */
          stp->st_data = *(struct xxxdata *)mp->b_cont->b_rptr;
          freemsg(mp->b_cont);
          mp->b_cont = NULL;
          /* Reuse M_IOCDATA to copyin data */
          mp->b_datap->db_type = M_COPYIN;
          cqp = (struct copyreq *)mp->b_rptr;
          cqp->cq_size = stp->st_data.x_inlen;
          cqp->cq_addr = stp->st_data.x_inaddr;
          cqp->cq_flag = 0;
          stp->st_state = GETINDATA;            /* next state */
          qreply(q, mp);
          break;
      case GETINDATA:            /* data successfully copied in */
          /* Process input, return output */
          if ((mp->b_cont = xxx_indata(mp->b_cont)) == NULL) {/* hypothetical */
              mp->b_datap->db_type = M_IOCNAK; /* fail xxx_indata */
              mp->b_wptr = mp->b_rptr + sizeof(struct iocblk);
              iocbp->ioc_error = EIO;
              qreply(q, mp);
              break;
          }
```

(continued on next page)

```
                mp->b_datap->db_type = M_COPYOUT;
                cqp = (struct copyreq *)mp->b_rptr;
                cqp->cq_size = min(msgdsize(mp->b_cont), stp->st_data.x_outlen);
                cqp->cq_addr = stp->st_data.x_outaddr;
                cqp->cq_flag = 0;
                stp->st_state = PUTOUTDATA;        /* next state */
                qreply(q, mp);
                break;
            case PUTOUTDATA:        /* data successfully copied out, ack ioctl */
                freemsg(csp->cp_private); /* state structure */
                mp->b_datap->db_type = M_IOCACK;
                mp->b_wtpr = mp->b_rptr + sizeof(struct iocblk);
                iocbp->ioc_error = 0; /* may have been overwritten */
                iocbp->ioc_count = 0; /* may have been overwritten */
                iocbp->ioc_rval = 0;   /* may have been overwritten */
                qreply(q, mp);
                break;
            default:                /* invalid state: can't happen */
                freemsg(mp->b_cont);
                mp->b_cont = NULL;
                mp->b_datap->db_type = M_IOCNAK;
                mp->b_wptr = mp->b_rptr + sizeof(struct iocblk);
                iocbp->ioc_error = EINVAL;
                qreply(q, mp);
                ASSERT (0);       /* panic if debugging mode */
                break;
            }  /* switch (stp->st_state) */
            break;
        default:        /* M_IOCDATA not for us */
            /* if module, pass message on */
            /* if driver, free message */
            break;
        }  /* switch (csp->cp_cmd) */
    }
```

At *case GETSTRUCT*, the user *xxxdata* structure is copied into the module's *state* structure (pointed at by *cp_private* in the message) and the M_IOCDATA message is reused to create a second M_COPYIN message to read in the user data. At *case GETINDATA*, the input user data are processed by the *xxx_indata* routine (not supplied in the example) which frees the linked M_DATA block and returns the output data message block. The M_IOCDATA message is reused to create an M_COPYOUT message to write the user data. At *case PUTOUTDATA*, the message block containing the state structure is freed and an acknowledgement is sent upstream.

Care must be taken at the "can't happen" *default* case since the message block containing the state structure (*cp_private*) is not returned to the pool because it might not be valid. This might result in a lost block. The ASSERT will help find errors in the module if a "can't happen" condition occurs.

I_LIST ioctl

The **ioctl** I_LIST supports the **strconf** and **strchg** commands [see **strchg**(1)] that are used to query or change the configuration of a Stream. Only the super-user or an owner of a STREAMS device may alter the configuration of that Stream.

The **strchg** command does the following:

- Push one or more modules on the Stream.

- Pop the topmost module off the Stream.

- Pop all the modules off the Stream.

- Pop all modules up to but not including a specified module.

The **strconf** command does the following:

- Indicate if the specified module is present on the Stream.

- Print the topmost module of the Stream.

- Print a list of all modules and topmost driver on the Stream.

If the Stream contains a multiplexing driver, the **strchg** and **strconf** commands will not recognize any modules below that driver.

The **ioctl** I_LIST performs two functions. When the third argument of the **ioctl** call is set to NULL, the return value of the call indicates the number of modules, including the driver, present on the Stream. For example, if there are two modules above the driver, 3 is returned. On failure, *errno* may be set to a value specified in **streamio**(7). The second function of the I_LIST **ioctl** is to copy the module names found on the Stream to the user supplied buffer. The address of the buffer in user space and the size of the buffer are passed to the **ioctl** through a structure **str_list** that is defined as:

```
struct  str_mlist {
   char l_name[FMNAMESZ+1];        /* space for holding a module name */
};
struct str_list {
   int sl_nmods;                    /* # of modules for which space is allocated */
   struct str_mlist  *sl_modlist;/* address of buffer for names */
};
```

where *sl_nmods* is the number of modules in the *sl_modlist* array that the user
has allocated. Each element in the array must be at least FMNAMESZ+1 bytes
long. FMNAMESZ is defined by <sys/conf.h>.

The user can find out how much space to allocate by first invoking the **ioctl**
I_LIST with *arg* set to NULL. The I_LIST call with *arg* pointing to the **str_list**
structure returns the number of entries that have been filled into the *sl_modlist*
array (the number includes the number of modules including the driver). If
there is not enough space in the *sl_modlist* array (see note) or *sl_nmods* is less
than 1, the I_LIST call will fail and *errno* is set to EINVAL. If *arg* or the
sl_modlist array points outside the allocated address space, EFAULT is returned.

 NOTE It is possible, but unlikely, that another module was pushed on the Stream
after the user invoked the I_LIST **ioctl** with the NULL argument and before
the I_LIST **ioctl** with the structure argument was invoked.

Flush Handling

All modules and drivers are expected to handle M_FLUSH messages. An M_FLUSH message can originate at the Stream head or from a module or a driver. The first byte of the M_FLUSH message is an option flag that can have following values:

FLUSHR	Flush read queue.
FLUSHW	Flush write queue.
FLUSHRW	Flush both, read and write, queues.
FLUSHBAND	Flush a specified priority band only.

The following example shows line discipline module flush handling:

```
ld_put (q, mp)
    queue_t *q;          /* pointer to read/write queue */
    mlkb_t *mp;          /* pointer to message being passed */
{
    switch (mp->_datap->db_type) {
            default:
                        putq(q, mp);    /* queue everything */
                        return;         /* except flush */

            case M_FLUSH:
                        if (*mp->b_rptr & FLUSHW)/* flush write queue */
                            flushq((q->q_flag & QREADR) ? WR(q) : q,FLUSHDATA);

                        if (*mp->b_rptr & FLUSHR)/* flush read queue */
                            flushq((q->q_flag & QREADQ) ? q : RD(q),FLUSHDATA);

                        putnext(q, mp);    /* pass it on */
                        return;
    }
}
```

The Stream head turns around the M_FLUSH message if FLUSHW is set (FLUSHR will be cleared). A driver turns around M_FLUSH if FLUSHR is set (should mask off FLUSHW).

The next example shows the line discipline module flushing due to break:

```
ld_put(q, mp)
    queue_t *q;         /* pointer to read/write queue */
    mblk_t *mp;         /* pointer to message being passed */
{
    switch (mp->b_datap->db_type) {
            default:
                    putq(q, mp);    /* queue everything except flush */
                    return;

            case M_FLUSH:
                    if (*mp->b_rptr & FLUSHW)/* flush write queue */
                        flushq((q->q_flag & QREADR) ? WR(q) : q, FLUSHDATA);

                    if (*mp->b_rptr & FLUSHR)/* flush read queue */
                        flushq((q->q_flag & QREADR) ? q : RD(q), FLUSHDATA);
                    putnext(q, mp);    /* pass it on */
                    return;

            case M_BREAK:
                    if (q->q_flag & QREADR) {/* read side only */
                            /* it doesn't make sense for write side */

                    putctll(q->q_next, M_PCSIG, SIGINT);
                    putctll(q->q_next, M_FLUSH, FLUSHW);
                    putctll(WR(q)->q_next, M_FLUSH, FLUSHR);
                    }
                    return;
    }
}
```

The next two figures further demonstrate flushing the entire Stream due to a line break. Figure 7-1 shows the flushing of the write-side of a Stream, and Figure 7-2 shows the flushing of the read-side of a Stream. In the figures dotted boxes indicate flushed queues.

Figure 7-1: Flushing The Write-Side of A Stream

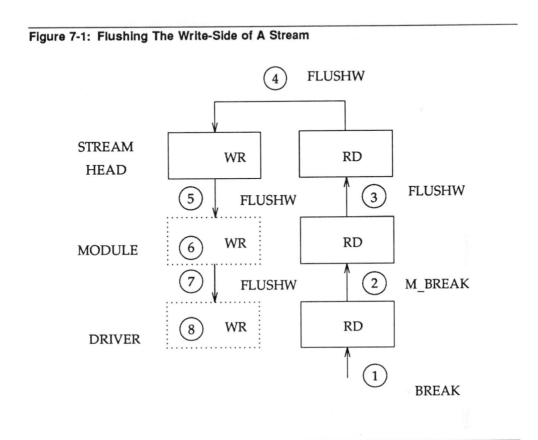

The following takes place:

1. A break is detected by a driver.

2. The driver generates an M_BREAK message and sends it upstream.

3. The module translates the M_BREAK into an M_FLUSH message with FLUSHW set and sends it upstream.

4. The Stream head does **not** flush the write queue (no messages are ever queued there).

5. The Stream head turns the message around (sends it down the write-side).

6. The module flushes its write queue.

7. The message is passed downstream.

8. The driver flushes its write queue and frees the message.

This figure shows flushing read-side of a Stream.

Figure 7-2: Flushing The Read-Side of A Stream

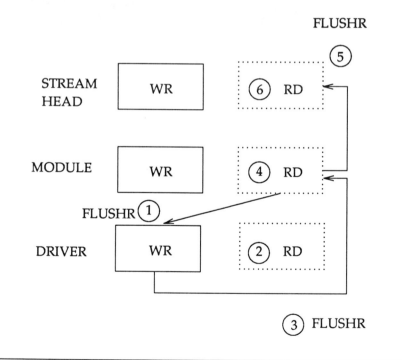

The events taking place are:

1. After generating the first M_FLUSH message, the module generates an M_FLUSH with FLUSHR set and sends it downstream.

2. The driver flushes its read queue.

3. The driver turns the message around (sends it up the read-side).

4. The module flushes its read queue.

5. The message is passed upstream.

6. The Stream head flushes the read queue and frees the message.

The **flushband**() routine (see Appendix C) provides the module and driver with the capability to flush messages associated with a given priority band. A user can flush a particular band of messages by issuing:

```
ioctl(fd, I_FLUSHBAND, bandp);
```

where *bandp* is a pointer to a structure **bandinfo** that has a format:

```
struct bandinfo {
        unsigned char       bi_pri;
        int                 bi_flag;
};
```

The *bi_flag* field may be one of FLUSHR, FLUSHW, or FLUSHRW.

The following example shows flushing according to the priority band:

```
queue_t *rdq;              /* read queue */
queue_t *wrq;              /* write queue */

case M_FLUSH:
    if (*bp->b_rptr & FLUSHBAND) {
            if (*bp->b_rptr & FLUSHW)
                        flushband(wrq, FLUSHDATA, *(bp->b_rptr + 1));
            if (*bp->b_rptr & FLUSHR)
                        flushband(rdq, FLUSHDATA, *(bp->b_rptr + 1));
    } else {
            if (*bp->b_rptr & FLUSHW)
                        flushq(wrq, FLUSHDATA);
            if (*bp->b_rptr & FLUSHR)
                        flushq(rdq, FLUSHDATA);
    }
    /*
     * modules pass the message on;
     * drivers shut off FLUSHW and loop the message
     * up the read-side if FLUSHR is set; otherwise,
     * drivers free the message.
     */
    break;
```

Note that modules and drivers are not required to treat messages as flowing in separate bands. Modules and drivers can view the queue having only two bands of flow, normal and high priority. However, the latter alternative will flush the entire queue whenever an M_FLUSH message is received.

One use of the field *b_flag* of the **msgb** structure is provided to give the Stream head a way to stop M_FLUSH messages from being reflected forever when the Stream is being used as a pipe. When the Stream head receives an M_FLUSH message, it sets the MSGNOLOOP flag in the *b_flag* field before reflecting the message down the write-side of the Stream. If the Stream head receives an M_FLUSH message with this flag set, the message is freed rather than reflected.

Driver–Kernel Interface

The Driver–Kernel Interface (DKI) is an interface between the UNIX system kernel and drivers. These drivers are block interface drivers, character interface drivers, and drivers and modules supporting a STREAMS interface. Each driver type supports an interface from the kernel to the driver. This kernel-to-driver interface consists of a set of driver-defined functions that are called by the kernel. These functions are the entry points into the driver.

One benefit of defining the DKI is increased portability of driver source code between various UNIX System V implementations. Another benefit is a gain in modularity that results in extending the potential for changes in the kernel without breaking driver code.

The interaction between a driver and the kernel can be described as occurring along two paths. (See Figure 7-3).

One path includes those functions in the driver that are called by the kernel. These are entry points into the driver. The other path consists of the functions in the kernel that are called by the driver. These are kernel utility functions used by the driver. Along both paths, information is exchanged between the kernel and drivers in the form of data structures. The DKI identifies these structures and specifies a set of contents for each. The DKI also defines the common set of entry points expected to be supported in each driver type and their calling and return syntaxes. For each driver type, the DKI lists a set of kernel utility functions that can be called by that driver and also specifies their calling and return syntaxes.

Figure 7-3: Interfaces Affecting Drivers

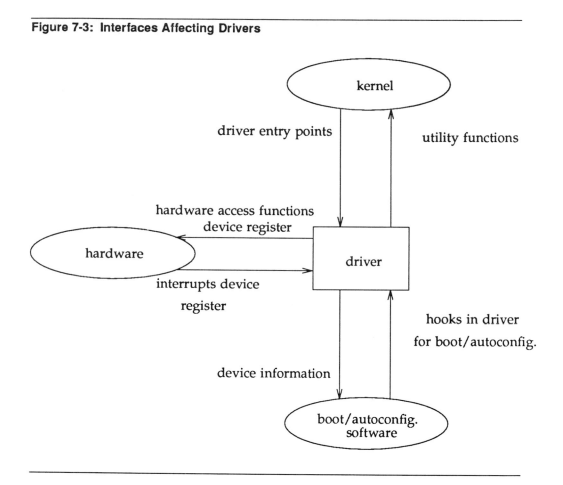

The set of STREAMS utilities available to drivers are listed in Appendix C. No system-defined macros that manipulate global kernel data or introduce structure size dependencies are permitted in these utilities. Therefore, some utilities that have been implemented as *macros* in the prior UNIX system releases are implemented as *functions* in UNIX System V Release 4.0. This does not preclude the existence of both *macro* and *function* versions of these utilities. It is envisioned that driver source code will include a header file (see "Header Files" later in this chapter) that picks up *function* declarations while the core operating system source includes a header file that defines the *macros*. With the DKI interface the following STREAMS utilities are implemented as C programming language functions: **datamsg, OTHERQ, putnext, RD, splstr,** and **WR.**

Replacing *macros* such as **RD**() with *function* equivalents in the driver source code allows driver objects to be insulated from changes in the data structures and their size, further increasing the useful lifetime of driver source code and objects.

The DKI interface defines an interface suitable for drivers and there is no need for drivers to access global kernel data structures directly. The kernel functions **drv_getparm** and **drv_setparm** are provided for reading and writing information in these structures. This restriction has an important consequence. Since drivers are not permitted to access global kernel data structures directly, changes in the contents/offsets of information within these structures will not break objects. The **drv_getparm** and **drv_setparm** functions are described in more detail in the *Device Driver Interface/Driver–Kernel Interface (DDI/DKI) Reference Manual.*

Device Driver Interface and Driver–Kernel Interface

The Device Driver Interface (DDI) is an AT&T interface that facilitates driver portability across different UNIX system versions on the AT&T 3B2 hardware. The Driver–Kernel Interface (DKI) is an interface that also facilitates driver source code portability across implementations of UNIX System V Release 4.0 on all machines. DKI driver code, however, will have to be recompiled on the machine on which it is to run.

The most important distinction between the DDI and the DKI lies in scope. The DDI addresses complete interfaces (see note below) for block, character, and STREAMS interface drivers and modules. The DKI defines only driver interfaces with the kernel with the addition of the kernel interface for file system type (FST) modules. The DKI interface does not specify the system initialization driver interface [i.e., **init**() and **start**() driver routines] nor hardware related interfaces such as **getvec** for the AT&T 3B2.

NOTE The "complete interface" refers to hardware- and boot/configuration-related driver interface in addition to the interface with the kernel.

STREAMS Interface

The entry points from the kernel into STREAMS drivers and modules are through the **qinit** structures (see Appendix A) pointed to by the **streamtab** structure, *prefix*info. STREAMS drivers may need to define additional entry points to support the interface with boot/autoconfiguration software and the hardware (for example, an interrupt handler).

If the STREAMS module has prefix *mod* then the declaration is of the form:

```
static int modrput(), modrsrv(), modopen(), modclose();

static int modwput(), modwsrv();

static struct qinit rdinit =
        {modrput, modrsrv, modopen, modclose, NULL, struct module_info, NULL};

static struct qinit wrinit =
        {modwput, modwsrv, NULL, NULL, NULL, struct module_info, NULL};

struct streamtab modinfo = { &rdinit, &wrinit, NULL, NULL };

extern int moddevflag = 0;
```

where
modrput is the module's read queue **put** procedure,
modrsrv is the module's read queue **service** procedure,
modopen is the **open** routine for the module,
modclose is the **close** routine for the module,
modwput is the **put** procedure for the module's write queue, and
modwsrv is the **service** procedure for the module's write queue.

Each **qinit** structure can point to four entry points. (An additional function pointer has been reserved for future use and must not be used by drivers or modules.) These four function pointer fields in the **qinit** structure are: *qi_putp*, *qi_srvp*, *qi_qopen*, and *qi_close*.

The utility functions that can be called by STREAMS drivers and modules are listed in Appendix C. They must follow the call and return syntaxes specified in the appendix. Manual pages relating to the Driver–Kernel Interface and Device Driver Interface are provided in the *Device Driver Interface/Driver–Kernel Interface (DDI/DKI) Reference Manual*.

Design Guidelines

This section summarizes guidelines common to the design of STREAMS modules and drivers. Additional rules pertaining to modules and drivers can be found in Chapter 8 for modules and Chapter 9 for drivers.

Modules and Drivers

1. Modules and drivers cannot access information in the **u_area** of a process. Modules and drivers are not associated with any process, and therefore have no concept of process or user context, except during open and close routines (see "Rules for Open/Close Routines").

2. Every module and driver must process an M_FLUSH message according to the value of the argument passed in the message.

3. A module or a driver should not change the contents of a data block whose reference count is greater than 1 [see **dupmsg()** in Appendix C] because other modules/drivers that have references to the block may not want the data changed. To avoid problems, data should be copied to a new block and then changed in the new one.

4. Modules and drivers should manipulate queues and manage buffers only with the routines provided for that purpose, (see Appendix C).

5. Modules and drivers should not require the data in an M_DATA message to follow a particular format, such as a specific alignment.

6. Care must be taken when modules are mixed and matched, because one module may place different semantics on the priority bands than another module. The specific use of each band by a module should be included in the service interface specification.

   When designing modules and drivers that make use of priority bands one should keep in mind that priority bands merely provide a way to impose an ordering of messages on a queue. The priority band is not used to determine the service primitive. Instead, the service interface should rely on the data contained in the message to determine the service primitive.

Rules for Open/Close Routines

1. **open** and **close** routines may sleep, but the sleep must return to the routine in the event of a signal. That is, if they sleep, they must be at priority <= PZERO, or with PCATCH set in the sleep priority.

2. The **open** routine should return zero on success or an error number on failure. If the **open** routine is called with the CLONEOPEN flag, the device number should be set by the driver to an unused device number accessible to that driver. This should be an entire device number (major/minor).

3. **open** and **close** routines have user context and can access the **u_area**.

4. Only the following fields can be accessed in the **u_area** (**user.h**): *u_procp, u_ttyp, u_uid, u_gid, u_ruid,* and *u_rgid*. The fields *u_uid, u_gid, u_ruid,* and *u_rgid* are for backward compatibility with previously designed device drivers. The actual user credentials are passed directly to the driver and need not be accessed in the **u_area**. These fields may not support valid *uid*s or *gid*s when the system is configured with large user ids. See note.

5. Only the following fields can be accessed in the process table (**proc.h**): *p_pid, p_pgrp*. See note.

6. If a module or a driver wants to allocate a controlling terminal, it should send an M_SETOPTS message to the Stream head with the SO_ISTTY flag set. Otherwise signaling will not work on the Stream.

 NOTE The DKI interface provides the **drv_getparm** and **drv_setparm** functions to read/write these data and the driver/module need not access them directly.

Rules for ioctls

- Do not change the *ioc_id, ioc_uid, ioc_gid,* or *ioc_cmd* fields in an M_IOCTL message.

- The above rule also applies to fields in an M_IOCDATA, M_COPYIN, and M_COPYOUT message. (Field names are different; see Appendix A)

- Always validate *ioc_count* to see whether the **ioctl** is the transparent or I_STR form.

Rules for Put and Service Procedures

To ensure proper data flow between modules and drivers, the following rules should be observed in **put** and **service** procedures:

- **Put** and **service** procedure must not sleep.

- Return codes can be sent with STREAMS messages M_IOCACK, M_IOCNAK, and M_ERROR.

- Protect data structures common to **put** and **service** procedures by using **splstr()**.

- **Put** and **service** procedures cannot access the information in the **u_area** of a process.

- Processing M_DATA messages by both **put** and **service** procedures could lead to messages going out of sequence. The **put** procedure should check if any messages were queued before processing the current message.

On the read-side, it is usually a good idea to have the **put** procedure check if the **service** procedure is running because of the possibility of a race condition. That is, if there are unprotected sections in the **service** procedure, the **put** procedure can be called and run to completion while the **service** procedure is running (the **put** procedure can interrupt the **service** procedure on the read-side). For example, the **service** procedure is running and it removes the last message from the queue, but before it puts the message upstream the **put** procedure is called (e.g., from an interrupt routine) at an unprotected section in the **service** procedure. The **put** procedure sees that the queue is empty and processes the message. The **put** procedure then returns and the **service** procedure resumes; but at this point data are out of order because the **put** procedure sent upstream the message that was received after the data the **service** procedure was processing.

Put Procedures

1. Each queue must define a **put** procedure in its **qinit** structure for passing messages between modules.

2. A **put** procedure must use the **putq()** (see Appendix C) utility to enqueue a message on its own queue. This is necessary to ensure that the various fields of the **queue** structure are maintained consistently.

3. When passing messages to a neighboring module, a module may not call **putq()** directly, but must call its neighbor module's **put** procedure [see **putnext()** in Appendix C].

   However, the **q_qinfo** structure that points to a module's **put** procedure may point to **putq()** [i.e., **putq()** is used as the **put** procedure for that module]. When a module calls a neighbor module's **put** procedure that is defined in this manner, it will be calling **putq()** indirectly. If any module uses **putq()** as its **put** procedure in this manner, the module must define a **service** procedure. Otherwise, no messages will ever be processed by the next module. Also, because **putq()** does not process M_FLUSH messages, any module that uses **putq()** as its **put** procedure must define a **service** procedure to process M_FLUSH messages.

4. The **put** procedure of a queue with no **service** procedure must call the **put** procedure of the next queue using **putnext()**, if a message is to be passed to that queue.

5. Processing many function calls with the **put** procedure could lead to interrupt stack overflow. In that case, switch to **service** procedure processing whenever appropriate to switch to a different stack.

Service Procedures

1. If flow control is desired, a **service** procedure is required. The **canput()** or **bcanput()** routines should be used by **service** procedures before doing **putnext()** to honor flow control.

2. The **service** procedure must use **getq()** to remove a message from its message queue, so that the flow control mechanism is maintained.

3. The **service** procedure should process all messages on its queue. The only exception is if the Stream ahead is blocked [i.e., **canput()** fails] or some other failure like buffer allocation failure. Adherence to this rule is the only guarantee that STREAMS will enable (schedule for execution) the

service procedure when necessary, and that the flow control mechanism will not fail.

If a **service** procedure exits for other reasons, it must take explicit steps to assure it will be re-enabled.

4. The **service** procedure should not put a high priority message back on the queue, because of the possibility of getting into an infinite loop.

5. The **service** procedure must follow the steps below for each message that it processes. STREAMS flow control relies on strict adherence to these steps.

Step 1:   Remove the next message from the queue using **getq**(). It is possible that the **service** procedure could be called when no messages exist on the queue, so the **service** procedure should never assume that there is a message on its queue. If there is no message, return.

Step 2:   If all of the following conditions are met:

■ **canput**() or **bcanput**() fails and

■ the message type is not a high priority type and

■ the message is to be put on the next queue,

continue at Step 3. Otherwise, continue at Step 4.

Step 3:   The message must be replaced on the head of the queue from which it was removed using **putbq**() (see Appendix C). Following this, the **service** procedure is exited. The **service** procedure should not be re-enabled at this point. It will be automatically back-enabled by flow control.

Step 4:   If all of the conditions of Step 2 are not met, the message should not be returned to the queue. It should be processed as necessary. Then, return to Step 1.

Data Structures

Only the contents of *q_ptr, q_minpsz, q_maxpsz, q_hiwat*, and *q_lowat* in the **queue** structure may be altered. *q_minpsz, q_maxpsz, q_hiwat*, and *q_lowat* are set when the module or driver is opened, but they may be modified subsequently.

Drivers and modules should not change any fields in the **equeue** structure. The only field of the **equeue** structure they are allowed to reference is *eq_bandp*. (Note that *_STYPES* must be defined to use the **equeue** structure.)

Drivers and modules are allowed to change the *qb_hiwat* and *qb_lowat* fields of the **qband** structure. They may only read the *qb_count, qb_first, qb_last*, and *qb_flag* fields.

The routines **strqget**() and **strqset**() can be used to get and set the fields associated with the queue. They insulate modules and drivers from changes in the **queue** structure and also enforce the previous rules.

Dynamic Allocation of STREAMS Data Structures

Prior to UNIX System V Release 4.0, STREAMS data structures were statically configured to support a fixed number of Streams, read and write queues, message and data blocks, link block data structures, and Stream event cells. The only way to change this configuration was to reconfigure and reboot the system. Resources were also wasted because data structures were allocated but not necessarily needed.

With Release 4.0 the STREAMS mechanism has been enhanced to dynamically allocate the following STREAMS data structures: **stdata**, **queue**, **linkblk**, **strevent**, **datab**, and **msgb**. STREAMS allocates memory to cover these structures as needed.

Dynamic data structure allocation has the advantage of the kernel being initially smaller than a system with static configuration. The performance of the system may also improve because of better memory utilization and added flexibility. However, **allocb**(), **bufcall**(), and **freeb**(), the routines that manage these data structures, may be slower at times because of extra overhead needed for dynamic allocation.

Header Files

The following header files are generally required in modules and drivers:

types.h	contains type definitions used in the STREAMS header files
stream.h	contains required structure and constant definitions
stropts.h	primarily for users, but contains definitions of the arguments to the M_FLUSH message type also required by modules
ddi.h	contains definitions and declarations needed by drivers to use functions for the UNIX System V Device Driver Interface or Driver–Kernel Interface. This header file should be the last header file included in the driver source code (after all #include statements).

One or more of the header files described next may also be included. No standard UNIX system header files should be included except as described in the following section. The intent is to prevent attempts to access data that cannot or should not be accessed.

errno.h	defines various system error conditions, and is needed if errors are to be returned upstream to the user
sysmacros.h	contains miscellaneous system macro definitions
param.h	defines various system parameters, particularly the value of the PCATCH sleep flag
signal.h	defines the system signal values, and should be used if signals are to be processed or sent upstream
file.h	defines the file open flags, and is needed if O_NDELAY (or O_NONBLOCK) is interpreted

Accessible Symbols and Functions

The following lists the only symbols and functions that modules or drivers may refer to (in addition to those defined by STREAMS; see Appendices A and C), if hardware and system release independence is to be maintained. Use of symbols not listed here is unsupported.

- **user.h** (from open/close procedures only)

u_procp	process structure pointer
u_ttyp	tty group ID pointer

- **proc.h** (from open/close procedures only)

p_pid	process ID
p_pgrp	process group ID

- **functions accessible from open/close procedures only**

sleep(chan, pri)	sleep until wakeup
delay(ticks)	delay for a specified time

- **universally accessible functions**

bcopy(from, to, nbytes)	copy data quickly
bzero(buffer, nbytes)	zero data quickly
max(a, b)	return max of args
min(a, b)	return min of args
rmalloc(mp, size)	allocate memory space
rmfree(mp, size, i)	de-allocate memory space
rminit(mp, mapsize)	initialize map structure
vtop(vaddr, NULL)	translate from virtual to physical address
cmn_err(level, ...)	print message and optional panic
spl$n$()	set priority level
splstr()	set processor level for Streams
timeout(func, arg, ticks)	schedule event
untimeout(id)	cancel event
wakeup(chan)	wake up sleeper

- **sysmacros.h**

The first four functions are used to get the major/minor part of the expanded device number.

getemajor(x)	return external major part
getmajor(x)	return internal major part

geteminor(x)	return external minor part
getminor(x)	return internal minor part
makedev(x, y)	create a old device number
makedevice(x, y)	create a new device number
cmpdev(x)	convert to old device format
expdev(x)	convert to new device format

- **systm.h**

lbolt	clock ticks since boot in HZ
time	seconds since epoch

- **param.h**

PZERO	zero sleep priority
PCATCH	catch signal sleep flag
HZ	clock ticks per second
NULL	0

- **types.h**

Everything in **types.h** can be used.

8 Modules

Modules   8-1
Module Routines   8-1
Filter Module Example   8-5

Flow Control   8-11

Design Guidelines   8-14

Modules

A STREAMS module is a pair of queues and a defined set of kernel-level rou-
tines and data structures used to process data, status, and control information.
A Stream may have zero or more modules. User processes push (insert)
modules on a Stream using the I_PUSH **ioctl** and pop (remove) them using the
I_POP **ioctl**. Pushing and popping of modules happens in a LIFO (Last-In-
First-Out) fashion. Modules manipulate messages as they flow through the
Stream.

Module Routines

STREAMS module routines (**open, close, put, service**) have already been
described in the previous chapters. This section shows some examples and
further describes attributes common to module **put** and **service** routines.

A module's **put** routine is called by the preceding module, driver, or Stream
head and before the corresponding **service** routine. The **put** routine should do
any processing that needs to be done immediately (for example, processing of
high priority messages). Any processing that can be deferred should be left for
the corresponding **service** routine.

The **service** routine is used to implement flow control, handle de-packetization
of messages, perform deferred processing, and handle resource allocation. Once
the **service** routine is enabled, it always runs before any user level code. The
put and **service** routines must not call **sleep**() and cannot access the **u_area** area,
because they are executed asynchronously with respect to any process.

The following example shows a STREAMS module read-side **put** routine:

```
modrput (q, mp)
    queue_t *q;
    mblk_t   *mp;
{
    struct mod_prv *modptr;

    modptr = (struct mod_prv *) q->q_ptr;      /* for state information */
    if (mp->b_datap->db_type >= QPCTL) {        /* process priority message */
            putnext (q, mp);                     /* and pass it on */
            return;
    }
    switch (mp->b_datap->db_type) {
    case M_DATA:                    /* may process message data */
            putq (q, mp);           /* queue message for service routine */
            return;
    case M_PROTO:                   /* handle protocol control message */
            .
            .
            .
    default:
            putnext (q, mp);
            return;
    }
}
```

The following briefly describes the code:

- A pointer to a queue defining an instance of the module and a pointer to a message are passed to the **put** routine.

- The **put** routine switches on the type of the message. For each message type, the **put** routine either enqueues the message for further processing by the module **service** routine, or passes the message to the next module in the Stream.

- High priority messages are processed immediately by the **put** routine and passed to the next module.

- Ordinary (or normal) messages are either enqueued or passed along the Stream.

This example shows a module write-side **put** routine:

```
modwput (q, mp)
    queue_t  *q;
    mblk_t   *mp;
{
    struct mod_prv *modptr;
    modptr = (struct mod_prv *) q->q_ptr;      /* for state information */
    if (mp->b_datap->db_type >= QPCTL) {       /* process priority message */
            putnext (q, mp);                   /* and pass it on */
            return;
    }
    switch (mp->b_datap->db_type) {
    case M_DATA:                    /* may process message data */
            putq (q, mp);           /* queue message for service routine */
                                    /* or pass message along */
                                    /* putnext (q, mp); */
            return;
    case M_PROTO:
            .
            .
            .
    case M_IOCTL:         /* if command in message is recognized */
                         /* process message and send back reply */
                         /* else pass message downstream */
    default:
            putnext (q, mp);
            return;
    }
}
```

The write-side **put** routine, unlike the read-side, may be passed M_IOCTL messages. It is up to the module to recognize and process the **ioctl** command, or pass the message downstream if it does not recognize the command.

The following example shows a general scenario employed by the module's **service** routine:

```
modrsrv(q)
   queue_t *q;
{
   mblk_t *mp;

   while ((mp = getq(q)) != (mblk_t *) NULL) {
         if (!(mp->b_datap->db_type >= QPCTL) &&
            !canput(q->q_next)) {          /* flow control check */
                  putbq(q, mp);           /* return message */
                  return;
         }
                                          /* process the message */
         switch(mp->b_datap->db_type) {
                  .
                  .
                  .
                  putnext(q, mp);          /* pass the result */
         }
   } /* while */
}
```

The steps are:

- Retrieve the first message from the queue using **getq()**.

- If the message is high priority, process it immediately, and pass it along the Stream.

- Otherwise, the **service** routine should use the **canput()** utility to determine if the next module or driver that enqueues messages is within acceptable flow control limits. The **canput()** routine goes down (or up on the read-side) the Stream until it reaches a module, a driver, or the Stream head with a **service** routine. When it reaches one, it looks at the total message space currently allocated at that queue for enqueued messages. If the amount of space currently used at that queue exceeds the high water mark, the **canput()** routine returns false (zero). If the next queue with a **service** routine is within acceptable flow control limits, **canput()** returns true (nonzero).

- If **canput()** returns false, the **service** routine should return the message to its own queue using the **putbq()** routine. The **service** routine can do no further processing at this time, and it should return.

Programmer's Guide: STREAMS

- If **canput**() returns true, the **service** routine should complete any processing of the message. This may involve retrieving more messages from the queue, (de)-allocating header and trailer information, and performing control function for the module.

- When the **service** routine is finished processing the message, it may call the **putnext**() routine to pass the resulting message to the next queue.

- Above steps are repeated until there are no messages left on the queue (that is, **getq**() returns NULL) or **canput**() returns false.

Filter Module Example

The module shown next, *crmod*, is an asymmetric filter. On the write-side, newline is converted to carriage return followed by newline. On the read-side, no conversion is done. The declarations of this module are essentially the same as those of the null module presented in the previous chapter:

```
/* Simple filter - converts newline -> carriage return, newline */

#include "sys/types.h"
#include "sys/param.h"
#include "sys/stream.h"
#include "sys/stropts.h"

static struct module_info minfo = { 0x09, "crmod", 0, INFPSZ, 512, 128 };

static int modopen(), modrput(), modwput(), modwsrv(), modclose();

static struct qinit rinit = {
    modrput, NULL, modopen, modclose, NULL, &minfo, NULL };

static struct qinit winit = {
    modwput, modwsrv, NULL, NULL, NULL, NULL, &minfo, NULL };

struct streamtab crmdinfo = { &rinit, &winit, NULL, NULL };

extern int moddevflag = 0;
```

A **master.d** file to configure *crmod* is shown in Appendix E. **stropts.h** includes definitions of flush message options common to user level, modules and drivers. *modopen* and *modclose* are unchanged from the null module example shown in Chapter 7. *modrput* is like *modput* from the null module.

Note that, in contrast to the null module example, a single **module_info** structure is shared by the read-side and write-side. The **module_info** includes the flow control high and low water marks (512 and 128) for the write queue. (Though the same **module_info** is used on the read queue side, the read-side has no **service** procedure so flow control is not used.) The **qinit** contains the **service** procedure pointer.

The write-side **put** procedure, the beginning of the **service** procedure, and an example of flushing a queue are shown next:

```
static int modwput(q, mp)
   queue_t  *q;
   register mblk_t  *mp;
(
   if (mp->b_datap->db_type >= QPCTL && mp->b_datap->db_type != M_FLUSH)
      putnext(q, mp);
   else
      putq(q, mp);     /* Put it on the queue */
}

static int modwsrv(q)
   queue_t  *q;
(
   mblk_t *mp;

   while ((mp = getq(q) != NULL) {
      switch (mp->b_datap->db_type) {

         default:
            if (canput(q->q_next)) {
               putnext(q, mp);
               break;
            } else {
               putbq(q, mp);
            return;
            }

         case M_FLUSH:
            if (*mp->b_rptr & FLUSHW)
               flushq(q, FLUSHDATA);
            putnext(q, mp);
            break;
```

modwput, the write **put** procedure, switches on the message type. High priority messages that are not type M_FLUSH are **putnext** to avoid scheduling. The others are queued for the **service** procedure. An M_FLUSH message is a request to remove messages on one or both queues. It can be processed in the **put** or **service** procedure.

modwsrv is the write **service** procedure. It takes a single argument, a pointer to the write **queue**. *modwsrv* processes only one high priority message, M_FLUSH. No other high priority messages should reach *modwsrv*.

For an M_FLUSH message, *modwsrv* checks the first data byte. If FLUSHW (defined in **stropts.h**) is set, the write queue is flushed by use of the **flushq()** utility (see Appendix C). **flushq()** takes two arguments, the queue pointer and a flag. The flag indicates what should be flushed, data messages (FLUSHDATA) or everything (FLUSHALL). In the example, data includes M_DATA, M_DELAY, M_PROTO, and M_PCPROTO messages. The choice of what types of messages to flush is module specific.

Ordinary messages will be returned to the queue if

> canput (q->q_next)

returns false, indicating the downstream path is blocked. The example continues with the remaining part of *modwsrv* processing M_DATA messages:

Programmer's Guide: STREAMS

```
        case M_DATA: {
            mblk_t *nbp = NULL;
            mblk_t *next;

            if (!canput(q->q_next)) {
                putbq(q, mp);
                return;
            }
            /* Filter data, appending to queue */
            for (; mp != NULL; mp = next) {
                while (mp->b_rptr < mp->b_wptr) {
                    if (*mp->b_rptr == '\n')
                        if (!bappend(&nbp, '\r'))
                            goto push;
                    if (!bappend(&nbp, *mp->b_rptr))
                        goto push;
                    mp->b_rptr++;
                    continue;

                push:
                    if (nbp)
                    putnext(q, nbp);
                    nbp = NULL;
                    if (!canput(q->q_next)) {
                        if (mp->b_rptr >= mp->b_wptr) {
                            next = mp->b_cont;
                            freeb(mp);
                            mp=next;
                        }
                        if (mp)
                            putbq(q, mp);
                        return;
                    }
                } /* while */
                next = mp->b_cont;
                freeb(mp);
            } /* for */
            if (nbp)
                putnext(q, nbp);
        } /* case M_DATA */
    } /* switch */
} /* while */
}
```

The differences in M_DATA processing between this and the example in Chapter 5 (see "Message Allocation and Freeing") relate to the manner in which the new messages are forwarded and flow controlled. For the purpose of demonstrating alternative means of processing messages, this version creates individual new messages rather than a single message containing multiple message blocks. When a new message block is full, it is immediately forwarded with the **putnext()** routine rather than being linked into a single, large message (as was done in the Chapter 5 example). This alternative may not be desirable because message boundaries will be altered and because of the additional overhead of handling and scheduling multiple messages.

When the filter processing is performed (following push), flow control is checked [with **canput()**] after, rather than before, each new message is forwarded. This is done because there is no provision to hold the new message until the queue becomes unblocked. If the downstream path is blocked, the remaining part of the original message is returned to the queue. Otherwise, processing continues.

Flow Control

To utilize the STREAMS flow control mechanism, modules must use **service** procedures, invoke **canput()** before calling **putnext()**, and use appropriate values for the high and low water marks.

Module flow control limits the amount of data that can be placed on a queue. It prevents depletion of buffers in the buffer pool. Flow control is advisory in nature and it can be bypassed. It is managed by high and low water marks and regulated by QWANTW and QFULL flags. Module flow control is implemented by using the **canput()**, **getq()**, **putq()**, **putbq()**, **insq()**, and **rmvq()** routines.

The following scenario takes place normally in flow control when a module and driver are in sync:

- A driver sends data to a module using the **putnext()** routine, and the module's **put** procedure queues data using **putq()**. The **putq()** routine then increments the module's q_count by the number of bytes in the message and enables the **service** procedure. When STREAMS scheduling runs the **service** procedure, the **service** procedure then retrieves the data by calling the **getq()** utility, and **getq()** decrements q_count by an appropriate value.

If the module cannot process data at the rate at which the driver is sending the data, the following happens:

- The module's q_count goes above its high water mark, and the QFULL flag is set by **putq()**. The driver's **canput()** fails, and **canput()** sets QWANTW flag in the module's queue. The driver may send a command to the device to stop input, queue the data in its own queue, or drop the data. In the meanwhile, the module's q_count falls below its low water mark [by **getq()**] and **getq()** finds the nearest back queue with a **service** procedure and enables it. The scheduler then runs the **service** procedure.

The next two examples show a line discipline module's flow control. The first example is a read-side line discipline module:

```
/* read-side line discipline module flow control */

ld_read_srv(q)
   queue_t *q;                /* pointer to read queue */
{
  mblk_t *mp;                 /* original message */
  mblk_t *bp;                 /* canonicalized message */

  while ((mp = getq(q)) != NULL) {
     switch (mp->b_datap->db_type) {       /* type of message */
       case M_DATA:                        /* data message */
          if (canput(q->q_next)) {
                     bp = read_canon(mp);
                     putnext(q, bp);
          } else {
                     putbq(q, mp);        /* put message back in queue */
                     return;
          }
          break;

       default:
          if (mp->b_datap->db_type >= QPCTL)
                     putnext(q, mp);         /* high priority message */
          else {                            /* ordinary message */
                     if (canput(q->q_next))
                        putnext(q, mp);
                     else {
                        putbq(q, mp);
                        return;
                     }
          }
          break;
   }
 }
}
```

The following shows a write-side line discipline module:

```
/* write-side line discipline module flow control */

ld_write_srv(q)
    queue_t  *q;              /* pointer to write queue */
{
    mlbk_t *mp;          /* original message */
    mblk_t *bp;          /* canonicalized message */

    while ((mp = getq(q)) != NULL) {
        switch (mp->b_datap->db_type) {  /* type of message */
        case M_DATA:                     /* data message */
            if (canput(q->q_next)) {
                    bp = write_canon(mp);
                    putnext(q, bp);
            } else {
                    putbq(q, mp);
                    return;
            }
            break;

        case M_IOCTL:
            ld_ioctl(q, mp);
            break:

        default:
            if (mp->b_datap->db_type >= QPCTL)
                    putnext(q, mp);          /* high priority message */
            else {                           /* ordinary message */
                    if (canput(q->q_next))
                        putnext(q, mp);
                    else {
                        putbq(q, mp);
                        return;
                    }
            }
            break;
        }
    }
)
```

Design Guidelines

Module developers should follow these guidelines:

- Messages types that are not understood by the modules should be passed to the next module.

- The module that acts on an M_IOCTL message should send an M_IOCACK or M_IOCNAK message in response to the **ioctl**. If the module does not understand the **ioctl**, it should pass the M_IOCTL message to the next module.

- Modules should be designed in such way that they don't pertain to any particular driver but can be used by all drivers.

- In general, modules should not require the data in an M_DATA message to follow a particular format, such as a specific alignment. This makes it easier to arbitrarily push modules on top of each other in a sensible fashion. Not following this rule may limit module reusability.

- Filter modules pushed between a service user and a service provider may not alter the contents of the M_PROTO or M_PCPROTO block in messages. The contents of the data blocks may be manipulated, but the message boundaries must be preserved.

Also see "Design Guidelines" in Chapter 7.

9 Drivers

Drivers   9-1

Overview of Drivers   9-1
- ■ Driver Classification   9-1
- ■ Driver Configuration   9-2
- ■ Writing a Driver   9-3
- ■ Major and Minor Device Numbers   9-5

STREAMS Drivers   9-6
- ■ Printer Driver Example   9-9
- ■ Driver Flow Control   9-16

Cloning   9-18

Loop-Around Driver   9-20

Design Guidelines   9-30

Drivers

This chapter describes the operation of a STREAMS driver and also discusses some of the processing typically required in drivers.

Unlike a module, a device driver must have an interrupt routine so that it is accessible from a hardware interrupt as well as from the Stream. A driver can have multiple Streams connected to it. Multiple connections occur when more than one minor device of the same driver is in use and in the case of multiplexors (multiplexing is discussed in Chapter 10). However, these particular differences are not recognized by the STREAMS mechanism. They are handled by developer-provided code included in the driver procedures.

Overview of Drivers

This section provides a brief overview of the UNIX® system drivers. This is not an all-inclusive description, but an introduction and general information on drivers. For more detailed information, see *Block and Character Interface (BCI) Driver Development Guide* and *Block and Character Interface (BCI) Driver Reference Manual*.

A driver is software that provides an interface between the operating system and a device. The driver controls the device in response to kernel commands, and user-level programs access the device through system calls. The system calls interface with the file system and process control system, which in turn access the drivers. The driver provides and manages a path for the data to and from the hardware device, and services interrupts issued by the device controller.

Driver Classification

In general, drivers are grouped according to the **type** of the device they control, the **access** method (the way data are transferred), and the **interface** between the driver and the device.

The type can be hardware or software. A hardware driver controls a physical device such as a disk. A software driver, also called a pseudo device, controls software, which in turn may interface with a hardware device. The software driver may also support pseudo devices that have no associated physical device.

Drivers can be character-type or block-type, but many support both access methods. In character-type transfer, data are read a character at a time or as a variable length stream of bytes, the size of which is determined by the device. In block-type access, data transfer is performed on fixed-length blocks of data. Devices that support both block- and character-type access must have a separate special device file for each access method. Character access devices can also use "raw" (also called unbuffered) data transfer that takes place directly between user address space and the device. Unbuffered data transfer is used mainly for administrative functions where the speed of the specific operation is more important than overall system performance.

The driver interface refers to the system structures and kernel interfaces used by the driver. For example, STREAMS is an interface.

Driver Configuration

For a driver to be recognized as part of the system, information on driver type, where object code resides, interrupts, and so on, must be stored in appropriate files.

The following summarizes information needed to include a driver in the system (this information is unique to the AT&T 3B2):

/etc/master.d	This directory contains the master files. A master file supplies information to the system initialization software to describe different attributes of a driver. There is one master file for each driver in the system.
/stand/system	This file contains entries for each driver and indicates to the system initialization software whether a driver is to be included or excluded during configuration.
/dev	This directory contains special files that provide applications with a way to access drivers via file operators.
/boot	This directory contains bootable object files that are used to create a new version of the UNIX operating system when the processor is booted.

Writing a Driver

All drivers are identified by a string of up to four characters called the *prefix*. The prefix is defined in the master file for the driver and is added to the name of the driver routines. For example, the **open** routine for the driver with the "xyz" prefix is **xyzopen**.

The location of the driver source code is determined by whether the driver is a part of the core operating system or an add-on to the core operating system.

Writing a driver differs from writing other C programs in the following ways:

- A driver does not have a **main.c** routine. Rather, driver entry points are given specific names and accessed through switch tables.

- A driver functions as a part of the kernel. Consequently, a poorly written driver can degrade system performance or corrupt the system.

- A driver cannot use system calls or the C library, because the driver functions at a lower level.

- A driver cannot use floating point arithmetic.

- A driver cannot use archives or shared libraries, but frequently used subroutines can be put in separate files in the source code directory for the driver.

Driver code, like other system software, uses the advanced C language capabilities. These include: bit-manipulation capabilities, casting of data types, and use of header files for defining and declaring global data structures.

Driver code includes a set of entry point routines:

- **initialization entry points** that are accessed through io_init and io_start arrays during system initialization.

- **switch table entry points** that are accessed through **bdevsw** (block-access) and **cdevsw** (character-access) switch tables when the appropriate system call is issued.

- **interrupt entry points** that are accessed through the interrupt vector table when the hardware generates an interrupt.

The following lists rules of driver development:

- All drivers must have an associated file in the **master.d** directory.

- All drivers should have `#include` system header files that define data structures used in the driver.

- Drivers may have an **init** and/or a **start** routine to initialize the driver.

  Software drivers will usually have little to initialize, because there is no hardware involved. An **init** routine is used when a driver needs to initialize but does not need any system services. **init** routines are run before system services are initialized (like the kernel memory allocator, for example). When a driver needs to do initialization that requires system services, a **start** routine is used. The **start** routines are run after system services have been initialized.

- Drivers will have **open** and **close** routines.

- Most drivers will have an interrupt handler routine.

  The driver developer is responsible for supplying an interrupt routine for the device's driver. The UNIX system provides a few interrupt handling routines for hardware interrupts, but the developer has to supply the specifics about the device.

  In general, a *prefix*int interrupt routine should be written for any device that does not send separate transmit and receive interrupts. TTY devices that request separate transmit and receive interrupts can have two separate interrupt routines associated with them; *prefix*xinit to transmit an interrupt, and *prefix*rint to receive an interrupt.

  In addition to hardware interrupts, many computers also support software interrupts. For example, AT&T computers support Programmed Interrupt Requests (PIRs). A PIR is generated by writing an integer into a logical register address assigned to the interrupt vector table.

- Most drivers will have **static** subordinate driver routines to provide the functionality for the specific device. The names of these routines should include the driver *prefix*, although this is not absolutely required since the routine is declared as **static**.

■ A bootable object file and special device files are also needed for a driver to be fully functional.

Major and Minor Device Numbers

The UNIX System V operating system identifies and accesses peripheral devices by major and minor numbers. When a driver is installed and a special device file is created, a device then appears to the user application as a file. A device is accessed by opening, reading, writing, and closing a special device file that has the proper major and minor device numbers.

The major number identifies a driver for a controller. The minor number identifies a specific device. Major numbers are assigned sequentially by either the system initialization software at boot time for hardware devices, by a program such as **drvinstall**, or by administrator direction. The major number for a software device is assigned automatically by the **drvinstall** command. Minor numbers are designated by the driver developer.

Major and minor numbers can be external or internal.

External major numbers for software devices are static and assigned sequentially to the appropriate field in the master file by the **drvinstall**(1M) command. External major numbers for hardware devices correspond to the board slot and are dynamically assigned by the **autoconfig** process at system boot time. The **mknod**(1M) command is then used to create the files (or nodes) to be associated with the device. External major numbers are those visible to the user.

Internal major numbers serve as an index into the **cdevsw** and **bdevsw** switch tables. These are assigned by the autoconfiguration process when drivers are loaded and they may change every time a full-configuration boot is done. The system uses the MAJOR table to translate external major numbers to the internal major numbers needed to access the switch tables.

One driver may control several devices, but each device will have its own external major number and all those external major numbers are mapped to one internal major number for the driver.

Minor numbers are determined differently for different types of devices. Typically, minor numbers are an encoding of information needed by the controller board.

External minor numbers are controlled by a driver developer, although there are conventions enforced for some types of devices by some utilities. For example, a tape drive may interface with a hardware controller (device) to which several tape drives (subdevices) are attached. All tape drives attached to one controller will have the same external major number, but each drive will have a different external minor number.

Internal minor numbers are used with hardware drivers to identify the logical controller that is being addressed. Since drivers that control multiple devices (controllers) usually require a data structure for each configured device, drivers address the per-controller data structure by the internal minor number rather than the external major number.

The logical controller numbers are assigned sequentially by the central controller firmware at self-configuration time. The internal minor device number is calculated from the MINOR array in the kernel by multiplying the logical controller number by the value of the #DEV field (number of devices per controller) in the master file.

The internal minor number for all software drivers is 0.

The MAJOR and MINOR tables map external major and minor numbers to the internal major number. The switch tables will have only as many entries as required to support the drivers installed on the system. Switch table entry points are activated by system calls that reference a special device file that supplies the external major number and instructions on whether to use **bdevsw** or **cdevsw**. By mapping the external major number to the corresponding internal major number in the MAJOR table, the system knows which driver routine to activate. The routines **getmajor()** and **getminor()** return an internal major and minor number for the device. The routines **getemajor()** and **geteminor()** return an external major and minor number for the device.

STREAMS Drivers

At the interface to hardware devices, character I/O drivers have interrupt entry points; at the system interface, those same drivers generally have direct entry points (routines) to process **open**, **close**, **read**, **write**, **poll**, and **ioctl** system calls.

STREAMS device drivers have interrupt entry points at the hardware device interface and have direct entry points only for the **open** and **close** system calls. These entry points are accessed via STREAMS, and the call formats differ from traditional character device drivers. (STREAMS drivers are character drivers, too. We call the non-STREAMS character drivers traditional character drivers or non-STREAMS character drivers.) The **put** procedure is a driver's third entry point, but it is a message (not system) interface. The Stream head translates **write** and **ioctl** calls into messages and sends them downstream to be processed by the driver's write queue **put** procedure. **read** is seen directly only by the Stream head, which contains the functions required to process system calls. A driver does not know about system interfaces other than **open** and **close**, but it can detect the absence of a **read** indirectly if flow control propagates from the Stream head to the driver and affects the driver's ability to send messages upstream.

For input processing, when the driver is ready to send data or other information to a user process, it does not wake up the process. It prepares a message and sends it to the read queue of the appropriate (minor device) Stream. The driver's open routine generally stores the queue address corresponding to this Stream.

For output processing, the driver receives messages in place of a **write** call. If the message can not be sent immediately to the hardware, it may be stored on the driver's write message queue. Subsequent output interrupts can remove messages from this queue.

Figure 9-1 shows multiple Streams (corresponding to minor devices) to a common driver. There are two distinct Streams opened from the same major device. Consequently, they have the same **streamtab** and the same driver procedures.

The configuration mechanism distinguishes between STREAMS devices and traditional character devices, because system calls to STREAMS drivers are processed by STREAMS routines, not by the UNIX system driver routines. In the **cdevsw** file, the field d_str provides this distinction. See Appendix E for details.

Multiple instantiations (minor devices) of the same driver are handled during the initial open for each device. Typically, the **queue** address is stored in a driver-private structure array indexed by the minor device number. This is for use by the interrupt routine which needs to translate from device number to a particular Stream. The q_ptr of the **queue** will point to the private data structure entry. When the messages are received by the queue, the calls to the driver put and **service** procedures pass the address of the **queue**, allowing the procedures to determine the associated device.

A driver is at the end of a Stream. As a result, drivers must include standard processing for certain message types that a module might simply be able to pass to the next component.

During the open and close routine the kernel locks the device **snode**. Thus only one **open** or **close** can be active at a time per major/minor device pair.

Figure 9-1: Device Driver Streams

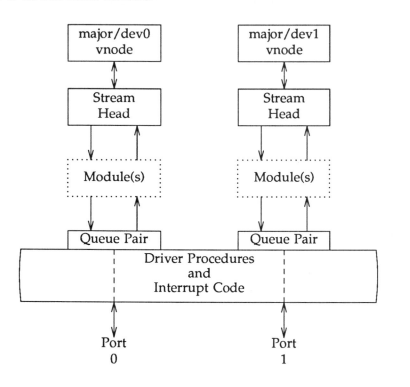

Printer Driver Example

The next example shows how a simple interrupt-per-character line printer driver could be written. The driver is unidirectional and has no read-side processing. It demonstrates some differences between module and driver programming, including the following:

Open handling   A driver is passed a device number or is asked to select one.

Flush handling   A driver must loop M_FLUSH messages back upstream.

ioctl handling   A driver must send a negative acknowledgement for ioctl messages it does not understand. This is discussed under "Module and Driver ioctls" in Chapter 7.

Declarations

The driver declarations are as follows (see also "Module and Driver Declarations" in Chapter 7):

```
/* Simple line printer driver */

#include "sys/types.h"
#include "sys/param.h"
#include "sys/sysmacros.h"
#ifdef u3b2
#include "sys/psw.h"     /* required for user.h */
#include "sys/pcb.h"     /* required for user.h */
#endif
#include "sys/stream.h"
#include "sys/stropts.h"
#include "sys/dir.h"     /* required for user.h */
#include "sys/signal.h"  /* required for user.h */
#include "sys/user.h"
#include "sys/errno.h"
#include "sys/cred.h"
#include "sys/ddi.h"

static struct module_info minfo = {
    0xaabb, "lp", 0, INFPSZ, 150, 50 };

static int lpopen(), lpclose(), lpwput();
```

(continued on next page)

```
static struct qinit rinit = {
    NULL, NULL, lpopen, lpclose, NULL, &minfo, NULL };

static struct qinit winit = {
    lpwput, NULL, NULL, NULL, NULL, &minfo, NULL };

struct streamtab lpinfo = { &rinit, &winit, NULL, NULL };

#define SET_OPTIONS  (('1'<<8)|1)/* should be in a .h file */

/* This is a private data structure, one per minor device number. */

struct lp {
    short flags;     /* flags -- see below */
    mblk_t *msg;     /* current message being output */
    queue_t *qptr;   /* back pointer to write queue */
};
/* Flags bits */
#define BUSY  1     /* device is running and interrupt is pending */

extern struct lp lp_lp[];   /* per device lp structure array */
extern int lp_cnt;          /* number of valid minor devices */
int lpdevflag = 0;
```

Configuring a STREAMS driver requires only the **streamtab** structure to be externally accessible. For hardware drivers, the interrupt handler must also be externally accessible. All other STREAMS driver procedures would typically be declared `static`.

The **streamtab** structure must be defined as *prefix*info, where *prefix* is the value of the prefix field in the master file for this driver. The values in the module name and ID fields in the **module_info** structure should be unique in the system. Note that, as in character I/O drivers, `extern` variables are assigned values in the master file when configuring drivers or modules.

There is no read-side **put** or **service** procedure. The flow control limits for use on the write-side are 50 bytes for the low water mark and 150 bytes for the high water mark. The private *lp* structure is indexed by the minor device number and contains these elements:

flags   A set of flags. Only one bit is used: BUSY indicates that output is active and a device interrupt is pending.

msg   A pointer to the current message being output.

qptr   A back pointer to the write queue. This is needed to find the write queue during interrupt processing.

Driver Open

The STREAMS mechanism allows only one Stream per minor device. The driver open routine is called whenever a STREAMS device is opened. Opening also allocates a private data structure. The driver open, *lpopen* in this example, has the same interface as the module open:

```
static int lpopen(q, devp, flag, sflag, credp)
    queue_t  *q;        /* read queue */
    dev_t    *devp;
    int      flag;
    int      sflag;
    cred_t   *credp;
{
    struct lp *lp;
        dev_t  device;

    if (sflag)                    /* check if non-driver open */
        return ENXIO;

    device = getminor(*devp);
    if (device >= lp_cnt)
        return ENXIO;

                    /* Check if open already. q_ptr is assigned below */
    if (q->q_ptr) {
        return EBUSY;
    }

    lp = &lp_lp[device];
    lp->qptr = WR(q);
    q->q_ptr = (char *) lp;
    WR(q)->q_ptr = (char *) lp;
    return 0;
}
```

The Stream flag, *sflag*, must have the value 0, indicating a normal driver open. *devp* is a pointer to the major/minor device number for this port. After checking *sflag*, the STREAMS open flag, *lpopen* extracts the minor device pointed to by *devp*, using the **getminor()** function. *credp* is a pointer to a credentials structure.

The minor device number selects a printer. The device number pointed to by *devp* must be less than *lp_cnt*, the number of configured printers. Otherwise failure occurs.

The next check, if (q->q_ptr) ..., determines if this printer is already open. If it is, EBUSY is returned to avoid merging printouts from multiple users. *q_ptr* is a driver/module private data pointer. It can be used by the driver for any purpose and is initialized to zero by STREAMS. In this example, the driver sets the value of *q_ptr*, in both the read and write **queue** structures, to point to a private data structure for the minor device, *lp_lp[device]*.

There are no physical pointers between queues. **WR** is a queue pointer macro. **WR**(q) generates the write pointer from the read pointer. **RD** and **OTHER** are also the queue pointer macros. **RD**(q) generates the read pointer from the write pointer, and **OTHER**(q) generates the mate pointer from either. With the DDI, **WR**, **RD**, and **OTHER** are functions.

Driver Flush Handling

The following write **put** procedure, *lpwput*, illustrates driver M_FLUSH handling. Note that all drivers are expected to incorporate flush handling.

If FLUSHW is set, the write message queue is flushed, and (in this example) the leading message (lp->msg) is also flushed. sp15 is used to protect the critical code, assuming the device interrupts at level 5.

Normally, if FLUSHR is set, the read queue would be flushed. However, in this example, no messages are ever placed on the read queue, so it is not necessary to flush it. The FLUSHW bit is cleared and the message is sent upstream using **qreply()**. If FLUSHR is not set, the message is discarded.

The Stream head always performs the following actions on flush requests received on the read-side from downstream. If FLUSHR is set, messages waiting to be sent to user space are flushed. If FLUSHW is set, the Stream head clears the FLUSHR bit and sends the M_FLUSH message downstream. In this manner, a single M_FLUSH message sent from the driver can reach all queues in a Stream. A module must send two M_FLUSH messages to have the same affect.

lpwput enqueues M_DATA and M_IOCTL messages and, if the device is not busy, starts output by calling *lpout*. Messages types that are not recognized are discarded.

```
static int lpwput(q, mp)
   queue_t  *q;          /* write queue */
   register mblk_t *mp;  /* message pointer */
{
   register struct lp *lp;
   int s;

   lp = (struct lp *)q->q_ptr;
   switch (mp->b_datap->db_type) {

   default:
       freemsg(mp);
       break;

   case M_FLUSH:                /* Canonical flush handling */
       if (*mp->b_rptr & FLUSHW) {
           flushq(q, FLUSHDATA);
           s = spl5();   /* also flush lp->msg since it is logically
                          * at the head of the write queue */
           if (lp->msg) {
               freemsg(lp->msg);
               lp->msg = NULL;
           }
           splx(s);
       }
       if (*mp->b_rptr & FLUSHR) {
           *mp->b_rptr &= ~FLUSHW;
           qreply(q, mp);
       } else
           freemsg(mp);
       break;

   case M_IOCTL:

   case M_DATA:
       putq(q, mp);
       s = spl5();
       if (!(lp->flags & BUSY))
           lpout(lp);
       splx(s);
   }
}
```

Driver Interrupt

The following example shows the interrupt routine in the printer driver.

lpint is the driver interrupt handler routine.

lpout simply takes a character from the queue and sends it to the printer. For convenience, the message currently being output is stored in `lp->msg`.

lpoutchar sends a character to the printer and interrupts when complete. Printer interface options need to be set before being able to print.

```
/* Device interrupt routine */

lpint(device)
   int device;       /* minor device number of lp */
{
   register struct lp *lp;

   lp = &lp_lp[device];
   if (!(lp->flags & BUSY)) {
       cmn_err(CE_WARN, "^lp: unexpected interrupt\n");
       return;
   }
   lp->flags &= ~BUSY;
   lpout(lp);
}
/* Start output to device - used by put procedure and driver */

lpout(lp)
   register struct lp *lp;
{
   register mblk_t *bp;
   queue_t *q;

   q = lp->qptr;

loop:
   if ((bp = lp->msg) == NULL) {          /* no current message */
       if ((bp = getq(q)) == NULL) {
           lp->flags &= NBUSY;
           return;
           }

       if (bp->b_datap->db_type == M_IOCTL) {
           lpdoioctl(lp, bp);
           goto loop;
       }
       lp->msg = bp;                       /* new message */
   }
   if (bp->b_rptr >= bp->b_wptr) {        /* validate message */
       bp = lp->msg->b_cont;
       lp->msg->b_cont = NULL;
       freeb(lp->msg);
       lp->msg = bp;
       goto loop;
   }
```

(continued on next page)

```
    lpoutchar(lp, *bp->b_rptr++);        /* output one character */
    lp->flags |= BUSY;
}
```

Driver Close

The driver close routine is called by the Stream head. Any messages left on the queue will be automatically removed by STREAMS. The Stream is dismantled and the data structures are de-allocated.

```
static int lpclose(q, flag, credp)
    queue_t  *q;   /* read queue */
    int      flag;
    cred_t   *credp;
{
    struct lp *lp;
    int s;

    lp = (struct lp *) q->q_ptr;

    /* Free message, queue is automatically flushed by STREAMS */

    s = spl5();
    if (lp->msg) {
        freemsg(lp->msg);
        lp->msg = NULL;
    }
    splx(s);
    lp->flags = 0;
}
```

Driver Flow Control

The same utilities (described in Chapter 8) and mechanisms used for module flow control are used by drivers.

When the message is queued, **putq**() increments the value of q_count by the size of the message and compares the result against the driver's write high water limit (q_hiwat) value. If the count exceeds q_hiwat, the **putq**() utility routine will set the internal FULL indicator for the driver write queue. This will cause messages from upstream to be halted [**canput**() returns FALSE] until the write queue count reaches q_lowat. The driver messages waiting to be output are dequeued by the driver output interrupt routine with **getq**(), which decrements the count. If the resulting count is below q_lowat, the **getq**() routine will back-enable any upstream queue that had been blocked.

Device drivers typically discard input when unable to send it to a user process. However, STREAMS allows flow control to be used on the driver read-side to handle temporary upstream blocks.

To some extent, a driver or a module can control when its upstream transmission will become blocked. Control is available through the M_SETOPTS message (see Appendix B) to modify the Stream head read-side flow control limits.

Cloning

In many earlier examples, each user process connected a Stream to a driver by opening a particular minor device of that driver. Often, however, a user process wants to connect a new Stream to a driver regardless of which minor device is used to access the driver. In the past, this typically forced the user process to poll the various minor device nodes of the driver for an available minor device. To alleviate this task, a facility called **clone open** is supported for STREAMS drivers. If a STREAMS driver is implemented as a cloneable device, a single node in the file system may be opened to access any unused device that the driver controls. This special node guarantees that the user will be allocated a separate Stream to the driver on every **open** call. Each Stream will be associated with an unused major/minor device, so the total number of Streams that may be connected to a particular cloneable driver is limited by the number of minor devices configured for that driver.

The clone device may be useful, for example, in a networking environment where a protocol pseudo-device driver requires each user to open a separate Stream over which it will establish communication.

> **NOTE**
>
> The decision to implement a STREAMS driver as a cloneable device is made by the designers of the device driver.
>
> Knowledge of clone driver implementation is not required to use it. A description is presented here for completeness and to assist developers who must implement their own clone driver.

There are two ways to create a clone device node in the file system. The first is to have a node with major number 63 (major of the clone driver) and with a minor number equal to the major number of the real device one wants to open. For example, **/dev/starlan00** might be major 40, minor 0 (normal open), and **/dev/starlan** might be major 63, minor 40 (clone open).

The second way to create a clone device node is for the driver to designate a special minor device as its clone entry point. Here, **/dev/starlan** might be major 40, minor 0 (clone open).

The former example will cause *sflag* to be set to CLONEOPEN in the open routine when **/dev/starlan** is opened. The latter will not. Instead, in the latter case the driver has decided to designate a special minor device as its clone interface. When the clone is opened, the driver knows that it should look for an unused minor device. This implies that the reserved minor for the clone entry point will never be given out.

Programmer's Guide: STREAMS

In either case, the driver returns the new device number as:

```
*devp = makedevice(getmajor(*devp), newminor);
```

 makedevice is unique to the DDI interface. If the DDI interface is not used, **makedev** can be used instead of **makedevice**.

Loop-Around Driver

The loop-around driver is a pseudo driver that loops data from one open Stream to another open Stream. The user processes see the associated files almost like a full-duplex pipe. The Streams are not physically linked. The driver is a simple multiplexor that passes messages from one Stream's write queue to the other Stream's read queue.

To create a connection, a process opens two Streams, obtains the minor device number associated with one of the returned file descriptors, and sends the device number in an I_STR ioctl(2) to the other Stream. For each **open**, the driver open places the passed **queue** pointer in a driver interconnection table, indexed by the device number. When the driver later receives the I_STR as an M_IOCTL message, it uses the device number to locate the other Stream's interconnection table entry, and stores the appropriate **queue** pointers in both of the Streams' interconnection table entries.

Subsequently, when messages other than M_IOCTL or M_FLUSH are received by the driver on either Stream's write-side, the messages are switched to the read queue following the driver on the other Stream's read-side. The resultant logical connection is shown in Figure 9-2 (in the figure, the abbreviation QP represents a queue pair). Flow control between the two Streams must be handled by special code since STREAMS will not automatically propagate flow control information between two Streams that are not physically interconnected.

Figure 9-2: Loop-Around Streams

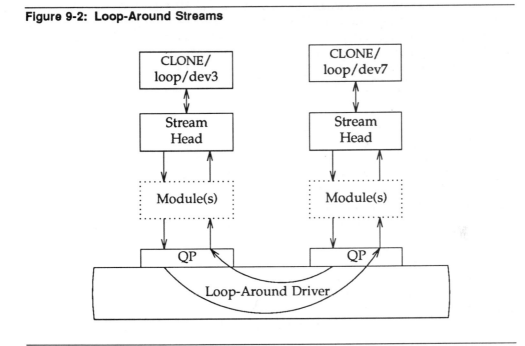

The next example shows the loop-around driver code. A master file to configure the *loop* driver is shown in Appendix E. The *loop* structure contains the interconnection information for a pair of Streams. *loop_loop* is indexed by the minor device number. When a Stream is opened to the driver, the address of the corresponding *loop_loop* element is placed in *q_ptr* (private data structure pointer) of the read-side and write-side **queues**. Since STREAMS clears *q_ptr* when the **queue** is allocated, a NULL value of *q_ptr* indicates an initial **open**. *loop_loop* is used to verify that this Stream is connected to another open Stream.

The declarations for the driver are:

```
/* Loop-around driver */

#include "sys/types.h"
#include "sys/param.h"
#include "sys/sysmacros.h"
#ifdef u3b2
#include "sys/psw.h"
#include "sys/pcb.h"
#endif
#include "sys/stream.h"
#include "sys/stropts.h"
#include "sys/dir.h"
#include "sys/signal.h"
#include "sys/user.h"
#include "sys/errno.h"
#include "sys/cred.h"
#include "sys/ddi.h"

static struct module_info minfo = {
    0xee12, "loop", 0, INFPSZ, 512, 128 };

static int loopopen(), loopclose(), loopwput(), loopwsrv(), looprsrv();

static struct qinit rinit = {
    NULL, looprsrv, loopopen, loopclose, NULL, &minfo, NULL };

static struct qinit winit = {
    loopwput, loopwsrv, NULL, NULL, NULL, &minfo, NULL };

struct streamtab loopinfo = { &rinit, &winit, NULL, NULL };

struct loop {
    queue_t *qptr;      /* back pointer to write queue */
    queue_t *oqptr;     /* pointer to connected read queue */
};

#define LOOP_SET (('l'<<8)|1)     /* should be in a .h file */

extern struct loop loop_loop[];
extern int loop_cnt;
int loopdevflag = 0;
```

The open procedure includes canonical clone processing which enables a single
file system node to yield a new minor device/vnode each time the driver is
opened:

```
static int loopopen(q, devp, flag, sflag, credp)
    queue_t   *q;
    dev_t     *devp;
    int       flag;
    int       sflag;
    cred_t    *credp;
{
    struct loop *loop;

    dev_t newminor;
    /*
     * If CLONEOPEN, pick a minor device number to use.
     * Otherwise, check the minor device range.
     */
    if (sflag == CLONEOPEN) {
        for (newminor = 0; newminor < loop_cnt; newminor++) {
            if (loop_loop[newminor].qptr == NULL) break;
        }
    } else
        newminor = getminor(*devp);

    if (newminor >= loop_cnt)
        return ENXIO;

    /* construct new device number and reset devp */

    /* getmajor gets the external major number, if (sflag == CLONEOPEN) */

    if (q->q_ptr)            /* already open */
        return 0;

    *devp = makedev(getemajor(*devp), newminor);
    loop = &loop_loop[newminor];
    WR(q)->q_ptr = (char *) loop;
    q->q_ptr = (char *) loop;
    loop->qptr = WR(q);
    loop->oqptr = NULL;

    return 0;
}
```

In *loopopen*, *sflag* can be CLONEOPEN, indicating that the driver should pick an
unused minor device (i.e., the user does not care which minor device is used).
In this case, the driver scans its private *loop_loop* data structure to find an
unused minor device number. If *sflag* has not been set to CLONEOPEN, the
passed-in minor device specified by `getminor->(*devp)` is used.

Since the messages are switched to the read queue following the other Stream's read-side, the driver needs a **put** procedure only on its write-side:

```
static int loopwput(q, mp)
   queue_t  *q;
   mblk_t   *mp;
{
   register struct loop *loop;

   loop = (struct loop *)q->q_ptr;

   switch (mp->b_datap->db_type) {
   case M_IOCTL: {
      struct iocblk *iocp;
      int error;

      iocp = (struct iocblk *)mp->b_rptr;
      switch (iocp->ioc_cmd) {
      case LOOP_SET: {
         int to;    /* other minor device */
         /*
          * Sanity check.  ioc_count contains the amount of
          * user supplied data which must equal the size of an int.
          */

         if (iocp->ioc_count != sizeof(int)) {
            error = EINVAL;
            goto iocnak;
         }
            /* fetch other dev from 2nd message block */
         to = *(int *)mp->b_cont->b_rptr;
         /*
          * More sanity checks.  The minor must be in range, open already.
          * Also, this device and the other one must be disconnected.
          */

         if (to >= loop_cnt || to < 0 || !loop_loop[to].qptr) {
            error = ENXIO;
            goto iocnak;
         }

         if (loop->oqptr || loop_loop[to].oqptr) {
            error = EBUSY;
            goto iocnak;
         }
         /* Cross connect streams via the loop structures */
```

(continued on next page)

```
            loop->oqptr = RD(loop_loop[to].qptr);
            loop_loop[to].oqptr = RD(q);
            /*
             * Return successful ioctl. Set ioc_count
             * to zero, since no data are returned.
             */

            mp->b_datap->db_type = M_IOCACK;
            iocp->ioc_count = 0;
            qreply(q, mp);
            break;
        }

    default:
        error = EINVAL;

    iocnak:
        /*
         * Bad ioctl. Setting ioc_error causes the
         * ioctl call to return that particular errno.
         * By default, ioctl will return EINVAL on failure
         */
        mp->b_datap->db_type = M_IOCNAK;
        iocp->ioc_error = error;   /* set returned errno */
        qreply(q, mp);

        }
        break;

    }
```

loopwput shows another use of an I_STR **ioctl** call (see Chapter 7, "Module and Driver ioctls"). The driver supports a *LOOP_SET* value of *ioc_cmd* in the **iocblk** of the M_IOCTL message. *LOOP_SET* instructs the driver to connect the current open Stream to the Stream indicated in the message. The second block of the M_IOCTL message holds an integer that specifies the minor device number of the Stream to connect to.

The driver performs several sanity checks: Does the second block have the proper amount of data? Is the "to" device in range? Is the "to" device open? Is the current Stream disconnected? Is the "to" Stream disconnected?

If everything checks out, the read **queue** pointers for the two Streams are stored in the respective *oqptr* fields. This cross-connects the two Streams indirectly, via *loop_loop*.

Canonical flush handling is incorporated in the **put** procedure:

```
case M_FLUSH:
    if (*mp->b_rptr & FLUSHW) {
        flushq(q, FLUSHALL);    /* write */
        flushq(loop->optr, FLUSHALL);
            /* read on other side equals write on this side */
    }
    if (*mp->b_rptr & FLUSHR) {
        flushq(RD(q), FLUSHALL);
        flushq(WR(loop->oqptr), FLUSHALL);
    }
    switch(*mp->b_rptr) {

    case FLUSHW:
        *mp->b_rptr = FLUSHR;
        break;

    case FLUSHR:
        *mp->b_rptr = FLUSHW:
        break;
    }
    putnext(loop->oqptr, mp);
    break;

default:    /* If this Stream isn't connected, send M_ERROR upstream. */
    if (loop->oqptr == NULL) {
        freemsg(mp);
        putctl1(RD(q)->q_next, M_ERROR, ENXIO);
        break;
    }
    putq(q, mp);
}
}
```

Finally, *loopwput* enqueues all other messages (e.g., M_DATA or M_PROTO) for processing by its **service** procedure. A check is made to see if the Stream is connected. If not, an M_ERROR is sent upstream to the Stream head.

Certain message types can be sent upstream by drivers and modules to the Stream head where they are translated into actions detectable by user process(es). The messages may also modify the state of the Stream head:

M_ERROR   Causes the Stream head to lock up. Message transmission between Stream and user processes is terminated. All subsequent system calls except **close**(2) and **poll**(2) will fail. Also causes an M_FLUSH clearing all message queues to be sent downstream by the Stream head.

M_HANGUP   Terminates input from a user process to the Stream. All subsequent system calls that would send messages downstream will fail. Once the Stream head read message queue is empty, EOF is returned on reads. Can also result in the SIGHUP signal being sent to the process group.

M_SIG/M_PCSIG   Causes a specified signal to be sent to a process.

putctl1() and **putctl**() are utilities that allocate a non-data (i.e., not M_DATA, M_DELAY, M_PROTO, or M_PCPROTO) type message, place one byte in the message (for **putctl1**) and call the **put** procedure of the specified queue.

Service procedures are required in this example on both the write-side and read-side for flow control:

```
static int loopwsrv(q)
   register queue_t *q;
{
  mblk_t *mp;
  register struct loop *loop;

  loop = (struct loop *)q->q_ptr;

  while ((mp = getq(q)) != NULL) {

     /* Check if we can put the message up the other Stream read queue */

     if (mp->b_datap->db_type <= QPCTL && !canput(loop->oqptr->q_next)) {
        putbq(q, mp);            /* read-side is blocked */
        break;
     }
     /* send message */

     putnext(loop->oqptr, mp); /* To queue following other Stream read queue */
  }
}
static int looprsrv(q)
   queue_t *q;
{
/*  Enter only when "back enabled" by flow control */

  struct loop *loop;

  loop = (struct loop *)q->q_ptr;
  if (loop->oqptr == NULL)
     return;

  /* manually enable write service procedure */

  qenable(WR(loop->oqptr));
}
```

The write **service** procedure, *loopwsrv*, takes on the canonical form. The queue being written to is not downstream, but upstream (found via *oqptr*) on the other Stream.

In this case, there is no read-side **put** procedure so the read **service** procedure, *looprsrv*, is not scheduled by an associated **put** procedure, as has been done previously. *looprsrv* is scheduled only by being back-enabled when its upstream becomes unstuck from flow control blockage. The purpose of the procedure is

to re-enable the writer (*loopwsrv*) by using *oqptr* to find the related **queue**.
loopwsrv can not be directly back-enabled by STREAMS because there is no
direct **queue** linkage between the two Streams. Note that no message ever gets
queued to the read **service** procedure. Messages are kept on the write-side so
that flow control can propagate up to the Stream head. The **qenable**() routine
schedules the write-side **service** procedure of the other Stream.

loopclose breaks the connection between the Streams:

```
static int loopclose(q, flag, credp)
    queue_t    *q;
    int        flag;
    cred_t     *credp;
{
    register struct loop *loop;

    loop = (struct loop *)q->q_ptr;
    loop->qptr = NULL;

    /* If we are connected to another stream, break the
     * linkage, and send a hangup message.
     * The hangup message causes the stream head to fail writes,
     * allow the queued data to be read completely, and then
     * return EOF on subsequent reads.
     */
    if (loop->oqptr) {
        ((struct loop *)loop->oqptr->q_ptr)->oqptr = NULL;
        putctl(loop->oqptr->q_next, M_HANGUP);
        loop->oqptr = NULL;
    }
}
```

loopclose sends an M_HANGUP message up the connected Stream to the Stream
head.

NOTE This driver can be implemented much more cleanly by actually linking the
q_next pointers of the queue pairs of the two Streams.

Design Guidelines

Driver developers should follow these guidelines:

- Messages that are not understood by the drivers should be freed.

- A driver must process an M_IOCTL message. Otherwise, the Stream head will block for an M_IOCNAK or M_IOCACK until the timeout (potentially infinite) expires.

- If a driver does not understand an ioctl, an M_IOCNAK message must be sent to upstream.

- Terminal drivers must always acknowledge the EUC ioctls whether they understand them or not.

- The Stream head locks up the Stream when it receives an M_ERROR message, so driver developers should be careful when using the M_ERROR message.

- A hardware driver must have an interrupt routine.

- If a driver wants to allocate a controlling terminal, it should send an M_SETOPTS message with the SO_ISTTY flag set upstream.

- A driver must be a part of the kernel for it to be opened.

Also see "Design Guidelines" in Chapter 7.

10 Multiplexing

Multiplexing   10-1
Building a Multiplexor   10-2
Dismantling a Multiplexor   10-11
Routing Data Through a Multiplexor   10-12

Connecting/Disconnecting Lower Streams   10-13
Connecting Lower Streams   10-13
Disconnecting Lower Streams   10-15

Multiplexor Construction Example   10-16

Multiplexing Driver   10-19
Upper Write Put Procedure   10-23
Upper Write Service Procedure   10-27
Lower Write Service Procedure   10-28
Lower Read Put Procedure   10-28

Persistent Links   10-32

Design Guidelines   10-37

Multiplexing

This chapter describes how STREAMS multiplexing configurations are created and also discusses multiplexing drivers. A STREAMS multiplexor is a driver with multiple Streams connected to it. The primary function of the multiplexing driver is to switch messages among the connected Streams. Multiplexor configurations are created from user level by system calls.

STREAMS related system calls are used to set up the "plumbing," or Stream interconnections, for multiplexing drivers. The subset of these calls that allows a user to connect (and disconnect) Streams below a driver is referred to as the multiplexing facility. This type of connection is referred to as a 1-to-M, or lower, multiplexor configuration. This configuration must always contain a multiplexing driver, which is recognized by STREAMS as having special characteristics.

Multiple Streams can be connected above a driver by use of **open**(2) calls. This was done for the loop-around driver and for the driver handling multiple minor devices in Chapter 9. There is no difference between the connections to these drivers, only the functions performed by the driver are different. In the multiplexing case, the driver routes data between multiple Streams. In the device driver case, the driver routes data between user processes and associated physical ports. Multiplexing with Streams connected above is referred to as an N-to-1, or upper, multiplexor. STREAMS does not provide any facilities beyond **open**(2) and **close**(2) to connect or disconnect upper Streams for multiplexing purposes.

From the driver's perspective, upper and lower configurations differ only in the way they are initially connected to the driver. The implementation requirements are the same: route the data and handle flow control. All multiplexor drivers require special developer-provided software to perform the multiplexing data routing and to handle flow control. STREAMS does not directly support flow control among multiplexed Streams.

M-to-N multiplexing configurations are implemented by using both of the above mechanisms in a driver.

As discussed in Chapter 9, the multiple Streams that represent minor devices are actually distinct Streams in which the driver keeps track of each Stream attached to it. The STREAMS subsystem does not recognize any relationship between the Streams. The same is true for STREAMS multiplexors of any configuration. The multiplexed Streams are distinct and the driver must be implemented to do most of the work.

In addition to upper and lower multiplexors, more complex configurations can be created by connecting Streams containing multiplexors to other multiplexor drivers. With such a diversity of needs for multiplexors, it is not possible to provide general purpose multiplexor drivers. Rather, STREAMS provides a general purpose multiplexing facility. The facility allows users to set up the inter-module/driver plumbing to create multiplexor configurations of generally unlimited interconnection.

Building a Multiplexor

This section builds a protocol multiplexor with the multiplexing configuration shown in Figure 10-1. To free users from the need to know about the underlying protocol structure, a user-level daemon process will be built to maintain the multiplexing configuration. Users can then access the transport protocol directly by opening the transport protocol (TP) driver device node.

An internetworking protocol driver (IP) routes data from a single upper Stream to one of two lower Streams. This driver supports two STREAMS connection beneath it. These connections are to two distinct networks; one for the IEEE 802.3 standard via the 802.3 driver, and other to the IEEE 802.4 standard via the 802.4 driver. The TP driver multiplexes upper Streams over a single Stream to the IP driver.

Figure 10-1: Protocol Multiplexor

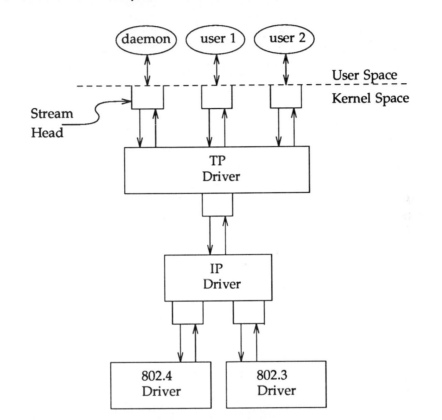

The following example shows how this daemon process sets up the protocol multiplexor. The necessary declarations and initialization for the daemon program are as follows:

```
#include <fcntl.h>
#include <stropts.h>

main()
{
    int fd_802_4,
        fd_802_3,
        fd_ip,
        fd_tp;

    /* daemon-ize this process */

    switch (fork()) {
    case 0:
        break;
    case -1:
        perror("fork failed");
        exit(2);
    default:
        exit(0);
    }
    setsid();
```

This multi-level multiplexed Stream configuration will be built from the bottom up. Therefore, the example begins by first constructing the Internel Protocol (IP) multiplexor. This multiplexing device driver is treated like any other software driver. It owns a node in the UNIX file system and is opened just like any other STREAMS device driver.

The first step is to open the multiplexing driver and the 802.4 driver, thus creating separate Streams above each driver as shown in Figure 10-2. The Stream to the 802.4 driver may now be connected below the multiplexing IP driver using the I_LINK **ioctl** call.

Figure 10-2: Before Link

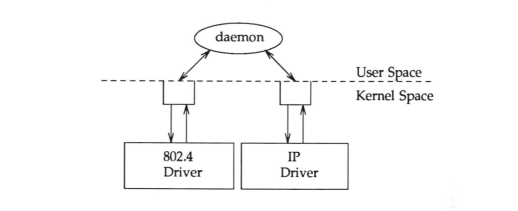

The sequence of instructions to this point is:

```
if ((fd_802_4 = open ("/dev/802_4", O_RDWR)) < 0) {
    perror("open of /dev/802_4 failed");
    exit(1);
}

if ((fd_ip = open ("/dev/ip", O_RDWR)) < 0) {
    perror("open of /dev/ip failed");
    exit(2);
}

/* now link 802.4 to underside of IP */

if (ioctl(fd_ip, I_LINK, fd_802_4) < 0) {
    perror("I_LINK ioctl failed");
    exit(3);
}
```

I_LINK takes two file descriptors as arguments. The first file descriptor, *fd_ip*, must reference the Stream connected to the multiplexing driver, and the second file descriptor, *fd_802_4*, must reference the Stream to be connected below the multiplexor. Figure 10-3 shows the state of these Streams following the I_LINK call. The complete Stream to the 802.4 driver has been connected below the IP driver. The Stream head's queues of the 802.4 driver will be used by the IP driver to manage the lower half of the multiplexor.

Figure 10-3: IP Multiplexor After First Link

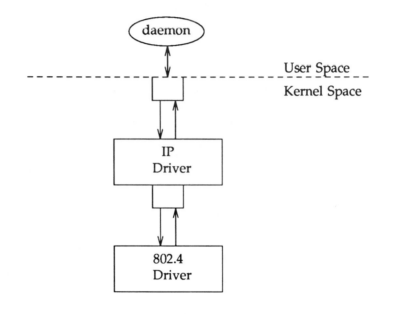

I_LINK will return an integer value, called *muxid*, which is used by the multiplexing driver to identify the Stream just connected below it. This *muxid* is ignored in the example, but it is useful for dismantling a multiplexor or routing data through the multiplexor. Its significance is discussed later.

The following sequence of system calls is used to continue building the internetworking protocol multiplexor (IP):

```
if ((fd_802_3 = open("/dev/802_3", O_RDWR)) < 0) {
    perror("open of /dev/802_3 failed");
    exit(4);
}

if (ioctl(fd_ip, I_LINK, fd_802_3) < 0) {
    perror("I_LINK ioctl failed");
    exit(5);
}
```

All links below the IP driver have now been established, giving the configuration in Figure 10-4.

Figure 10-4: IP Multiplexor

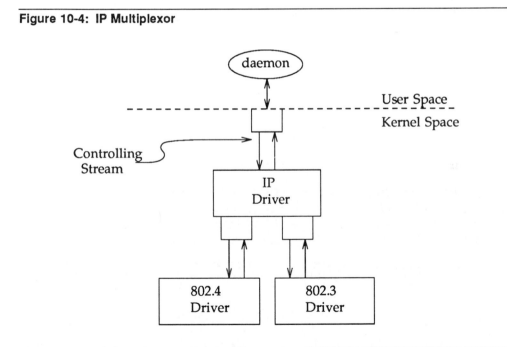

The Stream above the multiplexing driver used to establish the lower connections is the controlling Stream and has special significance when dismantling the multiplexing configuration. This will be illustrated later in this chapter. The Stream referenced by *fd_ip* is the controlling Stream for the IP multiplexor.

 NOTE The order in which the Streams in the multiplexing configuration are opened is unimportant. If it is necessary to have intermediate modules in the Stream between the IP driver and media drivers, these modules must be added to the Streams associated with the media drivers (using I_PUSH) before the media drivers are attached below the multiplexor.

The number of Streams that can be linked to a multiplexor is restricted by the design of the particular multiplexor. The manual page describing each driver (typically found in section 7) describes such restrictions. However, only one I_LINK operation is allowed for each lower Stream; a single Stream cannot be linked below two multiplexors simultaneously.

Continuing with the example, the IP driver will now be linked below the transport protocol (TP) multiplexing driver. As seen earlier in Figure 10-1, only one link will be supported below the transport driver. This link is formed by the following sequence of system calls:

```
if ((fd_tp = open("/dev/tp", O_RDWR)) < 0) {
    perror("open of /dev/tp failed");
    exit(6);
}

if (ioctl(fd_tp, I_LINK, fd_ip) < 0) {
    perror("I_LINK ioctl failed");
    exit(7);
}
```

The multi-level multiplexing configuration shown in Figure 10-5 has now been created.

Figure 10-5: TP Multiplexor

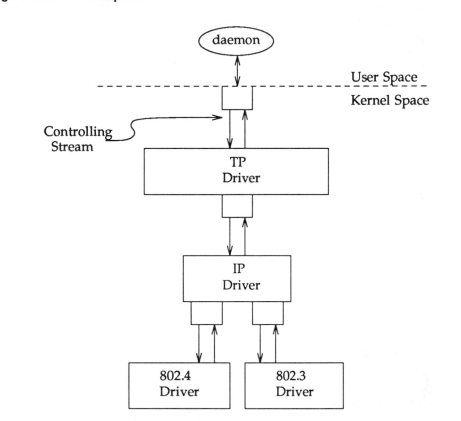

Because the controlling Stream of the IP multiplexor has been linked below the
TP multiplexor, the controlling Stream for the new multi-level multiplexor
configuration is the Stream above the TP multiplexor.

At this point the file descriptors associated with the lower drivers can be closed
without affecting the operation of the multiplexor. If these file descriptors are
not closed, all subsequent **read, write, ioctl, poll, getmsg,** and **putmsg** system
calls issued to them will fail. That is because I_LINK associates the Stream head
of each linked Stream with the multiplexor, so the user may not access that
Stream directly for the duration of the link.

The following sequence of system calls completes the daemon example:

```
    close(fd_802_4);
    close(fd_802_3);
    close(fd_ip);

    /* Hold multiplexor open forever */
    pause();
}
```

To summarize, Figure 10-5 shows the multi-level protocol multiplexor. The transport driver supports several simultaneous Streams. These Streams are multiplexed over the single Stream connected to the IP multiplexor. The mechanism for establishing multiple Streams above the transport multiplexor is actually a by-product of the way in which Streams are created between a user process and a driver. By opening different minor devices of a STREAMS driver, separate Streams will be connected to that driver. Of course, the driver must be designed with the intelligence to route data from the single lower Stream to the appropriate upper Stream.

The daemon process maintains the multiplexed Stream configuration through an open Stream (the controlling Stream) to the transport driver. Meanwhile, other users can access the services of the transport protocol by opening new Streams to the transport driver; they are freed from the need for any unnecessary knowledge of the underlying protocol configurations and sub-networks that support the transport service.

Multi-level multiplexing configurations should be assembled from the bottom up. That is because the passing of **ioctls** through the multiplexor is determined by the nature of the multiplexing driver and cannot generally be relied on.

Dismantling a Multiplexor

Streams connected to a multiplexing driver from above with **open**, can be dismantled by closing each Stream with **close**. The mechanism for dismantling Streams that have been linked below a multiplexing driver is less obvious, and is described below.

The I_UNLINK **ioctl** call is used to disconnect each multiplexor link below a multiplexing driver individually. This command has the form:

```
ioctl(fd, I_UNLINK, muxid);
```

where *fd* is a file descriptor associated with a Stream connected to the multiplexing driver from above, and *muxid* is the identifier that was returned by I_LINK when a driver was linked below the multiplexor. Each lower driver may be disconnected individually in this way, or a special *muxid* value of -1 may be used to disconnect all drivers from the multiplexor simultaneously.

In the multiplexing daemon program presented earlier, the multiplexor is never explicitly dismantled. That is because all links associated with a multiplexing driver are automatically dismantled when the controlling Stream associated with that multiplexor is closed. Because the controlling Stream is open to a driver, only the final call of **close** for that Stream will close it. In this case, the daemon is the only process that has opened the controlling Stream, so the multiplexing configuration will be dismantled when the daemon exits.

For the automatic dismantling mechanism to work in the multi-level, multiplexed Stream configuration, the controlling Stream for each multiplexor at each level must be linked under the next higher level multiplexor. In the example, the controlling Stream for the IP driver was linked under the TP driver. This resulted in a single controlling Stream for the full, multi-level configuration. Because the multiplexing program relied on closing the controlling Stream to dismantle the multiplexed Stream configuration instead of using explicit I_UNLINK calls, the *muxid* values returned by I_LINK could be ignored.

An important side effect of automatic dismantling on the close is that it is not possible for a process to build a multiplexing configuration with I_LINK and then exit. That is because **exit**(2) will close all files associated with the process, including the controlling Stream. To keep the configuration intact, the process must exist for the life of that multiplexor. That is the motivation for implementing the example as a daemon process.

However, if the process uses persistent links via the I_PLINK **ioctl** call, the multiplexor configuration would remain intact after the process exits. Persistent links are described later in this chapter.

Routing Data Through a Multiplexor

As demonstrated, STREAMS provides a mechanism for building multiplexed Stream configurations. However, the criteria on which a multiplexor routes data is driver dependent. For example, the protocol multiplexor shown before might use address information found in a protocol header to determine over which sub-network data should be routed. It is the multiplexing driver's responsibility to define its routing criteria.

One routing option available to the multiplexor is to use the *muxid* value to determine to which Stream data should be routed (remember that each multiplexor link is associated with a *muxid*). I_LINK passes the *muxid* value to the driver and returns this value to the user. The driver can therefore specify that the *muxid* value must accompany data routed through it. For example, if a multiplexor routed data from a single upper Stream to one of several lower Streams (as did the IP driver), the multiplexor could require the user to insert the *muxid* of the desired lower Stream into the first four bytes of each message passed to it. The driver could then match the *muxid* in each message with the *muxid* of each lower Stream, and route the data accordingly.

Connecting/Disconnecting Lower Streams

Multiple Streams are created above a driver/multiplexor by use of the **open** system call on either different minor devices, or on a cloneable device file. Note that any driver that handles more than one minor device is considered an upper multiplexor.

To connect Streams below a multiplexor requires additional software within the multiplexor. The main difference between STREAMS lower multiplexors and STREAMS device drivers are that multiplexors are pseudo-devices and that multiplexors have two additional **qinit** structures, pointed to by fields in the **streamtab** structure: the *lower half read-side* **qinit** and the *lower half write-side* **qinit**.

The multiplexor is conceptually divided into two parts: the lower half (bottom) and the upper half (top). The multiplexor **queue** structures that have been allocated when the multiplexor was opened, use the usual **qinit** entries from the multiplexor's **streamtab**. This is the same as any open of the STREAMS device. When a lower Stream is linked beneath the multiplexor, the **qinit** structures at the Stream head are substituted by the bottom half **qinit** structures of the multiplexors. Once the linkage is made, the multiplexor switches messages between upper and lower Streams. When messages reach the top of the lower Stream, they are handled by **put** and **service** routines specified in the bottom half of the multiplexor.

Connecting Lower Streams

A lower multiplexor is connected as follows: the initial **open** to a multiplexing driver creates a Stream, as in any other driver. **open** uses the first two **streamtab** structure entries to create the driver queues. At this point, the only distinguishing characteristic of this Stream are non-NULL entries in the **streamtab** *st_muxrinit* and *st_muxwinit* fields.

These fields are ignored by **open** (see the rightmost Stream in Figure 10-6). Any other Stream subsequently opened to this driver will have the same **streamtab** and thereby the same mux fields.

Next, another file is opened to create a (soon to be) lower Stream. The driver for the lower Stream is typically a device driver (see the leftmost Stream in Figure 10-6). This Stream has no distinguishing characteristics. It can include any driver compatible with the multiplexor. Any modules required on the lower Stream must be pushed onto it now.

Next, this lower Stream is connected below the multiplexing driver with an
I_LINK **ioctl** call [see **streamio**(7)]. The Stream head points to the Stream head
routines as its procedures (known via its **queue**). An I_LINK to the upper
Stream, referencing the lower Stream, causes STREAMS to modify the contents
of the Stream head's queues in the lower Stream. The pointers to the Stream
head routines, and other values, in the Stream head's queues are replaced with
those contained in the mux fields of the multiplexing driver's **streamtab**.
Changing the Stream head routines on the lower Stream means that all subsequent messages sent upstream by the lower Stream's driver will, ultimately, be
passed to the **put** procedure designated in *st_muxrinit*, the multiplexing driver.
The I_LINK also establishes this upper Stream as the control Stream for this
lower Stream. STREAMS remembers the relationship between these two
Streams until the upper Stream is closed, or the lower Stream is unlinked.

Finally, the Stream head sends an M_IOCTL message with *ioc_cmd* set to
I_LINK to the multiplexing driver. The M_DATA part of the M_IOCTL contains a **linkblk** structure. The multiplexing driver stores information from the
linkblk structure in private storage and returns an M_IOCACK message (acknowledgement). *l_index* is returned to the process requesting the I_LINK. This
value can be used later by the process to disconnect this Stream.

An I_LINK is required for each lower Stream connected to the driver. Additional upper Streams can be connected to the multiplexing driver by **open** calls.
Any message type can be sent from a lower Stream to user processes along any
of the upper Streams. The upper Streams provide the only interface between
the user processes and the multiplexor.

Note that no direct data structure linkage is established for the linked Streams.
The read queue's *q_next* will be NULL and the write queue's *q_next* will point to
the first entity on the lower Stream. Messages flowing upstream from a lower
driver (a device driver or another multiplexor) will enter the multiplexing driver
put procedure with *l_qbot* as the **queue** value. The multiplexing driver has to
route the messages to the appropriate upper (or lower) Stream. Similarly, a
message coming downstream from user space on any upper Stream has to be
processed and routed, if required, by the driver.

Also note that the lower Stream (see the headers and file descriptors in Figure
10-7) is no longer accessible from user space. This causes all system calls to the
lower Stream to return EINVAL, with the exception of **close**. This is why all
modules have to be in place before the lower Stream is linked to the multiplexing driver.

Finally, note that the absence of direct linkage between the upper and lower Streams means that STREAMS flow control has to be handled by special code in the multiplexing driver. The flow control mechanism cannot see across the driver.

In general, multiplexing drivers should be implemented so that new Streams can be dynamically connected to (and existing Streams disconnected from) the driver without interfering with its ongoing operation. The number of Streams that can be connected to a multiplexor is developer dependent.

Disconnecting Lower Streams

Dismantling a lower multiplexor is accomplished by disconnecting (unlinking) the lower Streams. Unlinking can be initiated in three ways: an I_UNLINK ioctl referencing a specific Stream, an I_UNLINK indicating all lower Streams, or the last **close** of the control Stream. As in the link, an unlink sends a **linkblk** structure to the driver in an M_IOCTL message. The I_UNLINK call, which unlinks a single Stream, uses the *l_index* value returned in the I_LINK to specify the lower Stream to be unlinked. The latter two calls must designate a file corresponding to a control Stream which causes all the lower Streams that were previously linked by this control Stream to be unlinked. However, the driver sees a series of individual unlinks.

If no open references exist for a lower Stream, a subsequent unlink will automatically close the Stream. Otherwise, the lower Stream must be closed by **close** following the unlink. STREAMS will automatically dismantle all cascaded multiplexors (below other multiplexing Streams) if their controlling Stream is closed. An I_UNLINK will leave lower, cascaded multiplexing Streams intact unless the Stream file descriptor was previously closed.

Multiplexor Construction Example

This section describes an example of multiplexor construction and usage. Figure 10-6 shows the Streams before their connection to create the multiplexing configuration of Figure 10-7. Multiple upper and lower Streams interface to the multiplexor driver. The user processes of Figure 10-7 are not shown in Figure 10-6.

Figure 10-6: Internet Multiplexor Before Connecting

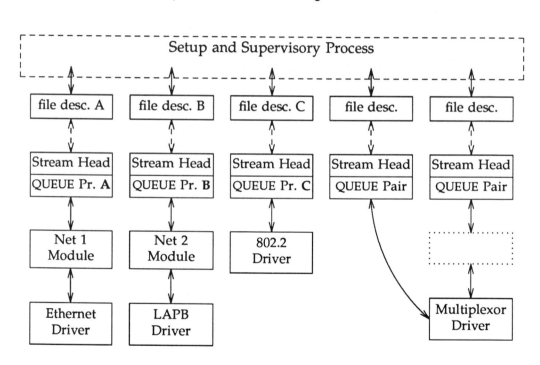

The Ethernet, LAPB and IEEE 802.2 device drivers terminate links to other nodes. The multiplexor driver is an Internet Protocol (IP) multiplexor that switches data among the various nodes or sends data upstream to a user(s) in the system. The Net modules would typically provide a convergence function which matches the multiplexor driver and device driver interface.

Figure 10-6 depicts only a portion of the full, larger Stream. In the dotted rectangle above the IP multiplexor, there generally would be an upper transport control protocol (TCP) multiplexor, additional modules and, possibly, additional multiplexors in the Stream. Multiplexors could also be cascaded below the IP driver if the device drivers were replaced by multiplexor drivers.

Figure 10-7: Internet Multiplexor After Connecting

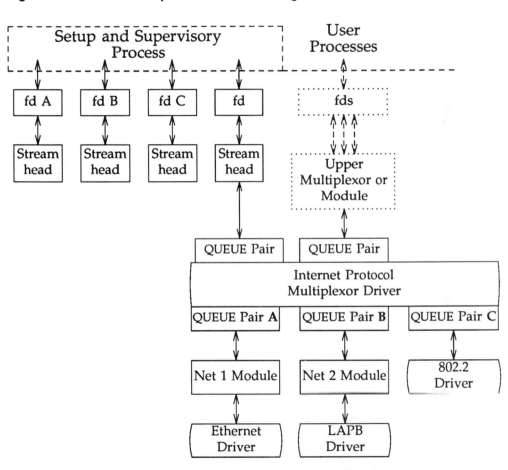

Streams A, B, and C are opened by the process, and modules are pushed as needed. Two upper Streams are opened to the IP multiplexor. The rightmost Stream represents multiple Streams, each connected to a process using the network. The Stream second from the right provides a direct path to the multiplexor for supervisory functions. It is the control Stream, leading to a process which sets up and supervises this configuration. It is always directly connected to the IP driver. Although not shown, modules can be pushed on the control Stream.

After the Streams are opened, the supervisory process typically transfers routing information to the IP drivers (and any other multiplexors above the IP), and initializes the links. As each link becomes operational, its Stream is connected below the IP driver. If a more complex multiplexing configuration is required, the IP multiplexor Stream with all its connected links can be connected below another multiplexor driver.

Figure 10-7 shows that the file descriptors for the lower device driver Streams are left dangling. The primary purpose in creating these Streams was to provide parts for the multiplexor. Those not used for control and not required for error recovery (by reconnecting them through an I_UNLINK ioctl) have no further function. These lower Streams can be closed to free the file descriptor without any effect on the multiplexor.

Multiplexing Driver

This section contains an example of a multiplexing driver that implements an N-to-1 configuration. This configuration might be used for terminal windows, where each transmission to or from the terminal identifies the window. This resembles a typical device driver, with two differences: the device handling functions are performed by a separate driver, connected as a lower Stream, and the device information (i.e., relevant user process) is contained in the input data rather than in an interrupt call.

Each upper Stream is created by **open**(2). A single lower Stream is opened and then it is linked by use of the multiplexing facility. This lower Stream might connect to the tty driver. The implementation of this example is a foundation for an M-to-N multiplexor.

As in the loop-around driver (in Chapter 9), flow control requires the use of standard and special code, since physical connectivity among the Streams is broken at the driver. Different approaches are used for flow control on the lower Stream, for messages coming upstream from the device driver, and on the upper Streams, for messages coming downstream from the user processes.

The multiplexor declarations are:

```
#include "sys/types.h"
#include "sys/param.h"
#include "sys/sysmacros.h"
#include "sys/stream.h"
#include "sys/stropts.h"
#include "sys/errno.h"
#include "sys/cred.h"
#include "sys/ddi.h"

static int muxopen(), muxclose(), muxuwput(), muxlwsrv(), muxlrput(),
        muxuwsrv();

static struct module_info info = {
    0xaabb, "mux", 0, INFPSZ, 512, 128 };

static struct qinit urinit = {    /* upper read */
    NULL, NULL, muxopen, muxclose, NULL, &info, NULL };

static struct qinit uwinit = {    /* upper write */
    muxuwput, muxuwsrv, NULL, NULL, NULL, &info, NULL };

static struct qinit lrinit = {    /* lower read */
    muxlrput, NULL, NULL, NULL, NULL, &info, NULL };

static struct qinit lwinit = {    /* lower write */
    NULL, muxlwsrv, NULL, NULL, NULL, &info, NULL };

struct streamtab muxinfo = { &urinit, &uwinit, &lrinit, &lwinit };

struct mux {
    queue_t *qptr; /* back pointer to read queue */
};

extern struct mux mux_mux[];
extern int mux_cnt;

queue_t *muxbot; /* linked lower queue */
int muxerr;      /* set if error of hangup on lower stream */
```

The four **streamtab** entries correspond to the upper read, upper write, lower read, and lower write **qinit** structures. The multiplexing **qinit** structures replace those in each (in this case there is only one) lower Stream head after the I_LINK has completed successfully. In a multiplexing configuration, the processing performed by the multiplexing driver can be partitioned between the upper and lower queues. There must be an upper Stream write **put** procedure and lower

Stream read **put** procedure. If the queue procedures of the opposite upper/lower queue are not needed, the queue can be skipped over, and the message put to the following queue.

In the example, the upper read-side procedures are not used. The lower Stream read queue **put** procedure transfers the message directly to the read queue upstream from the multiplexor. There is no lower write **put** procedure because the upper write **put** procedure directly feeds the lower write queue downstream from the multiplexor.

The driver uses a private data structure, *mux*. *mux_mux[dev]* points back to the opened upper read queue. This is used to route messages coming upstream from the driver to the appropriate upper queue. It is also used to find a free major/minor device for a CLONEOPEN driver open case.

The upper queue open contains the canonical driver open code:

```
static int muxopen(q, devp, flag, sflag, credp)
    queue_t    *q;
    dev_t      *devp;
    int        flag;
    int        sflag;
    cred_t     *credp;
{
    struct mux *mux;
    dev_t device;

    if (sflag == CLONEOPEN) {
        for (device = 0; device < mux_cnt; device++)
            if (mux_mux[device].qptr == 0)
                break;
        }
    }
    else
        device = getminor(*devp);

    if (device >= mux_cnt)
        return ENXIO;

    mux = &mux_mux[device];
    mux->qptr = q;
    q->q_ptr = (char *) mux;
    WR(q)->q_ptr = (char *) mux;
    return 0;
}
```

muxopen checks for a clone or ordinary open call. It initializes *q_ptr* to point at the *mux_mux[]* structure.

The core multiplexor processing is the following: downstream data written to an upper Stream is queued on the corresponding upper write message queue if the lower Stream is flow controlled. This allows flow control to propagate towards the Stream head for each upper Stream. A lower write **service** procedure, rather than a write **put** procedure, is used so that flow control, coming up from the driver below, may be handled.

On the lower read-side, data coming up the lower Stream are passed to the lower read **put** procedure. The procedure routes the data to an upper Stream based on the first byte of the message. This byte holds the minor device number of an upper Stream. The **put** procedure handles flow control by testing the upper Stream at the first upper read queue beyond the driver. That is, the **put** procedure treats the Stream component above the driver as the next queue.

Upper Write Put Procedure

muxuwput, the upper queue write **put** procedure, traps **ioctls**, in particular I_LINK and I_UNLINK:

```
static int muxuwput(q, mp);
    queue_t    *q;
    mblk_t     *mp;

{

    int s;
    struct mux *mux;

    mux = (struct mux *)q->q_ptr;
    switch (mp->b_datap->db_type) {
    case M_IOCTL: {
        struct iocblk *iocp;
        struct linkblk *linkp;

        /*
         * ioctl. Only channel 0 can do ioctls.  Two
         * calls are recognized: LINK, and UNLINK
         */

        if (mux != mux_mux)
            goto iocnak;

        iocp = (struct iocblk *) mp->b_rptr;
        switch (iocp->ioc_cmd) {
        case I_LINK:

            /*
             * Link.  The data contains a linkblk structure
             * Remember the bottom queue in muxbot.
             */

            if (muxbot != NULL)
                goto iocnak;
```

(continued on next page)

```
            linkp = (struct linkblk *) mp->b_cont->b_rptr;
            muxbot = linkp->l_qbot;
            muxerr = 0;
            mp->b_datap->db_type = M_IOCACK;
            iocp->ioc_count = 0;
            qreply(q, mp);
            break;
        case I_UNLINK:
            /*
             * Unlink.  The data contains a linkblk structure.
             * Should not fail an unlink.  Null out muxbot.
             */

            linkp = (struct linkblk *) mp->b_cont->b_rptr;
            muxbot = NULL;
            mp->b_datap->db_type = M_IOCACK;
            iocp->ioc_count = 0;
            qreply(q, mp);
            break;
        default:
        iocnak:

            /* fail ioctl */

            mp->b_datap->db_type = M_IOCNAK;
            qreply(q, mp);
        }

        break;

    }
```

First, there is a check to enforce that the Stream associated with minor device 0 will be the single, controlling Stream. The **ioctls** are only accepted on this Stream. As described previously, a controlling Stream is the one that issues the I_LINK. Having a single control Stream is a recommended practice. I_LINK and I_UNLINK include a **linkblk** structure containing:

l_qtop   The upper write queue from which the **ioctl** is coming. It should always equal *q*.

l_qbot   The new lower write queue. It is the former Stream head write queue. It is of most interest since that is where the multiplexor gets and puts its data.

l_index   A unique (system wide) identifier for the link. It can be used for routing or during selective unlinks. Since the example only supports a single link, *l_index* is not used.

For I_LINK, *l_qbot* is saved in *muxbot* and a positive acknowledgment is generated. From this point on, until an I_UNLINK occurs, data from upper queues will be routed through *muxbot*. Note that when an I_LINK, is received, the lower Stream has already been connected. This allows the driver to send messages downstream to perform any initialization functions. Returning an M_IOCNAK message (negative acknowledgment) in response to an I_LINK will cause the lower Stream to be disconnected.

The I_UNLINK handling code nulls out *muxbot* and generates a positive acknowledgment. A negative acknowledgment should not be returned to an I_UNLINK. The Stream head assures that the lower Stream is connected to a multiplexor before sending an I_UNLINK M_IOCTL.

muxuwput handles M_FLUSH messages as a normal driver would:

```
case M_FLUSH:
    if (*mp->b_rptr & FLUSHW)
        flushq(q, FLUSHDATA);
    if (*mp->b_rptr & FLUSHR) {
        *mp->b_rptr &= ~FLUSHW;
        qreply(q, mp);
    } else
        freemsg(mp);
    break;
case M_DATA:
    /*
     * Data.  If we have no bottom queue --> fail
     * Otherwise, queue the data and invoke the lower
     * service procedure.
     */
    if (muxerr || muxbot == NULL)
        goto bad;
    if (canput(muxbot->q_next)){
        mblk_t *bp;
        if((bp = allocb(1, BPRI_MED)) == NULL) {
            putq(q, mp);
            bufcall(1, BPRI_MED, qenable, q);
                break;
        }
        *bp->b_wptr++ = (struct mux *)q->q_ptr - mux_mux;
        bp->b_cont = mp;
        putnext(muxbot, bp);
    } else
        putq(q, mp);
    break;
default:
bad:
    /*
     * Send an error message upstream.
     */
    mp->b_datap->db_type = M_ERROR;
    mp->b_rptr = mp->b_wptr = mp->b_datap->db_base;
    *mp->b_wptr++ = EINVAL;
    qreply(q, mp);
    }
}
```

M_DATA messages are not placed on the lower write message queue. They are queued on the upper write message queue. When flow control subsides on the lower Stream, the lower **service** procedure, *muxlwsrv,* is scheduled to start output. This is similar to starting output on a device driver.

Upper Write Service Procedure

The following example shows the code for the upper multiplexor write **service** procedure:

```
static int muxuwsrv(q)
    queue_t  *q;
{
    struct mux  *muxp;
    mblk_t  *mp;
    muxp = (struct mux *)q->q_ptr;

    if (!muxbot && q->q_first) {
        flushq(q, FLUSHALL);
        return;
    }
    if (muxerr) {
        flushq(q, FLUSHALL);
        return;
    }
    while (mp = getq(q)) {
        if (canput(muxbot->q_next))
            putnext(muxbot, mp);
        else {
            putbq(q, mp);
            return;
        }
    }
}
```

As long as there is a Stream still linked under the multiplexor and there are no errors, the **service** procedure will take a message off the queue and send it downstream, if flow control allows.

Lower Write Service Procedure

muxlwsrv, the lower (linked) queue write **service** procedure is scheduled as a result of flow control subsiding downstream (it is back-enabled).

```
static int muxlwsrv(q)
   queue_t *q;
{
   register int i;
   for (i = 0; i < mux_cnt; i++)
      if (mux_mux[i].qptr && mux_mux[i].qptr->q_first)
         qenable(mux_mux[i].qptr);
}
```

muxlwsrv steps through all possible upper queues. If a queue is active and there are messages on the queue, then its the upper write **service** procedure is enabled via **qenable()**.

Lower Read Put Procedure

The lower (linked) queue read **put** procedure is:

```
static int muxlrput(q, mp)
   queue_t   *q;
   mblk_t    *mp;
{
   queue_t *uq;
   mblk_t *b_cont;
   int device;

   if(muxerr) {
       freemsg(mp);
       return;
   }
   switch(mp->b_datap->db_type) {
   case M_FLUSH:
       /*
        * Flush queues. NOTE: sense of tests is reversed
        * since we are acting like a "stream head"
        */
       if (*mp->b_rptr & FLUSHW) {
           *mp->b_rptr &= ~FLUSHR;
           qreply(q, mp);
       } else
           freemsg(mp);
       break;

   case M_ERROR:
   case M_HANGUP:
       muxerr = 1;
       freemsg(mp);
       break;

   case M_DATA:
       /*
        * Route message.  First byte indicates
        * device to send to.  No flow control.
        *
        * Extract and delete device number.  If the leading block is
        * now empty and more blocks follow, strip the leading block.
        */

       device = *mp->b_rptr++;

       /* Sanity check.  Device must be in range */

       if (device < 0 || device >= mux_cnt) {
           freemsg(mp);
```

(continued on next page)

```
            break;
        }

        /*
         * If upper stream is open and not backed up,
         * send the message there, otherwise discard it.
         */

        uq = mux_mux[device].qptr;
        if (uq != NULL && canput(uq->q_next))
            putnext(uq, mp);
        else
            freemsg(mp);
        break;
    default:
        freemsg(mp);
    }
}
```

muxlrput receives messages from the linked Stream. In this case, it is acting as a Stream head. It handles M_FLUSH messages. Note the code is reversed from that of a driver, handling M_FLUSH messages from upstream. There is no need to flush the read queue because no data are ever placed on it.

muxlrput also handles M_ERROR and M_HANGUP messages. If one is received, it locks-up the upper Streams by setting *muxerr*.

M_DATA messages are routed by looking at the first data byte of the message. This byte contains the minor device of the upper Stream. Several sanity checks are made: Is the device in range? Is the upper Stream open? Is the upper Stream not full?

This multiplexor does not support flow control on the read-side. It is merely a router. If everything checks out, the message is put to the proper upper queue. Otherwise, the message is discarded.

The upper Stream close routine simply clears the mux entry so this queue will no longer be found.

```
/*
 * Upper queue close
 */
static int muxclose(q, flag, credp)
   queue_t  *q;
   int      flag;
   cred_t   *credp;
{
   ((struct mux *)q->q_ptr)->qptr = NULL;
   q->q->ptr = NULL;
   WR(q)->q_ptr = NULL;
}
```

Persistent Links

With I_LINK and I_UNLINK **ioctls** the file descriptor associated with the Stream above the multiplexor used to set up the lower multiplexor connections must remain open for the duration of the configuration. Closing the file descriptor associated with the controlling Stream will dismantle the whole multiplexing configuration. Some applications may not want to keep a process running merely to hold the multiplexor configuration together. Therefore, "freestanding" links below a multiplexor are needed. A persistent link is such a link. It is similar to a STREAMS multiplexor link, except that a process is not needed to hold the links together. After the multiplexor has been set up, the process may close all file descriptors and exit, and the multiplexor will remain intact.

Two **ioctls**, I_PLINK and I_PUNLINK, are used to create and remove persistent links that are associated with the Stream above the multiplexor. **close**(2) and I_UNLINK are not able to disconnect the persistent links.

The format of I_PLINK is:

```
ioctl(fd0, I_PLINK, fd1)
```

The first file descriptor, *fd0,* must reference the Stream connected to the multiplexing driver and the second file descriptor, *fd1,* must reference the Stream to be connected below the multiplexor. The persistent link can be created in the following way:

```
upper_stream_fd = open("/dev/mux", O_RDWR);
lower_stream_fd = open("/dev/driver", O_RDWR);
muxid = ioctl(upper_stream_fd, I_PLINK, lower_stream_fd);
/*
 * save muxid in a file
 */
exit(0);
```

Figure 10-8 shows how **open**(2) establishes a Stream between the device and the Stream head.

Figure 10-8: open() of MUXdriver and Driver1

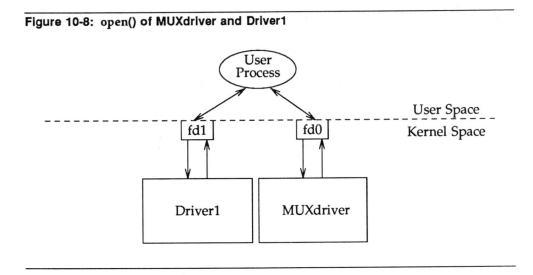

The persistent link can still exist even if the file descriptor associated with the upper Stream to the multiplexing driver is closed. The I_PLINK **ioctl** returns an integer value, *muxid*, that can be used for dismantling the multiplexing configuration. If the process that created the persistent link still exists, it may pass the *muxid* value to some other process to dismantle the link, if the dismantling is desired, or it can leave the *muxid* value in a file so that other processes may find it later. Figure 10-9 shows a multiplexor after I_PLINK.

Figure 10-9: Multiplexor After I_PLINK

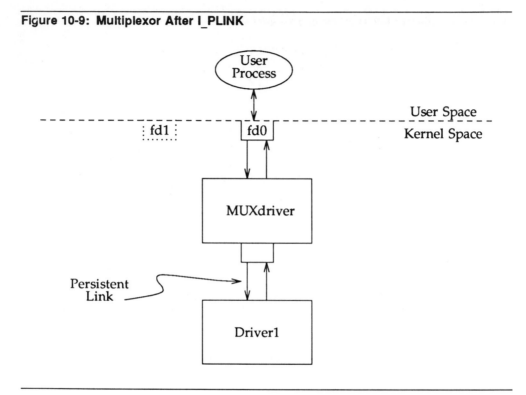

Several users can open the MUXdriver and send data to the Driver1 since the persistent link to the Driver1 remains intact. This is shown in the following figure.

Figure 10-10: Other Users Opening a MUXdriver

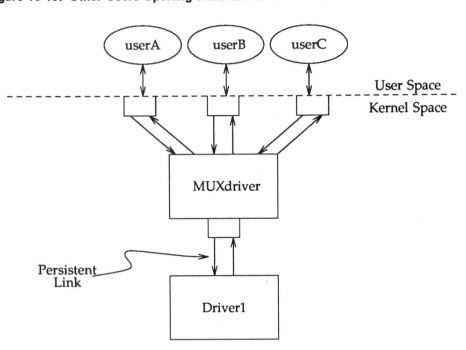

The **ioctl** I_PUNLINK is used for dismantling the persistent link. Its format is:

```
ioctl(fd0, I_PUNLINK, muxid)
```

where the *fd0* is the file descriptor associated with Stream connected to the multiplexing driver from above. The *muxid* is returned by the **ioctl** I_PLINK for the Stream that was connected below the multiplexor. The I_PUNLINK removes the persistent link between the multiplexor referenced by the *fd0* and the Stream to the driver designated by the *muxid*. Each of the bottom persistent links can be disconnected individually. An I_PUNLINK **ioctl** with the *muxid* value of MUXID_ALL will remove all persistent links below the multiplexing driver referenced by the *fd0*.

The following will dismantle the previously given configuration:

```
fd = open ("/dev/mux", O_RDWR);
/*
 * retrieve muxid from the file
 */
ioctl (fd, I_PUNLINK, muxid);
exit (0);
```

The use of the **ioctls** I_PLINK and I_PUNLINK should not be intermixed with the I_LINK and I_UNLINK. Any attempt to unlink a regular link via the I_PUNLINK or to unlink a persistent link via the I_UNLINK **ioctl** will cause the *errno* value of EINVAL to be returned.

Since multi-level multiplexing configurations are allowed in STREAMS, it is possible to have a situation where persistent links exist below a multiplexor whose Stream is connected to the above multiplexor by regular links. Closing the file descriptor associated with the controlling Stream will remove the regular link but not the persistent links below it. On the other hand, regular links are allowed to exist below a multiplexor whose Stream is connected to the above multiplexor via persistent links. In this case, the regular links will be removed if the persistent link above is removed and no other references to the lower Streams exist.

The construction of cycles is not allowed when creating links. A cycle could be constructed by creating a persistent link of multiplexor 2 below multiplexor 1 and then closing the controlling file descriptor associated with the multiplexor 2 and reopening it again and then linking the multiplexor 1 below the multiplexor 2. This is not allowed. The operating system prevents a multiplexor configuration from containing a cycle to ensure that messages can not be routed infinitely, thus creating an infinite loop or overflowing the kernel stack.

Design Guidelines

The following lists general multiplexor design guidelines:

- The upper half of the multiplexor acts like the end of the upper Stream.

- The lower half of the multiplexor acts like the head of the lower Stream.

- **Service** procedures are used for flow control.

- Message routing is based on multiplexor specific criteria.

- When one Stream is being fed by many Streams, flow control may have to take place. Then all feeding Streams on the other end of the multiplexor will have to be enabled when the flow control is relieved.

- When one Stream is feeding many Streams, flow control may also have to take place. Be careful not to starve other Streams when one becomes flow controlled.

11 STREAMS-Based Pipes and FIFOS

STREAMS-based Pipes and FIFOs   11-1
Creating and Opening Pipes and FIFOs   11-1
Accessing Pipes and FIFOs   11-3
  ■ Reading from a Pipe or FIFO   11-4
  ■ Writing to a Pipe or FIFO   11-4
  ■ Closing a Pipe or FIFO   11-5
Flushing Pipes and FIFOs   11-6
Named Streams   11-7
  ■ fattach   11-7
  ■ fdetach   11-8
  ■ isastream   11-9
  ■ File Descriptor Passing   11-9
  ■ Named Streams in A Remote Environment   11-10
Unique Connections   11-10

STREAMS-based Pipes and FIFOs

A pipe in the UNIX system is a mechanism that provides a communication path between multiple processes. Prior to Release 4.0 UNIX System V had "standard" pipes and named pipes (also called FIFOs). With standard pipes, one end was opened for reading and the other end for writing, thus data flow was uni-directional. FIFOs had only one end and typically one process opened the file for reading and another process opened the file for writing. Data written into the FIFO by the writer could then be read by the reader.

To provide greater support and development flexibility for networked applications, pipes and FIFOs have become STREAMS-based in UNIX System V Release 4.0. The basic interface remains the same but the underlying implementation has changed. Pipes now provide a bi-directional mechanism for process communication. When a pipe is created via the **pipe**(2) system call, two Streams are opened and connected together, thus providing a full-duplex mechanism. Data flow is on First-In-First-Out basis. Previously pipes were associated with character devices and the creation of a pipe was limited to the capacity and configuration of the device. STREAMS-based pipes and FIFOs are not attached to STREAMS-based character devices. This eliminates configuration constraints and limits the number of opened pipes to the number of file descriptors for that process.

The remainder of this chapter uses the terms pipe and STREAMS-based pipe interchangeably for a STREAMS-based pipe.

Creating and Opening Pipes and FIFOs

FIFOs are created via **mknod**(2) or **mkfifo**(3C). FIFOs behave like regular file system nodes but are distinguished from other file system nodes by the p in the first column when the ls −l command is executed. Data written to the FIFO or read from the FIFO flow up and down the Stream in STREAMS buffers. Data written by one process can be read by another process.

FIFOs are opened in the same manner as other file system nodes via the **open**(2) system call. Any data written to the FIFO can be read from the same file descriptor in the First-In-First-Out manner. Modules can also be pushed on the FIFO. See **open**(2) for the restrictions that apply when opening a FIFO.

A STREAMS-based pipe is created via the **pipe**(2) system call that returns two file descriptors, *fd[0]* and *fd[1]*. Both file descriptors are opened for reading and writing. Data written to *fd[0]* becomes data read from *fd[1]* and vice versa.

Each end of the pipe has knowledge of the other end through internal data structures. Subsequent reads, writes, and closes are aware of if the other end of the pipe is open or closed. When one end of the pipe is closed, the internal data structures provide a way to access the Stream for the other end so that an M_HANGUP message can be sent to its Stream head.

After successful creation of a STREAMS-based pipe, 0 is returned. If **pipe**(2) is unable to create and open a STREAMS-based pipe, it will fail with *errno* set as follows:

- ENOMEM - could not allocate two **vnodes**.

- ENFILE - file table is overflowed.

- EMFILE - can't allocate more file descriptors for the process.

- ENOSR - could not allocate resources for both Stream heads.

- EINTR - signal was caught while creating the Stream heads.

STREAMS modules can be added to a STREAMS-based pipe with the **ioctl**(2) I_PUSH. A module can be pushed onto one or both ends of the pipe (see Figure 11-1). However, a pipe maintains the concept of a midpoint so that if a module is pushed onto one end of the pipe, that module cannot be popped from the other end.

Figure 11-1: Pushing Modules on a STREAMS-based Pipe

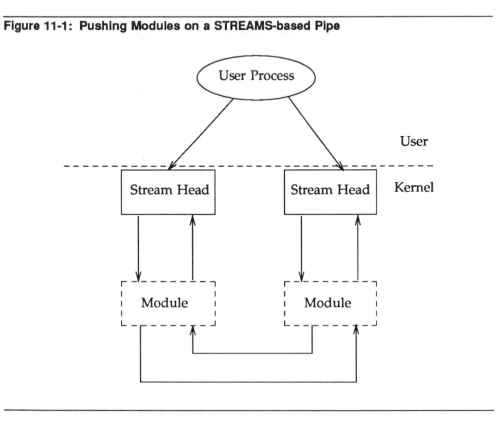

Accessing Pipes and FIFOs

STREAMS-based pipes and FIFOs can be accessed through the operating system routines read(2), write(2), ioctl(2), close(2), putmsg(2), getmsg(2), and poll(2). In case of FIFOs open(2) is also used.

Reading from a Pipe or FIFO

The **read**(2) [or **getmsg**(2)] system call is used to read from a pipe or FIFO. A user reads data from a Stream (not from a data buffer as was done prior to Release 4.0). Data can be read from either end of a pipe.

On success, the **read** returns the number of bytes read and placed in the buffer. When the end of the data is reached, the **read** returns 0.

When a user process attempts to read from an empty pipe (or FIFO), the following will happen:

- If one end of the pipe is closed, 0 is returned indicating the end of the file.

- If no process has the FIFO open for writing, **read**(2) returns 0 to indicate the end of the file.

- If some process has the FIFO open for writing, or both ends of the pipe are open, and O_NDELAY is set, **read**(2) returns 0.

- If some process has the FIFO open for writing, or both ends of the pipe are open, and O_NONBLOCK is set, **read**(2) returns -1 and set *errno* to EAGAIN.

- If O_NDELAY and O_NONBLOCK are not set, the **read** call will block until data are written to the pipe, until one end of the pipe is closed, or the FIFO is no longer open for writing.

Writing to a Pipe or FIFO

When a user process calls the **write**(2) system call, data are sent down the associated Stream. If the pipe or FIFO is empty (no modules pushed), data written are placed on the read queue of the other Stream for STREAMS-based pipes, and on the read queue of the same Stream for FIFOs. Since the size of a pipe is the number of unread data bytes, the written data are reflected in the size of the other end of the pipe.

Zero Length Writes

If a user process issues **write**(2) with 0 as the number of bytes to send down a STREAMS-based pipe or FIFO, 0 is returned, and by default no message is sent down the Stream. However, if a user requires that a 0-length message be sent downstream, an **ioctl** call may be used to change this default behavior. The flag SNDZERO supports this. If SNDZERO is set in the Stream head, **write**(2) requests of 0 bytes will generate a 0-length message and send the message down the Stream. If SNDZERO is not set, no message is generated and 0 is returned to the user.

To toggle the SNDZERO bit, the **ioctl** I_SWROPT is used. If *arg* in the **ioctl** call is set to SNDZERO and the SNDZERO bit is off, the bit is turned on. If *arg* is set to 0 and the SNDZERO bit is on, the bit is turned off.

The **ioctl** I_GWROPT is used to return the current write settings.

Atomic Writes

If multiple processes simultaneously write to the same pipe, data from one process can be interleaved with data from another process, if modules are pushed on the pipe or the write is greater than PIPE_BUF. The order of data written is not necessarily the order of data read. To ensure that writes of less than PIPE_BUF bytes will not be interleaved with data written from other processes, any modules pushed on the pipe should have a maximum packet size of at least PIPE_BUF.

> **NOTE** PIPE_BUF is an implementation specific constant that specifies the maximum number of bytes that are atomic in a write to a pipe. When writing to a pipe, write requests of PIPE_BUF or less bytes will not be interleaved with data from other processes doing writes on the same pipe. However, write requests greater than PIPE_BUF bytes may have data interleaved on arbitrary byte boundaries with writes by other processes whether or not the O_NONBLOCK or O_NDELAY flag is set.

If the module packet size is at least the size of PIPE_BUF, the Stream head packages the data in such a way that the first message is at least PIPE_BUF bytes. The remaining data may be packaged into smaller or larger blocks depending on buffer availability. If the first module on the Stream cannot support a packet of PIPE_BUF, atomic writes on the pipe cannot be guaranteed.

Closing a Pipe or FIFO

The **close**(2) system call closes a pipe or FIFO and dismantles its associated Streams. On the last close of one end of a pipe, an M_HANGUP message is sent upstream to the other end of the pipe. Subsequent **read**(2) or **getmsg**(2) calls on that Stream head will return the number of bytes read and zero when there are no more data. Subsequent **write**(2) or **putmsg**(2) requests will fail with *errno* set to ENXIO. If the pipe has been mounted via **fattach**() the pipe must be unmounted prior to calling **close**, otherwise the Stream will not be dismantled. If the other end of the pipe is mounted, the last close of the pipe will force it to be unmounted.

Flushing Pipes and FIFOs

When the flush request is initiated from a user **ioctl** or from a **flushq**() routine, the FLUSHR and/or FLUSHW bits of an M_FLUSH message will have to be switched. The point of switching the bits is the point where the M_FLUSH message is passed from a write queue to a read queue. This point is also known as the mid-point of the pipe.

The mid-point of a pipe is not always easily detectable, especially if there are numerous modules pushed on either end of the pipe. In that case, there needs to be a mechanism to intercept all messages passing through the Stream. If the message is an M_FLUSH message and it is at the Streams mid-point, the flush bits need to switched.

This bit switching is handled by the **pipemod** module. **pipemod** should be pushed onto a pipe or FIFO where flushing of any kind will take place. The **pipemod** module can be pushed on either end of the pipe. The only requirement is that it is pushed onto an end that previously did not have modules on it. That is, **pipemod** must be the first module pushed onto a pipe so that it is at the mid-point of the pipe itself.

The **pipemod** module handles only M_FLUSH messages. All other messages are passed on to the next module via the **putnext**() utility routine. If an M_FLUSH message is passed to **pipemod** and the FLUSHR and FLUSHW bits are set, the message is not processed but is passed to the next module via the **putnext**() routine. If only the FLUSHR bit is set, the FLUSHR bit is turned off and the FLUSHW bit is set. The message is then passed to the next module via **putnext**. Similarly, if the FLUSHW bit was the only bit set in the M_FLUSH message, the FLUSHW bit is turned off and the FLUSHR bit is turned on. The message is then passed to the next module on the Stream.

The **pipemod** module can be pushed on any Stream that desires the bit switching. It must be pushed onto a pipe or FIFO if any form of flushing must take place.

Programmer's Guide: STREAMS

Named Streams

Some applications may want to associate a Stream or STREAMS-based pipe with an existing node in the file system name space. For example, a server process may create a pipe, name one end of the pipe, and allow unrelated processes to communicate with it over that named end.

fattach

A STREAMS file descriptor can be named by attaching that file descriptor to a node in the file system name space. The routine **fattach**() [see also **fattach**(3C)] is used to name a STREAMS file descriptor. Its format is:

```
int fattach (int fildes, char *path)
```

where *fildes* is an open file descriptor that refers to either a STREAMS-based pipe or a STREAMS device driver (or a pseudo device driver), and *path* is an existing node in the file system name space (for example, regular file, directory, character special file, etc).

The *path* cannot have a Stream already attached to it. It cannot be a mount point for a file system nor the root of a file system. A user must be an owner of the *path* with write permission or a user with the appropriate privileges in order to attach the file descriptor.

If the *path* is in use when the routine **fattach**() is executed, those processes accessing the *path* will not be interrupted and any data associated with the *path* before the call to the **fattach**() routine will continue to be accessible by those processes.

After a Stream is named, all subsequent operations [for example, **open**(2)] on the *path* will operate on the named Stream. Thus, it is possible that a user process has one file descriptor pointing to the data originally associated with the *path* and another file descriptor pointing to a named Stream.

Once the Stream has been named, the **stat**(2) system call on *path* will show information for the Stream. If the named Stream is a pipe, the **stat**(2) information will show that *path* is a pipe. If the Stream is a device driver or a pseudo device driver, *path* appears as a device. The initial modes, permissions, and ownership of the named Stream are taken from the attributes of the *path*. The user can issue the system calls **chmod**(2) and **chown**(2) to alter the attributes of the named Stream and not affect the original attributes of the *path* nor the original attributes of the STREAMS file.

The size represented in the **stat**(2) information will reflect the number of unread bytes of data currently at the Stream head. This size is not necessarily the number of bytes written to the Stream.

A STREAMS-based file descriptor can be attached to many different *path*s at the same time (i.e., a Stream can have many names attached to it). The modes, ownership, and permissions of these *path*s may vary, but operations on any of these *path*s will access the same Stream.

Named Streams can have modules pushed on them, be polled, be passed as file descriptors, and be used for any other STREAMS operation.

fdetach

A named Stream can be disassociated from a file name with the fdetach() routine [see also **fdetach**(3C)] that has the following format:

```
int fdetach (char *path)
```

where *path* is the name of the previously named Stream. Only the owner of *path* or the user with the appropriate privileges may disassociate the Stream from its name. The Stream may be disassociated from its name while processes are accessing it. If these processes have the named Stream open at the time of the fdetach() call, the processes will not get an error, and will continue to access the Stream. However, after the disassociation, subsequent operations on *path* access the underlying file rather than the named Stream.

If only one end of the pipe is named, the last close of the other end will cause the named end to be automatically detached. If the named Stream is a device and not a pipe, the last close will not cause the Stream to be detached.

If there is no named Stream or the user does not have access permissions on *path* or on the named Stream, fdetach() returns -1 with *errno* set to EINVAL. Otherwise, fdetach() returns 0 for success.

A Stream will remain attached with or without an active server process. If a server aborted, the only way a named Stream is cleaned up is if the server executed a clean up routine that explicitly detached and closed down the Stream.

If the named Stream is that of a pipe with only one end attached, clean up will occur automatically. The named end of the pipe is forced to be detached when the other end closes down. If there are no other references after the pipe is detached, the Stream is deallocated and cleaned up. Thus, a forced detach of a pipe end will occur when the server is aborted.

If the both ends of the pipe are named, the pipe remains attached even after all processes have exited. In order for the pipe to become detached, a server process would have to explicitly invoke a program that executed the **fdetach**() routine.

To eliminate the need for the server process to invoke the program, the **fdetach**(1M) command can be used. This command accepts a path name that is a path to a named Stream. When the command is invoked, the Stream is detached from the path. If the name was the only reference to the Stream, the Stream is also deallocated.

A user invoking the **fdetach**(1M) command must be an owner of the named Stream or a user with the appropriate permissions.

isastream

The function **isastream**() [see also **isastream**(3C)] may be used to determine if a file descriptor is associated with a STREAMS device. Its format is:

```
int isastream (int fildes);
```

where *fildes* refers to an open file. **isastream**() returns 1 if *fildes* represents a STREAMS file, and 0 if not. On failure, **isastream**() returns -1 with *errno* set to EBADF.

This function is useful for client processes communicating with a server process over a named Stream to check whether the file has been overlaid by a Stream before sending any data over the file.

File Descriptor Passing

Named Streams are useful for passing file descriptors between unrelated processes. A user process can send a file descriptor to another process by invoking the **ioctl**(2) I_SENDFD on one end of a named Stream. This sends a message containing a file pointer to the Stream head at the other end of the pipe. Another process can retrieve that message containing the file pointer by invoking the **ioctl**(2) I_RECVFD on the other end of the pipe.

Named Streams in A Remote Environment

If a user on the server machine creates a pipe and mounts it over a file that is part of an advertised resource, a user on the client machine (that has remotely named the resource) may access the remote named Stream. A user on the client machine is not allowed to pass file descriptors across the named Stream and will get an error when the **ioctl** request is attempted. If a user on the client machine creates a pipe and attempts to attach it to a file that is a remotely named resource, the system call will fail.

The following three examples are given as illustrations:

Suppose the server advertised a resource */dev/foo*, created a STREAMS-based pipe, and attached one end of the pipe onto */dev/foo/spipe*. All processes on the server machine will be able to access the pipe when they open */dev/foo/spipe*. Now suppose that client XYZ mounts the advertised resource */dev/foo* onto its */mnt* directory. All processes on client XYZ will be able to access the STREAMS-based pipe when they open */mnt/spipe*.

If the server advertised another resource */dev/fog* and client XYZ mounts that resource onto its */install* directory and then attaches a STREAMS-based pipe onto */install*, the mount would fail with *errno* set to EBUSY, because */install* is already a mount point. If client XYZ attached a pipe onto */install/spipe*, the mount would also fail with *errno* set to EREMOTE, because the mount would require crossing an RFS (Remote File System) mount point.

Suppose the server advertised its */usr/control* directory and client XYZ mounts that resource onto its */tmp* directory. The server now creates a STREAMS-based pipe and attaches one end over its */usr* directory. When the server opens */usr* it will access the pipe. On the other hand, when the client opens */tmp* it will access what is in the server's */usr/control* directory.

Programmer's Guide: STREAMS

Unique Connections

With named pipes, client processes may communicate with a server process via a module called **connld** that enables a client process to gain a unique, non-multiplexed connection to a server. The **connld** module can be pushed onto the named end of the pipe. If **connld** is pushed on the named end of the pipe and that end is opened by a client, a new pipe will be created. One file descriptor for the new pipe is passed back to a client (named Stream) as the file descriptor from the **open**(2) system call and the other file descriptor is passed to the server. The server and the client may now communicate through a new pipe.

Figure 11-2: Server Sets Up a Pipe

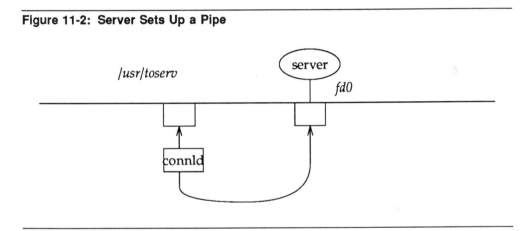

Figure 11-2 illustrates a server process that has created a pipe and pushed the **connld** module on the other end. The server then invokes the **fattach()** routine to name the other end */usr/toserv*.

Figure 11-3: Processes X and Y Open /usr/toserv

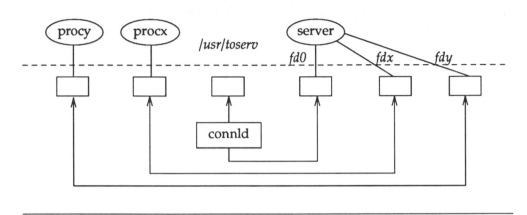

When process X (procx) opens /usr/toserv, it gains a unique connection to the server process that was at one end of the original STREAMS-based pipe. When process Y (procy) does the same, it also gains a unique connection to the server. As shown in Figure 11-3, the server process has access to three separate STREAMS-based pipes via three file descriptors.

connld is a STREAMS-based module that has an open, close, and **put** procedure. **connld** is opened when the module is pushed onto the pipe for the first time and whenever the named end of the pipe is opened. The **connld** module distinguishes between these two opens by use of the *q_ptr* field of its read queue. On the first open, this field is set to 1 and the routine returns without further processing. On subsequent opens, the field is checked for 1 or 0. If the 1 is present, the **connld** module creates a pipe and sends the file descriptor to a client and a server.

> **NOTE** Making use of the *q_ptr* field eliminates the need to configure the **connld** module at boot time. It also eliminates the need to manage the number of times the module is either pushed and/or popped.

When the named Stream is opened, the open routine of **connld** is called. The **connld** open will fail if:

- The pipe ends can not be created.
- A file pointer and file descriptor can not be allocated.
- The Stream head can not stream the two pipe ends.
- **strioctl()** fails while sending the file descriptor to the server.

The open is not complete until the server process has received the file descriptor using the **ioctl** I_RECVFD. The setting of the O_NDELAY or O_NONBLOCK flag has no impact on the open.

The **connld** module does not process messages. All messages are passed to the next object in the Stream. The read and write **put** routines call **putnext()** (see Appendix C) to send the message up or down the Stream.

12 STREAMS-Based Terminal Subsystem

STREAMS-based Terminal Subsystem 12-1
Line Discipline Module 12-3
- Default Settings 12-3
- Data Structure 12-4
- Open and Close Routines 12-5
- Read-Side Processing 12-5
- Write-Side Processing 12-7
- EUC Handling in ldterm 12-8
Support of termiox(7) 12-12
Hardware Emulation Module 12-13

STREAMS-based Pseudo-Terminal Subsystem 12-15
Line Discipline Module 12-15
Pseudo-tty Emulation Module - PTEM 12-17
- Data Structure 12-19
- Open and Close Routines 12-19
Remote Mode 12-20
Packet Mode 12-21
Pseudo-tty Drivers - ptm and pts 12-22
- grantpt 12-25
- unlockpt 12-26
- ptsname 12-26

STREAMS-based Terminal Subsystem

STREAMS provides a uniform interface for implementing character I/O devices and networking protocols in the kernel. UNIX System V Release 4.0 implements the terminal subsystem in STREAMS. The STREAMS-based terminal subsystem (see Figure 12-1) provides many benefits:

- Reusable line discipline modules. The same module can be used in many STREAMS where the configuration of these STREAMS may be different.

- Line discipline substitution. Although UNIX System V provides a standard terminal line discipline module, another one conforming to the interface may be substituted. For example, a remote login feature may use the terminal subsystem line discipline module to provide a terminal interface to the user.

- Internationalization. The modularity and flexibility of the STREAMS-based terminal subsystem enables an easy implementation of a system that supports multiple byte characters for internationalization. This modularity also allows easy addition of new features to the terminal subsystem.

- Easy customizing. Users may customize their terminal subsystem environment by adding and removing modules of their choice.

- The pseudo-terminal subsystem. The pseudo-terminal subsystem can be easily supported (this is discussed in more detail later in this chapter).

- Merge with networking. By pushing a line discipline module on a network line, one can make the network look like a terminal line.

Figure 12-1: STREAMS-based Terminal Subsystem

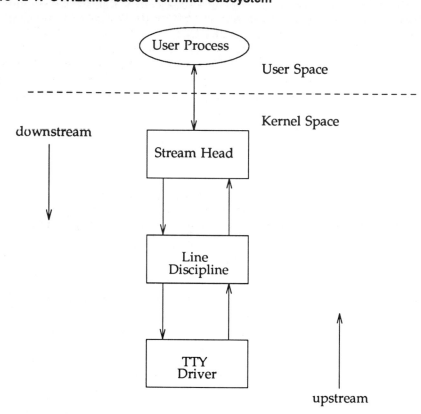

The initial setup of the STREAMS-based terminal subsystem is handled with the **ttymon**(1M) command within the framework of the Service Access Facility or the autopush feature. The autopush facility is discussed in Appendix E.

The STREAMS-based terminal subsystem supports **termio**(7), the **termios**(2) specification of the POSIX standard, multiple byte characters for internationalization, the interface to asynchronous hardware flow control [see **termiox**(7)], and peripheral controllers for asynchronous terminals. XENIX® and BSD compatibility can also be provided by pushing the **ttcompat** module. In order to use **shl** with the STREAMS-based terminal subsystem, the **sxt** driver is implemented as a STREAMS-based driver. However, the **sxt** feature is being phased out and users are encouraged to use the job control mechanism. Both **shl** and job control should not be run simultaneously.

Line Discipline Module

A STREAMS line discipline module called **ldterm** [see **ldterm**(7)] is a key part of the STREAMS-based terminal subsystem. Throughout this chapter, the terms *line discipline* and **ldterm** are used interchangeably and refer to the STREAMS version of the standard line discipline and not the traditional character version. **ldterm** performs the standard terminal I/O processing which was traditionally done through the *linesw* mechanism.

The **termio** and **termios** specifications describe four flags which are used to control the terminal: *c_iflag* (defines input modes), *c_oflag* (defines output modes), *c_cflag* (defines hardware control modes), and *c_lflag* (defines terminal functions used by **ldterm**). In order to process these flags elsewhere (for example, in the firmware or in another process), a mechanism is in place to turn on and off the processing of these flags. When **ldterm** is pushed, it sends an M_CTL message downstream which asks the driver which flags the driver will process. The driver sends back that message in response if it needs to change **ldterm**'s default processing. By default, **ldterm** assumes that it must process all flags except *c_cflag*, unless it receives a message telling otherwise.

Default Settings

When **ldterm** is pushed on the Stream, the open routine initializes the settings of the **termio** flags. The default settings are:

> *c_iflag* = BRKINT|ICRNL|IXON|ISTRIP|IXANY
> *c_oflag* = OPOST|ONLCR|TAB3
> *c_cflag* = 0
> *c_lflag* = ISIG|ICANON|ECHO|ECHOK

In canonical mode (ICANON flag in *c_lflag* is turned on), **read** from the terminal file descriptor is in message non-discard (RMSGN) mode [see **streamio**(7)]. This implies that in canonical mode, **read** on the terminal file descriptor always returns at most one line regardless how many characters have been requested. In non-canonical mode, **read** is in byte-stream (RNORM) mode.

Data Structure

The **ldterm** module uses the following structure to maintain state information:

```
struct ldterm_mod {
    mblk_t    *t_savbp;        /* saved mblk that holds ld structure */
    struct    termios t_modes;  /* effective modes set by the provider */
    struct    termios t_amodes; /* apparent modes for user programs */
    struct    termios t_dmodes; /* modes that driver wishes to process */
    unsigned  long    t_state;  /* internal state of tty module */
    int       t_line;          /* output line of tty */
    int       t_col;           /* output column of tty */
    int       t_rocount;       /* # of characters echoed since last output */
    int       t_rocol;         /* column in which first such character appeared */
    mblk_t    *t_message;      /* pointer to 1st mblk in message being built */
    mblk_t    *t_endmsg;       /* pointer to last mblk in that message */
    int       t_msglen;        /* number of characters in that message */
    mblk_t    *t_echomp;       /* echoed output being assembled */
    int       t_rd_request;    /* # of bytes requested by M_READ during
                                  vmin/vtime read */

/*
 * The following are for EUC processing.
 */

    unchar    t_codeset;  /* current code set indicator - read-side */
    unchar    t_eucleft;  /* bytes left to get in current character */
    unchar    t_eucign;   /* bytes left to ignore - output post proc */
    unchar    t_eucpad;   /* padding for eucwioc */
    eucioc_t  eucwioc;    /* eucioc structure (have to use bcopy) */
    unchar    *t_eucp;    /* pointer to parallel array of column widths */
    mblk_t    *t_eucp_mp; /* message block that holds parallel array */
    unchar    t_maxeuc;   /* maximum length in memory bytes of an EUC *?
    int       t_eucwarn;  /* bad EUC counter */
};
```

Programmer's Guide: STREAMS

Open and Close Routines

The open routine of the **ldterm** module allocates space for holding the **tty** structure (see **tty.h**) by allocating a buffer from the STREAMS buffer pool. The number of modules that can be pushed depends on the availability of buffers. The open also sends an M_SETOPTS message upstream to set the Stream head high and low water marks to 300 and 200 respectively.

The **ldterm** module establishes a controlling tty for the line when an M_SETOPTS message (*so_flags* is set to SO_ISTTY) is sent upstream. The Stream head allocates the controlling tty on the open, if one is not already allocated.

To maintain compatibility with existing applications that use the O_NDELAY flag, the open routine sets the SO_NDLEON flag on in the *so_flags* field of the **stroptions** structure in the M_SETOPTS message.

The open routine fails if there are no buffers available (cannot allocate the **tty** structure) or when an interrupt occurs while sleeping for a buffer to become available.

The close routine frees all the outstanding buffers allocated by this Stream. It also sends an M_SETOPTS message to the Stream head to undo the changes made by the open routine. The **ldterm** module also sends M_START and M_STARTI messages downstream to undo the effect of any previous M_STOP and M_STOPI messages.

Read-Side Processing

The **ldterm** module's read-side processing has **put** and **service** procedures. High and low water marks for the read queue are 128 and 64 respectively.

ldterm can send the following messages upstream:

M_DATA, M_BREAK, M_PCSIG, M_SIG, M_FLUSH, M_ERROR, M_IOCACK, M_IOCNAK, M_HANGUP, M_CTL, M_SETOPTS, M_COPYOUT, and M_COPYIN (see Appendix B).

The **ldterm** module's read-side processes M_BREAK, M_DATA, M_CTL, M_FLUSH, M_HANGUP, and M_IOCACK messages. All other messages are sent upstream unchanged.

The **put** procedure scans the message for flow control characters (IXON), signal generating characters, and after (possible) transformation of the message, queues the message for the **service** procedure. Echoing is handled completely by the **service** procedure.

In canonical mode if the ICANON flag is on in *c_lflag*, canonical processing is performed. If the ICANON flag is off, non-canonical processing is performed [see **termio**(7) for more details]. Handling of VMIN/VTIME in the STREAMS environment is somewhat complicated, because **read** needs to activate a timer in the **ldterm** module in some cases; hence, read notification becomes necessary. When a user issues an **ioctl** to put **ldterm** in non-canonical mode, the **ldterm** module sends an M_SETOPTS message to the Stream head to register read notification. Further reads on the terminal file descriptor will cause the Stream head to issue an M_READ message downstream and data will be sent upstream in response to the M_READ message. With read notification, buffering of raw data is performed by **ldterm**. It is possible to canonize the raw data, when the user has switched from raw to canonical mode. However, the reverse is not possible.

To summarize, in non-canonical mode, the **ldterm** module buffers all data until a request for the data arrives in the form of an M_READ message. The number of bytes sent upstream will be the argument of the M_READ message.

The **service** procedure of **ldterm** handles STREAMS related flow control. Since the read-side high and low water marks are 128 and 64 respectively, placing more than 128 characters on the **ldterm**'s read queue will cause the QFULL flag be turned on indicating that the module below should not send more data upstream.

Input flow control is regulated by the line discipline module by generating M_STARTI and M_STOPI high priority messages. When sent downstream, receiving drivers or modules take appropriate action to regulate the sending of data upstream. Output flow control is activated when **ldterm** receives flow control characters in its data stream. The **ldterm** module then sets an internal flag indicating that output processing is to be restarted/stopped and sends an M_START/M_STOP message downstream.

Write-Side Processing

Write-side processing of the **ldterm** module is performed by the write-side **put** and **service** procedures.

The **ldterm** module supports the following **ioctls**:

TCSETA, TCSETAW, TCSETAF, TCSETS, TCSETSW, TCSETSF, TCGETA, TCGETS, TCXONC, TCFLSH, TCSBRK, TIOCSWINSZ, TIOCGWINSZ, and JWINSIZE.

All **ioctls** not recognized by the **ldterm** module are passed downstream to the neighboring module or driver. BSD functionality is turned off by IEXTEN [see **termio**(7) for more details].

The following messages can be received on the write-side:

M_DATA, M_DELAY, M_BREAK, M_FLUSH, M_STOP, M_START, M_STOPI, M_STARTI, M_READ, M_IOCDATA, M_CTL, and M_IOCTL.

On the write-side, the **ldterm** module processes M_FLUSH, M_DATA, M_IOCTL, and M_READ messages, and all other message are passed downstream unchanged.

An M_CTL message is generated by **ldterm** as a query to the driver for an intelligent peripheral and to decide on the functional split for **termio** processing. If all or part of **termio** processing is done by the intelligent peripheral, **ldterm** can turn off this processing to avoid computational overhead. This is done by sending an appropriate response to the M_CTL message, as follows: [see also **ldterm**(7)].

- If all of the **termio** processing is done by the peripheral hardware, the driver sends an M_CTL message back to **ldterm** with *ioc_cmd* of the structure iocblk set to MC_NO_CANON. If **ldterm** is to handle all **termio** processing, the driver sends an M_CTL message with *ioc_cmd* set to MC_DO_CANON. Default is MC_DO_CANON.

- If the peripheral hardware handles only part of the **termio** processing, it informs **ldterm** in the following way:

The driver for the peripheral device allocates an M_DATA message large enough to hold a **termios** structure. The driver then turns on those *c_iflag, c_oflag,* and *c_lflag* fields of the **termios** structure that are processed on the peripheral device by ORing the flag values. The M_DATA message is then attached to the *b_cont* field of the M_CTL message it received. The message is sent back to **ldterm** with *ioc_cmd* in the data buffer of the M_CTL message set to MC_PART_CANON.

The line discipline module does not check if write-side flow control is in effect before forwarding data downstream. It expects the downstream module or driver to queue the messages on its queue until flow control is lifted.

EUC Handling in ldterm

The idea of letting post-processing (the *o_flags*) happen off the host processor is not recommended unless the board software is prepared to deal with international (EUC) character sets properly. The reason for this is that post-processing must take the EUC information into account. **ldterm** knows about the screen width of characters (that is, how many columns are taken by characters from each given code set on the current physical display) and it takes this width into account when calculating tab expansions. When using multi-byte characters or multi-column characters **ldterm** automatically handles tab expansion (when TAB3 is set) and does not leave this handling to a lower module or driver.

As an example, consider the 3B2 PORTS board that has a processor and runs firmware on the board that can handle output post-processing. However, the firmware on the PORTS board has no knowledge of EUC unless one can change the firmware. Therefore, with some EUC code sets, particularly those where number of bytes in a character is not equivalent to the width of the character on the screen (for example, 3 byte codes that take only 2 screen columns), the PORTS board's firmware miscalculates the number of spaces required to expand the tab. Hence, if the board is allowed to handle tab expansion, it may get the expansion wrong in some cases.

By default multi-byte handling by **ldterm** is turned off. When **ldterm** receives an EUC_WSET **ioctl** call, it turns multi-byte processing on, if it is essential to properly handle the indicated code set. Thus, if one is using single byte 8-bit codes and has no special multi-column requirements, the special multi-column processing is not used at all. This means that multi-byte processing does not reduce the processing speed or efficiency of **ldterm** unless it is actually used.

The following describes how the EUC handling in **ldterm** works:

First, the multi-byte and multi-column character handling is only enabled when the EUC_WSET **ioctl** indicates that one of the following conditions is met:

- Code set consists of more than one byte (including the SS2 and/or SS3) of characters, or

- Code set requires more than one column to display on the current device, as indicated in the EUC_WSET structure.

Assuming that one or more of the above conditions, EUC handling is enabled. At this point, a parallel array (see **ldterm_mod** structure) used for other information, is allocated and a pointer to it is stored in *t_eucp_mp*. The parallel array which it holds is pointed to by *t_eucp*. The *t_codeset* field holds the flag that indicates which of the code sets is currently being processed on the read-side. When a byte with the high bit arrives, it is checked to see if it is SS2 or SS3. If so, it belongs to code set 2 or 3. Otherwise, it is a byte that comes from code set 1. Once the extended code set flag has been set, the input processor retrieves the subsequent bytes, as they arrive, to build one multi-byte character. The counter field *t_eucleft* tells the input processor how many bytes remain to be read for the current character. The parallel array *t_eucp* holds for each logical character in the canonical buffer its display width. During erase processing, positions in the parallel array are consulted to figure out how many backspaces need to be sent to erase each logical character. (In canonical mode, one backspace of input erases one logical character, no matter how many bytes or columns that character consumes.) This greatly simplifies erase processing for EUC.

The *t_maxeuc* field holds the maximum length, in memory bytes, of the EUC character mapping currently in use. The *eucwioc* field is a sub-structure that holds information about each extended code set.

The *t_eucign* field aids in output post-processing (tab expansion). When characters are output, **ldterm** keeps a column to indicate what the current cursor column is supposed to be. When it sends the first byte of an extended character, it adds the number of columns required for that character to the output column. It then subtracts one from the total width in memory bytes of that character and stores the result in *t_eucign*. This field tells **ldterm** how many subsequent bytes to ignore for the purposes of column calculation. (**ldterm** calculates the appropriate number of columns when it sees the first byte of the character.)

The field *t_eucwarn* is a counter for occurrences of bad extended characters. It is mostly useful for debugging. After receiving a certain number of illegal EUC characters (perhaps because of some problem on the line or with declared values), a warning is given on the system console.

There are two relevant files for handling multi-byte characters: **euc.h** and **eucioctl.h**. The **eucioctl.h** contains the structure that is passed with EUC_WSET and EUC_WGET calls. The normal way to use this structure is to get CSWIDTH (see note below) from the *locale* via a mechanism such as **getwidth** or **setlocale** and then copy the values into the structure in **eucioctl.h**, and send the structure via an I_STR **ioctl** call. The EUC_WSET call informs the **ldterm** module about the number of bytes in extended characters and how many columns the extended characters from each set consume on the screen. This allows **ldterm** to treat multi-byte characters as single entities for the purpose of erase processing and to correctly calculate tab expansions for multi-byte characters.

NOTE	LC_CTYPE (instead of CSWIDTH) should be used in the environment in UNIX System V Release 4.0 systems. See **chrtbl**(1M) for more information.

The file **euc.h** has the structure with fields for EUC width, screen width, and wide character width. The following functions are used to set and get EUC widths (these functions assume the environment where the **eucwidth_t** structure is needed and available):

```
#include <eucioctl.h>        /* need some other things too, like stropts.h */

struct eucioc eucw;          /* for EUC_WSET/EUC_WGET to line discipline */
eucwidth_t width;            /* return struct from _getwidth() */

/*
 * set_euc       Send EUC code widths to line discipline.
 */

set_euc(e)
        struct eucioc *e;
        {
        struct strioctl sb;

        sb.ic_cmd = EUC_WSET;
        sb.ic_timout = 15;
        sb.ic_len = sizeof(struct eucioc);
        sb.ic_dp = (char *) e;

        if (ioctl(0, I_STR, &sb) < 0)
                fail();
        }
/*
 * euclook       Get current EUC code widths from line discipline.
 */

euclook(e)
        struct eucioc *e;
        {
        struct strioctl sb;

        sb.ic_cmd = EUC_WGET;
        sb.ic_timout = 15;
        sb.ic_len = sizeof(struct eucioc);
        sb.ic_dp = (char *) e;
        if (ioctl(0, I_STR, &sb) < 0)
                fail();
        printf("CSWIDTH=%d:%d,%d:%d,%d:%d0,
                                        e->eucw[1], e->scrw[1],
                                        e->eucw[2], e->scrw[2],
                                        e->eucw[3], e->scrw[3]);
        }
```

The brief discussion of multiple byte character handling by the **ldterm** module was provided here for the those interested in internationalization applications in UNIX System V. More detailed descriptions may be obtained from product related documents, for example *UNIX® System V Multi-National Language Supplement Release 3.2 Product Overview*. This book (select code is 320-093) is available from AT&T Customer Information Center. To order this or other UNIX System V books, call one of the following numbers: 1-800-432-6600 in the continental U.S., 1-800-256-1242 outside the continental U.S., or 317-256-1242 outside the U.S.

Support of termiox(7)

UNIX System V Release 4.0 includes the extended general terminal interface [see **termiox**(7)] that supplements the **termio**(7) general terminal interface by adding for asynchronous hardware flow control, isochronous flow control and clock modes, and local implementations of additional asynchronous features. **termiox**(7) is handled by hardware drivers if the board (e.g., EPORTS) supports it.

Hardware flow control supplements the **termio**(7) IXON, IXOFF, and IXANY character flow control. The **termiox**(7) interface allows for both unidirectional and bidirectional hardware flow control. Isochronous communication is a variation of asynchronous communication where two communicating devices provide transmit and/or receive clock to each other. Incoming clock signals can be taken from the baud rate generator on the local isochronous port controller. Outgoing signals are sent on the receive and transmit baud rate generator on the local isochronous port controller.

Terminal parameters are specified in the **termiox** structure that is defined in the **termiox.h**.

Hardware Emulation Module

If a Stream supports a terminal interface, a driver or module that understands all **ioctls** to support terminal semantics (specified by **termio** and **termios**) is needed. If there is no hardware driver that understands all **ioctl** commands downstream from the **ldterm** module, a hardware emulation module must be placed downstream from the line discipline module. The function of the hardware emulation module is to understand and acknowledge the **ioctls** that may be sent to the process at the Stream head and to mediate the passage of control information downstream. The combination of the line discipline module and the hardware emulation module behaves as if there were an actual terminal on that Stream.

The hardware emulation module is necessary whenever there is no tty driver at the end of the Stream. For example, it is necessary in a pseudo-tty situation where there is process to process communication on one system (this is discussed later in this chapter) and in a network situation where a **termio** interface is expected (e.g., remote login) but there is no tty driver on the Stream.

Most of the actions taken by the hardware emulation module are the same regardless of the underlying architecture. However, there are some actions that are different depending on whether the communication is local or remote and whether the underlying transport protocol is used to support the remote connection. For example, NTTY is a hardware emulation module supported by AT&T in its Starlan® networking environment. This hardware emulation module behaves in a way understood by the URP protocol driver that exists below NTTY. On receipt of a TCSBRK **ioctl**, NTTY sends an M_BREAK message downstream. When the baud rate is 0, the hardware emulation module sends a TPI message requesting a disconnect. These actions are valid for a network situation but may not make sense in other environments when there is no module/driver below to understand the TPI messages or handle M_BREAK messages.

Each hardware emulation module has an open, close, read queue **put** procedure, and write queue **put** procedure.

The hardware emulation module does the following:

- Processes, if appropriate, and acknowledges receipt of the following **ioctls** on its write queue by sending an M_IOCACK message back upstream: TCSETA, TCSETAW, TCSETAF, TCSETS, TCSETSW, TCSETSF, TCGETA, TCGETS, and TCSBRK.

- Acknowledges the Extended UNIX Code (EUC) **ioctls**.

- If the environment supports windowing, it acknowledges the windowing **ioctls** TIOCSWINSZ, TIOCGWINSZ, and JWINSIZE. If the environment does not support windowing, an M_IOCNAK message is sent upstream.

- If any other **ioctls** are received on its write queue, it sends an M_IOCNAK message upstream.

- When the hardware emulation module receives an M_IOCTL message of type TCSBRK on its write queue, it sends an M_IOCACK message upstream and the appropriate message downstream. For example, an M_BREAK message could be sent downstream.

- When the hardware emulation module receives an M_IOCTL message on its write queue to set the baud rate to 0 (TCSETAW with CBAUD set to B0), it sends an M_IOCACK message upstream and an appropriate message downstream; for networking situations this will probably be an M_PROTO message which is a TPI T_DISCON_REQ message requesting the transport provider to disconnect.

- All other messages (M_DATA, etc.) not mentioned here are passed to the next module or driver in the Stream.

The hardware emulation module processes messages in a way consistent with the driver that exists below.

STREAMS-based Pseudo-Terminal Subsystem

The STREAMS-based pseudo-terminal subsystem provides the user with an interface that is identical to the STREAMS-based terminal subsystem described earlier in this chapter. The pseudo-terminal subsystem (pseudo-tty) supports a pair of STREAMS-based devices called the *master* device and *slave* device. The *slave* device provides processes with an interface that is identical to the terminal interface. However, where all devices, which provide the terminal interface, have some kind of hardware device behind them, the *slave* device has another process manipulating it through the master half of the pseudo terminal. Anything written on the *master* device is given to the *slave* as an input and anything written on the *slave* device is presented as an input on the master side.

Figure 12-2 illustrates the architecture of the STREAMS-based pseudo-terminal subsystem. The *master* driver called **ptm** is accessed through the clone driver [see **clone**(7)] and is the controlling part of the system. The *slave* driver called **pts** works with the line discipline module and the hardware emulation module to provide a terminal interface to the user process. An optional packetizing module called **pckt** is also provided. It can be pushed on the master side to support **packet mode** (this is discussed later).

The number of pseudo-tty devices that can be installed on a system is dependent on available memory.

Line Discipline Module

In the pseudo-tty subsystem, the line discipline module is pushed on the slave side to present the user with the terminal interface.

ldterm may turn off the processing of the c_iflag, c_oflag, and c_lflag fields to allow processing to take place elsewhere. The **ldterm** module may also turn off all canonical processing when it receives an M_CTL message with the MC_NO_CANON command in order to support **remote mode** (this is discussed later). Although **ldterm** passes through messages without processing them, the appropriate flags are set when a "get" **ioctl**, such as TCGETA or TCGETS, is issued to indicate that canonical processing is being performed.

Figure 12-2: Pseudo-tty Subsystem Architecture

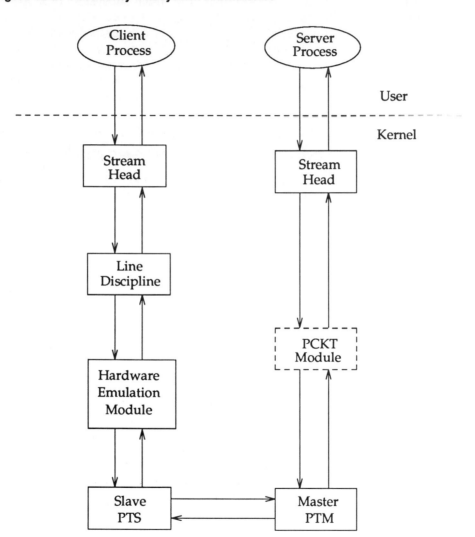

Pseudo-tty Emulation Module - PTEM

Since the pseudo-tty subsystem has no hardware driver downstream from the **ldterm** module to process the terminal **ioctl** calls, another module that understands the **ioctl** commands is placed downstream from the **ldterm**. This module, known as **ptem**, processes all of the terminal **ioctl** commands and mediates the passage of control information downstream.

ldterm and **ptem** together behave like a real terminal. Since there is no real terminal or modem in the pseudo-tty subsystem, some of the **ioctl** commands are ignored and cause only an acknowledgement of the command. The **ptem** module keeps track of the terminal parameters set by the various "set" commands such as TCSETA or TCSETAW but does not usually perform any action. For example, if one of the "set" **ioctls** is called, none of the bits in the c_cflag field of **termio** has any effect on the pseudo-terminal except if the baud rate is set to 0. When setting the baud rate to 0, it has the effect of hanging up the pseudo-terminal.

The pseudo-terminal has no concept of parity so none of the flags in the c_iflag that control the processing of parity errors have any effect. The delays specified in the c_oflag field are not also supported.

The **ptem** module does the following:

- Processes, if appropriate, and acknowledges receipt of the following ioctls on its write queue by sending an M_IOCACK message back upstream:

  TCSETA, TCSETAW, TCSETAF, TCSETS, TCSETSW, TCSETSF, TCGETA, TCGETS, and TCSBRK.

- Keeps track of the window size; information needed for the TIOCSWINSZ, TIOCGWINSZ, and JWINSIZE **ioctl** commands.

- When it receives any other **ioctl** on its write queue, it sends an M_IOCNAK message upstream.

- It passes downstream the following ioctls after processing them:

  TCSETA, TCSETAW, TCSETAF, TCSETS, TCSETSW, TCSETSF, TCSBRK, and TIOCSWINSZ.

- ptem frees any M_IOCNAK messages it receives on its read queue in case the **pckt** module (**pckt** is described later) is not on the pseudo terminal subsystem and the above **ioctls** get to the *master*'s Stream head which would then send an M_IOCNAK message.

- In its open routine, the **ptem** module sends an M_SETOPTS message upstream requesting allocation of a controlling tty.

- When the **ptem** module receives an M_IOCTL message of type TCSBRK on its read queue, it sends an M_IOCACK message downstream and an M_BREAK message upstream.

- When it receives an **ioctl** message on its write queue to set the baud rate to 0 (TCSETAW with CBAUD set to B0), it sends an M_IOCACK message upstream and a 0-length message downstream.

- When it receives an M_IOCTL of type TIOCSIGNAL on its read queue, it sends an M_IOCACK downstream and an M_PCSIG upstream where the signal number is the same as in the M_IOCTL message.

- When the **ptem** module receives an M_IOCTL of type TIOCREMOTE on its read queue, it sends an M_IOCACK message downstream and the appropriate M_CTL message upstream to enable/disable canonical processing.

- When it receives an M_DELAY message on its read or write queue, it discards the message and does not act on it.

- When it receives an M_IOCTL message with type JWINSIZE on its write queue and if the values in the **jwinsize** structure of **ptem** are not zero, it sends an M_IOCACK message upstream with the **jwinsize** structure. If the values are zero, it sends an M_IOCNAK message upstream.

- When it receives an M_IOCTL message of type TIOCGWINSZ on its write queue and if the values in the **winsize** structure are not zero, it sends an M_IOCACK message upstream with the **winsize** structure. If the values are zero, it sends an M_IOCNAK message upstream. It also saves the information passed to it in the **winsize** structure and sends a STREAMS signal message for signal SIGWINCH upstream to the slave process if the size changed.

- When the **ptem** module receives an M_IOCTL message with type TIOCGWINSZ on its read queue and if the values in the **winsize** structure are not zero, it sends an M_IOCACK message downstream with the **winsize** structure. If the values are zero, it sends an M_IOCNAK message downstream. It also saves the information passed to it in the **winsize** structure and sends a STREAMS signal message for signal SIGWINCH upstream to the slave process if the size changed.

- All other messages not mentioned above are passed to the next module or driver.

Data Structure

Each instantiation of the **ptem** module is associated with a local area. These data are held in a structure called **ptem** that has the following format:

```
struct ptem
{
    long cflags;            /* copy of c_flags */
    mblk_t *dack_ptr;       /* pointer to preallocated message block used to
                               send disconnect */
    queue_t *q_ptr;         /* pointer to ptem's read queue */
    struct winsize wsz;     /* structure to hold windowing information */
    unsigned short state;   /* state of ptem entry */
};
```

When the **ptem** module is pushed onto the slave side Stream, a search of the **ptem** structure is made for a free entry (*state* is not set to INUSE). The *c_cflags* of the **termio** structure and the windowing variables are stored in *cflags* and *wsz* respectively. The *dack_ptr* is a pointer to a message block used to send a 0-length message whenever a hang-up occurs on the slave side.

Open and Close Routines

In the open routine of **ptem** a STREAMS message block is allocated for a 0-length message for delivering a hang-up message; this allocation of a buffer is done before it is needed to ensure that a buffer is available. An M_SETOPTS message is sent upstream to set the read-side Stream head queues, to assign high and low water marks (512 and 256 respectively), and to establish a controlling terminal.

The default values B300, CS8, CREAD, and HUPCL are assigned to *cflags*, and INUSE to the *state* field.

The open routine fails if:

- No free entries are found when the **ptem** structure is searched.

- *sflag* is not set to MODOPEN.

- A 0-length message can not be allocated (no buffer is available).

- A **stroptions** structure can not be allocated.

The close routine is called on the last close of the slave side Stream. Pointers to read and write queue are cleared and the buffer for the 0-length message is freed.

Remote Mode

A feature known as **remote mode** is available with the pseudo-tty subsystem. This feature is used for applications that perform the canonical function normally done by the **ldterm** module and tty driver. The **remote mode** allows applications on the master side to turn off the canonical processing. An **ioctl** TIOCREMOTE with a nonzero parameter [ioctl(fd, TIOCREMOTE, 1)] is issued on the master side to enter the **remote mode**. When this occurs, an M_CTL message with the command MC_NO_CANON is sent to the **ldterm** module indicating that data should be passed when received on the read-side and no canonical processing is to take place. The **remote mode** may be disabled by ioctl(fd, TIOCREMOTE, 0).

Packet Mode

The STREAMS-based pseudo-terminal subsystem also supports a feature called **packet mode**. This is used to inform the process on the master side when *state* changes have occurred in the pseudo-tty. **Packet mode** is enabled by pushing the **pckt** module on the master side. Data written on the master side is processed normally. When data are written on the slave side or when other messages are encountered by the **pckt** module, a header is added to the message so it can be subsequently retrieved by the master side with a **getmsg** operation.

The **pckt** module does the following:

- When a message is passed to this module on its write queue, the module does no processing and passes the message to the next module or driver.

- The **pckt** module creates an M_PROTO message when one of the following messages is passed to it:

  M_DATA, M_IOCTL, M_PROTO/M_PCPROTO, M_FLUSH, M_START/M_STOP, M_STARTI/M_STOPI, and M_READ.

  All other messages are passed through. The M_PROTO message is passed upstream and retrieved when the user issues **getmsg**(2).

- If the message is an M_FLUSH message, **pckt** does the following:

  If the flag is FLUSHW, it is changed to FLUSHR (because FLUSHR was the original flag before the **pts** driver changed it), packetized into an M_PROTO message, and passed upstream. To prevent the Stream head's read queue from being flushed, the original M_FLUSH message must not be passed upstream.

  If the flag is FLUSHR, it is changed to FLUSHW, packetized into an M_PROTO message, and passed upstream. In order to flush of the write queues properly, an M_FLUSH message with the FLUSHW flag set is also sent upstream.

  If the flag is FLUSHRW, the message with both flags set is packetized and passed upstream. An M_FLUSH message with the FLUSHW flag set is also sent upstream.

Pseudo-tty Drivers - ptm and pts

In order to use the pseudo-tty subsystem, a node for the master side driver **/dev/ptmx** and N number of slave drivers (N is determined at installation time) must be installed. The names of the slave devices are **/dev/pts/**M where M has the values 0 through N-1. A user accesses a pseudo-tty device through the *master* device (called **ptm**) that in turn is accessed through the clone driver [see **clone**(7)]. The *master* device is set up as a clone device where its major device number is the major for the clone device and its minor device number is the major for the **ptm** driver.

The *master* pseudo driver is opened via the **open**(2) system call with **/dev/ptmx** as the device to be opened. The clone open finds the next available minor device for that major device; a *master* device is available only if it and its corresponding *slave* device are not already open. There are no nodes in the file system for *master* devices.

When the *master* device is opened, the corresponding *slave* device is automatically locked out. No user may open that *slave* device until it is unlocked. A user may invoke a function **grantpt** that will change the owner of the *slave* device to that of the user who is running this process, change the group id to *tty*, and change the mode of the device to *0620*. Once the permissions have been changed, the device may be unlocked by the user. Only the owner or super-user can access the *slave* device. The user must then invoke the **unlockpt** function to unlock the *slave* device. Before opening the *slave* device, the user must call the **ptsname** function to obtain the name of the *slave* device. The functions **grantpt**, **unlockpt**, and **ptsname** are called with the file descriptor of the *master* device. The user may then invoke the **open** system call with the name that was returned by the **ptsname** function to open the *slave* device.

The following example shows how a user may invoke the pseudo-tty subsystem:

```
int fdm fds;
char *slavename;
extern char *ptsname();

fdm = open("/dev/ptmx", O_RDWR);    /* open master */
grantpt(fdm);                        /* change permission of slave */
unlockpt(fdm);                       /* unlock slave */
slavename = ptsname(fdm);            /* get name of slave */
fds = open(slavename, O_RDWR);       /* open slave */
ioctl(fds, I_PUSH, "ptem");          /* push ptem */
ioctl(fds, I_PUSH, "ldterm");        /* push ldterm */
```

Unrelated processes may open the pseudo device. The initial user may pass the master file descriptor using a STREAMS-based pipe or a slave name to another process to enable it to open the *slave*. After the *slave* device is open, the owner is free to change the permissions.

> **NOTE** Certain programs such as **write** and **wall** are set group-id (**setgid**) to *tty* and are also able to access the slave device.

After both the *master* and *slave* have been opened, the user has two file descriptors which provide full-duplex communication using two Streams. The two Streams are automatically connected. The user may then push modules onto either side of the Stream. The user also needs to push the **ptem** and **ldterm** modules onto the slave side of the pseudo-terminal subsystem to get terminal semantics.

The *master* and *slave* drivers pass all STREAMS messages to their adjacent queues. Only the M_FLUSH needs some processing. Because the read queue of one side is connected to the write queue of the other, the FLUSHR flag is changed to FLUSHW flag and vice versa.

When the *master* device is closed, an M_HANGUP message is sent to the *slave* device which will render the device unusable. The process on the slave side gets the *errno* ENXIO when attempting to write on that Stream but it will be able to read any data remaining on the Stream head read queue. When all the data have been read, **read** returns 0 indicating that the Stream can no longer be used.

On the last close of the *slave* device, a 0-length message is sent to the *master* device. When the application on the master side issues a **read** or **getmsg** and 0 is returned, the user of the *master* device decides whether to issue a close that dismantles the pseudo-terminal subsystem. If the *master* device is not closed, the pseudo-tty subsystem will be available to another user to open the *slave* device.

Since 0-length messages are used to indicate that the process on the slave side has closed and should be interpreted that way by the process on the master side, applications on the slave side should not **write** 0-length messages. If that occurs, the **write** returns 0, and the 0-length message is discarded by the **ptem** module.

The standard STREAMS system calls can access the pseudo-tty devices. The *slave* devices support the O_NDELAY and O_NONBLOCK flags. Since the master side does not act like the terminal, if O_NONBLOCK or O_NDELAY is set, **read** on the master side returns -1 with *errno* set to EAGAIN if no data are available, and **write** returns -1 with *errno* set to EAGAIN if there is internal flow control.

The *master* driver supports the ISPTM and UNLKPT **ioctls** that are used by the functions **grantpt, unlockpt,** and **ptsname** [see **grantpt**(3C), **unlockpt**(3C), **ptsname**(3C)]. The **ioctl** ISPTM determines whether the file descriptor is that of an open *master* device. On success, it returns the major/minor number (type **dev_t**) of the *master* device which can be used to determine the name of the corresponding *slave* device. The **ioctl** UNLKPT unlocks the *master* and *slave* devices. It returns 0 on success. On failure, the *errno* is set to EINVAL indicating that the *master* device is not open.

The format of these commands is:

```
int ioctl (fd, command, arg)
int fd, command, arg;
```

where *command* is either ISPTM or UNLKPT and *arg* is 0. On failure, -1 is returned.

When data are written to the master side, the entire block of data written is treated as a single line. The slave side process reading the terminal receives the entire block of data. Data are not input edited by the **ldterm** module regardless of the terminal mode. The master side application is responsible for detecting an interrupt character and sending an interrupt signal SIGINT to the process in the slave side. This can be done as follows:

```
ioctl (fd, TIOCSIGNAL, SIGINT)
```

where SIGINT is defined in the file <signal.h>. When a process on the master side issues this **ioctl**, the argument is the number of the signal that should be sent. The specified signal is then sent to the process group on the slave side.

To summarize, the *master* driver and *slave* driver have the following characteristics:

- Each *master* driver has one-to-one relationship with a *slave* device based on major/minor device numbers.

- Only one open is allowed on a *master* device. Multiple opens are allowed on the *slave* device according to standard file mode and ownership permissions.

- Each *slave* driver minor device has a node in the file system.

- An open on a *master* device automatically locks out an open on the corresponding *slave* driver.

- A *slave* cannot be opened unless the corresponding *master* is open and has unlocked the *slave*.

- To provide a tty interface to the user, the **ldterm** and **ptem** modules are pushed on the slave side.

- A close on the *master* sends a hang-up to the *slave* and renders both Streams unusable after all data have been consumed by the process on the slave side.

- The last close on the slave side sends a 0-length message to the *master* but does not sever the connection between the *master* and *slave* drivers.

grantpt

The **grantpt** function changes the mode and the ownership of the *slave* device that is associated with the given *master* device. Given a file descriptor *fd*, **grantpt** first checks that the file descriptor is that of the *master* device. If so, it obtains the name of the associated *slave* device and sets the user id to that of the user running the process and the group id to *tty*. The mode of the *slave* device is set to *0620*.

If the process is already running as root, the permission of the *slave* can be changed directly without invoking this function. The interface is:

```
grantpt (int fd);
```

The **grantpt** function returns 0 on success and -1 on failure. It fails if one or more of the following occurs: *fd* is not an open file descriptor, *fd* is not associated with a *master* device, the corresponding *slave* could not be accessed, or a system call failed because no more processes could be created.

unlockpt

The **unlockpt** function clears a lock flag associated with a *master/slave* device pair. Its interface is:

```
unlockpt (int fd);
```

The **unlockpt** returns 0 on success and -1 on failure. It fails if one or more of the following occurs: *fd* is not an open file descriptor or *fd* is not associated with a *master* device.

ptsname

The **ptsname** function returns the name of the *slave* device that is associated with the given *master* device. It first checks that the file descriptor is that of the *master*. If it is, it then determines the name of the corresponding *slave* device /dev/pts/M and returns a pointer to a string containing the null-terminated path name. The return value points to static data whose content is overwritten by each call. The interface is:

```
char *ptsname (int fd);
```

The **ptsname** function returns a non-NULL path name upon success and a NULL pointer upon failure. It fails if one or more of the following occurs: *fd* is not an open file descriptor or *fd* is not associated with the *master* device.

A Appendix A: STREAMS Data Structures

STREAMS Data Structures   A-1

streamtab   A-1

QUEUE Structures   A-1
- queue   A-2
- qinit   A-3
- module_info   A-4
- module_stat   A-4
- equeue   A-5
- qband   A-6

Message Structures   A-6

iocblk   A-9

copyreq   A-10

copyresp   A-11

strioctl   A-12

linkblk   A-12

stroptions   A-12

STREAMS Data Structures

This appendix summarizes data structures commonly encountered in STREAMS
module and driver development. Most of the data structures given in this
appendix are contained in <sys/stream.h>.

streamtab

This structure defines a module or a driver.

```
struct streamtab {
    struct qinit *st_rdinit;    /* defines read queue */
    struct qinit *st_wrinit;    /* defines write queue */
    struct qinit *st_muxrinit;  /* for multiplexing drivers only */
    struct qinit *st_muxwinit;  /* for multiplexing drivers only */
};
```

QUEUE Structures

Two sets of queue structures form a module. The structures are **queue, qband,
qinit, module_info,** and **module_stat** (optional).

queue

queue structure has the following format:

```
#ifdef   _STYPES

struct queue {
    struct qinit     *q_qinfo;   /* procedures and limits for queue */
    struct msgb      *q_first;   /* head of message queue for this queue */
    struct msgb      *q_last;    /* tail of message queue for this queue */
    struct queue     *q_next;    /* next queue in Stream*/
    struct equeue    *q_eq;      /* pointer to an extended queue structure */
    _VOID            *q_ptr;     /* to private data structure */
    ushort           q_count;    /* number of bytes in queue */
    ushort           q_flag;     /* queue state */
    short            q_minpsz;   /* min packet size accepted by this module */
    short            q_maxpsz;   /* max packet size accepted by this module */
    ushort           q_hiwat;    /* queue high water mark for flow control */
    ushort           q_lowat;    /* queue low water mark for flow control */
};

#else  /* large definition */

struct queue {
    struct qinit     *q_qinfo;   /* procedures and limits for queue */
    struct msgb      *q_first;   /* head of message queue for this queue */
    struct msgb      *q_last;    /* tail of message queue for this queue */
    struct queue     *q_next;    /* next queue in Stream*/
    struct queue     *q_link;    /* to next queue for scheduling */
    _VOID            *q_ptr;     /* to private data structure */
    ulong            q_count;    /* number of bytes in queue */
    ulong            q_flag;     /* queue state */
    long             q_minpsz;   /* min packet size accepted by this module */
    long             q_maxpsz;   /* max packet size accepted by this module */
    ulong            q_hiwat;    /* queue high water mark for flow control */
    ulong            q_lowat;    /* queue low water mark for flow control */
    struct qband     *q_bandp;   /* separate flow information */
    unsigned char    q_nband;    /* number of priority bands */
    unsigned char    q_pad1[3];  /* reserved for future use */
    long             q_pad2[2];  /* reserved for future use */
};

#endif  /* _STYPES */

typedef struct queue queue_t;
```

When a **queue** pair is allocated, their contents are zero unless specifically initialized. The following fields are initialized:

- q_qinfo: st_rdinit and st_wrinit (or st_muxrinit and st_muxwinit) - from **streamtab**

- q_minpsz, q_maxpsz, q_hiwat, q_lowat - from **module_info**

- q_ptr - optionally, by the driver/module open routine

qinit

qinit format is as follows:

```
struct qinit {
    int                    (*qi_putp) ();     /* put procedure */
    int                    (*qi_srvp) ();     /* service procedure */
    int                    (*qi_qopen) ();    /* called on each open or a push */
    int                    (*qi_qclose) ();   /* called on last close or a pop */
    int                    (*qi_qadmin) ();   /* reserved for future use */
    struct module_info     *qi_minfo;         /* information structure */
    struct module_stat     *qi_mstat;         /* statistics structure - optional */
};
```

module_info

module_info has the following format:

```
#ifdef _STYPES

struct module_info {
    ushort   mi_idnum;    /* module ID number */
    char     *mi_idname;  /* module name */
    short    mi_minpsz;   /* min packet size accepted */
    short    mi_maxpsz;   /* max packet size accepted */
    ushort   mi_hiwat;    /* high water mark, for flow control */
    ushort   mi_lowat;    /* low water mark, for flow control */
};

#else /* large definition */

struct module_info {
    ushort   mi_idnum;    /* module ID number */
    char     *mi_idname;  /* module name */
    long     mi_minpsz;   /* min packet size accepted */
    long     mi_maxpsz;   /* max packet size accepted */
    ulong    mi_hiwat;    /* high water mark, for flow control */
    ulong    mi_lowat;    /* low water mark, for flow control */
};

#endif /* _STYPES */
```

module_stat

The format of **module_stat** is:

```
struct module_stat {
    long     ms_pcnt;     /* count of calls to put proc */
    long     ms_scnt;     /* count of calls to service proc */
    long     ms_ocnt;     /* count of calls to open proc */
    long     ms_ccnt;     /* count of calls to close proc */
    long     ms_acnt;     /* count of calls to admin proc */
    char     *ms_xptr;    /* pointer to private statistics */
    short    ms_xsize;    /* length of private statistics buffer */
};
```

Note that in the event these counts are calculated by modules or drivers, the counts will be cumulative over all instantiations of modules with the same **fmodsw** entry and drivers with the same **cdevsw** entry. (cdevsw and fmodsw tables are described in Appendix E.)

equeue

The format of the extended queue structure is:

```
/* the extended queue structure contains a link to next queue on STREAMS
 * scheduling queue, a pointer to an array of structures containing the
 * flow control parameters for each priority, and number of priority bands
 *
 * NOTE: The extended queue structure is only present for non-EFT systems
 *
 * /

#ifdef  _STYPES

struct equeue {
    struct queue    *eq_link;    /* to next queue for scheduling */
    struct qband    *eq_bandp;   /* separate flow information */
    unsigned char    eq_nband;   /* number of priority bands > 0 */
};

#define q_link    q_eq->eq_link
#define q_bandp   q_eq->eq_bandp
#define q_nband   q_eq->eq_nband

#endif  /* _STYPES */
```

qband

The queue flow information for each band is contained in the following structure:

```
/* Structure that describes the separate information for each priority
 * band in the queue
 */

struct qband {
    struct qband    *qb_next;    /* next band's info */
    ulong           qb_count;    /* number of bytes in band */
    struct msgb     *qb_first;   /* beginning of band's data */
    struct msgb     *qb_last;    /* end of band's data */
    ulong           qb_hiwat;    /* high water mark for band */
    ulong           qb_lowat;    /* low water mark for band */
    ulong           qb_flag;     /* flag, QB_FULL, denotes that a band of
                                    data flow is flow controlled */
    long            qb_pad1;     /* reserved for future use */
};

typedef struct qband qband_t;

/*
 * qband flags
 */
#define QB_FULL     0x01         /* band is considered full */
#define QB_WANTW    0x02         /* someone wants to write to band */
#define QB_BACK     0x04         /* queue has been back-enabled */
```

Message Structures

A message is composed of a linked list of triples, consisting of two structures (**msgb** and **datab**) and a data buffer.

```
/* the message block, msgb, structure */
#ifdef _STYPES

struct      msgb {
    struct   msgb   *b_next;      /* next message on queue */
    struct   msgb   *b_prev;      /* previous message on queue */
    struct   msgb   *b_cont;      /* next message block of message */
    unsigned char   *b_rptr;      /* first unread data byte in buffer */
    unsigned char   *b_wptr;      /* first unwritten data byte in buffer  */
    struct   datab  *b_datap;     /* data block */
};
#define b_band      b_datap->db_band
#define b_flag      b_datap->db_flag

#else   /* large definition */

struct      msgb {
    struct   msgb   *b_next;      /* next message on queue */
    struct   msgb   *b_prev;      /* previous message on queue */
    struct   msgb   *b_cont;      /* next message block of message */
    unsigned char   *b_rptr;      /* first unread data byte in buffer */
    unsigned char   *b_wptr;      /* first unwritten data byte in buffer  */
    struct   datab  *b_datap;     /* data block */
    unsigned char   b_band;       /* message priority */
    unsigned char   b_pad1;
    unsigned short  b_flag;
    long            b_pad2;
};
#endif    /* _STYPES */

typedef struct msgb mblk_t;
typedef struct datab dblk_t;
typedef struct free_rtn frtn_t;

};
/* Message flags. These are interpreted by the Stream head. */

#define MSGMARK   0x01        /* last byte of message is "marked" */
#define MSGNOLOOP 0x02        /* don't loop message around to write-side of Stream */
#define MSGDELIM  0x04        /* message is delimited */
```

```
/* data block, datab, structure */
#ifdef _STYPES
struct datab {
    union {
        struct datab    *freep;
        struct free_rtn *frtnp;
    } db_f;                         /* used internally */
        unsigned char    *db_base;  /* first byte of buffer * */
        unsigned char    *db_lim;   /* last byte+1 of buffer */
        unsigned char    db_ref;    /* count of messages pointing to this block */
        unsigned char    db_type;   /* message type */
        unsigned char    db_band;   /* message priority, determines where a
                                       message is placed when enqueued */
        unsigned char    db_iswhat; /* status of message/data/buffer triplet */
        unsigned int     db_size;   /* used internally */
        unsigned short   db_flag;   /* data block flag */
        unsigned short   db_pad;
        caddr_t          db_msgaddr;/* triplet message header pointing to datab */
};
#else    /*  large definition */

struct datab {
    union {
        struct datab    *freep;
        struct free_rtn *frtnp;
    } db_f;                         /* used internally */
        unsigned char    *db_base;  /* first byte of buffer * */
        unsigned char    *db_lim;   /* last byte+1 of buffer */
        unsigned char    db_ref;    /* count of messages pointing to this block */
        unsigned char    db_type;   /* message type */
        unsigned char    db_iswhat; /* status of message/data/buffer triplet */
        unsigned int     db_size;   /* used internally */
        caddr_t          db_msgaddr; /* triplet message header pointing to datab */
        long             db_filler;  /* reserved for future use */
};
#endif /* _STYPES */

#define db_freep db_f.freep
#define db_frtnp db_f.frtnp

typedef struct datab dblk_t;
```

iocblk

This is contained in an M_IOCTL message block:

```
#ifdef _STYPES

struct iocblk {
    int      ioc_cmd;      /* ioctl command type */
    o_uid_t  ioc_uid;      /* effective uid of user */
    o_gid_t  ioc_gid;      /* effective gid of user */
    uint     ioc_id;       /* ioctl id */
    uint     ioc_count;    /* count of bytes in data field */
    int      ioc_error;    /* error code */
    int      ioc_rval;     /* return value  */
};

#else /* large definition */

struct iocblk {
    int      ioc_cmd;      /* ioctl command type */
    cred_t   *ioc_cr;      /* full credentials */
    uint     ioc_id;       /* ioctl id */
    uint     ioc_count;    /* count of bytes in data field */
    int      ioc_error;    /* error code */
    int      ioc_rval;     /* return value */
    long     ioc_filler[4];/* reserved for future use */
};

#define ioc_uid ioc_cr->cr_uid
#define ioc_gid ioc_cr->cr_gid

#endif /* _STYPES */
```

copyreq

This is used in M_COPYIN/M_COPYOUT messages:

```
#ifdef _STYPES

struct copyreq {
    int         cq_cmd;       /* ioctl command (from ioc_cmd) */
    o_uid_t     cq_uid;       /* effective uid of user */
    o_gid_t     cq_gid;       /* effective gid of user */
    uint        cq_id;        /* ioctl id (from ioc_id) */
    caddr_t     cq_addr;      /* address to copy data to/from */
    uint        cq_size;      /* number of bytes to copy */
    int         cq_flag;      /* see below */
    mblk_t      *cq_private;  /* private state information */
};

#else /* large definition */

struct copyreq {
    int         cq_cmd;       /* ioctl command (from ioc_cmd) */
    cred_t      *cq_cr;       /* full credentials */
    uint        cq_id;        /* ioctl id (from ioc_id) */
    caddr_t     cq_addr;      /* address to copy data to/from */
    uint        cq_size;      /* number of bytes to copy */
    int         cq_flag;      /* see below */
    mblk_t      *cq_private;  /* private state information */
    long        cq_filler[4]; /* reserved for future use */
};

#define cq_uid cq_cr->cr_uid
#define cq_gid cq_cr->cr_gid

#endif /* _STYPES */

/* cq_flag values */

#define STRCANON    0x01   /* b_cont data block contains canonical format specifier */
#define RECOPY      0x02   /* perform I_STR copyin again this time using canonical
                             format specifier */
```

copyresp

This structure is used in M_IOCDATA:

```
#ifdef _STYPES

struct copyresp {
    int        cp_cmd;       /* ioctl command (from ioc_cmd) */
    o_uid_t    cp_uid;       /* effective uid of user */
    o_gid_t    cp_gid;       /* effective gid of user */
    uint       cp_id;        /* ioctl id (from ioc_id) */
    caddr_t    cp_rval;      /* status of request: 0 for success
                                non-zero for failure */
    uint       cp_pad1;      /* reserved */
    int        cp_pad2;      /* reserved */
    mblk_t     *cp_private;  /* private state information */
};

#else /* large definition */

struct copyresp {
    int        cp_cmd;       /* ioctl command (from ioc_cmd) */
    cred_t     *cp_cr;       /* full credentials */
    uint       cp_id;        /* ioctl id (from ioc_id) */
    caddr_t    cp_rval;      /* status of request; 0 for success
                                non-zero for failure */
    uint       cp_pad1;      /* reserved */
    int        cp_pad2;      /* reserved */
    mblk_t     *cp_private;  /* private state information */
    long       cp_filler[4]; /* reserved for future use */
};

#define cp_uid cp_cr->cr_uid
#define cp_gid cp_cr->cr_gid

#endif /* _STYPES */
```

strioctl

This structure supplies user values as an argument to the **ioctl** call I_STR in
streamio(7).

```
struct strioctl {
    int     ic_cmd;        /* downstream request */
    int     ic_timout;     /* timeout acknowledgement - ACK/NAK */
    int     ic_len;        /* length of data argument */
    char    *ic_dp;        /* pointer to data argument */
};
```

linkblk

```
/* this is used in lower multiplexor drivers to indicate a link */
#ifdef _STYPES

struct linkblk {
    queue_t *l_qtop;       /* lowest level write queue of upper Stream */
                           /* set to NULL for persistent links */
    queue_t *l_qbot;       /* highest level write queue of lower Stream */
    int      l_index;      /* system-unique index for lower Stream */
};
#else /* large definition */

struct linkblk {
    queue_t *l_qtop;       /* lowest level write queue for upper Stream */
                           /* set to NULL for persistent links */
    queue_t *l_qbot;       /* highest level write queue of lower Stream */
    int      l_index;      /* system-unique index for lower Stream */
    long     l_pad[5];     /* reserved for future use */
};
#endif /* _STYPES */
```

stroptions

```
#ifdef  _STYPES
struct stroptions {
    short          so_flags;      /* options to set */
    short          so_readopt;    /* read option */
    ushort         so_wroff;      /* write offset */
    short          so_minpsz;     /* minimum read packet size */
    short          so_maxpsz;     /* maximum read packet size */
    ushort         so_hiwat;      /* read queue high water mark */
    ushort         so_lowat;      /* read queue low water mark */
    unsigned char  so_band;       /* band for water marks */
};
#else  /* large definition */
struct stroptions {
    ulong          so_flags;      /* options to set */
    short          so_readopt;    /* read option */
    ushort         so_wroff;      /* write offset */
    long           so_minpsz;     /* minimum read packet size */
    long           so_maxpsz;     /* maximum read packet size */
    ulong          so_hiwat;      /* read queue high water mark */
    ulong          so_lowat;      /* read queue low water mark */
    unsigned char  so_band;       /* band for water marks */
};
#endif  /* _STYPES */
/* flags for Stream options set message */
#define  SO_ALL        0x003f  /* set all options */
#define  SO_READOPT    0x0001  /* set read option */
#define  SO_WROFF      0x0002  /* set write offset */
#define  SO_MINPSZ     0x0004  /* set minimum packet size */
#define  SO_MAXPSZ     0x0008  /* set maximum packet size */
#define  SO_HIWAT      0x0010  /* set high water mark */
#define  SO_LOWAT      0x0020  /* set low water mark */
#define  SO_MREADON    0x0040  /* set read notification on */
#define  SO_MREADOFF   0x0080  /* set read notification off */
#define  SO_NDELON     0x0100  /* old TTY semantics for NDELAY reads/writes */
#define  SO_NDELOFF    0x0200  /* STREAMS semantics for NDELAY reads/writes */
#define  SO_ISTTY      0x0400  /* Stream is acting as terminal */
#define  SO_ISNTTY     0x0800  /* Stream is not acting as a terminal */
#define  SO_TOSTOP     0x1000  /* stop on background writes to Stream */
#define  SO_TONSTOP    0x2000  /* don't stop on background jobs to Stream */
#define  SO_BAND       0x4000  /* water marks that affect band */
```

B Appendix B: Message Types

Message Types   B-1

Ordinary Messages   B-2

High Priority Messages   B-14

Message Types

Defined STREAMS message types differ in their intended purposes, their treatment at the Stream head, and in their message queueing priority.

STREAMS does not prevent a module or driver from generating any message type and sending it in any direction on the Stream. However, established processing and direction rules should be observed. Stream head processing according to message type is fixed, although certain parameters can be altered.

The message types are described in this appendix, classified according to their message queueing priority. Ordinary messages are described first, with high priority messages following. In certain cases, two message types may perform similar functions, differing only in priority. Message construction is described in Chapter 5. The use of the word module will generally imply "module or driver."

Ordinary messages are also called normal or non-priority messages. Ordinary messages are subject to flow control whereas high priority messages are not.

Ordinary Messages

M_BREAK   Sent to a driver to request that BREAK be transmitted on whatever media the driver is controlling.

  The message format is not defined by STREAMS and its use is developer dependent. This message may be considered a special case of an M_CTL message. An M_BREAK message cannot be generated by a user-level process and is always discarded if passed to the Stream head.

M_CTL   Generated by modules that wish to send information to a particular module or type of module. M_CTL messages are typically used for inter-module communication, as when adjacent STREAMS protocol modules negotiate the terms of their interface. An M_CTL message cannot be generated by a user-level process and is always discarded if passed to the Stream head.

M_DATA   Intended to contain ordinary data. Messages allocated by the **allocb**() routine (see Appendix C) are type M_DATA by default. M_DATA messages are generally sent bidirectionally on a Stream and their contents can be passed between a process and the Stream head. In the **getmsg**(2) and **putmsg**(2) system calls, the contents of M_DATA message blocks are referred to as the data part. Messages composed of multiple message blocks will typically have M_DATA as the message type for all message blocks following the first.

M_DELAY   Sent to a media driver to request a real-time delay on output. The data buffer associated with this message is expected to contain an integer to indicate the number of machine ticks of delay desired. M_DELAY messages are typically used to prevent transmitted data from exceeding the buffering capacity of slower terminals.

  The message format is not defined by STREAMS and its use is developer dependent. Not all media drivers may understand this message. This message may be considered a special case of an M_CTL message. An M_DELAY message cannot be generated by a user-level process and is always discarded if passed to the Stream head.

M_IOCTL Generated by the Stream head in response to I_STR, I_LINK,
I_UNLINK, I_PLINK, and I_PUNLINK [ioctl(2) STREAMS
system calls, see streamio(7)], and in response to ioctl calls
which contain a *command* argument value not defined in
streamio(7). When one of these ioctls is received from a user
process, the Stream head uses values supplied in the call and
values from the process to create an M_IOCTL message containing them, and sends the message downstream.
M_IOCTL messages are intended to perform the general ioctl
functions of character device drivers.

For an I_STR ioctl, the user values are supplied in a structure
of the following form, provided as an argument to the ioctl
call [see I_STR in streamio(7)]:

```
struct strioctl
{
        int     ic_cmd;     /* downstream request */
        int     ic_timout;  /* ACK/NAK timeout    */
        int     ic_len;     /* length of data arg */
        char *ic_dp;        /* ptr to data arg    */
};
```

where *ic_cmd* is the request (or command) defined by a
downstream module or driver, *ic_timout* is the time the
Stream head will wait for acknowledgement to the M_IOCTL
message before timing out, and *ic_dp* is a pointer to an
optional data buffer. On input, *ic_len* contains the length of
the data in the buffer passed in and, on return from the call,
it contains the length of the data, if any, being returned to
the user in the same buffer.

The M_IOCTL message format is one M_IOCTL message
block followed by zero or more M_DATA message blocks.
STREAMS constructs an M_IOCTL message block by placing
an iocblk structure, defined in <sys/stream.h>, in its data
buffer (see Appendix A for a complete iocblk structure):

```
struct iocblk
{
    int     ioc_cmd;    /* ioctl command type */
    cred_t  *ioc_cr;    /* full credentials */
    uint    ioc_id;     /* ioctl identifier */
    uint    ioc_count;  /* byte count for ioctl data */
    int     ioc_error;  /* error code for M_IOCACK or M_IOCNAK */
    int     ioc_rval;   /* return value for M_IOCACK */
    long    ioc_filler[4]; /* reserved for future use */
};
```

For an I_STR **ioctl**, *ioc_cmd* corresponds to *ic_cmd* of the **strioctl** structure. *ioc_cr* points to a credentials structure defining the user process's permissions (see <**cred.h**>). Its contents can be tested to determine if the user issuing the **ioctl** call is authorized to do so. For an I_STR **ioctl**, *ioc_count* is the number of data bytes, if any, contained in the message and corresponds to *ic_len*.

ioc_id is an identifier generated internally, and is used by the Stream head to match each M_IOCTL message sent downstream with response messages sent upstream to the Stream head. The response message which completes the Stream head processing for the **ioctl** is an M_IOCACK (positive acknowledgement) or an M_IOCNAK (negative acknowledgement) message.

For an I_STR **ioctl**, if a user supplies data to be sent downstream, the Stream head copies the data, pointed to by *ic_dp* in the **strioctl** structure, into M_DATA message blocks and links the blocks to the initial M_IOCTL message block. *ioc_count* is copied from *ic_len*. If there are no data, *ioc_count* is zero.

If the Stream head does not recognize the *command* argument of an **ioctl**, it creates a transparent M_IOCTL message. The format of a transparent M_IOCTL message is one M_IOCTL message block followed by one M_DATA block. The form of the **iocblk** structure is the same as above. However, *ioc_cmd* is set to the value of the *command* argument in the **ioctl** system call and *ioc_count* is set to TRANSPARENT, defined in <**sys/stream.h**>. TRANSPARENT distinguishes the case where an I_STR **ioctl** may specify a value of *ioc_cmd* equivalent to the *command* argument of a transparent **ioctl**.

The M_DATA block of the message contains the value of the *arg* parameter in the **ioctl** call.

The first module or driver that understands the *ioc_cmd* request contained in the M_IOCTL acts on it. For an I_STR **ioctl**, this action generally includes an immediate upstream transmission of an M_IOCACK message. For transparent M_IOCTLs, this action generally includes the upstream transmission of an M_COPYIN or M_COPYOUT message.

Intermediate modules that do not recognize a particular request must pass the message on. If a driver does not recognize the request, or the receiving module can not acknowledge it, an M_IOCNAK message must be returned.

M_IOCACK and M_IOCNAK message types have the same format as an M_IOCTL message and contain an **iocblk** structure in the first block. An M_IOCACK block may be linked to following M_DATA blocks. If one of these messages reaches the Stream head with an identifier which does not match that of the currently-outstanding M_IOCTL message, the response message is discarded. A common means of assuring that the correct identifier is returned is for the replying module to convert the M_IOCTL message into the appropriate response type and set *ioc_count* to 0, if no data are returned. Then, the **qreply**() utility (see Appendix C) is used to send the response to the Stream head.

In an M_IOCACK or M_IOCNAK message, *ioc_error* holds any return error condition set by a downstream module. If this value is non-zero, it is returned to the user in *errno*. Note that both an M_IOCNAK and an M_IOCACK may return an error. However, only an M_IOCACK can have a return value. For an M_IOCACK, *ioc_rval* holds any return value set by a responding module. For an M_IOCNAK, *ioc_rval* is ignored by the Stream head.

If a module processing an I_STR **ioctl** wants to send data to a user process, it must use the M_IOCACK message which it constructs such that the M_IOCACK block is linked to one or more following M_DATA blocks containing the user data. The module must set *ioc_count* to the number of data bytes sent. The Stream head places the data in the address pointed to by *ic_dp* in the user I_STR **strioctl** structure.

If a module processing a transparent **ioctl** (i.e., it received a transparent M_IOCTL) wants to send data to a user process, it can use only an M_COPYOUT message. For a transparent **ioctl**, no data can be sent to the user process in an M_IOCACK message. All data must have been sent in a preceding M_COPYOUT message. The Stream head will ignore any data contained in an M_IOCACK message (in M_DATA blocks) and will free the blocks.

No data can be sent with an M_IOCNAK message for any type of M_IOCTL. The Stream head will ignore and will free any M_DATA blocks.

The Stream head blocks the user process until an M_IOCACK or M_IOCNAK response to the M_IOCTL (same *ioc_id*) is received. For an M_IOCTL generated from an I_STR **ioctl**, the Stream head will "time out" if no response is received in *ic_timout* interval (the user may specify an explicit interval or specify use of the default interval). For M_IOCTL messages generated from all other **ioctls**, the default (infinite) is used.

M_PASSFP   Used by STREAMS to pass a file pointer from the Stream head at one end of a Stream pipe to the Stream head at the other end of the same Stream pipe.

The message is generated as a result of an I_SENDFD **ioctl** [see **streamio**(7)] issued by a process to the sending Stream head. STREAMS places the M_PASSFP message directly on the destination Stream head's read queue to be retrieved by an I_RECVFD **ioctl** [see **streamio**(7)]. The message is placed without passing it through the Stream (i.e., it is not seen by any modules or drivers in the Stream). This message should never be present on any queue except the read queue of a Stream head. Consequently, modules and drivers do not need to recognize this message, and it can be ignored by module and driver developers.

M_PROTO   Intended to contain control information and associated data. The message format is one or more (see note) M_PROTO message blocks followed by zero or more M_DATA message blocks as shown in Figure B-1. The semantics of the M_DATA and M_PROTO message block are determined by the STREAMS module that receives the message.

The M_PROTO message block will typically contain implementation dependent control information. M_PROTO messages are generally sent bidirectionally on a Stream, and their contents can be passed between a process and the Stream head. The contents of the first message block of an M_PROTO message is generally referred to as the control part, and the contents of any following M_DATA message blocks are referred to as the data part. In the **getmsg**(2) and **putmsg**(2) system calls, the control and data parts are passed separately.

NOTE: On the write-side, the user can only generate M_PROTO messages containing one M_PROTO message block.

Although its use is not recommended, the format of M_PROTO and M_PCPROTO (generically PROTO) messages sent upstream to the Stream head allows multiple PROTO blocks at the beginning of the message. **getmsg**(2) will compact the blocks into a single control part when passing them to the user process.

Figure B-1: **M_PROTO and M_PCPROTO Message Structure**

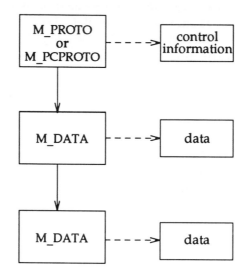

M_RSE   Reserved for internal use. Modules that do not recognize this message must pass it on. Drivers that do not recognize it must free it.

M_SETOPTS   Used to alter some characteristics of the Stream head. It is generated by any downstream module, and is interpreted by the Stream head. The data buffer of the message has the following structure (see Appendix A for a complete **stroptions** structure):

```
struct stroptions
{
    ulong   so_flags;   /* options to set */
    short   so_readopt; /* read option */
    ushort  so_wroff;   /* write offset */
    long    so_minpsz;  /* minimum read packet size */
    long    so_maxpsz;  /* maximum read packet size */
    ulong   so_hiwat;   /* read queue high-water mark */
    ulong   so_lowat;   /* read queue low-water mark */
    unsigned char so_band; /* update water marks for this band */
};
```

where *so_flags* specifies which options are to be altered, and
can be any combination of the following:

- SO_ALL: Update all options according to the
  values specified in the remaining fields of the
  stroptions structure.

- SO_READOPT: Set the read mode [see **read**(2)] to
  RNORM (byte stream), RMSGD (message discard),
  RMSGN (message non-discard), RPROTNORM (nor-
  mal protocol), RPROTDAT (turn M_PROTO and
  M_PCPROTO messages into M_DATA messages), or
  RPROTDIS (discard M_PROTO and M_PCPROTO
  blocks in a message and retain any linked M_DATA
  blocks) as specified by the value of *so_readopt*.

- SO_WROFF: Direct the Stream head to insert an
  offset (unwritten area, see "Write Offset" in Chapter
  5) specified by *so_wroff* into the first message block
  of all M_DATA messages created as a result of a
  write(2) system call. The same offset is inserted into
  the first M_DATA message block, if any, of all messages created by a **putmsg** system call. The default
  offset is zero.

  The offset must be less than the maximum message
  buffer size (system dependent). Under certain cir-
  cumstances, a write offset may not be inserted. A
  module or driver must test that *b_rptr* in the **msgb**
  structure is greater than *db_base* in the **datab** structure to determine that an offset has been inserted in
  the first message block.

- SO_MINPSZ: Change the minimum packet size value associated with the Stream head read queue to *so_minpsz* (see *q_minpsz* in the **queue** structure, Appendix A). This value is advisory for the module immediately below the Stream head. It is intended to limit the size of M_DATA messages that the module should put to the Stream head. There is no intended minimum size for other message types. The default value in the Stream head is zero.

- SO_MAXPSZ: Change the maximum packet size value associated with the Stream head read queue to *so_maxpsz* (see *q_maxpsz* in the **queue** structure, Appendix A). This value is advisory for the module immediately below the Stream head. It is intended to limit the size of M_DATA messages that the module should put to the Stream head. There is no intended maximum size for other message types. The default value in the Stream head is INFPSZ, the maximum STREAMS allows.

- SO_HIWAT: Change the flow control high water mark (*q_hiwat* in the **queue** structure, *qb_hiwat* in the **qband** structure) on the Stream head read queue to the value specified in *so_hiwat*.

- SO_LOWAT: Change the flow control low water mark (*q_lowat* in the **queue** structure, *qb_lowat* in the **qband** structure) on the Stream head read queue to the value specified in *so_lowat*.

- SO_MREADON: Enable the Stream head to generate M_READ messages when processing a **read**(2) system call. If both SO_MREADON and SO_MREADOFF are set in *so_flags*, SO_MREADOFF will have precedence.

- SO_MREADOFF: Disable the Stream head generation of M_READ messages when processing a **read**(2) system call. This is the default. If both SO_MREADON and SO_MREADOFF are set in *so_flags*, SO_MREADOFF will have precedence.

- SO_NDELON: Set non-STREAMS tty semantics for O_NDELAY (or O_NONBLOCK) processing on **read**(2) and **write**(2) system calls. If O_NDELAY (or O_NONBLOCK) is set, a **read**(2) will return 0 if no data are waiting to be read at the Stream head. If O_NDELAY (or O_NONBLOCK) is clear, a **read**(2) will block until data become available at the Stream head. (See note below)

  Regardless of the state of O_NDELAY (or O_NONBLOCK), a **write**(2) will block on flow control and will block if buffers are not available.

  If both SO_NDELON and SO_NDELOFF are set in *so_flags*, SO_NDELOFF will have precedence.

  NOTE: For conformance with the POSIX standard, it is recommended that new applications use the O_NONBLOCK flag whose behavior is the same as that of O_NDELAY unless otherwise noted.

- SO_NDELOFF: Set STREAMS semantics for O_NDELAY (or O_NONBLOCK) processing on **read**(2) and **write**(2) system calls. If O_NDELAY (or O_NONBLOCK) is set, a **read**(2) will return -1 and set EAGAIN if no data are waiting to be read at the Stream head. If O_NDELAY (or O_NONBLOCK) is clear, a **read**(2) will block until data become available at the Stream head. (See note above)

  If O_NDELAY (or O_NONBLOCK) is set, a **write**(2) will return -1 and set EAGAIN if flow control is in effect when the call is received. It will block if buffers are not available. If O_NDELAY (or O_NONBLOCK) is set and part of the buffer has been written and a flow control or buffers not available condition is encountered, **write**(2) will terminate and return the number of bytes written. If O_NDELAY (or O_NONBLOCK) is clear, a **write**(2) will block on flow control and will block if buffers are not available.

This is the default. If both SO_NDELON and
SO_NDELOFF are set in *so_flags*, SO_NDELOFF will
have precedence.

In the STREAMS-based pipe mechanism, the
behavior of **read**(2) and **write**(2) is different for the
O_NDELAY and O_NONBLOCK flags. See **read**(2)
and **write**(2) for details.

■ SO_BAND: Set water marks in a band. If the
SO_BAND flag is set with the SO_HIWAT or
SO_LOWAT flag, the *so_band* field contains the
priority band number the *so_hiwat* and *so_lowat*
fields pertain to.

If the SO_BAND flag is not set and the SO_HIWAT
and SO_LOWAT flags are on, the normal high and
low water marks are affected. The SO_BAND flag
has no effect if SO_HIWAT and SO_LOWAT flags
are off.

Only one band's water marks can be updated with a
single M_SETOPTS message.

■ SO_ISTTY: Inform the Stream head that the Stream
is acting like a controlling terminal.

■ SO_ISNTTY: Inform the Stream head that the
Stream is no longer acting like a controlling terminal.

For SO_ISTTY, the Stream may or may not be allocated as a controlling terminal via an M_SETOPTS
message arriving upstream during open processing.
If the Stream head is opened before receiving this
message, the Stream will not be allocated as a controlling terminal until it is queued again by a session leader.

■ SO_TOSTOP: Stop on background writes to the
Stream.

- SO_TONSTOP: Do not stop on background writes to the Stream.

  SO_TOSTOP and SO_TONSTOP are used in conjunction with job control.

M_SIG Sent upstream by modules or drivers to post a signal to a process. When the message reaches the front of the Stream head read queue, it evaluates the first data byte of the message as a signal number, defined in **<sys/signal.h>**. (Note that the signal is not generated until it reaches the front of the Stream head read queue.) The associated signal will be sent to process(es) under the following conditions:

If the signal is SIGPOLL, it will be sent only to those processes that have explicitly registered to receive the signal [see I_SETSIG in **streamio**(7)].

If the signal is not SIGPOLL and the Stream containing the sending module or driver is a controlling tty, the signal is sent to the associated process group. A Stream becomes the controlling tty for its process group if, on **open**(2), a module or driver sends an M_SETOPTS message to the Stream head with the SO_ISTTY flag set.

If the signal is not SIGPOLL and the Stream is not a controlling tty, no signal is sent, except in case of SIOCSPGRP and TIOCSPGRP. These two **ioctls** set the process group field in the Stream head so the Stream can generate signals even if it is not a controlling tty.

High Priority Messages

M_COPYIN Generated by a module or driver and sent upstream to request that the Stream head perform a **copyin**() on behalf of the module or driver. It is valid only after receiving an M_IOCTL message and before an M_IOCACK or M_IOCNAK.

The message format is one M_COPYIN message block containing a **copyreq** structure, defined in **<sys/stream.h>** (see Appendix A for a complete **copyreq** structure):

```
struct copyreq {
    int     cq_cmd;          /* ioctl command (from ioc_cmd) */
    cred_t  *cq_cr;          /* full credentials */
    uint    cq_id;           /* ioctl id (from ioc_id) */
    caddr_t cq_addr;         /* address to copy data to/from */
    uint    cq_size;         /* number of bytes to copy */
    int     cq_flag;         /* reserved */
    mblk_t  *cq_private;     /* private state information */
    long    cp_filler[4];    /* reserved for future use */
};
```

The first four members of the structure correspond to those of the **iocblk** structure in the M_IOCTL message which allows the same message block to be reused for both structures. The Stream head will guarantee that the message block allocated for the M_IOCTL message is large enough to contain a **copyreq** structure. The *cq_addr* field contains the user space address from which the data are to be copied. The *cq_size* field is the number of bytes to copy from user space. The *cq_flag* field is reserved for future use and should be set to zero.

The *cq_private* field can be used by a module to point to a message block containing the module's state information relating to this **ioctl**. The Stream head will copy (without processing) the contents of this field to the M_IOCDATA response message so that the module can resume the associated state. If an M_COPYIN or M_COPYOUT message is freed, STREAMS will not free any message block pointed to by *cq_private*. This is the module's responsibility.

This message should not be queued by a module or driver unless it intends to process the data for the **ioctl**.

M_COPYOUT   Generated by a module or driver and sent upstream to request that the Stream head perform a **copyout**() on behalf of the module or driver. It is valid only after receiving an M_IOCTL message and before an M_IOCACK or M_IOCNAK.

The message format is one M_COPYOUT message block followed by one or more M_DATA blocks. The M_COPYOUT message block contains a **copyreq** structure as described in the M_COPYIN message with the following differences: The *cq_addr* field contains the user space address to which the data are to be copied. The *cq_size* field is the number of bytes to copy to user space.

Data to be copied to user space is contained in the linked M_DATA blocks.

This message should not be queued by a module or driver unless it intends to process the data for the **ioctl** in some way.

M_ERROR   Sent upstream by modules or drivers to report some downstream error condition. When the message reaches the Stream head, the Stream is marked so that all subsequent system calls issued to the Stream, excluding **close**(2) and **poll**(2), will fail with *errno* set to the first data byte of the message. POLLERR is set if the Stream is being **polled** [see **poll**(2)]. All processes sleeping on a system call to the Stream are awakened. An M_FLUSH message with FLUSHRW is sent downstream.

The Stream head maintains two error fields, one for the read-side and one for the write-side. The one-byte format M_ERROR message sets both of these fields to the error specified by the first byte in the message.

The second style of the M_ERROR message is two bytes long. The first byte is the read error and the second byte is the write error. This allows modules to set a different error on the read-side and write-side. If one of the bytes is set to NOERROR, then the field for the corresponding side of the Stream is unchanged. This allows a module to just an error on one side of the Stream. For example, if the Stream head was not in an error state and a module sent an M_ERROR message upstream with the first byte set to EPROTO and the second byte set to NOERROR, all subsequent read-like system calls (for example, **read, getmsg**) will fail with EPROTO, but all write-like system calls (for example, **write, putmsg**) will still succeed. If a byte is set to 0, the error state is cleared for the corresponding side of the Stream. The values NOERROR and 0 are not valid for the one-byte form of the M_ERROR message.

M_FLUSH   Requests all modules and drivers that receive it to flush their message queues (discard all messages in those queues) as indicated in the message. An M_FLUSH can originate at the Stream head, or in any module or driver. The first byte of the message contains flags that specify one of the following actions:

- FLUSHR: Flush the read queue of the module.

- FLUSHW: Flush the write queue of the module.

- FLUSHRW: Flush both the read queue and the write queue of the module.

- FLUSHBAND: Flush the message according to the priority associated with the band.

Each module passes this message to its neighbor after flushing its appropriate queue(s), until the message reaches one of the ends of the Stream.

Drivers are expected to include the following processing for M_FLUSH messages. When an M_FLUSH message is sent downstream through the write queues in a Stream, the driver at the Stream end discards it if the message action indicates that the read queues in the Stream are not to be flushed (only FLUSHW set). If the message indicates that the read queues are to be flushed, the driver shuts off the FLUSHW flag, and sends the message up the Stream's read queues. When a flush message is sent up a Stream's read-side, the Stream head checks to see if the write-side of the Stream is to be flushed. If only FLUSHR is set, the Stream head discards the message. However, if the write-side of the Stream is to be flushed, the Stream head sets the M_FLUSH flag to

FLUSHW and sends the message down the Stream's write side. *All modules that enqueue messages must identify and process this message type.*

If FLUSHBAND is set, the second byte of the message contains the value of the priority band to flush.

M_HANGUP
Sent upstream by a driver to report that it can no longer send data upstream. As example, this might be due to an error, or to a remote line connection being dropped. When the message reaches the Stream head, the Stream is marked so that all subsequent **write**(2) and **putmsg**(2) system calls issued to the Stream will fail and return an ENXIO error. Those **ioctls** that cause messages to be sent downstream are also failed. POLLHUP is set if the Stream is being **polled** [see **poll**(2)].

However, subsequent **read**(2) or **getmsg**(2) calls to the Stream will not generate an error. These calls will return any messages (according to their function) that were on, or in transit to, the Stream head read queue before the M_HANGUP message was received. When all such messages have been read, **read**(2) will return 0 and **getmsg**(2) will set each of its two length fields to 0.

This message also causes a SIGHUP signal to be sent to the controlling process instead of the foreground process group, since the allocation and deallocation of controlling terminals to a session is the responsibility of the controlling process.

M_IOCACK
Signals the positive acknowledgement of a previous M_IOCTL message. The message format is one M_IOCACK block (containing an **iocblk** structure, see M_IOCTL) followed by zero or more M_DATA blocks. The **iocblk** data structure may contain a value in *ioc_rval* to be returned to the user process. It may also contain a value in *ioc_error* to be returned to the user process in *errno*.

If this message is responding to an I_STR **ioctl** [see **streamio**(7)], it may contain data from the receiving module or driver to be sent to the user process. In this case, message format is one M_IOCACK block followed by one or more M_DATA blocks containing the user data. The Stream head returns the data to the user if there is a corresponding outstanding M_IOCTL request. Otherwise, the M_IOCACK message is ignored and all blocks in the message are freed.

Data can not be returned in an M_IOCACK message responding to a transparent M_IOCTL. The data must have been sent with preceding M_COPYOUT message(s). If any M_DATA blocks follow the M_IOCACK block, the Stream head will ignore and free them.

The format and use of this message type is described further under M_IOCTL.

M_IOCDATA   Generated by the Stream head and sent downstream as a response to an M_COPYIN or M_COPYOUT message. The message format is one M_IOCDATA message block followed by zero or more M_DATA blocks. The M_IOCDATA message block contains a **copyresp** structure, defined in **<sys/stream.h>** (see Appendix A for a complete **copyresp** structure):

```
struct copyresp {
        int      cp_cmd;       /* ioctl command (from ioc_cmd) */
        cred_t  *cp_cr;        /* full credentials */
        uint     cp_id;        /* ioctl id (from ioc_id) */
        caddr_t  cp_rval;      /* status of request: 0 -> success
                                                  non_zero -> failure */
        uint     cp_pad1;      /* reserved */
        int      cp_pad2;      /* reserved */
        mblk_t  *cp_private;   /* private state info (from cq_private) */
        long     cp_filler[4]; /* reserved for future use */
};
```

The first three members of the structure correspond to those of the **iocblk** structure in the M_IOCTL message which allows the same message blocks to be reused for all of the related transparent messages (M_COPYIN, M_COPYOUT, M_IOCACK, M_IOCNAK). The *cp_rval* field contains the result of the request at the Stream head. Zero indicates success and non-zero indicates failure. If failure is indicated, the module should not generate an M_IOCNAK message. It must abort all **ioctl** processing, clean up its data structures, and return.

The *cp_private* field is copied from the *cq_private* field in the associated M_COPYIN or M_COPYOUT message. It is included in the M_IOCDATA message so the message can be self-describing. This is intended to simplify **ioctl** processing by modules and drivers.

If the message is in response to an M_COPYIN message and success is indicated, the M_IOCDATA block will be followed by M_DATA blocks containing the data copied in.

If an M_IOCDATA block is reused, any unused fields defined for the resultant message block should be cleared (particularly in an M_IOCACK or M_IOCNAK).

This message should not be queued by a module or driver unless it intends to process the data for the **ioctl** in some way.

M_IOCNAK Signals the negative acknowledgement (failure) of a previous M_IOCTL message. Its form is one M_IOCNAK block containing an **iocblk** data structure (see M_IOCTL). The **iocblk** structure may contain a value in *ioc_error* to be returned to the user process in *errno*. Unlike the M_IOCACK, no user data or return value can be sent with this message. If any M_DATA blocks follow the M_IOCNAK block, the Stream head will ignore and free them. When the Stream head receives an M_IOCNAK, the outstanding **ioctl** request, if any, will fail. The format and usage of this message type is described further under M_IOCTL.

M_PCPROTO As the M_PROTO message type, except for the priority and the following additional attributes.

When an M_PCPROTO message is placed on a queue, its **service** procedure is always enabled. The Stream head will allow only one M_PCPROTO message to be placed in its read queue at a time. If an M_PCPROTO message is already in the queue when another arrives, the second message is silently discarded and its message blocks freed.

This message is intended to allow data and control information to be sent outside the normal flow control constraints.

The **getmsg**(2) and **putmsg**(2) system calls refer to M_PCPROTO messages as high priority messages.

M_PCRSE	Reserved for internal use. Modules that do not recognize this message must pass it on. Drivers that do not recognize it must free it.
M_PCSIG	As the M_SIG message, except for the priority.

M_PCSIG is often preferable to the M_SIG message especially in tty applications, because M_SIG may be queued while M_PCSIG is more guaranteed to get through quickly. For example, if one generates an M_SIG message when the *DEL* (delete) key is hit on the terminal and one has already typed ahead, the M_SIG message becomes queued and the user doesn't get the call until it's too late; it becomes impossible to kill or interrupt a process by hitting a delete key.

M_READ	Generated by the Stream head and sent downstream for a **read**(2) system call if no messages are waiting to be read at the Stream head and if read notification has been enabled. Read notification is enabled with the SO_MREADON flag of the M_SETOPTS message and disabled by use of the SO_MREADOFF flag.

The message content is set to the value of the *nbyte* parameter (the number of bytes to be read) in the **read**(2) call.

M_READ is intended to notify modules and drivers of the occurrence of a **read**. It is also intended to support communication between Streams that reside in separate processors. The use of the M_READ message is developer dependent. Modules may take specific action and pass on or free the M_READ message. Modules that do not recognize this message must pass it on. All other drivers may or may not take action and then free the message.

This message cannot be generated by a user-level process and should not be generated by a module or driver. It is always discarded if passed to the Stream head.

M_START and M_STOP

Request devices to start or stop their output. They are intended to produce momentary pauses in a device's output, not to turn devices on or off.

The message format is not defined by STREAMS and its use is developer dependent. These messages may be considered special cases of an M_CTL message. These messages cannot be generated by a user-level process and each is always discarded if passed to the Stream head.

M_STARTI and **M_STOPI**

As M_START and M_STOP except that M_STARTI and M_STOPI are used to start and stop input.

C Appendix C: STREAMS Utilities

STREAMS Utilities   C-1

Utility Descriptions   C-3
- **adjmsg** – trim bytes in a message   C-3
- **allocb** – allocate a message and data block   C-3
- **backq** – get pointer to the queue behind a given queue   C-4
- **bcanput** – test for flow control in the given priority band C-4
- **bufcall** – recover from failure of **allocb**   C-4
- **canput** – test for room in a queue   C-5
- **copyb** – copy a message block   C-5
- **copymsg** – copy a message   C-6
- **datamsg** – test whether message is a data message   C-6
- **dupb** – duplicate a message block descriptor   C-6
- **dupmsg** – duplicate a message   C-7
- **enableok** – re-allow a queue to be scheduled for service C-7
- **esballoc** – allocate message and data blocks   C-8
- **flushband** – flush the messages in a given priority band C-8
- **flushq** – flush a queue   C-8
- **freeb** – free a single message block   C-9
- **freemsg** – free all message blocks in a message   C-9
- **getadmin()** – return the pointer to the module   C-10
- **getmid** – return a module id   C-10
- **getq** – get a message from a queue   C-10
- **insq** – put a message at a specific place in a queue   C-11
- **linkb** – concatenate two messages into one   C-11
- **msgdsize** – get the number of data bytes in a message   C-12
- **nocnable** – prevent a queue from being scheduled   C-12
- **OTHERQ** – get pointer to the mate queue   C-12
- **pullupmsg** – concatenate and aling bytes in a message   C-12
- **putbq** – return a message to the beginning of a queue   C-13
- **putctl** – put a control message   C-13
- **putctl1** – put a control message with a one-byte parameter C-14
- **putnext** – put a message to the next queue   C-14

- **putq** – put a message on a queue   C-14
- **qenable** – enable a queue   C-15
- **qreply** – send a message on a Stream in the reverse direction   C-16
- **qsize** – find the number of messages on a queue   C-16
- **RD** – get pointer to the read queue   C-16
- **rmvb** – remove a message block from a message   C-16
- **rmvq** – remove a message from a queue   C-17
- **splstr** – set processor level   C-17
- **strlog** – submit messages for logging   C-17
- **strqget** – obtain information about a queue or band of the queue   C-18
- **strqset** – change information about a queue or band of the queue   C-19
- **testb** – check for an available buffer   C-19
- **unbufcall** – cancel a **bufcall** request   C-20
- **unlinkb** – remove a message block from the head of a message   C-20
- **WR** – get pointer to the write queue   C-20

DKI Interface   C-21

Utility Routine Summary   C-22

STREAMS Utilities

This appendix specifies the set of utility routines provided by STREAMS to assist development of modules and drivers.

The general purpose of the utilities is to perform functions that are commonly used in modules and drivers. However, some utilities also provide the required interrupt environment. A utility routine must always be used when operating on a message queue and when accessing the buffer pool.

Most of these utility routines are contained in either the system source file **io/stream.c** or, if they are macros, in **<sys/stream.h>**.

 NOTE The utility routines contained in this appendix represent an interface that will be maintained in subsequent versions of UNIX® System V. Other than these utilities (also see the section titled "Accessible Symbols and Functions" in Chapter 7), functions contained in the STREAMS kernel code may change between versions.

Structure definitions are contained in Appendix A. Routine references are found in this appendix. The following definitions are used:

Blocked	A queue that can not be enabled due to flow control.
Enable	To schedule a queue's **service** procedure to run.
Free	To deallocate a STREAMS message or other data structure.
Message block (bp)	
	A triplet consisting of an **msgb** structure, a **datab** structure, and a data buffer. It is referenced by its type definition **mblk_t**.
Message (mp)	One or more linked message blocks. A message is referenced by its first message block.
Message queue	Zero or more linked messages associated with a queue (**queue** structure).
Queue (q)	A **queue** structure. When it appears with "message" in certain utility description lines, it means "message queue."
Schedule	To place a queue on the internal linked list of queues which will subsequently have their **service** procedure called by the STREAMS scheduler.

The word module will generally mean "module and/or driver". The phrase "next/following module" will generally refer to a module, driver, or Stream head.

Utility Descriptions

The STREAMS utility routines are described below. A summary table is contained at the end of this appendix.

adjmsg – trim bytes in a message

```
int
adjmsg(mp, len)
        mblk_t   *mp;
        register int   len;
```

adjmsg() trims bytes from either the head or tail of the message specified by *mp*. If *len* is greater than zero, it removes *len* bytes from the beginning of *mp*. If *len* is less than zero, it removes (-)*len* bytes from the end of *mp*. If *len* is zero, adjmsg() does nothing.

adjmsg() only trims bytes across message blocks of the same type. It fails if *mp* points to a message containing fewer than *len* bytes of similar type at the message position indicated.

adjmsg() returns 1 on success and 0 on failure.

allocb – allocate a message and data block

```
struct msgb   *
allocb(size, pri)
        register  int  size;
        uint       pri;
```

allocb() returns a pointer to a message block of type M_DATA, in which the data buffer contains at least *size* bytes. *pri* is one of BPRI_LO, BPRI_MED, or BPRI_HI and indicates how critically the module needs the buffer. *pri* is currently unused and is maintained only for compatibility with applications developed prior to UNIX® System V Release 4.0. If a block can not be allocated as requested, allocb() returns a NULL pointer.

When a message is allocated via allocb() the *b_band* field of the mblk_t is initially set to zero. Modules and drivers may set this field if so desired.

backq – get pointer to the queue behind a given queue

```
queue_t  *
backq(q)
        register  queue_t  *q;
```

backq() returns a pointer to the queue behind a given queue. That is, it returns a pointer to the queue whose *q_next* (see **queue** structure in Appendix A) pointer is *q*. If no such queue exists (as when *q* is at a Stream end), backq() returns NULL.

bcanput – test for flow control in the given priority band

```
int
bcanput(q, pri)
        register  queue_t  *q;
        unsigned  char  pri;
```

bcanput() provides modules and drivers with a way to test flow control in the given priority band. It returns 1 if a message of priority *pri* can be placed on the queue. It returns 0 if the priority band is flow controlled and sets the QWANTW flag to zero band (QB_WANTW to nonzero band).

If the band does not yet exist on the queue in question, 1 is returned.

The call bcanput (q, 0) is equivalent to the call canput (q).

bufcall – recover from failure of **allocb**

```
int
bufcall(size, pri, func, arg)
        uint  size;
        int  pri;
        void  (*func)();
        long  arg;
```

bufcall() is provided to assist in the event of a block allocation failure. If allocb() returns NULL, indicating a message block is not currently available, bufcall() may be invoked.

bufcall() arranges for (*func)(arg) to be called when a buffer of *size* bytes is available. *pri* is as described in **allocb()**. When *func* is called, it has no user context.

Programmer's Guide: STREAMS

It cannot reference the **u_area** and must return without sleeping. **bufcall()** does not guarantee that the desired buffer will be available when *func* is called since interrupt processing may acquire it.

bufcall() returns 1 on success, indicating that the request has been successfully recorded, and 0 on failure. On a failure return, *func* will never be called. A failure indicates a (temporary) inability to allocate required internal data structures.

canput − test for room in a queue

int
canput(q)
      register queue_t *q;

canput() determines if there is room left in a message queue. If *q* does not have a **service** procedure, **canput()** will search further in the same direction in the Stream until it finds a queue containing a **service** procedure (this is the first queue on which the passed message can actually be enqueued). If such a queue cannot be found, the search terminates on the queue at the end of the Stream. **canput()** tests the queue found by the search. If the message queue in this queue is not full, **canput()** returns 1. This return indicates that a message can be put to queue *q*. If the message queue is full, **canput()** returns 0. In this case, the caller is generally referred to as blocked.

canput() only takes into account normal data flow control.

copyb − copy a message block

mblk_t *
copyb(bp)
      register mblk_t *bp;

copyb() copies the contents of the message block pointed at by *bp* into a newly-allocated message block of at least the same size. **copyb()** allocates a new block by calling **allocb()**. All data between the *b_rptr* and *b_wptr* pointers of a message block are copied to the new block, and these pointers in the new block are given the same offset values they had in the original message block.

On successful completion, **copyb()** returns a pointer to the new message block containing the copied data. Otherwise, it returns a NULL pointer. The copy is rounded to full word boundary.

copymsg – copy a message

```
mblk_t  *
copymsg(bp)
     register  mblk_t  *bp;
```

copymsg() uses **copyb()** to copy the message blocks contained in the message pointed at by *bp* to newly-allocated message blocks, and links the new message blocks to form the new message.

On successful completion, **copymsg()** returns a pointer to the new message. Otherwise, it returns a NULL pointer.

datamsg – test whether message is a data message

```
#define  datamsg(type) ((type) == M_DATA || (type) == M_PROTO ||
     (type) == M_PCPROTO || (type) == M_DELAY)
```

The **datamsg()** macro returns TRUE if mp->b_datap->db_type (where *mp* is declared as mblk_t *mp) is a data type message (i.e., not a control message). In this case, a data type is M_DATA, M_PROTO, M_PCPROTO, or M_DELAY. If mp->b_datap->db_type is any other message type, **datamsg()** returns FALSE.

dupb – duplicate a message block descriptor

```
mblk_t  *
dupb(bp)
     register  mblk_t  *bp;
```

dupb() duplicates the message block descriptor (**mblk_t**) pointed at by *bp* by copying it into a newly allocated message block descriptor. A message block is formed with the new message block descriptor pointing to the same data block as the original descriptor. The reference count in the data block descriptor (**dblk_t**) is incremented. **dupb()** does not copy the data buffer, only the message block descriptor.

On successful completion, **dupb()** returns a pointer to the new message block. If **dupb()** cannot allocate a new message block descriptor, it returns NULL.

This routine allows message blocks that exist on different queues to reference the same data block. In general, if the contents of a message block with a reference count greater than 1 are to be modified, **copymsg()** should be used to create a new message block and only the new message block should be modified. This insures that other references to the original message block are not invalidated by unwanted changes.

dupmsg – duplicate a message

mblk_t *
dupmsg(bp)
         register mblk_t *bp;

dupmsg() calls **dupb()** to duplicate the message pointed at by *bp*, by copying all individual message block descriptors, and then linking the new message blocks to form the new message. **dupmsg()** does not copy data buffers, only message block descriptors.

On successful completion, **dupmsg()** returns a pointer to the new message. Otherwise, it returns NULL.

enableok – re-allow a queue to be scheduled for service

void
enableok(q)
         queue_t *q;

enableok() cancels the effect of an earlier **noenable()** on the same queue *q*. It allows a queue to be scheduled for service that had previously been excluded from queue service by a call to **nocnable()**.

esballoc – allocate message and data blocks

```
mblk_t  *
esballoc(base, size, pri, fr_rtn)
        unsigned char  *base;
        int   size, pri;
        frtn_t  *fr_rtn;
```

esballoc() allocates message and data blocks that point directly to a client-supplied buffer. esballoc() sets *db_base*, *b_rptr*, and *b_wptr* fields to *base* (data buffer size) and *db_lim* to *base + size*. The pointer to **struct free_rtn** is placed in the *db_freep* field of the data block.

The success of **esballoc()** depends on the success of **allocb()** and that *base*, *size*, and *fr_rtn* are not NULL, in which case **esballoc()** returns a pointer to a message block. If an error occurs, **esballoc()** returns NULL.

flushband – flush the messages in a given priority band

```
void
flushband(q, pri, flag)
        register  queue_t  *q;
        unsigned  char  pri;
        int  flag;
```

flushband() provides modules and drivers with the capability to flush the messages associated in a given priority band. *flag* is defined the same as in **flushq()**. If *pri* is zero, only ordinary messages are flushed. Otherwise, messages are flushed from the band specified by *pri* according to the value of *flag*.

flushq – flush a queue

```
void
flushq(q, flag)
        register  queue_t  *q;
        int  flag;
```

flushq() removes messages from the message queue in queue *q* and frees them, using **freemsg()**. If *flag* is set to FLUSHDATA, **flushq()** discards all M_DATA, M_PROTO, M_PCPROTO, and M_DELAY messages, but leaves all other messages on the queue. If *flag* is set to FLUSHALL, all messages are removed from the message queue and freed. FLUSHALL and FLUSHDATA are defined in

<sys/stream.h>.

If a queue behind *q* is blocked, **flushq()** may enable the blocked queue, as described in **putq()**.

freeb – free a single message block

void
freeb(bp)
      register struct msgb *bp;

freeb() will free (deallocate) the message block descriptor pointed at by *bp*, and free the corresponding data block if the reference count [see **dupb()**] in the data block descriptor (**datab** structure) is equal to 1. If the reference count is greater than 1, **freeb()** will not free the data block, but will decrement the reference count.

If the reference count is 1 and if the message was allocated by **esballoc()**, the function specified by the db_frtnp->free_func pointer is called with the parameter specified by db_frtnp->free_arg.

freeb() can't be used to free a multi-block message [see **freemsg()**]. Note that results will be unpredictable if the **freeb()** is called with a null argument. One should always check that pointer is non-NULL before using **freeb()**.

freemsg – free all message blocks in a message

void
freemsg(bp)
      register mblk_t *bp;

freemsg() uses **freeb()** to free all message blocks and their corresponding data blocks for the message pointed at by *bp*.

getadmin() − return the pointer to the module

```
int
(*getadmin(mid))()
        ushort  mid;
```

getadmin() returns the *qadmin* pointer to the module identified by *mid*. It returns NULL on error.

getmid − return a module id

```
ushort
getmid(name)
        char  name;
```

getmid() returns the module id for the module identified by *name*. It returns 0 on error.

getq − get a message from a queue

```
mblk_t  *
getq(q)
        register  queue_t  *q;
```

getq() gets the next available message from the queue pointed at by *q*. getq() returns a pointer to the message and removes that message from the queue. If no message is queued, **getq()** returns NULL.

getq(), and certain other utility routines, affect flow control in the Stream as follows: If **getq()** returns NULL, the queue is marked with QWANTR so that the next time a message is placed on it, it will be scheduled for service [enabled, see qenable()]. If the data in the enqueued messages in the queue drop below the low water mark, *q_lowat*, and a queue behind the current queue had previously attempted to place a message in the queue and failed [i.e., was blocked, see canput()], then the queue behind the current queue is scheduled for service.

The queue count is maintained on a per-band basis. Priority band 0 (normal messages) uses *q_count, q_lowat*, etc. Nonzero priority bands use the fields in their respective **qband** structures (*qb_count, qb_lowat*, etc). All messages appear on the same list, linked via their *b_next* pointers.

q_count does not reflect the size of all messages on the queue; it only reflects those messages in the normal band of flow.

insq – put a message at a specific place in a queue

```
int
insq(q, emp, mp)
        register queue_t  *q;
        register mblk_t   *emp;
        register mblk_t   *mp;
```

insq() places the message pointed at by *mp* in the message queue contained in the queue pointed at by *q* immediately before the already enqueued message pointed at by *emp*. If *emp* is NULL, the message is placed at the end of the queue. If *emp* is non-NULL, it must point to a message that exists on the queue *q*, or a system panic could result.

If an attempt is made to insert a message out of order in a queue via insq(), the message will not be inserted and the routine fails.

The queue class of the new message is ignored. However, the priority band of the new message must adhere to the following ordering:

    emp->b_prev->b_band >= mp->b_band >= emp->b_band.

This routine returns 1 on success and 0 on failure.

linkb – concatenate two messages into one

```
void
linkb(mp, bp)
        register  mblk_t *mp;
        register  mblk_t *bp;
```

linkb() puts the message pointed at by *bp* at the tail of the message pointed at by *mp*.

msgdsize – get the number of data bytes in a message

```
int
msgdsize(bp)
      register  mblk_t  *bp;
```

msgdsize() returns the number of bytes of data in the message pointed at by *bp*. Only bytes included in data blocks of type M_DATA are included in the total.

noenable – prevent a queue from being scheduled

```
void
noenable(q)
      queue_t  *q;
```

noenable() prevents the queue *q* from being scheduled for service by putq() or putbq() when these routines enqueue an ordinary priority message, or by insq() when it enqueues any message. noenable() does not prevent the scheduling of queues when a high priority message is enqueued, unless it is enqueued by insq().

OTHERQ – get pointer to the mate queue

```
#define  OTHERQ(q)  ((q)->q_flag&QREADR? (q)+1: (q)-1)
```

The OTHERQ() macro returns a pointer to the mate queue of *q*.

If *q* is the read queue for the module, it returns a pointer to the module's write queue. If *q* is the write queue for the module, it returns a pointer to the read queue.

pullupmsg – concatenate and aling bytes in a message

```
int
pullupmsg(mp, len)
      register  struct msgb  *mp;
      register  int  len;
```

pullupmsg() concatenates and aligns the first *len* data bytes of the passed message into a single, contiguous message block. Proper alignment is hardware-

Programmer's Guide: STREAMS

dependent. **pullupmsg()** only concatenates across message blocks of similar type. It fails if *mp* points to a message of less than *len* bytes of similar type. If *len* is -1 **pullupmsg()** concatenates all the like-type blocks in the beginning of the message pointed at by *mp*.

On success, **pullupmsg()** returns 1 and, as a result of the concatenation, it may have altered the contents of the message pointed to by *mp*. On failure, it returns 0.

putbq – return a message to the beginning of a queue

```
int
putbq(q, bp)
        register  queue_t   *q;
        register  mblk_t   *bp;
```

putbq() puts the message pointed at by *bp* at the beginning of the queue pointed at by *q*, in a position in accordance with the message type. High priority messages are placed at the head of the queue, followed by priority band messages and ordinary messages. Ordinary messages are placed after all high priority and priority band messages, but before all other ordinary messages already in a queue. The queue will be scheduled in accordance with the same rules described in **putq()**. This utility is typically used to replace a message on a queue from which it was just removed.

A **service** procedure must never put a high priority message back on its own queue, as this would result in an infinitive loop.

putbq() returns 1 on success and 0 on failure.

putctl – put a control message

```
int
putctl(q, type)
        queue_t   *q;
```

putctl() creates a control message of type *type*, and calls the **put** procedure of the queue pointed at by *q*, with a pointer to the created message as an argument. **putctl()** allocates new blocks by calling **allocb()**.

On successful completion, **putctl()** returns 1. It returns 0, if it cannot allocate a message block, or if *type* M_DATA, M_PROTO, M_PCPROTO, or M_DELAY was specified.

putctl1 − put a control message with a one-byte parameter

int
putctl1(q, type, param)
      queue_t *q;

putctl1() creates a control message of type *type* with a one-byte parameter *param*, and calls the **put** procedure of the queue pointed at by *q*, with a pointer to the created message as an argument. **putctl1()** allocates new blocks by calling **allocb()**.

On successful completion, **putctl1()** returns 1. It returns 0, if it cannot allocate a message block, or if *type* M_DATA, M_PROTO, or M_PCPROTO was specified. M_DELAY is allowed.

putnext − put a message to the next queue

#define putnext(q, mp) ((*(q)->q_next->q_qinfo->qi_putp)((q)->q_next, (mp)))

The **putnext()** macro calls the **put** procedure of the next queue in a Stream and passes it a message pointer as an argument. *q* is the calling queue (not the next queue) and *mp* is the message to be passed. **putnext()** is the typical means of passing messages to the next queue in a Stream.

putq − put a message on a queue

int
putq(q, bp)
      register queue_t   *q;
      register mblk_t   *bp;

putq() puts the message pointed at by *bp* on the message queue contained in the queue pointed at by *q* and enables that queue. **putq()** queues messages based on message queueing priority.

The priority classes are high priority (type >= QPCTL), priority band (type < QPCTL && band > 0), and normal (type < QPCTL && band == 0).

putq() always enables the queue when a high priority message is queued. putq() is allowed to enable the queue (QNOENAB is not set) if the message is the priority band message, or the QWANTR flag is set indicating that the ser-vice procedure is ready to read the queue. Note that the **service** procedure must never put a priority message back on its own queue, as this would result in an infinite loop. **putq()** enables the queue when an ordinary message is queued if the following condition is set, and enabling is not inhibited by **noen-able()**: the condition is set if the module has just been pushed, or if no message was queued on the last **getq()** call, and no message has been queued since.

putq() only looks at the priority band in the first message block of a message. If a high priority message is passed to putq() with a nonzero b_band value, b_band is reset to 0 before placing the message on the queue. If the message is passed to putq() with b_band value that is greater than the number of **qband** structures associated with the queue, **putq()** tries to allocate a new **qband** structure for each band up to and including the band of the message.

putq() is intended to be used from the **put** procedure in the same queue in which the message will be queued. A module should not call **putq()** directly to pass messages to a neighboring module. **putq()** may be used as the $qi\_putp()$ **put** procedure value in either or both of a module's **qinit** structures. This effec-tively bypasses any **put** procedure processing and uses only the module's **ser-vice** procedure(s).

putq() returns 1 on success and 0 on failure.

qenable – enable a queue

void
qenable(q)
        register queue_t *q;

qenable() places the queue pointed at by q on the linked list of queues that are ready to be called by the STREAMS scheduler.

qreply – send a message on a Stream in the reverse direction

```
void
qreply(q, bp)
      register  queue_t  *q;
      mblk_t  *bp;
```

qreply() sends the message pointed at by *bp* up (or down) the Stream in the reverse direction from the queue pointed at by *q*. This is done by locating the partner of *q* [see **OTHERQ()**], and then calling the **put** procedure of that queue's neighbor [as in **putnext()**]. qreply() is typically used to send back a response (M_IOCACK or M_IOCNAK message) to an M_IOCTL message.

qsize – find the number of messages on a queue

```
int
qsize(qp)
      register  queue_t  *qp;
```

qsize() returns the number of messages present in queue *qp*. If there are no messages on the queue, **qsize()** returns 0.

RD – get pointer to the read queue

```
#define  RD(q) ((q)-1)
```

The **RD()** macro accepts a write queue pointer, *q*, as an argument and returns a pointer to the read queue for the same module.

rmvb – remove a message block from a message

```
mblk_t  *
rmvb(mp, bp)
      register  mblk_t  *mp;
      register  mblk_t  *bp;
```

rmvb() removes the message block pointed at by *bp* from the message pointed at by *mp*, and then restores the linkage of the message blocks remaining in the message. **rmvb()** does not free the removed message block. **rmvb()** returns a pointer to the head of the resulting message. If *bp* is not contained in *mp*, rmvb() returns a -1. If there are no message blocks in the resulting message, rmvb() returns a NULL pointer.

rmvq – remove a message from a queue

void
rmvq(q, mp)
      register queue_t *q;
      register mblk_t *mp;

rmvq() removes the message pointed at by *mp* from the message queue in the queue pointed at by *q*, and then restores the linkage of the messages remaining on the queue. If *mp* does not point to a message that is present on the queue *q*, a system panic could result.

splstr – set processor level

#define splstr() spltty()

splstr() increases the system processor level to block interrupts at a level appropriate for STREAMS modules and drivers when they are executing critical portions of their code. splstr() returns the processor level at the time of its invocation. Module developers are expected to use the standard kernel function splx(s), where *s* is the integer value returned by splstr(), to restore the processor level to its previous value after the critical portions of code are passed.

strlog – submit messages for logging

int
strlog(mid, sid, level, flags, fmt, arg1, ...)
      short mid, sid;
      char   level;
      unsigned short flags;
      char   *fmt;
      unsigned arg1;

strlog() submits messages containing specified information to the **log**(7) driver. Required definitions are contained in **<sys/strlog.h>** and **<sys/log.h>**. *mid* is the STREAMS module id number for the module or driver submitting the log message. *sid* is an internal sub-id number usually used to identify a particular minor device of a driver. *level* is a tracing level that allows selective screening of messages from the tracer. *flags* are any combination of:

- SL_ERROR (the message is for the error logger),

- SL_TRACE (the message is for the tracer),

- SL_FATAL (advisory notification of a fatal error),

- SL_NOTIFY (request that a copy of the message be mailed to the system administrator) (Note that SL_NOTIFY is not an option by itself, but rather a modifier to the SL_ERROR flag),

- SL_CONSOLE (log the message to the console),

- SL_WARN (warning message), and

- SL_NOTE (notice the message).

fmt is a **printf**(3S) style format string, except that %s, %e, %E, %g, and %G conversion specifications are not handled. Up to NLOGARGS numeric or character arguments can be provided. [See **log**(7).]

strqget – obtain information about a queue or band of the queue

```
int
strqget(q, what, pri, valp)
        register  queue_t  *q;
        qfields_t  what;
        register  unsigned char  pri;
        long  *valp;
```

strqget() allows modules and drivers to get information about a queue or particular band of the queue. The information is returned in the *long* referenced by *valp*. The fields that can be obtained are defined by the following:

```
typedef enum qfields {
        QHIWAT          = 0,
        QLOWAT          = 1,
        QMAXPSZ         = 2,
        QMINPSZ         = 3,
        QCOUNT          = 4,
        QFIRST          = 5,
        QLAST           = 6,
        QFLAG           = 7,
        QBAD            = 8
} qfields_t;
```

strqget() returns 0 on success and an error number on failure.

strqset – change information about a queue or band of the queue

int
strqset(q, what, pri, val)
        register queue_t *q;
        qfields_t what;
        register unsigned char pri;
        long val;

strqset() allows modules and drivers to change information about a queue or particular band of the queue. The updated information is provided by *val*. This routine returns 0 on success and an error number on failure. If the field is intended to be read-only, then the error EPERM is returned and the field is left unchanged.

testb – check for an available buffer

int
testb(size, pri)
        register size;
        uint pri;

testb() checks for the availability of a message buffer of size *size* without actually retrieving the buffer. **testb()** returns 1 if the buffer is available, and 0 if no buffer is available. A successful return value from **testb()** does not guarantee that a subsequent **allocb()** call will succeed (e.g., in the case of an interrupt routine taking buffers).

pri is as described in **allocb()**.

unbufcall – cancel a **bufcall** request

void
unbufcall(id)
      register int id;

unbufcall() cancels a **bufcall** request. *id* identifies an event in the **bufcall** request.

unlinkb – remove a message block from the head of a message

mblk_t *
unlinkb(bp)
      register mblk_t *bp;

unlinkb() removes the first message block pointed at by *bp* and returns a pointer to the head of the resulting message. **unlinkb()** returns a NULL pointer if there are no more message blocks in the message.

WR – get pointer to the write queue

#define WR(q) ((q)+1)

The **WR()** macro accepts a read queue pointer, *q*, as an argument and returns a pointer to the write queue for the same module.

DKI Interface

With the DKI interface (see Chapter 7), the following STREAMS utilities are implemented as functions: **datamsg, OTHERQ, putnext, RD, splstr,** and **WR.** **<sys/ddi.h>** must be included after **<sys/stream.h>** to get function definitions instead of the macros.

Utility Routine Summary

ROUTINE	DESCRIPTION
adjmsg	trim bytes in a message
allocb	allocate a message block
backq	get pointer to the queue behind a given queue
bcanput	test for flow control in a given priority band
bufcall	recover from failure of allocb
canput	test for room in a queue
copyb	copy a message block
copymsg	copy a message
datamsg	test whether message is a data message
dupb	duplicate a message block descriptor
dupmsg	duplicate a message
enableok	re-allow a queue to be scheduled for service
esballoc	allocate message and data blocks
flushband	flush messages in a given priority band
flushq	flush a queue
freeb	free a message block
freemsg	free all message blocks in a message
getadmin	return a pointer to a module
getmid	return the module id
getq	get a message from a queue
insq	put a message at a specific place in a queue
linkb	concatenate two messages into one
msgdsize	get the number of data bytes in a message
noenable	prevent a queue from being scheduled
OTHERQ	get pointer to the mate queue
pullupmsg	concatenate and align bytes in a message
putbq	return a message to the beginning of a queue
putctl	put a control message
putctl1	put a control message with a one-byte parameter
putnext	put a message to the next queue
putq	put a message on a queue
qenable	enable a queue
qreply	send a message on a Stream in the reverse direction
qsize	find the number of messages on a queue
RD	get pointer to the read queue
rmvb	remove a message block from a message
rmvq	remove a message from a queue
splstr	set processor level

strlog	submit messages for logging
strqget	obtain information on a queue or a band of the queue
strqset	change information on a queue or a band of the queue
testb	check for an available buffer
unbufcall	cancel **bufcall** request
unlinkb	remove a message block from the head of a message
WR	get pointer to the write queue

D Appendix D: Debugging

Debugging   D-1
crash(1M) Command   D-2
Dump Module Example   D-6
Error and Trace Logging   D-17

Debugging

This appendix provides some tools to assist in debugging STREAMS-based applications.

The kernel routine **cmn_err()** allows printing of formatted strings on a system console. It displays a specified message on the console and/or stores it in the **putbuf** that is a circular array in the kernel and contains output from **cmn_err()**. Its format is:

```
#include <sys/cmn_err.h>
cmn_err (level, fmt, ARGS)
int level;
char *fmt;
int ARGS;
```

where *level* can take the following values:

- CE_CONT - may be used as simple **printf()**. It is used to continue another message or to display an informative message not associated with an error.

- CE_NOTE - report system events. It is used to display a message preceded with NOTICE:. This message is used to report system events that do not necessarily require user action, but may interest the system administrator. For example, a sector on a disk needing to be accessed repeatedly before it can be accessed correctly might be such an event.

- CE_WARN - system events that require user action. This is used to display a message preceded with WARNING:. This message is used to report system events that require immediate attention, such as those where if an action is not taken, the system may panic. For example, when a peripheral device does not initialize correctly, this level should be used.

- CE_PANIC - system panic. This is used to display a message preceded with PANIC:. Drivers should specify this level only under the most severe conditions. A valid use of this level is when the system cannot continue to function. If the error is recoverable, not essential to continued system operation, do not panic the system. This level halts all processing.

fmt and *ARGS* are passed to the kernel routine **printf()** that runs at **splhi()** and should be used sparingly. If the first character of *fmt* begins with ! (an exclamation point) output is directed to **putbuf**. **putbuf** can be accessed with the **crash(1M)** command. If the destination character begins with ^ (a caret) output goes to the console. If no destination character is specified, the message is directed to both the **putbuf** array and the console.

cmn_err() appends each *fmt* with "\n", except for the CE_CONT level, even when a message is sent to the **putbuf** array. *ARGS* specifies a set arguments passed when the message is displayed. Valid specifications are *%s* (string), *%u* (unsigned decimal), *%d* (decimal), *%o* (octal), and *%x* (hexadecimal). cmn_err() does not accept length specifications in conversion specifications. For example, *%3d* is ignored.

crash(1M) Command

The **crash**(1M) command is used to examine kernel structures interactively. It can be used on system dump and on active system.

The following lists **crash** functions related to STREAMS:

- **dbfree** - print data block header free list.
- **dblock** - print allocated Streams data block headers.
- **linkblk** - print the **linkblk** table.
- **mbfree** - print free Streams message block headers.
- **mblock** - print allocated Streams message block headers.
- **pty** - print pseudo ttys presently configured. The -l option gives information on the line discipline module **ldterm**, the -h option provides information on the pseudo-tty emulation module **ptem**, and the -s option gives information on the packet module **pckt**.
- **qrun** - print a list of scheduled queues.
- **queue** - print STREAMS queues.
- **stream** - print the **stdata** table.
- **strstat** - print STREAMS statistics.
- **tty** - print the tty table. The -l option prints out details about the line discipline module.

Programmer's Guide: STREAMS

The **crash** functions **dblock, linkblk, mblock, queue,** and **stream** take an optional table entry argument or address that is the address of the data structure. The **strstat** command gives information about STREAMS event cells and **linkblks** in addition to message blocks, data blocks, queues, and Streams. On the output report, the CONFIG column represents the number of structures currently configured. It may change because resources are allocated as needed.

The following example is a sample output from **crash**(1M):

NOTE
Output from **crash**(1M) may look different depending on what version of UNIX System V is used. Examples in the section were produced using UNIX System V Release 3.2, and they were also formatted for easier reference.

```
# /usr/sbin/crash
dumpfile = /dev/mem, namelist = /stand/unix, outfile = stdout

> strstat
ITEM                        CONFIGURED      ALLOCATED       FREE
streams                     36              13              23
queues                      288             62              226
message blocks              5441            21              5420
data block totals           4353            22              4332
data block size    4        2048            1               2048
data block size    16       1024            0               1024
data block size    64       1024            16              1008
data block size    128      128             0               128
data block size    256      64              0               64
data block size    512      32              0               32
data block size    1024     12              1               11
data block size    2048     20              4               16
data block size    4096     1               0               1

Count of scheduled queues:  0

> dblock
DATA BLOCK TABLE SIZE = 4353
SLOT     CLASS     SIZE     RCNT     TYPE     BASE       LIMIT        FREEP
15       7         2048     1        data     4030a000   4030a800     -
16       7         2048     1        data     4030a800   4030b000     -
> mblock
MESSAGE BLOCK TABLE SIZE = 5441
SLOT     NEXT      CONT     PREV     RPTR               WPTR             DATAB
5384     5429      -        5371     4032bd80           4032bdac         1271
5391     -         -        -        4032be40           4032be40         1274
5433     5394      -        5360     4032bb00           4043bb2c         1261

> stream
STREAM TABLE SIZE = 36
SLOT WRQ IOCB VNODE     PGRP     IOCID     IOCWT WOFF      ERR     FLAG
0        1    -   42363177 4412     9616      0         0         0       rslp
1        7    -   42804683 0        213       0         0         0       plex
2        11   -   49648021 0        214       0         0         0
```

The following example illustrates debugging of a line printer. Knowledge of the data structures of the driver is needed for debugging. The example starts with the following data structure of the line printer driver:

```
struct lp {
        short lp_flags;
        queue_t *lp_qptr;   /* back pointer to write queue */
};

extern struct lp lp_lp[];
```

The first command nm lp_lp prints the value and type for the line printer
driver data structure. The second command rd 40275750 20 prints 20 values
starting from the location 40275750 (note that the function rd is alias of od).
The third command size queue gives the size of the **queue** structure. The
next two functions again give the 20 values starting at the specified locations in
the hexadecimal format. The command rd -c 4032bf40 32 gives the character representation of the value in the given location. The option -x gives a
value in the hexadecimal representation and the option -a produces the same
in the ASCII format.

```
/usr/sbin/crash
dumpfile - /dev/mem, namelist = /stand/unix, outfile = crash.out

> nm lp_lp
lp_lp   40275750   bss

> rd 40275750 20
40275750:  00000000  00000000  00000000  40262f60
40275760:  00000000  00000000  00000000  00000000
40275770:  00000000  00000000  00000000  00000000
40275780:  00000000  00000000  00000000  00000000
40275790:  00000000  00000000  00000000  00000000

> size queue
36

> rd 40262f60 20
40262f60:  4017315c  402624a4  4026257c  00000000
40262f70:  00000000  40275758  0200002e  00000200
40262f80:  02000100  00000000  00000000  00000000
40262f90:  00000000  00000000  00000000  00000000
40262fa0:  00000000  00000000  00000000  00000000
```

(continued on next page)

```
> rd 402624a4 20
402624a4:  40262624  00000000  00000000  4032bf40
402624b4:  4032bf5f  40236884  4026233c  00000000
402624c4:  00000000  40331fd9  40331fd9  00000000
402624d4:  00000000  00000000  00000000  4032bf80
402623e4:  4032bf80  40236894  40262564  00000000

> rd -c 4032bf40 32
4032bf40:  l i t t l e   r e d   l i g h t
4042bf50:  o n   t h e   h i g h w a y

> rd -x 40262624 20
40252624:  40262594  402624a4  00000000  4032bd40
40262634:  4032bd5f  40236804  00000000  00000000
40262644:  00000000  4030c800  4030c800  402319e4
40262654:  00000000  00000000  00000000  4032be40
40262664:  4032be40  40236844  4026239c  00000000

> rd -a 4032bd40 31
little red light on the highway
```

Dump Module Example

The following dump module example represents only one way of debugging STREAMS modules and drivers; using the **strlog** function is another way. **strlog** is discussed later in the chapter.

The dump module (its creator calls it "primitive but handy at times when a driver is not working properly or some other anomalies occur") has advantages over logging messages in that it will print all data passing to and from the module in the order they are received. One can modify this module to print more detailed information on the particular types of messages (e.g., special M_IOCTL messages) that a user is interested in.

This dump module is useful for looking at the sequence of messages passing on a Stream and to know who is doing what and when. For example, if a user is faced with a situation where a module is not passing through some messages correctly and user processes are hung waiting the messages to be returned, this module may help diagnose the problem. Another example is a situation where

M_IOCTL messages are causing problems in a driver. This module can help to pinpoint the messages and their sequence without going back to the source of the programs and trying to figure out what is happening in particular cases. This module is also useful in debugging inter-module communication protocols (e.g., M_CTL or M_PROTO between two cooperating modules).

This example should not be used *as is* for debugging in more than one place. However, it can be modified quite easily to print minor device numbers along with each message, so that it can be inserted in two places around a particular module for looking at both ends of the module simultaneously.

There are two disadvantages in this module approach: this module cannot be used to debug the console driver, and it drastically alters the timing characteristics of the machine and the Stream in which it is running. Therefore, this example module is not meant to be used for discovering timing-related problems such as interrupt timing and priority level changes.

The dump module is given here only as an illustration and a possible aid to developers in debugging their applications. First the appropriate header file is provided followed by the master file and the code.

```
/*
 * dump.h Header for DUMP module.
 */
#define DUMPIOC              ('Q' << 8)          /* define to be unique */

#define DUMP_VERB  (DUMPIOC | 1)
#define DUMP_TERSE (DUMPIOC | 2)

#define D_FREE      0          /* slot free */
#define D_USED      1          /* slot in use */

#define D_OUT       1          /* outgoing data */
#define D_IN        2          /* incoming data */

#define D_VERB      0x01     /* verbose option on */

struct dm_str {
        char  dm_use;                   /* non-zero if in use */
        char  dm_state;                 /* for state during console output */
        char  dm_flags;                 /* flags */
};
```

```
*
* DUMP - STREAMS message dump module
*
*FLAG    #VEC     PREFIX    SOFT    #DEV    IPL    DEPENDENCIES/VARIABLES
m        -        dump
                                                   dm_users[#C] (%c%c%c)
                                                   dm_ucnt (%i) - (#C)
```

```
/*
 *         DUMP module.  This module prints data and ioctls going to and
 *         from a device in real time. Printout is on the console.
 *         Usage is to push it into a Stream between any other modules.
 *
 *         DUMP_VERB    Verbose printing of M_DATA (default)
 *         DUMP_TERSE   Terse printing of data (optional)
 *
 *         The messages it prints begin with "I:" for incoming, "O:" for
 *         outgoing data.  "Ci" or "Co" are for non-data (control) messages.
 *         Data is printed in character or hexadecimal format delimited
 *         by (( and )) at message boundaries.
 */

#include "sys/types.h"              /* required in all modules and drivers */
#include "sys/stream.h"             /* required in all modules and drivers */
#include "sys/param.h"
#include "sys/fcntl.h"
#include "sys/cmn_err.h"
#include "dump.h"  /* local ioctls */
#include <sys/termio.h>

static struct module_info dumprinfo = { 0x6475, "dump", 0, INFPSZ, 0, 0 };
static struct module_info dumpwinfo = { 0x6475, "dump", 0, INFPSZ, 0, 0 };
static int dumpopen(), dumprput(), dumpwput(), dumpclose();

static struct qinit rinit = {
        dumprput, NULL, dumpopen, dumpclose, NULL, &dumprinfo, NULL };

static struct qinit winit = {
        dumpwput, NULL, NULL,     NULL,      NULL, &dumpwinfo, NULL };

struct streamtab dumpinfo = { &rinit, &winit, NULL, NULL };
```

(continued on next page)

Programmer's Guide: STREAMS

```
extern int dm_ucnt;                              /* count of dm_users */

extern struct dm_str dm_users[];      /* 1 dm_str per user */

/*
 * dumpopen        Open us and turn us on.
 */
static int
dumpopen(q, dev, flag, sflag)
        queue_t  *q;       /* pointer to read queue */
        dev_t    dev;      /* major/minor device number */
        int      flag;     /* file open flag */
        int      sflag;    /* stream open flag */
{
        register int i;

        if (q->q_ptr != NULL) {
                cmn_err(CE_CONT, "^DUMP: re-open slot %d0,
                    ((struct dm_str *)q->q_ptr - dm_users));
                if (flag & O_NDELAY)
                        cmn_err(CE_CONT, "^DUMP: re-open: O_NDELAY set0);
                return 0;
        }
        for (i = 0; i < dm_ucnt; i++) {
                if (dm_users[i].dm_use == D_FREE) {
                        dm_users[i].dm_use = D_USED;
                        dm_users[i].dm_state = 0;
                        dm_users[i].dm_flags = D_VERB;
                        q->q_ptr = (caddr_t)&dm_users[i];
                        WR(q)->q_ptr = (caddr_t)&dm_users[i];
                        if (flag & O_NDELAY)
                                cmn_err(CE_CONT, "^DUMP: open: O_NDELAY set0);
                        return 0;
                }
        }
        return OPENFAIL;
}
/*
 * dumpclose       Close us down.
 */
static int
dumpclose(q, flag)
        queue_t  *q;       /* pointer to the read queue */
        int      flag;     /* file flags */
{
```

(continued on next page)

```
        struct dm_str *d;

        d = (struct dm_str *)q->q_ptr;
        d->dm_use = D_FREE;
        d->dm_flags = 0;
        q->q_ptr = 0;
        WR(q)->q_ptr = 0;
        return;
}
/*
 * dumpwput      Put procedure for WRITE side of module.  Gathers data
 *               from all passing M_DATA messages.  Calls routine to
 *               handle ioctl calls.
 */
static int
dumpwput(q, mp)
        queue_t *q;         /* pointer to the write queue */
        mblk_t *mp;         /* message pointer */
{
        struct iocblk *iocp;
        struct dm_str *d;

        d = (struct dm_str *)q->q_ptr;
        if (mp->b_datap->db_type == M_IOCTL) {
                iocp = (struct iocblk *)mp->b_rptr;
                if ((iocp->ioc_cmd & DUMPIOC) == DUMPIOC) {
                        dumpioc(q, mp);
                        return;
                } else {
                        cmn_err(CE_CONT, "^0o: M_IOCTL %x, cnt %d ",
                                iocp->ioc_cmd, iocp->ioc_count);
                        if ((d->dm_flags & D_VERB) && mp->b_cont)
                                dumpshow(mp->b_cont, iocp->ioc_cmd);
                        d->dm_state = 0;
                        putnext(q, mp);
                }
        } else if (mp->b_datap->db_type == M_DATA) {
                dumpgather(q, mp, D_OUT);
                putnext(q, mp);
        } else {
                dumpctl(q, mp, d, D_OUT);
                d->dm_state = 0;
                putnext(q, mp);     /* pass message through */
        }
}
/*
```

(continued on next page)

```
 * dumprput        Read side put procedure.  Snag all M_DATA messages.
 */
static int
dumprput(q, mp)
        queue_t *q;         /* pointer to the read queue */
        mblk_t *mp;         /* message pointer */
{
        struct dm_str *d;

        d = (struct dm_str *)q->q_ptr;
        if (mp->b_datap->db_type == M_DATA) {
                dumpgather(q, mp, D_IN);
        } else {
                dumpctl(q, mp, d, D_IN);
                d->dm_state = 0;
        }
        putnext(q, mp);     /* pass message through */
}
/*
 * dumpgather       Gather info from this data message and print it.
 *                  We don't "putnext", as that is done by the caller,
 *                  in the appropriate direction.
 */
dumpgather(q, mp, dir)
        queue_t *q;
        mblk_t *mp;
        int dir;
{
        register struct dm_str *d;
        register int sx;
        register unsigned char *readp;
        register mblk_t *tmp;
        int counter;
        char junk[2];

        d = (struct dm_str *)q->q_ptr;
        /*
         * when dumping to console, check state & print I/O if it
         * changes.
         */
        if (d->dm_state != dir) {
                d->dm_state = dir;
                cmn_err(CE_CONT, "^11s", ((dir == D_IN) ? "I:" : "O:"));
        }
        if ((!mp->b_datap) ||
            ((mp->b_rptr == mp->b_wptr) && (mp->b_cont == NULL))) {
```

(continued on next page)

```
                    /* Trap zero length messages going past! */
                    cmn_err(CE_CONT, "^DUMP: 0 len data msg %s.0,
                            (dir == D_OUT) ? "OUT" : "IN");
                    return;
            }
            cmn_err(CE_CONT, "^ ({");
            tmp = mp;
            counter = 0;
            sx = splstr();
            junk[1] = ' ';
more:
            readp = tmp->b_rptr;
            while (readp < tmp->b_wptr) {
                if (d->dm_flags & D_VERB) {
                    if ((*readp >= ' ') && (*readp <= '~') && !(*readp & 0x80)) {
                            junk[0] = *readp;
                            cmn_err(CE_CONT, "^ %s", junk);
                    } else
                            cmn_err(CE_CONT, "^ 0x%x", *readp);
                } else {
                    ++counter;
                }
                ++readp;
            }
            if ((tmp->b_cont) && (tmp->b_datap->db_type == M_DATA)) {
                    tmp = tmp->b_cont;
                    goto more;
            }
            if (!(d->dm_flags & D_VERB))
                    cmn_err(CE_CONT, "^%d ", counter);
            cmn_err(CE_CONT, "^}} ");
            if (tmp->b_cont && (tmp->b_datap->db_type != M_DATA))
                    cmn_err(CE_CONT, "^0UMP: non-data b_cont0);
            splx(sx);
}
/*
 * dumpioc       Completely handle one of our ioctl calls, including the
 *               qreply of the message.
 */
dumpioc(q, mp)

        queue_t *q;
        mblk_t *mp;
{
        register struct iocblk *iocp;
        register struct dm_str *d, *ret;
```

(continued on next page)

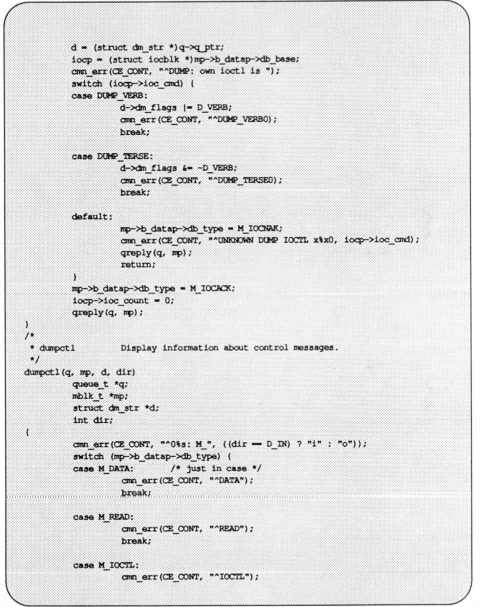

```
        d = (struct dm_str *)q->q_ptr;
        iocp = (struct ioclk *)mp->b_datap->db_base;
        cmn_err(CE_CONT, "^DUMP: own ioctl is ");
        switch (iocp->ioc_cmd) {
        case DUMP_VERB:
                d->dm_flags |= D_VERB;
                cmn_err(CE_CONT, "^DUMP_VERB0);
                break;

        case DUMP_TERSE:
                d->dm_flags &= ~D_VERB;
                cmn_err(CE_CONT, "^DUMP_TERSE0);
                break;

        default:
                mp->b_datap->db_type = M_IOCNAK;
                cmn_err(CE_CONT, "^UNKNOWN DUMP IOCTL x%x0, iocp->ioc_cmd);
                qreply(q, mp);
                return;
        }
        mp->b_datap->db_type = M_IOCACK;
        iocp->ioc_count = 0;
        qreply(q, mp);
}
/*
 * dumpctl        Display information about control messages.
 */
dumpctl(q, mp, d, dir)
        queue_t *q;
        mblk_t *mp;
        struct dm_str *d;
        int dir;
{
        cmn_err(CE_CONT, "^0%s: M_", ((dir == D_IN) ? "i" : "o"));
        switch (mp->b_datap->db_type) {
        case M_DATA:        /* just in case */
                cmn_err(CE_CONT, "^DATA");
                break;

        case M_READ:
                cmn_err(CE_CONT, "^READ");
                break;

        case M_IOCTL:
                cmn_err(CE_CONT, "^IOCTL");
```

(continued on next page)

```
                break;
        case M_IOCACK:
                cmn_err(CE_CONT, "^IOCACK");
                break;

        case M_IOCNAK:
                cmn_err(CE_CONT, "^IOCNAK");
                break;

        case M_IOCDATA:
                cmn_err(CE_CONT, "^IOCDATA");
                break;

        case M_CTL:
                cmn_err(CE_CONT, "^CTL");
                break;

        case M_PROTO:
                cmn_err(CE_CONT, "^PROTO");
                break;

        case M_PCPROTO:
                cmn_err(CE_CONT, "^PCPROTO");
                break;

        case M_BREAK:
                cmn_err(CE_CONT, "^BREAK");
                break;

        case M_DELAY:
                cmn_err(CE_CONT, "^DELAY");
                break;

        case M_PASSFP:
                cmn_err(CE_CONT, "^PASSFP");
                break;

        case M_SETOPTS:
                cmn_err(CE_CONT, "^SETOPTS");
                break;

        case M_SIG:
                cmn_err(CE_CONT, "^SIG");
                cmn_err(CE_CONT, "^ (%d) ", (int)*mp->b_rptr);
                break;
```

(continued on next page)

Programmer's Guide: STREAMS

```
        case M_ERROR:
                cmn_err(CE_CONT, "^ERROR");
                break;

        case M_HANGUP:
                cmn_err(CE_CONT, "^HANGUP");
                break;

        case M_FLUSH:
                cmn_err(CE_CONT, "^FLUSH");
                break;

        case M_PCSIG:
                cmn_err(CE_CONT, "^PCSIG");
                cmn_err(CE_CONT, "^ (%d) ", (int)*mp->b_rptr);
                break;

        case M_COPYOUT:
                cmn_err(CE_CONT, "^COPYOUT");
                break;

        case M_COPYIN:
                cmn_err(CE_CONT, "^COPYIN");
                break;

        case M_START:
                cmn_err(CE_CONT, "^START");
                break;

        case M_STOP:
                cmn_err(CE_CONT, "^STOP");
                break;

        case M_STARTI:
                cmn_err(CE_CONT, "^STARTI");
                break;

        case M_STOPI:
                cmn_err(CE_CONT, "^STOPI");
                break;

        default:
                cmn_err(CE_CONT, "^Unknown! 07 07");
        }
}
```

(continued on next page)

```
/*
 * dumpshow          Display information about known ioctls.
 */
dumpshow(mp, cmd)
        mblk_t *mp;          /* pointer to cont block of ioctl message */
        int cmd; /* ioc_cmd field */
{
        int i;
        struct termio *t;

        /*
         * This is an example of printing data from IOCTL messages that
         * we're interested in.  Add others as needed.
         */
        switch (cmd) {
        case TCSETAF:
                cmn_err(CE_CONT, "^TCSETAF ");
                goto prtall;

        case TCSETA:
                cmn_err(CE_CONT, "^TCSETA ");
                goto prtall;

        case TCSETAW:
                cmn_err(CE_CONT, "^TCSETAW ");
prtall:
                t = (struct termio *)mp->b_rptr;
                cmn_err(CE_CONT, "^if=%x ; of=%x ; cf=%x ; lf=%x0_cc=",
                        t->c_iflag, t->c_oflag, t->c_cflag, t->c_lflag);
                for (i = 0; i < NCC; i++)
                        cmn_err(CE_CONT, "^0x%x ", (int) t->c_cc[i]);
                cmn_err(CE_CONT, "^0);
                break;
        default:
                return;
        }
}
```

The situation with "cooperating modules" that seems to contradict the basic idea of reusability and independence of modules has risen in the internationalization context (see Chapter 12) related to input methods of languages. It turns out that some back-end processing for input methods can be re-used and the size of the kernel reduced from what would be necessary by having two different full modules when only front-end processing needs to be different for different input methods. In this situation, one will save as much space as the size of the back-end module. The way this relates to the dump module is that this dump module can be used to help debug the protocol between the front-end and back-end modules. (The protocol is standard across various front-ends.)

Error and Trace Logging

STREAMS error and trace loggers are provided for debugging and for administering STREAMS modules and drivers. This facility consists of **log**(7), **strace**(1M), **strclean**(1M) **strerr**(1M), and the **strlog** function.

Any module or driver in any Stream can call the STREAMS logging function **strlog**, described in **log**(7). **strlog** is also described in Appendix C. When called, **strlog** will send formatted text to the error logger **strerr**(1M), the trace logger **strace**(1M), or the console logger.

Figure D-1: Error and Trace Logging

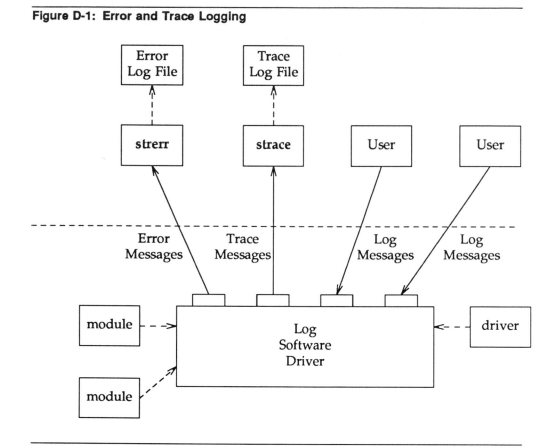

strerr is intended to operate as a daemon process initiated at system startup. A call to **strlog** requesting an error to be logged causes an M_PROTO message to be sent to **strerr**, which formats the contents and places them in a daily file. The utility **strclean**(1M) is provided to purge daily log files that have not been modified for 3 days.

A call to **strlog** requesting trace information to be logged causes a similar M_PROTO message to be sent to **strace**(1M), which places it in a user designated file. **strace** is intended to be initiated by a user. The user can designate the modules/drivers and severity level of the messages to be accepted for logging by **strace**.

A user process can submit its own M_PROTO messages to the log driver for inclusion in the logger of its choice through **putmsg**(2). The messages must be in the same format required by the logging processes and will be switched to the logger(s) requested in the message.

The output to the log files is formatted, ASCII text. The files can be processed by standard system commands such as **grep**(1) or **ed**(1), or by developer-provided routines.

E   Appendix E: Configuration

Configuration

Configuration	E-1
Configuring STREAMS Modules and Drivers	E-1
■ Configuration Examples	E-2
■ Tunable Parameters	E-5
Autopush Facility	E-6
■ User Interface	E-7

Configuration

This appendix contains information about configuring STREAMS modules and drivers into UNIX System V Release 4.0. The information is incremental and presumes the reader is familiar with the configuration mechanism, which may vary on different processors. An example of how to configure a driver and a module is included.

This appendix also includes a list of STREAMS related tunable parameters and describes the autopush facility.

Configuring STREAMS Modules and Drivers

Each character device that is configured into a UNIX system results in an entry being placed in the kernel **cdevsw** table. Entries for STREAMS drivers are also placed in this table. However, because system calls to STREAMS drivers must be processed by the STREAMS routines, the configuration mechanism distinguishes between STREAMS drivers and character device drivers in their associated **cdevsw** entries.

The distinction is contained in the d_str field of the **cdevsw** structure. The d_str field provides the appropriate single entry point for all system calls on STREAMS files, as shown below:

```
extern  struct  cdevsw  {
    .

    .
    struct streamtab *d_str;
} cdevsw[];
```

The configuration mechanism forms the d_str entry name by appending the string "info" to the STREAMS driver prefix. The "info" entry is a pointer to a **streamtab** structure (see Appendix A) that contains pointers to the **qinit** structures for the read and write queues of the driver. The driver must contain the external definition:

```
struct streamtab prefixinfo = { ...
```

If the d_str entry contains a non-null pointer, the operating system will recognize the device as a STREAMS driver and will call the appropriate STREAMS routine. If the entry is null, a traditional character I/O device **cdevsw** interface is used. Note that only the **streamtab** structure must be externally defined in STREAMS drivers and modules. The **streamtab** is used to identify the appropriate **open, close, put, service,** and administration routines. These driver and module routines should generally be declared `static`.

The configuration mechanism supports various combinations of block, character, STREAMS devices, and STREAMS modules. For example, it is possible to identify a device as a block *and* STREAMS device (although this is very unlikely), and entries will be inserted in the appropriate system switch tables.

When a STREAMS module is configured, an **fmodsw** table entry is generated by the configuration mechanism. The **fmodsw** contains the following:

```
#define FMNAMESZ 8


extern struct fmodsw {
        char    f_name[FMNAMESZ+1];
        struct  streamtab *f_str;
        int     *f_flag;   /* same as device flag */
} fmodsw[];
```

where *f_name* is the name of the module used in STREAMS related **ioctl** calls. *f_str* is similar to the *d_str* entry in the **cdevsw** table. It is a pointer to a **streamtab** structure which contains pointers to the **qinit** structures for the read and write queues of this STREAMS module (as in STREAMS drivers). The module must contain the external definition:

```
struct streamtab prefixinfo = { ...
```

Configuration Examples

This section shows examples of configuring the following STREAMS driver and module:

loop　　　　the STREAMS loop-around software driver of Chapter 9

crmod　　　the conversion module of Chapter 8

To configure the STREAMS software (pseudo device) driver, *loop*, and assign values to the driver **extern** variables, the following must appear in the file **/etc/master.d/loop** [see **master(4)**]:

```
* LOOP - STREAMS loop-around software driver
*
*FLAG  #VEC  PREFIX  SOFT  #DEV  IPL   DEPENDENCIES/VARIABLES
fs     -     loop    62    -     -
                                       loop_loop[NLP]  (%i%i)
                                       loop_cnt  (%i)  ={NLP}
$$$
NLP = 2
```

The *flag* field is set to "fs" which signifies that it is a STREAMS driver and a software driver. The *prefix* "loop" requires that the **streamtab** structure for the driver be defined as *loopinfo*. (The prefix cannot exceed four characters.) "62" is an arbitrary, software driver major number. If this field contained "-", an unused software driver major number would be assigned by **drvinstall**(1M). The #*dev* field is "-" which shows that there are no sub-devices. The "-" in the *ipl* field indicates that there is no interrupt priority level for this device. The next field, *dependencies/variables,* is optional and contains a list of other drivers and modules that must be present in the configuration of this driver.

To configure the STREAMS module *crmod*, the following must appear in the file **/etc/master.d/crmod**:

```
* CRMOD stream conversion module
*
*FLAG  #VEC  PREFIX  SOFT  #DEV  IPL   DEPENDENCIES/VARIABLES
m      -     crmd
```

The *flag* field is set to "m" which signifies that it is a STREAMS module. The *prefix* "crmd" (recall that the prefix cannot exceed four characters) requires that the **streamtab** structure for the module be defined as *crmdinfo*. The configuration mechanism uses the name of the **master.d** file (*crmod* in this case) to create the module name field (*f_name*) of the associated **fmodsw** entry. The prefix and module name can be different. However, the module name should be the same as the **master.d** name.

mkboot(1M) should be run on the corresponding object files in the appropriate directories for these master files. Also, if it is desired to have these objects loaded at boot time, then the file **/stand/system** must contain the following entries:

```
INCLUDE: LOOP
INCLUDE: CRMOD
```

Neither of the given examples are hardware drivers. Configuring a STREAMS hardware driver is similar to configuring a character I/O hardware driver.

At times, it is useful to make a module both a module and a driver. There are not many good reasons to do so, but in some cases it's a good way to solve odd problems. It is done in the following way:

We called our module-driver combination *thing* in this description. First, the module open routine is handled differently. We also need to keep the state flag *sflag* that tells for any particular instantiation whether *thing* is to behave as a module or a driver, because **ioctl** handling is usually different depending on whether the *thing* is a driver or a module. Then, we need to make sure that the flags are set properly in the master file. Here is a sample master file for *thing*:

```
*
*FLAG  #VEC   PREFIX SOFT   #DEV   IPL    DEPENDENCIES/VARIABLES
fsm    -      can    52     -      -
                                          canstr[#C]  (%0x40)
                                          can_cnt  (%i) ={#C}

$$$
```

Notice the *flag* field contains "f" for being a Streams driver, "s" for being a software driver, and "m" for being a Streams module. We need to do **drvinstall** (or **mkboot**) and make sure that the module has a character device node in the file system, either as a cloneable driver or a regular driver. Once we have rebooted our system, *thing* can be opened by its name /**dev**/*thing*, or we can push it with `ioctl(fd, I_PUSH, "thing")`.

There is a trick in the open routine where *sflag* is checked:

```
        .
        .
        .
    if (sflag == MODOPEN)
            /* then the module is being pushed */

    else if (sflag == CLONEOPEN)
            /* then its being opened as a cloneable driver */

    else
            /* its being opened as a regular driver */
        .
        .
        .
```

File systems that support STREAMS devices go through **cdevsw** to get the driver open routine. If *d_str* is set, then *thing* is a STREAMS driver, and it goes to the **fmodsw** to get the open routine. When one pushes a Streams module, the push code also goes to the **fmodsw** looking for the module by name. Depending on which way the open routine is called the *sflag* argument will be MODOPEN, CLONEOPEN, or zero.

Tunable Parameters

Certain system parameters referenced by STREAMS are configurable when building a new operating system (see the *System Administrator's Guide* for further details). This can be done by including the appropriate entry in the kernel master file. These parameters are:

NSTRPUSH   Maximum number (should be at least 8) of modules that may be pushed onto a single Stream.

STRMSGSZ   Maximum number of bytes of information that a single system call can pass to a Stream to be placed into the data part of a message (in M_DATA blocks). Any **write**(2) exceeding this size will be broken into multiple messages. A **putmsg**(2) with a data part exceeding this size will fail with ERANGE.

                    If STRMSGSZ is set to 0, then the number of bytes passed to a Stream is effectively infinitive.

STRCTLSZ   Maximum number of bytes of information that a single system call can pass to a Stream to be placed into the control part of a message (in an M_PROTO or M_PCPROTO block). A **putmsg**(2) with a control part exceeding this size will fail with ERANGE.

STRTHRESH   Maximum number of bytes Streams are normally allowed to allocate. When the threshold is passed, users without the appropriate privilege will not be allowed to open Streams, push modules, or write to Streams devices, and ENOSR is returned. The threshold applies only to output side, thus data coming into the system (e.g., console) is not affected and will continue work properly. A value of zero means that there is no threshold.

Autopush Facility

The Autopush facility [see **autopush**(1M)] is a general mechanism that configures the list of modules for a STREAMS device. It automatically pushes a pre-specified list of modules onto the Stream when the STREAMS device is opened and the device is not already open.

The STREAMS Administrative Driver (SAD) [see **sad**(7)] provides an interface to the autopush mechanism. System administrators can open the SAD driver and set or get autopush information on other drivers. The SAD driver caches the list of modules to push for each driver. When the driver is opened, if not already open, the Stream head checks the SAD's cache to see if the device opened has been configured to have modules pushed automatically. If an entry is found, the modules are pushed. If the device has already been opened but has not yet been closed, another open would not cause the list of the pre-specified modules to be pushed again.

Three options are available to configure the module list:

■ Configure for each minor device - that is, a specific major and minor device number.

- Configure for a range of minor devices within a major device.

- Configure for all minor devices within a major device.

When the configuration list is cleared, a range of minor devices has to be cleared as a range and not in parts.

User Interface

The SAD driver can be accessed via the node **/dev/sad/admin** or **/dev/sad/user**. After the device is initialized, a program can be run to perform any needed autopush configuration. The program should open the SAD driver, read a configuration file to find out what modules are needed to be configured for which devices, format the information into **strapush** structures, and perform the necessary SAD_SAP ioctls.

All autopush operations are performed through an **ioctl(2)** command to set or get autopush information. Only the superuser may set autopush information, but any user may get the autopush information for a device.

The **ioctl** is a form of `ioctl(fd, cmd, arg)`, where *fd* is the file descriptor of the SAD driver, *cmd* is either SAD_SAP (set autopush information) or SAD_GAP (get autopush information), and *arg* is a pointer to the structure **strapush**.

The structure **strapush** is defined as:

```
/*
 * maximum number of modules that can be pushed on a Stream using the
 * autopush feature should be less than NSTRPUSH
 */
#define MAXAPUSH  8

/* autopush information common to user and kernel */

struct apcommon {
    uint  apc_cmd;         /* command - see below */
    long  apc_major;       /* major device number */
    long  apc_minor;       /* minor device number */
    long  apc_lastminor;   /* last minor device number for range */
    uint  apc_npush;       /* number of modules to push */
};

/* ap_cmd - various options of autopush */

#define SAP_CLEAR  0    /* remove configuration list */
#define SAP_ONE    1    /* configure one minor device */
#define SAP_RANGE  2    /* configure range of minor devices */
#define SAP_ALL    3    /* configure all minor devices */

/* format of autopush ioctls */

struct strapush {
    struct apcommon sap_common;
    char    sap_list[MAXAPUSH] [FMNAMESZ + 1];/* module list */
};

#define sap_cmd           sap_common.apc_cmd
#define sap_major         sap_common.apc_major
#define sap_minor         sap_common.apc_minor
#define sap_lastminor     sap_common.apc_lastminor
#define sap_npush         sap_common.apc_npush
```

A device is identified by its major device number, *sap_major*. The SAD_SAP
ioctl (*sap_cmd*) can take the following options:

- SAP_ONE configures a single minor device, *sap_minor*, of a driver.

- SAP_RANGE configures a range of minor devices from *sap_minor* to
  sap_lastminor, inclusive.

- SAP_ALL configures all minor devices of a device.

- SAP_CLEAR clears the previous settings by removing the entry with the matching *sap_major* and *sap_minor* fields.

The list of modules is specified as a list of module names in *sap_list*. The maximum number of modules to push automatically is defined by MAXAPUSH.

A user may query the current configuration status of a given major/minor device by issuing the SAD_GAP **ioctl** with *sap_major* and *sap_minor* values of the device set. On successful return from this system call, the **strapush** structure will be filled in with the corresponding information for that device.

The following is an example of an autopush configuration file:

```
21  5  0 mod1 mod2        # configure a single minor device
22 -1  0 mod0 mod5 mod9   # configure all minor devices for
                            major 22
39  3 18 mod7             # configure a range of minor
                            devices
```

The first line represents the configuration for a single minor device whose major and minor numbers are 21 and 5 respectively. Two modules, *mod1* and *mod2*, are automatically pushed on the Stream for this minor device. *mod1* is pushed first, and *mod2* is pushed next. The second line represents the configuration for all minor devices whose major number is 22. Three modules, *mod0*, *mod5*, and *mod9*, are pushed automatically on the Stream. The last line represents the configuration for the range of minor devices from 3 to 18 whose major device number is 39. Only the module, *mod7*, is pushed with this configuration.

The maximum number of entries the SAD driver can cache is determined by the tunable parameter NAUTOPUSH found in the SAD driver's master file.

Manual Pages

This appendix has STREAMS related manual pages. The manual pages are given here for easier reference. Some of them are also included in the appropriate sections of the *Programmer's Reference Manual* or *System Administrator's Reference Manual*.

The following manual pages are included:

- **autopush(1M)** - configure automatically pushed STREAMS modules
- **fdetach(1M)** - detach a name from a STREAMS-based file descriptor
- **strace(1M)** - print STREAMS trace messages
- **strchg(1)** - change or query Stream configuration
- **strclean(1M)** - STREAMS error logger cleanup program
- **strerr(1M)** - STREAMS error logger daemon
- **getmsg(2)** - get next message off a Stream
- **poll(2)** - STREAMS input/output multiplexing
- **putmsg(2)** - send a message on a Stream
- **fattach(3C)** - name (attach) a STREAMS file descriptor
- **fdetach(3C)** - disassociate a file name from a named Stream
- **grantpt(3C)** - grant access to the slave pseudo-terminal device
- **isastream(3C)** - determine if a file descriptor is associated with a STREAMS device
- **ptsname(3C)** - get the slave pseudo-terminal device name
- **unlockpt(3C)** - unlock a pseudo-terminal master/slave pair
- **clone(7)** - open a major/minor device a STREAMS driver
- **connld(7)** - gain a unique, non-multiplexed connection to a server
- **console(7)** - STREAMS-based console interface
- **ldterm(7)** - standard STREAMS terminal line discipline module
- **log(7)** - interface to STREAMS error logging and event tracing

- **pckt(7)** - push a PCKT module (packet mode) on the master side
- **ports(7)** - asynchronous communications interface STREAMS driver
- **ptem(7)** - process terminal **ioctl** messages
- **sad(7)** - STREAMS Administrative Driver
- **streamio(7)** - STREAMS **ioctl** commands
- **sxt(7)** - STREAMS-based pseudo-device driver
- **timod(7)** - Transport Interface cooperating STREAMS module
- **tirdwr(7)** - Transport Interface read/write interface STREAMS module
- **xt(7)** - STREAMS-based multiplexed tty driver

NAME

autopush – configures lists of automatically pushed STREAMS modules.

SYNOPSIS

autopush −f *file*

autopush −r −M *major* −m *minor*

autopush −g −M *major* −m *minor*

DESCRIPTION

This command allows one to configure the list of modules to be automatically pushed onto the stream when a device is opened. It can also be used to remove a previous setting or get information on a setting.

The following options apply to autopush:

−f   This option sets up the autopush configuration for each driver according to the information stored in the specified file. An autopush file consists of lines of at least four fields each where the fields are separated by a space as shown below:

       maj_   min_   last_min_   mod1 mod2 ... modn

The first three fields are integers that specify the major device number, minor device number, and last minor device number. The fields following represent the names of modules. If *min_* is -1, then all minor devices of a major driver specified by *maj_* are configured and the value for *last_min_* is ignored. If *last_min_* is 0, then only a single minor device is configured. To configure a range of minor devices for a particular major, *min_* must be less than *last_min_*.

The last fields of a line in the autopush file represent the list of module names where each is separated by a space. The maximum number of modules that can be automatically pushed on a stream is defined to be eight. The modules are pushed in the order they are specified. Comment lines start with a # sign.

−r   This option removes the previous configuration setting of the particular *major* and *minor* device number specified with the −M and −m options respectively. If the values of *major* and *minor* correspond to a setting of a range of minor devices, where *minor* matches the first minor device number in the range, the configuration would be removed for the entire range.

−g   This option gets the current configuration setting of a particular *major* and *minor* device number specified with the −M and −m options respectively. It will also return the starting minor device number if the request corresponds to a setting of a range (as described with the −f option).

SEE ALSO

streamio(7)

Programmer's Guide: STREAMS

NAME

    fdetach – detach a name from a STREAMS-based file descriptor

SYNOPSIS

    fdetach path

DESCRIPTION

    The **fdetach** command detaches a STREAMS-based file descriptor from a name in the file system. *path* is the path name of the object in the file system name space, which was previously attached [see **fattach**(3C)]. The user must be the owner of the file or a user with the appropriate privileges. All subsequent operations on *path* will operate on the file system node and not on the STREAMS file. The permissions and status of the node are restored to the state the node was in before the STREAMS file was attached to it.

SEE ALSO

    fattach(3C), **fdetach**(3C), **streamio**(7).
    Programmer's Guide: STREAMS

NAME

strace – print STREAMS trace messages

SYNOPSIS

strace [*mid sid level*] ...

DESCRIPTION

strace without arguments writes all STREAMS event trace messages from all drivers and modules to its standard output. These messages are obtained from the STREAMS log driver [log(7)]. If arguments are provided they must be in triplets of the form *mid, sid, level*, where *mid* is a STREAMS module ID number, *sid* is a sub-ID number, and *level* is a tracing priority level. Each triplet indicates that tracing messages are to be received from the given module/driver, sub-ID (usually indicating minor device), and priority level equal to or less than the given level. The token all may be used for any member to indicate no restriction for that attribute.

The format of each trace message output is:

<seq> <time> <ticks> <level> <flags> <mid> <sid> <text>

       <seq>   trace sequence number

       <time>   time of message in *hh:mm:ss*

       <ticks>   time of message in machine ticks since boot

       <level>   tracing priority level

       <flags>   E : message is also in the error log
                    F : indicates a fatal error
                    N : mail was sent to the system administrator

       <mid>   module ID number of source

       <sid>   sub-ID number of source

       <text>   formatted text of the trace message

Once initiated, strace will continue to execute until terminated by the user.

EXAMPLES

Output all trace messages from the module or driver whose module ID is 41:

      strace 41 all all

Output those trace messages from driver/module ID 41 with sub-IDs 0, 1, or 2:

      strace 41 0 1 41 1 1 41 2 0

Messages from sub-IDs 0 and 1 must have a tracing level less than or equal to 1. Those from sub-ID 2 must have a tracing level of 0.

SEE ALSO

log(7)
Programmer's Guide: STREAMS

NOTES

Due to performance considerations, only one strace process is permitted to open the STREAMS log driver at a time. The log driver has a list of the triplets specified in the command invocation, and compares each potential trace message against this list to decide if it should be formatted and sent up to the **strace** process. Hence, long lists of triplets will have a greater impact on overall STREAMS performance. Running **strace** will have the most impact on the timing of the modules and drivers generating the trace messages that are sent to the **strace** process. If trace messages are generated faster than the **strace** process can handle them, then some of the messages will be lost. This last case can be determined by examining the sequence numbers on the trace messages output.

NAME

strchg, strconf – change or query stream configuration

SYNOPSIS

strchg –h *module1* [, *module2* . . .]
strchg –p [–a | –u *module*]
strchg –f *file*
strconf [–t | –m *module*]

DESCRIPTION

These commands are used to alter or query the configuration of the stream associated with the user's standard input. The strchg command pushes modules on
and/or pops modules off the stream. The strconf command queries the
configuration of the stream. Only the super-user or owner of a STREAMS device
may alter the configuration of that stream.

With the –h option, strchg pushes modules onto a stream; it takes as arguments
the names of one or more pushable streams modules. These modules are pushed
in order; that is, *module1* is pushed first, *module2* is pushed second, etc.

The –p option pops modules off the stream. With the –p option alone, strchg
pops the topmost module from the stream. With the –p and –a options, all the
modules above the topmost driver are popped. When the –p option is followed
by –u *module*, then all modules above but not including *module* are popped off the
stream. The –a and –u options are mutually exclusive.

With the –f option, the user can specify a *file* that contains a list of modules
representing the desired configuration of the stream. Each module name must
appear on a separate line where the first name represents the topmost module
and the last name represents the module that should be closest to the driver. The
strchg command will determine the current configuration of the stream and pop
and push the necessary modules in order to end up with the desired
configuration.

The –h, –f and –p options are mutually exclusive.

Invoked without any arguments, strconf prints a list of all the modules in the
stream as well as the topmost driver. The list is printed with one name per line
where the first name printed is the topmost module on the stream (if one exists)
and the last item printed is the name of the driver. With the –t option, only the
topmost module (if one exists) is printed. The –m option determines if the named
module is present on a stream. If it is, strconf prints the message yes and
returns zero. If not, strconf prints the message no and returns a non-zero value.
The –t and –m options are mutually exclusive.

EXAMPLES

The following command pushes the module ldterm on the stream associated
with the user's standard input:

       strchg –h ldterm

The following command pops the topmost module from the stream associated
with /dev/term/24. The user must be the owner of this device or the super-
user.

        strchg -p < /dev/term/24

If the file fileconf contains the following:

        compat
        ldterm
        ptem

then the command

        strchg -f fileconf

will configure the user's standard input stream so that the module ptem is pushed over the driver, followed by ldterm and compat closest to the stream head.

The strconf command with no arguments lists the modules and topmost driver on the stream; for a stream that has only the module ldterm pushed above the ports driver, it would produce the following output:

        ldterm
        ports

The following command asks if ldterm is on the stream

        strconf -m ldterm

and produces the following output while returning an exit status of 0:

        yes

SEE ALSO

streamio(7) in the *Programmer's Guide: STREAMS*.

DIAGNOSTICS

strchg returns zero on success. It prints an error message and returns non-zero status for various error conditions, including usage error, bad module name, too many modules to push, failure of an ioctl on the stream, or failure to open *file* from the -f option.

strconf returns zero on success (for the -m or -t option, "success" means the named or topmost module is present). It returns a non-zero status if invoked with the -m or -t option and the module is not present. It prints an error message and returns non-zero status for various error conditions, including usage error or failure of an ioctl on the stream.

NOTES

If the user is neither the owner of the stream nor the super-user, the strchg command will fail. If the user does not have read permissions on the stream and is not the super-user, the strconf command will fail.

If modules are pushed in the wrong order, one could end up with a stream that does not function as expected. For ttys, if the line discipline module is not pushed in the correct place, one could have a terminal that does not respond to any commands.

NAME
strclean – STREAMS error logger cleanup program

SYNOPSIS
strclean [–d *logdir*] [–a *age*]

DESCRIPTION
strclean is used to clean up the STREAMS error logger directory on a regular basis (for example, by using cron. By default, all files with names matching error.* in /var/adm/streams that have not been modified in the last three days are removed. A directory other than /var/adm/streams can be specified using the –d option. The maximum age in days for a log file can be changed using the –a option.

EXAMPLE
strclean –d /var/adm/streams –a 3

has the same result as running strclean with no arguments.

FILES
/var/adm/streams/error.*

SEE ALSO
cron(1M), strerr(1M)
Programmer's Guide: STREAMS

NOTES
strclean is typically run from cron on a daily or weekly basis.

NAME

strerr – STREAMS error logger daemon

SYNOPSIS

strerr

DESCRIPTION

strerr receives error log messages from the STREAMS log driver [log(7)] and appends them to a log file. The error log files produced reside in the directory /var/adm/streams, and are named error.*mm–dd*, where *mm* is the month and *dd* is the day of the messages contained in each log file.

The format of an error log message is:

<seq> <time> <ticks> <flags> <mid> <sid> <text>

<seq>	error sequence number
<time>	time of message in hh:mm:ss
<ticks>	time of message in machine ticks since boot priority level
<flags>	T : the message was also sent to a tracing process F : indicates a fatal error N : send mail to the system administrator
<mid>	module ID number of source
<sid>	sub-ID number of source
<text>	formatted text of the error message

Messages that appear in the error log are intended to report exceptional conditions that require the attention of the system administrator. Those messages which indicate the total failure of a STREAMS driver or module should have the F flag set. Those messages requiring the immediate attention of the administrator will have the N flag set, which causes the error logger to send the message to the system administrator via mail. The priority level usually has no meaning in the error log but will have meaning if the message is also sent to a tracer process.

Once initiated, strerr continues to execute until terminated by the user. It is commonly executed asynchronously.

FILES

/var/adm/streams/error.*mm–dd*

SEE ALSO

log(7)
Programmer's Guide: STREAMS

NOTES

Only one strerr process at a time is permitted to open the STREAMS log driver.

If a module or driver is generating a large number of error messages, running the error logger will cause a degradation in STREAMS performance. If a large burst of messages are generated in a short time, the log driver may not be able to deliver some of the messages. This situation is indicated by gaps in the sequence numbering of the messages in the log files.

NAME

getmsg – get next message off a stream

SYNOPSIS

```
#include <stropts.h>

int getmsg(int fd, struct strbuf *ctlptr,
                struct strbuf *dataptr, int *flagsp);

int getpmsg(int fd, struct strbuf *ctlptr,
                struct strbuf *dataptr, int *bandp, int *flagsp);
```

DESCRIPTION

getmsg retrieves the contents of a message [see intro(2)] located at the stream head read queue from a STREAMS file, and places the contents into user specified buffer(s). The message must contain either a data part, a control part, or both. The data and control parts of the message are placed into separate buffers, as described below. The semantics of each part is defined by the STREAMS module that generated the message.

The function getpmsg does the same thing as getmsg, but provides finer control over the priority of the messages received. Except where noted, all information pertaining to getmsg also pertains to getpmsg.

fd specifies a file descriptor referencing an open stream. *ctlptr* and *dataptr* each point to a strbuf structure, which contains the following members:

```
int maxlen;     /* maximum buffer length */
int len;        /* length of data */
char *buf;      /* ptr to buffer */
```

buf points to a buffer in which the data or control information is to be placed, and maxlen indicates the maximum number of bytes this buffer can hold. On return, len contains the number of bytes of data or control information actually received, or 0 if there is a zero-length control or data part, or -1 if no data or control information is present in the message. *flagsp* should point to an integer that indicates the type of message the user is able to receive. This is described later.

ctlptr is used to hold the control part from the message and *dataptr* is used to hold the data part from the message. If *ctlptr* (or *dataptr*) is NULL or the maxlen field is −1, the control (or data) part of the message is not processed and is left on the stream head read queue. If *ctlptr* (or *dataptr*) is not NULL and there is no corresponding control (or data) part of the messages on the stream head read queue, len is set to −1. If the maxlen field is set to 0 and there is a zero-length control (or data) part, that zero-length part is removed from the read queue and len is set to 0. If the maxlen field is set to 0 and there are more than zero bytes of control (or data) information, that information is left on the read queue and len is set to 0. If the maxlen field in *ctlptr* or *dataptr* is less than, respectively, the control or data part of the message, maxlen bytes are retrieved. In this case, the remainder of the message is left on the stream head read queue and a non-zero return value is provided, as described below under DIAGNOSTICS.

By default, getmsg processes the first available message on the stream head read queue. However, a user may choose to retrieve only high priority messages by setting the integer pointed by *flagsp* to RS_HIPRI. In this case, getmsg processes the next message only if it is a high priority message. If the integer pointed by *flagsp* is 0, getmsg retrieves any message available on the stream head read queue. In this case, on return, the integer pointed to by *flagsp* will be set to RS_HIPRI if a high priority message was retrieved, or 0 otherwise.

For getpmsg, the flags are different. *flagsp* points to a bitmask with the following mutually-exclusive flags defined: MSG_HIPRI, MSG_BAND, and MSG_ANY. Like getmsg, getpmsg processes the first available message on the stream head read queue. A user may choose to retrieve only high-priority messages by setting the integer pointed to by *flagsp* to MSG_HIPRI and the integer pointed to by *bandp* to 0. In this case, getpmsg will only process the next message if it is a high-priority message. In a similar manner, a user may choose to retrieve a message from a particular priority band by setting the integer pointed to by *flagsp* to MSG_BAND and the integer pointed to by *bandp* to the priority band of interest. In this case, getpmsg will only process the next message if it is in a priority band equal to, or greater than, the integer pointed to by *bandp*, or if it is a high-priority message. If a user just wants to get the first message off the queue, the integer pointed to by *flagsp* should be set to MSG_ANY and the integer pointed to by *bandp* should be set to 0. On return, if the message retrieved was a high-priority message, the integer pointed to by *flagsp* will be set to MSG_HIPRI and the integer pointed to by *bandp* will be set to 0. Otherwise, the integer pointed to by *flagsp* will be set to MSG_BAND and the integer pointed to by *bandp* will be set to the priority band of the message.

If O_NDELAY and O_NONBLOCK are clear, getmsg blocks until a message of the type specified by *flagsp* is available on the stream head read queue. If O_NDELAY or O_NONBLOCK has been set and a message of the specified type is not present on the read queue, getmsg fails and sets errno to EAGAIN.

If a hangup occurs on the stream from which messages are to be retrieved, getmsg continues to operate normally, as described above, until the stream head read queue is empty. Thereafter, it returns 0 in the len fields of *ctlptr* and *dataptr*.

getmsg or getpmsg will fail if one or more of the following are true:

EAGAIN	The O_NDELAY or O_NONBLOCK flag is set, and no messages are available.
EBADF	*fd* is not a valid file descriptor open for reading.
EBADMSG	Queued message to be read is not valid for getmsg.
EFAULT	*ctlptr*, *dataptr*, *bandp*, or *flagsp* points to a location outside the allocated address space.
EINTR	A signal was caught during the getmsg system call.
EINVAL	An illegal value was specified in *flagsp*, or the stream referenced by *fd* is linked under a multiplexor.

ENOSTR   A stream is not associated with *fd*.

getmsg can also fail if a STREAMS error message had been received at the stream head before the call to getmsg. The error returned is the value contained in the STREAMS error message.

SEE ALSO
intro(2), poll(2), putmsg(2), read(2), write(2).
Programmer's Guide: STREAMS.

DIAGNOSTICS
Upon successful completion, a non-negative value is returned. A value of 0 indicates that a full message was read successfully. A return value of MORECTL indicates that more control information is waiting for retrieval. A return value of MOREDATA indicates that more data are waiting for retrieval. A return value of MORECTL | MOREDATA indicates that both types of information remain. Subsequent getmsg calls retrieve the remainder of the message. However, if a message of higher priority has come in on the stream head read queue, the next call to getmsg will retrieve that higher priority message before retrieving the remainder of the previously received partial message.

NAME

poll – input/output multiplexing

SYNOPSIS

```
#include <stropts.h>
#include <poll.h>

int poll(struct poll *fds, size_t nfds, int timeout);
```

DESCRIPTION

poll provides users with a mechanism for multiplexing input/output over a set of file descriptors that reference open files. poll identifies those files on which a user can send or receive messages, or on which certain events have occurred.

fds specifies the file descriptors to be examined and the events of interest for each file descriptor. It is a pointer to an array with one element for each open file descriptor of interest. The array's elements are pollfd structures, which contain the following members:

```
int fd;                    /* file descriptor */
short events;              /* requested events */
short revents;             /* returned events */
```

fd specifies an open file descriptor and events and revents are bitmasks constructed by an OR of any combination of the following event flags:

POLLIN   Data other than high priority data may be read without blocking. For STREAMS, this flag is set even if the message is of zero length.

POLLRDNORM   Normal data (priority band = 0) may be read without blocking. For STREAMS, this flag is set even if the message is of zero length.

POLLRDBAND   Data from a non-zero priority band may be read without blocking For STREAMS, this flag is set even if the message is of zero length.

POLLPRI   High priority data may be received without blocking. For STREAMS, this flag is set even if the message is of zero length.

POLLOUT   Normal data may be written without blocking.

POLLWRNORM   The same as POLLOUT.

POLLWRBAND   Priority data (priority band > 0) may be written. This event only examines bands that have been written to at least once.

POLLMSG   An M_SIG or M_PCSIG message containing the SIGPOLL signal has reached the front of the stream head read queue.

POLLERR   An error has occured on the device or stream. This flag is only valid in the revents bitmask; it is not used in the events field.

POLLHUP   A hangup has occurred on the stream. This event and POLLOUT are mutually exclusive; a stream can never be writable if a hangup has occurred. However, this event and POLLIN, POLLRDNORM, POLLRDBAND, or POLLPRI are not mutually exclusive. This flag is only valid in the revents bitmask; it is not used in the events field.

POLLNVAL   The specified fd value does not belong to an open file. This flag is only valid in the revents field; it is not used in the events field.

For each element of the array pointed to by *fds*, poll examines the given file descriptor for the event(s) specified in events. The number of file descriptors to be examined is specified by *nfds*.

If the value fd is less than zero, events is ignored and revents is set to 0 in that entry on return from poll .

The results of the poll query are stored in the revents field in the pollfd structure. Bits are set in the revents bitmask to indicate which of the requested events are true. If none are true, none of the specified bits are set in revents when the poll call returns. The event flags POLLHUP, POLLERR, and POLLNVAL are always set in revents if the conditions they indicate are true; this occurs even though these flags were not present in events.

If none of the defined events have occurred on any selected file descriptor, poll waits at least *timeout* milliseconds for an event to occur on any of the selected file descriptors. On a computer where millisecond timing accuracy is not available, *timeout* is rounded up to the nearest legal value available on that system. If the value *timeout* is 0, poll returns immediately. If the value of *timeout* is INFTIM (or −1), poll blocks until a requested event occurs or until the call is interrupted. poll is not affected by the O_NDELAY and O_NONBLOCK flags.

poll fails if one or more of the following are true:

EAGAIN   Allocation of internal data structures failed, but the request may be attempted again.

EFAULT   Some argument points outside the allocated address space.

EINTR   A signal was caught during the poll system call.

EINVAL   The argument *nfds* is greater than {OPEN_MAX}.

SEE ALSO

intro(2), getmsg(2), getrlimit(2), putmsg(2), read(2), write(2)
Programmer's Guide: STREAMS

DIAGNOSTICS

Upon successful completion, a non-negative value is returned. A positive value indicates the total number of file descriptors that has been selected (i.e., file descriptors for which the revents field is non-zero). A value of 0 indicates that the call timed out and no file descriptors have been selected. Upon failure, a value of −1 is returned and errno is set to indicate the error.

NAME

putmsg – send a message on a stream

SYNOPSIS

#include <stropts.h>

int putmsg(int fd, const struct strbuf *ctlptr,
        const struct strbuf *dataptr, int flags);

int putpmsg(int fd, const struct strbuf *ctlptr,
        const struct strbuf *dataptr, int band, int flags);

DESCRIPTION

putmsg creates a message from user-specified buffer(s) and sends the message to a STREAMS file. The message may contain either a data part, a control part, or both. The data and control parts to be sent are distinguished by placement in separate buffers, as described below. The semantics of each part is defined by the STREAMS module that receives the message.

The function putpmsg does the same thing as putmsg, but provides the user the ability to send messages in different priority bands. Except where noted, all information pertaining to putmsg also pertains to putpmsg.

fd specifies a file descriptor referencing an open stream. *ctlptr* and *dataptr* each point to a strbuf structure, which contains the following members:

        int maxlen;   /* not used */
        int len;   /* length of data */
        void *buf;   /* ptr to buffer */

ctlptr points to the structure describing the control part, if any, to be included in the message. The buf field in the strbuf structure points to the buffer where the control information resides, and the len field indicates the number of bytes to be sent. The maxlen field is not used in putmsg [see getmsg(2)]. In a similar manner, *dataptr* specifies the data, if any, to be included in the message. *flags* indicates what type of message should be sent and is described later.

To send the data part of a message, *dataptr* must not be NULL and the len field of *dataptr* must have a value of 0 or greater. To send the control part of a message, the corresponding values must be set for *ctlptr*. No data (control) part is sent if either *dataptr* (*ctlptr*) is NULL or the len field of *dataptr* (*ctlptr*) is set to −1.

For putmsg(), if a control part is specified, and *flags* is set to RS_HIPRI, a high priority message is sent. If no control part is specified, and *flags* is set to RS_HIPRI, putmsg fails and sets errno to EINVAL. If *flags* is set to 0, a normal (non-priority) message is sent. If no control part and no data part are specified, and *flags* is set to 0, no message is sent, and 0 is returned.

The stream head guarantees that the control part of a message generated by putmsg is at least 64 bytes in length.

For putpmsg, the flags are different. *flags* is a bitmask with the following mutually-exclusive flags defined: MSG_HIPRI and MSG_BAND. If *flags* is set to 0, putpmsg fails and sets errno to EINVAL. If a control part is specified and *flags* is set to MSG_HIPRI and *band* is set to 0, a high-priority message is sent. If *flags* is set to MSG_HIPRI and either no control part is specified or *band* is set to a non-zero value, putpmsg() fails and sets errno to EINVAL. If flags is set to MSG_BAND, then a message is sent in the priority band specified by *band*. If a control part and data part are not specified and *flags* is set to MSG_BAND, no message is sent and 0 is returned.

Normally, putmsg() will block if the stream write queue is full due to internal flow control conditions. For high-priority messages, putmsg() does not block on this condition. For other messages, putmsg() does not block when the write queue is full and O_NDELAY or O_NONBLOCK is set. Instead, it fails and sets errno to EAGAIN.

putmsg or putpmsg also blocks, unless prevented by lack of internal resources, waiting for the availability of message blocks in the stream, regardless of priority or whether O_NDELAY or O_NONBLOCK has been specified. No partial message is sent.

putmsg fails if one or more of the following are true:

EAGAIN	A non-priority message was specified, the O_NDELAY or O_NONBLOCK flag is set and the stream write queue is full due to internal flow control conditions.
EBADF	*fd* is not a valid file descriptor open for writing.
EFAULT	*ctlptr* or *dataptr* points outside the allocated address space.
EINTR	A signal was caught during the putmsg system call.
EINVAL	An undefined value was specified in *flags*, or *flags* is set to RS_HIPRI and no control part was supplied.
EINVAL	The stream referenced by *fd* is linked below a multiplexor.
EINVAL	For putpmsg, if *flags* is set to MSG_HIPRI and *band* is nonzero.
ENOSR	Buffers could not be allocated for the message that was to be created due to insufficient STREAMS memory resources.
ENOSTR	A stream is not associated with *fd*.
ENXIO	A hangup condition was generated downstream for the specified stream, or the other end of the pipe is closed.
ERANGE	The size of the data part of the message does not fall within the range specified by the maximum and minimum packet sizes of the topmost stream module. This value is also returned if the control part of the message is larger than the maximum configured size of the control part of a message, or if the data part of a message is larger than the maximum configured size of the data part of a message.

putmsg also fails if a STREAMS error message had been processed by the stream head before the call to putmsg. The error returned is the value contained in the STREAMS error message.

SEE ALSO
getmsg(2), intro(2), poll(2), putmsg(2), read(2), write(2).
Programmer's Guide: STREAMS.

DIAGNOSTICS
Upon successful completion, a value of 0 is returned. Otherwise, a value of −1 is returned and **errno** is set to indicate the error.

NAME

fattach – attach a STREAMS-based file descriptor to an object in the file system name space

SYNOPSIS

`int fattach(int fildes, const char *path);`

DESCRIPTION

The `fattach` routine attaches a STREAMS-based file descriptor to an object in the file system name space, effectively associating a name with *fildes*. *fildes* must be a valid open file descriptor representing a STREAMS file. *path* is a path name of an existing object and the user must have appropriate privileges or be the owner of the file and have write permissions. All subsequent operations on *path* will operate on the STREAMS file until the STREAMS file is detached from the node. *fildes* can be attached to more than one *path*, i.e., a stream can have several names associated with it.

The attributes of the named stream [see `stat(2)`], are initialized as follows: the permissions, user ID, group ID, and times are set to those of *path*, the number of links is set to 1, and the size and device identifier are set to those of the streams device associated with *fildes*. If any attributes of the named stream are subsequently changed [e.g., `chmod(2)`], the attributes of the underlying object are not affected.

RETURN VALUE

If successful, `fattach` returns 0; otherwise it returns -1 and sets `errno` to indicate an error.

ERRORS

Under the following conditions, the function `fattach` fails and sets `errno` to:

EACCES   The user is the owner of *path* but does not have write permissions on *path* or *fildes* is locked.

EBADF   *fildes* is not a valid open file descriptor.

ENOENT   *path* does not exist.

ENOTDIR   A component of a path prefix is not a directory.

EINVAL   *fildes* does not represent a STREAMS file.

EPERM   The effective user ID is not the owner of *path* or a user with the appropriate privileges.

EBUSY   *path* is currently a mount point or has a STREAMS file descriptor attached lt.

ENAMETOOLONG
                The size of *path* exceeds {PATH_MAX}, or the component of a path name is longer than {NAME_MAX} while {_POSIX_NO_TRUNC} is in effect.

ELOOP   Too many symbolic links were encountered in translating *path*.

       EREMOTE   *path* is a file in a remotely mounted directory.

SEE ALSO

    fdetach(1M), fdetach(3C), isastream(3C), streamio(7)
    in the *Programmer's Guide: STREAMS*

NAME
fdetach – detach a name from a STREAMS-based file descriptor

SYNOPSIS
```
int fdetach(const char *path);
```

DESCRIPTION
The fdetach routine detaches a STREAMS-based file descriptor from a name in the file system. *path* is the path name of the object in the file system name space, which was previously attached [see fattach(3C)]. The user must be the owner of the file or a user with the appropriate privileges. All subsequent operations on *path* will operate on the file system node and not on the STREAMS file. The permissions and status of the node are restored to the state the node was in before the STREAMS file was attached to it.

RETURN VALUE
If successful, fdetach returns 0; otherwise it returns -1 and sets errno to indicate an error.

ERRORS
Under the following conditions, the function fdetach fails and sets errno to:

EPERM   The effective user ID is not the owner of *path* or is not a user with appropriate permissions.

ENOTDIR   A component of the path prefix is not a directory.

ENOENT   *path* does not exist.

EINVAL   *path* is not attached to a STREAMS file.

ENAMETOOLONG
                The size of *path* exceeds {PATH_MAX}, or a path name component is longer than {NAME_MAX} while {_POSIX_NO_TRUNC} is in effect.

ELOOP   Too many symbolic links were encountered in translating *path*.

SEE ALSO
fdetach(1M), fattach(3C), streamio(7).
in the *Programmer's Guide: STREAMS*

NAME

grantpt − grant access to the slave pseudo-terminal device

SYNOPSIS

```
int grantpt(int fildes);
```

DESCRIPTION

The function grantpt changes the mode and ownership of the slave pseudo-terminal device associated with its master pseudo-terminal counter part. *fildes* is the file descriptor returned from a successful open of the master pseudo-terminal device. A setuid root program [see setuid(2)] is invoked to change the permissions. The user ID of the slave is set to the effective owner of the calling process and the group ID is set to a reserved group. The permission mode of the slave pseudo-terminal is set to readable, writeable by the owner and writeable by the group.

RETURN VALUE

Upon successful completion, the function grantpt returns 0; otherwise it returns −1. Failure could occur if *fildes* is not an open file descriptor, if *fildes* is not associated with a master pseudo-terminal device, or if the corresponding slave device could not be accessed.

SEE ALSO

open(2), setuid(2).

ptsname(3C), unlockpt(3C)
in the *Programmer's Guide: STREAMS*.

NAME
isastream – test a file descriptor

SYNOPSIS
```
int isastream(int fildes);
```

DESCRIPTION
The function isastream() determines if a file descriptor represents a STREAMS file. *fildes* refers to an open file.

RETURN VALUE
If successful, isastream() returns 1 if *fildes* represents a STREAMS file, and 0 if not. On failure, isastream() returns -1 with **errno** set to indicate an error.

ERRORS
Under the following conditions, isastream() fails and sets **errno** to:

EBADF   *fildes* is not a valid open file.

SEE ALSO
streamio(7).
in the *Programmer's Guide: STREAMS*

NAME

ptsname – get name of the slave pseudo-terminal device

SYNOPSIS

#include <stdio.h>

char *ptsname(int fildes);

DESCRIPTION

The function ptsname() returns the name of the slave pseudo-terminal device associated with a master pseudo-terminal device. *fildes* is a file descriptor returned from a successful open of the master device. ptsname() returns a pointer to a string containing the null-terminated path name of the slave device of the form /dev/pts/N, where N is an integer between 0 and 255.

RETURN VALUE

Upon successful completion, the function ptsname() returns a pointer to a string which is the name of the pseudo-terminal slave device. This value points to a static data area that is overwritten by each call to ptsname(). Upon failure, ptsname() returns NULL. This could occur if *fildes* is an invalid file descriptor or if the slave device name does not exist in the file system.

SEE ALSO

open(2), grantpt(3C), ttyname(3C), unlockpt(3C).
Programmer's Guide: STREAMS.

NAME

　　unlockpt – unlock a pseudo-terminal master/slave pair

SYNOPSIS

　　int unlockpt (int fildes);

DESCRIPTION

　　The function unlockpt() clears a lock flag associated with the slave pseudo-terminal device associated with its master pseudo-terminal counterpart so that the slave pseudo-terminal device can be opened. *fildes* is a file descriptor returned from a successful open of a master pseudo-terminal device.

RETURN VALUE

　　Upon successful completion, the function unlockpt() returns 0; otherwise it returns −1. A failure may occur if *fildes* is not an open file descriptor or is not associated with a master pseudo-terminal device.

SEE ALSO

　　open(2)

　　grantpt(3C), ptsname(3C)
　　in the *Programmer's Guide: STREAMS*.

NAME

clone – open any major/minor device pair on a STREAMS driver

DESCRIPTION

clone is a STREAMS software driver that finds and opens an unused major/minor device on another STREAMS driver. The major device number passed to clone during open corresponds to the clone driver and the minor device number corresponds to the target driver. Each open results in a separate stream to a previously unused major/minor device.

The clone driver consists solely of an open function. This open function performs all of the necessary work so that subsequent system calls [including close(2)] require no further involvement of clone.

clone will generate an ENXIO error, without opening the device, if the major/minor device number provided does not correspond to a valid major/minor device, or if the driver indicated is not a STREAMS driver.

SEE ALSO

log(7).
Programmer's Guide: STREAMS.

NOTES

Multiple opens of the same major/minor device cannot be done through the clone interface. Executing stat(2) on the file system node for a cloned device yields a different result from executing fstat(2) using a file descriptor obtained from opening the node.

NAME

  connld - line discipline for unique stream connections

DESCRIPTION

  connld is a STREAMS-based module that provides unique connections between
  server and client processes. It can only be pushed [see streamio(7)] onto one
  end of a STREAMS-based pipe that may subsequently be attached to a name in the
  file system name space. After the pipe end is attached, a new pipe is created
  internally when an originating process attempts to open(2) or creat(2) the file
  system name. A file descriptor for one end of the new pipe is packaged into a
  message identical to that for the ioctl I_SENDFD [see streamio(7)] and is
  transmitted along the stream to the server process on the other end. The originating process is blocked until the server responds.

  The server responds to the I_SENDFD request by accepting the file descriptor
  through the I_RECVFD ioctl message. When this happens, the file descriptor
  associated with the other end of the new pipe is transmitted to the originating
  process as the file descriptor returned from open(2) or creat(2).

  If the server does not respond to the I_SENDFD request, the stream that the
  connld module is pushed on becomes uni-directional because the server will not
  be able to retrieve any data off the stream until the I_RECVFD request is issued.
  If the server process exits before issuing the I_RECVFD request, the open(2) or the
  creat(2) system calls will fail and return -1 to the originating process.

  When the connld module is pushed onto a pipe, messages going back and forth
  through the pipe are ignored by connld.

  On success, an open of connld returns 0. On failure, errno is set to the following values:

  EINVAL   A stream onto which connld is being pushed is not a pipe or the
                  pipe does not have a write queue pointer pointing to a stream head
                  read queue.

  EINVAL   The other end of the pipe onto which connld is being pushed is
                  linked under a multiplexor.

  EPIPE   connld is being pushed onto a pipe end whose other end is no
                  longer there.

  ENOMEM   An internal pipe could not be created.

  ENXIO   An M_HANGUP message is at the stream head of the pipe onto which
                  connld is being pushed.

  EAGAIN   Internal data structures could not be allocated.

  ENFILE   A file table entry could not be allocated.

SEE ALSO

  streamio(7)
  Programmer's Guide: STREAMS

NAME

    console – STREAMS-based console interface

DESCRIPTION

    The file dev/console is the system console and refers to an asynchronous serial data line originating from the system board.

    The file **dev/contty** refers to a second asynchronous serial data line originating from the system board.

    Both **/dev/console** and **/dev/contty** access the STREAMS-based console driver, which when used in conjunction with the STREAMS line discipline module **ldterm**, supports the **termio**(7) and **termios**(2) processing.

FILES

    /dev/console
    /dev/contty

SEE ALSO

    crash(1M), termios(2), ldterm(7), termio(7).
    Programmer's Guide: STREAMS.

NAME

ldterm – standard STREAMS terminal line discipline module

DESCRIPTION

ldterm is a STREAMS module that provides most of the termio(7) terminal interface. This module does not perform the low-level device control functions
specified by flags in the c_cflag word of the termio/termios structure or by
the IGNBRK, IGNPAR, PARMRK, or INPCK flags in the c_iflag word of the
termio/termios structure; those functions must be performed by the driver or
by modules pushed below the ldterm module. All other termio/termios functions are performed by ldterm; some of them, however, require the cooperation
of the driver or modules pushed below ldterm and may not be performed in
some cases. These include the IXOFF flag in the c_iflag word and the delays
specified in the c_oflag word.

ldterm also handles EUC and multi-byte characters.

The remainder of this section describes the processing of various STREAMS messages on the read- and write-side.

Read-side Behavior

Various types of STREAMS messages are processed as follows:

M_BREAK
      When this message is received, either an interrupt signal is generated or
      the message is treated as if it were an M_DATA message containing a sin-
      gle ASCII NUL character, depending on the state of the BRKINT flag.

M_DATA This message is normally processed using the standard termio input
      processing. If the ICANON flag is set, a single input record ("line") is
      accumulated in an internal buffer and sent upstream when a line-
      terminating character is received. If the ICANON flag is not set, other
      input processing is performed and the processed data are passed
      upstream.

      If output is to be stopped or started as a result of the arrival of charac-
      ters (usually CNTRL–Q and CNTRL–S), M_STOP and M_START messages are
      sent downstream. If the IXOFF flag is set and input is to be stopped or
      started as a result of flow-control considerations, M_STOPI and M_STARTI
      messages are sent downstream.

      M_DATA messages are sent downstream, as necessary, to perform echoing.

      If a signal is to be generated, an M_FLUSH message with a flag byte of
      FLUSHR is placed on the read queue. If the signal is also to flush output,
      an M_FLUSH message with a flag byte of FLUSHW is sent downstream.

M_CTL   If the size of the data buffer associated with the message is the size of
      struct iocblk, ldterm will perform functional negotiation to deter-
      mine where the termio(7) processing is to be done. If the command field
      of the iocblk structure (ioc_cmd) is set to MC_NO_CANON, the input
      canonical processing normally performed on M_DATA messages is dis-
      abled and those messages are passed upstream unmodified; this is for
      the use of modules or drivers that perform their own input processing,
      such as a pseudo-terminal in TIOCREMOTE mode connected to a program

that performs this processing. If the command is MC_DO_CANON, all input processing is enabled. If the command is MC_PART_CANON, then an M_DATA message containing a termios structure is expected to be attached to the original M_CTL message. The ldterm module will examine the iflag, oflag, and lflag fields of the termios structure and from then on will process only those flags which have not been turned ON. If none of the above commands are found, the message is ignored; in any case, the message is passed upstream.

M_FLUSH

The read queue of the module is flushed of all its data messages and all data in the record being accumulated are also flushed. The message is passed upstream.

M_IOCACK

The data contained within the message, which is to be returned to the process, are augmented if necessary, and the message is passed upstream.

All other messages are passed upstream unchanged.

Write-side Behavior

Various types of STREAMS messages are processed as follows:

M_FLUSH

The write queue of the module is flushed of all its data messages and the message is passed downstream.

M_IOCTL

The function of this ioctl is performed and the message is passed downstream in most cases. The TCFLSH and TCXONC ioctls can be performed entirely in the ldterm module, so the reply is sent upstream and the message is not passed downstream.

M_DATA If the OPOST flag is set, or both the XCASE and ICANON flags are set, output processing is performed and the processed message is passed downstream along with any M_DELAY messages generated. Otherwise, the message is passed downstream without change.

All other messages are passed downstream unchanged.

IOCTLS

The following ioctls are processed by the ldterm module. All others are passed downstream. EUC_WSET and EUC_WGET are I_STR ioctl calls whereas other ioctls listed here are TRANPARENT ioctls.

TCGETS/TCGETA

The message is passed downstream; if an acknowledgment is seen, the data provided by the driver and modules downstream are augmented and the acknowledgement is passed upstream.

TCSETS/TCSETSW/TCSETSF/TCSETA/TCSETAW/TCSETAF

The parameters that control the behavior of the ldterm module are changed. If a mode change requires options at the stream head to be changed, an M_SETOPTS message is sent upstream. If the ICANON flag is turned on or off, the read mode at the stream head is changed to message-nondiscard or byte-stream mode, respectively. If the TOSTOP flag is turned on or off, the tostop mode at the stream head is turned on or off, respectively.

TCFLSH If the argument is 0, an M_FLUSH message with a flag byte of FLUSHR is sent downstream and placed on the read queue. If the argument is 1, the write queue is flushed of all its data messages and an M_FLUSH message with a flag byte of FLUSHW is sent upstream and downstream. If the argument is 2, the write queue is flushed of all its data messages and an M_FLUSH message with a flag byte of FLUSHRW is sent downstream and placed on the read queue.

TCXONC If the argument is 0 and output is not already stopped, an M_STOP message is sent downstream. If the argument is 1 and output is stopped, an M_START message is sent downstream. If the argument is 2 and input is not already stopped, an M_STOPI message is sent downstream. If the argument is 3 and input is stopped, an M_STARTI message is sent downstream.

TCSBRK The message is passed downstream, so the driver has a chance to drain the data and then send and an M_IOCACK message upstream.

EUC_WSET
        This call takes a pointer to an eucioc structure, and uses it to set the EUC line discipline's local definition for the code set widths to be used for subsequent operations. Within the stream, the line discipline may optionally notify other modules of this setting via M_CTL messages.

EUC_WGET
        This call takes a pointer to an eucioc structure, and returns in it the EUC code set widths currently in use by the EUC line discipline.

SEE ALSO

termios(2), console(7), ports(7), termio(7).
Programmer's Guide: STREAMS.

NAME

    log – interface to STREAMS error logging and event tracing

DESCRIPTION

    log is a STREAMS software device driver that provides an interface for console logging and for the STREAMS error logging and event tracing processes (strerr(1M), strace(1M)). log presents two separate interfaces: a function call interface in the kernel through which STREAMS drivers and modules submit log messages; and a subset of ioctl(2) system calls and STREAMS messages for interaction with a user level console logger, an error logger, a trace logger, or processes that need to submit their own log messages.

Kernel Interface

    log messages are generated within the kernel by calls to the function strlog:

```
strlog(mid, sid, level, flags, fmt, arg1, ...)
short mid, sid;
char level;
ushort flags;
char *fmt;
unsigned arg1;
```

Required definitions are contained in <sys/strlog.h>, <sys/log.h>, and <sys/syslog.h>. *mid* is the STREAMS module id number for the module or driver submitting the log message. *sid* is an internal sub-id number usually used to identify a particular minor device of a driver. *level* is a tracing level that allows for selective screening out of low priority messages from the tracer. *flags* are any combination of SL_ERROR (the message is for the error logger), SL_TRACE (the message is for the tracer), SL_CONSOLE (the message is for the console logger), SL_FATAL (advisory notification of a fatal error), and SL_NOTIFY (request that a copy of the message be mailed to the system administrator). *fmt* is a printf(3S) style format string, except that %s, %e, %E, %g, and %G conversion specifications are not handled. Up to NLOGARGS (currently 3) numeric or character arguments can be provided.

User Interface

    log is opened via the clone interface, /dev/log. Each open of /dev/log obtains a separate stream to log. In order to receive log messages, a process must first notify log whether it is an error logger, trace logger, or console logger via a STREAMS I_STR ioctl call (see below). For the console logger, the I_STR ioctl has an ic_cmd field of I_CONSLOG, with no accompanying data. For the error logger, the I_STR ioctl has an ic_cmd field of I_ERRLOG, with no accompanying data. For the trace logger, the ioctl has an ic_cmd field of I_TRCLOG, and must be accompanied by a data buffer containing an array of one or more struct trace_ids elements. Each trace_ids structure specifies an *mid*, *sid*, and *level* from which message will be accepted. strlog will accept messages whose *mid* and *sid* exactly match those in the trace_ids structure, and whose level is less than or equal to the level given in the trace_ids structure. A value of -1 in any of the fields of the trace_ids structure indicates that any value is accepted for that field.

Once the logger process has identified itself via the ioctl call, log will begin sending up messages subject to the restrictions noted above. These messages are obtained via the getmsg(2) system call. The control part of this message contains a log_ctl structure, which specifies the *mid*, *sid*, *level*, *flags*, time in ticks since boot that the message was submitted, the corresponding time in seconds since Jan. 1, 1970, a sequence number, and a priority. The time in seconds since 1970 is provided so that the date and time of the message can be easily computed, and the time in ticks since boot is provided so that the relative timing of log messages can be determined.

The priority is comprised of a priority code and a facility code, found in <sys/syslog.h>. If SL_CONSOLE is set in *flags*, the priority code is set as follows. If SL_WARN is set, the priority code is set to LOG_WARNING. If SL_FATAL is set, the priority code is set to LOG_CRIT. If SL_ERROR is set, the priority code is set to LOG_ERR. If SL_NOTE is set, the priority code is set to LOG_NOTICE. If SL_TRACE is set, the priority code is set to LOG_DEBUG. If only SL_CONSOLE is set, the priority code is set to LOG_INFO. Messages originating from the kernel have the facility code set to LOG_KERN. Most messages originating from user processes will have the facility code set to LOG_USER.

Different sequence numbers are maintained for the error and trace logging streams, and are provided so that gaps in the sequence of messages can be determined (during times of high message traffic some messages may not be delivered by the logger to avoid hogging system resources). The data part of the message contains the unexpanded text of the format string (null terminated), followed by NLOGARGS words for the arguments to the format string, aligned on the first word boundary following the format string.

A process may also send a message of the same structure to log, even if it is not an error or trace logger. The only fields of the log_ctl structure in the control part of the message that are accepted are the *level*, *flags*, and *pri* fields; all other fields are filled in by log before being forwarded to the appropriate logger. The data portion must contain a null terminated format string, and any arguments (up to NLOGARGS) must be packed one word each, on the next word boundary following the end of the format string.

ENXIO is returned for I_TRCLOG ioctls without any trace_ids structures, or for any unrecognized I_STR ioctl calls. Incorrectly formatted log messages sent to the driver by a user process are silently ignored (no error results).

Processes that wish to write a message to the console logger may direct their output to /dev/conslog, using either write(2) or putmsg(2).

EXAMPLES

Example of I_ERRLOG notification.

```
struct strioctl ioc;

ioc.ic_cmd = I_ERRLOG;
ioc.ic_timout = 0;    /* default timeout (15 secs.) */
ioc.ic_len = 0;
ioc.ic_dp = NULL;
```

```
            ioctl(log, I_STR, &ioc);
```

Example of I_TRCLOG notification.

```
        struct trace_ids tid[2];

        tid[0].ti_mid = 2;
        tid[0].ti_sid = 0;
        tid[0].ti_level = 1;

        tid[1].ti_mid = 1002;
        tid[1].ti_sid = -1;    /* any sub-id will be allowed */
        tid[1].ti_level = -1; /* any level will be allowed */

        ioc.ic_cmd = I_TRCLOG;
        ioc.ic_timout = 0;
        ioc.ic_len = 2 * sizeof(struct trace_ids);
        ioc.ic_dp = (char *)tid;

        ioctl(log, I_STR, &ioc);
```

Example of submitting a log message (no arguments).

```
        struct strbuf ctl, dat;
        struct log_ctl lc;
        char *message = "Don't forget to pick up some milk
                         on the way home";

        ctl.len = ctl.maxlen = sizeof(lc);
        ctl.buf = (char *)&lc;

        dat.len = dat.maxlen = strlen(message);
        dat.buf = message;

        lc.level = 0;
        lc.flags = SL_ERROR|SL_NOTIFY;

        putmsg(log, &ctl, &dat, 0);
```

FILES
      /dev/log
      /dev/conslog
      <sys/log.h>
      <sys/strlog.h>
      <sys/syslog.h>

SEE ALSO
      strace(1M), strerr(1M), getmsg(2), intro(2), putmsg(2), write(2), clone(7).
      Programmer's Guide: STREAMS.

NAME

    pckt – STREAMS Packet Mode module

DESCRIPTION

    pckt is a STREAMS module that may be used with a pseudo terminal to packetize certain messages. The pckt module should be pushed [see I_PUSH, streamio(7)] onto the master side of a pseudo terminal.

    Packetizing is performed by prefixing a message with an M_PROTO message. The original message type is stored in the 4 byte data portion of the M_PROTO message.

    On the read-side, only the M_PROTO, M_PCPROTO, M_STOP, M_START, M_STOPI, M_STARTI, M_IOCTL, M_DATA, M_FLUSH, and M_READ messages are packetized. All other message types are passed upstream unmodified.

    Since all unread state information is held in the master's stream head read queue, flushing of this queue is disabled.

    On the write-side, all messages are sent down unmodified.

    With this module in place, all reads from the master side of the pseudo terminal should be performed with the getmsg(2) or getpmsg() system call. The control part of the message contains the message type. The data part contains the actual data associated with that message type. The onus is on the application to separate the data into its component parts.

SEE ALSO

    crash(1M), getmsg(2), ioctl(2),
    ldterm(7), ptem(7), streamio(7), termio(7).
    Programmer's Guide: STREAMS.

NAME

ports – 5 line asynchronous communications interface STREAMS driver

DESCRIPTION

ports is a STREAMS-based driver that supports a five line asynchronous interface. Each device supports 4 RS232 lines and one parallel Centronics interface.

When used in conjuction with the STREAMS line discipline module, ldterm, behavior on all lines is as described in termio(7).

FILES

/dev/term/??   scrial interface
/dev/lp?   parallel interface

SEE ALSO

crash(1M), ldterm(7), termio(7).
Programmer's Guide: STREAMS

NAME

ptem – STREAMS Pseudo Terminal Emulation module

DESCRIPTION

ptem is a STREAMS module that when used in conjunction with a line discipline and pseudo terminal driver emulates a terminal.

The ptem module must be pushed [see I_PUSH, streamio(7)] onto the slave side of a pseudo terminal STREAM, before the ldterm module is pushed.

On the write-side, the TCSETA, TCSETAF, TCSETAW, TCGETA, TCSETS, TCSETSW, TCSETSF, TCGETS, TCSBRK, JWINSIZE, TIOCGWINSZ, and TIOCSWINSZ termio ioctl(2) messages are processed and acknowledged. A hang up (i.e. stty 0) is converted to a zero length M_DATA message and passed downstream. Termio cflags and window row and column information are stored locally one per stream. M_DELAY messages are discarded. All other messages are passed downstream unmodified.

On the read-side all messages are passed upstream unmodified with the following exceptions. All M_READ and M_DELAY messages are freed in both directions. An ioctl TCSBRK is converted to an M_BREAK message and passed upstream and an acknowledgement is returned downstream. An ioctl TIOCSIGNAL is converted into an M_PCSIG message, and passed upstream and an acknowledgement is returned downstream. Finally an ioctl TIOCREMOTE is converted into an M_CTL message, acknowledged, and passed upstream.

FILES

<sys/ptem.h>

SEE ALSO

stty(1), crash(1M), ioctl(2), ldterm(7), pckt(7), streamio(7), termio(7)
Programmer's Guide: STREAMS.

NAME

sad - STREAMS Administrative Driver

SYNOPSIS

```
#include <sys/types.h>
#include <sys/conf.h>
#include <sys/sad.h>
#include <sys/stropts.h>

int ioctl (fildes, command, arg);
int fildes, command;
```

DESCRIPTION

The STREAMS Administrative Driver provides an interface for applications to perform administrative operations on STREAMS modules and drivers. The interface is provided through ioctl(2) commands. Privileged operations may access the sad driver via /dev/sad/admin. Unprivileged operations may access the sad driver via /dev/sad/user.

fildes is an open file descriptor that refers to the sad driver. *command* determines the control function to be performed as described below. *arg* represents additional information that is needed by this command. The type of *arg* depends upon the command, but it is generally an integer or a pointer to a *command-specific* data structure.

COMMAND FUNCTIONS

The autopush facility [see autopush(1M)] allows one to configure a list of modules to be automatically pushed on a stream when a driver is first opened. Autopush is controlled by the next commands.

SAD_SAP   Allows the administrator to configure the autopush information for the given device. *arg* points to a strapush structure which contains the following members:

```
uint    sap_cmd;
long    sap_major;
long    sap_minor;
long    sap_lastminor;
long    sap_npush;
uint    sap_list[MAXAPUSH] [FMNAMESZ + 1];
```

The sap_cmd field indicates the type of configuration being done. It may take on one of the following values:

SAP_ONE   Configure one minor device of a driver.

SAP_RANGE   Configure a range of minor devices of a driver.

SAP_ALL   Configure all minor devices of a driver.

SAP_CLEAR   Undo configuration information for a driver.

The sap_major field is the major device number of the device to be configured. The sap_minor field is the minor device number of the device to be configured. The sap_lastminor field is used only with the SAP_RANGE command, with which a range of minor devices between **sap_minor** and **sap_lastminor**, inclusive, are to be configured. The minor fields have no meaning for the SAP_ALL command. The **sap_npush** field indicates the number of modules to be automatically pushed when the device is opened. It must be less than or equal to MAXAPUSH, defined in **sad.h**. It must also be less than or equal to NSTRPUSH, the maximum number of modules that can be pushed on a stream, defined in the kernel master file. The field **sap_list** is an array of module names to be pushed in the order in which they appear in the list.

When using the SAP_CLEAR command, the user sets only **sap_major** and **sap_minor**. This will undo the configuration information for any of the other commands. If a previous entry was configured as SAP_ALL, **sap_minor** should be set to zero. If a previous entry was configured as SAP_RANGE, **sap_minor** should be set to the lowest minor device number in the range configured.

On failure, **errno** is set to the following value:

EFAULT	*arg* points outside the allocated address space.
EINVAL	The major device number is invalid, the number of modules is invalid, or the list of module names is invalid.
ENOSTR	The major device number does not represent a STREAMS driver.
EEXIST	The major-minor device pair is already configured.
ERANGE	The command is SAP_RANGE and **sap_lastminor** is not greater than **sap_minor**, or the command is SAP_CLEAR and **sap_minor** is not equal to the first minor in the range.
ENODEV	The command is SAP_CLEAR and the device is not configured for autopush.
ENOSR	An internal autopush data structure cannot be allocated.

SAD_GAP   Allows any user to query the **sad** driver to get the autopush configuration information for a given device. *arg* points to a strapush structure as described in the previous command.

The user should set the **sap_major** and **sap_minor** fields of the strapush structure to the major and minor device numbers, respectively, of the device in question. On return, the strapush structure will be filled in with the entire information used to configure the device. Unused entries in the module list will be zero-filled.

On failure, **errno** is set to one of the following values:

EFAULT	*arg* points outside the allocated address space.
EINVAL	The major device number is invalid.
ENOSTR	The major device number does not represent a STREAMS driver.
ENODEV	The device is not configured for autopush.

SAD_VML   Allows any user to validate a list of modules (i.e., to see if they are installed on the system.) *arg* is a pointer to a **str_list** structure with the following members:

```
int             sl_nmods;
struct str_mlist  *sl_modlist;
```

The **str_mlist** structure has the following member:

```
char            l_name[FMNAMESZ+1];
```

sl_nmods indicates the number of entries the user has allocated in the array and **sl_modlist** points to the array of module names. The return value is 0 if the list is valid, 1 if the list contains an invalid module name, or −1 on failure. On failure, **errno** is set to one of the following values:

EFAULT	*arg* points outside the allocated address space.
EINVAL	The **sl_nmods** field of the **str_list** structure is less than or equal to zero.

SEE ALSO
intro(2), ioctl(2), open(2).
Programmer's Guide: STREAMS.

DIAGNOSTICS
Unless specified otherwise above, the return value from ioctl is 0 upon success and -1 upon failure with **errno** set as indicated.

NAME

streamio – STREAMS ioctl commands

SYNOPSIS

#include <sys/types.h>
#include <stropts.h>

int ioctl (int fildes, int command, ... /* arg */);

DESCRIPTION

STREAMS [see intro(2)] ioctl commands are a subset of the ioctl(2) system calls which perform a variety of control functions on streams.

fildes is an open file descriptor that refers to a stream. *command* determines the control function to be performed as described below. *arg* represents additional information that is needed by this command. The type of *arg* depends upon the command, but it is generally an integer or a pointer to a *command*-specific data structure. The *command* and *arg* are interpreted by the stream head. Certain combinations of these arguments may be passed to a module or driver in the stream.

Since these STREAMS commands are a subset of ioctl, they are subject to the errors described there. In addition to those errors, the call will fail with errno set to EINVAL, without processing a control function, if the stream referenced by *fildes* is linked below a multiplexor, or if *command* is not a valid value for a stream.

Also, as described in ioctl, STREAMS modules and drivers can detect errors. In this case, the module or driver sends an error message to the stream head containing an error value. This causes subsequent system calls to fail with errno set to this value.

COMMAND FUNCTIONS

The following ioctl commands, with error values indicated, are applicable to all STREAMS files:

I_PUSH   Pushes the module whose name is pointed to by *arg* onto the top of the current stream, just below the stream head. If the stream is a pipe, the module will be inserted between the stream heads of both ends of the pipe. It then calls the open routine of the newly-pushed module. On failure, errno is set to one of the following values:

        EINVAL   Invalid module name.

        EFAULT   *arg* points outside the allocated address space.

        ENXIO   Open routine of new module failed.

        ENXIO   Hangup received on *fildes*.

I_POP   Removes the module just below the stream head of the stream pointed to by *fildes*. To remove a module from a pipe requires that the module was pushed on the side it is being removed from. *arg* should be 0 in an I_POP request. On failure, errno is set to one of the following values:

	EINVAL	No module present in the stream.
	ENXIO	Hangup received on *fildes*.

I_LOOK
Retrieves the name of the module just below the stream head of the stream pointed to by *fildes*, and places it in a null terminated character string pointed at by *arg*. The buffer pointed to by *arg* should be at least FMNAMESZ+1 bytes long. An (#include <sys/conf.h>) declaration is required. On failure, errno is set to one of the following values:

	EFAULT	*arg* points outside the allocated address space.
	EINVAL	No module present in stream.

I_FLUSH
This request flushes all input and/or output queues, depending on the value of *arg*. Legal *arg* values are:

	FLUSHR	Flush read queues.
	FLUSHW	Flush write queues.
	FLUSHRW	Flush read and write queues.

If a pipe or FIFO does not have any modules pushed, the read queue of the stream head on either end is flushed depending on the value of *arg*.

If FLUSHR is set and *fildes* is a pipe, the read queue for that end of the pipe is flushed and the write queue for the other end is flushed. If *fildes* is a FIFO, both queues are flushed.

If FLUSHW is set and *fildes* is a pipe and the other end of the pipe exists, the read queue for the other end of the pipe is flushed and the write queue for this end is flushed. If *fildes* is a FIFO, both queues of the FIFO are flushed.

If FLUSHRW is set, all read queues are flushed, that is, the read queue for the FIFO and the read queue on both ends of the pipe are flushed.

Correct flush handling of a pipe or FIFO with modules pushed is achieved via the pipemod module. This module should be the first module pushed onto a pipe so that it is at the midpoint of the pipe itself.

On failure, errno is set to one of the following values:

	ENOSR	Unable to allocate buffers for flush message due to insufficient STREAMS memory resources.
	EINVAL	Invalid *arg* value.
	ENXIO	Hangup received on *fildes*.

I_FLUSHBAND
Flushes a particular band of messages. *arg* points to a bandinfo structure that has the following members:

```
unsigned char    bi_pri;
int              bi_flag;
```

The bi_flag field may be one of FLUSHR, FLUSHW, or FLUSHRW as described earlier.

I_SETSIG   Informs the stream head that the user wishes the kernel to issue the SIGPOLL signal [see signal(2)] when a particular event has occurred on the stream associated with *fildes*. I_SETSIG supports an asynchronous processing capability in STREAMS. The value of *arg* is a bitmask that specifies the events for which the user should be signaled. It is the bitwise-OR of any combination of the following constants:

S_INPUT   Any message other than an M_PCPROTO has arrived on a stream head read queue. This event is maintained for compatibility with prior UNIX System V releases. This is set even if the message is of zero length.

S_RDNORM   An ordinary (non-priority) message has arrived on a stream head read queue. This is set even if the message is of zero length.

S_RDBAND   A priority band message (band > 0) has arrived on a stream head read queue. This is set even if the message is of zero length.

S_HIPRI   A high priority message is present on the stream head read queue. This is set even if the message is of zero length.

S_OUTPUT   The write queue just below the stream head is no longer full. This notifies the user that there is room on the queue for sending (or writing) data downstream.

S_WRNORM   This event is the same as S_OUTPUT.

S_WRBAND   A priority band greater than 0 of a queue downstream exists and is writable. This notifies the user that there is room on the queue for sending (or writing) priority data downstream.

S_MSG   A STREAMS signal message that contains the SIGPOLL signal has reached the front of the stream head read queue.

S_ERROR   An M_ERROR message has reached the stream head.

S_HANGUP   An M_HANGUP message has reached the stream head.

S_BANDURG   When used in conjunction with S_RDBAND, SIGURG is generated instead of SIGPOLL when a priority message reaches the front of the stream head read queue.

A user process may choose to be signaled only of high priority messages by setting the *arg* bitmask to the value S_HIPRI.

Processes that wish to receive SIGPOLL signals must explicitly register to receive them using I_SETSIG. If several processes register to receive this signal for the same event on the same stream, each process will be signaled when the event occurs.

If the value of *arg* is zero, the calling process will be unregistered and will not receive further SIGPOLL signals. On failure, errno is set to one of the following values:

EINVAL   *arg* value is invalid or *arg* is zero and process is not registered to receive the SIGPOLL signal.

EAGAIN   Allocation of a data structure to store the signal request failed.

I_GETSIG   Returns the events for which the calling process is currently registered to be sent a SIGPOLL signal. The events are returned as a bitmask pointed to by *arg*, where the events are those specified in the description of I_SETSIG above. On failure, errno is set to one of the following values:

EINVAL   Process not registered to receive the SIGPOLL signal.

EFAULT   *arg* points outside the allocated address space.

I_FIND   Compares the names of all modules currently present in the stream to the name pointed to by *arg*, and returns 1 if the named module is present in the stream. It returns 0 if the named module is not present. On failure, errno is set to one of the following values:

EFAULT   *arg* points outside the allocated address space.

EINVAL   *arg* does not contain a valid module name.

I_PEEK   Allows a user to retrieve the information in the first message on the stream head read queue without taking the message off the queue. I_PEEK is analogous to getmsg(2) except that it does not remove the message from the queue. *arg* points to a strpeek structure which contains the following members:

```
struct strbuf      ctlbuf;
struct strbuf      databuf;
long               flags;
```

The maxlen field in the ctlbuf and databuf strbuf structures [see getmsg(2)] must be set to the number of bytes of control information and/or data information, respectively, to retrieve. flags may be set to RS_HIPRI or 0. If RS_HIPRI is set, I_PEEK will look for a high priority message on the stream head read queue. Otherwise, I_PEEK will look for the first message on the stream head read queue.

I_PEEK returns 1 if a message was retrieved, and returns 0 if no message was found on the stream head read queue. It does not wait for a message to arrive. On return, ctlbuf specifies information in the control buffer, databuf specifies information in the data buffer, and flags contains the value RS_HIPRI or 0. On failure, errno is set to the following value:

EFAULT	*arg* points, or the buffer area specified in ctlbuf or databuf is, outside the allocated address space.
EBADMSG	Queued message to be read is not valid for I_PEEK
EINVAL	Illegal value for flags.

I_SRDOPT   Sets the read mode [see read(2)] using the value of the argument *arg*. Legal *arg* values are:

RNORM	Byte-stream mode, the default.
RMSGD	Message-discard mode.
RMSGN	Message-nondiscard mode.

In addition, treatment of control messages by the stream head may be changed by setting the following flags in *arg*:

RPROTNORM	Fail read() with EBADMSG if a control message is at the front of the stream head read queue. This is the default behavior.
RPROTDAT	Deliver the control portion of a message as data when a user issues read().
RPROTDIS	Discard the control portion of a message, delivering any data portion, when a user issues a read().

On failure, errno is set to the following value:

EINVAL	*arg* is not one of the above legal values.

I_GRDOPT   Returns the current read mode setting in an int pointed to by the argument *arg*. Read modes are described in read(2). On failure, errno is set to the following value:

EFAULT	*arg* points outside the allocated address space.

I_NREAD   Counts the number of data bytes in data blocks in the first message on the stream head read queue, and places this value in the location pointed to by *arg*. The return value for the command is the number of messages on the stream head read queue. For example, if zero is returned in *arg*, but the ioctl return value is greater than zero, this indicates that a zero-length message is next on the queue. On failure, errno is set to the following value:

EFAULT	*arg* points outside the allocated address space.

I_FDINSERT   Creates a message from user specified buffer(s), adds information about another stream and sends the message downstream. The message contains a control part and an optional data part. The data and control parts to be sent are distinguished by placement in separate buffers, as described below.

arg points to a strfdinsert structure which contains the following members:

```
struct strbuf    ctlbuf;
```

```
struct strbuf      databuf;
long               flags;
int                fildes;
int                offset;
```

The len field in the ctlbuf strbuf structure [see putmsg(2)] must
be set to the size of a pointer plus the number of bytes of control
information to be sent with the message. *fildes* in the strfdinsert
structure specifies the file descriptor of the other stream. offset,
which must be word-aligned, specifies the number of bytes beyond
the beginning of the control buffer where I_FDINSERT will store a
pointer. This pointer will be the address of the read queue structure of the driver for the stream corresponding to fildes in the
strfdinsert structure. The len field in the databuf strbuf
structure must be set to the number of bytes of data information to
be sent with the message or zero if no data part is to be sent.

flags specifies the type of message to be created. An ordinary
(non-priority) message is created if flags is set to 0, a high priority
message is created if flags is set to RS_HIPRI. For normal messages, I_FDINSERT will block if the stream write queue is full due
to internal flow control conditions. For high priority messages,
I_FDINSERT does not block on this condition. For normal messages, I_FDINSERT does not block when the write queue is full and
O_NDELAY or O_NONBLOCK is set. Instead, it fails and sets errno to
EAGAIN.

I_FDINSERT also blocks, unless prevented by lack of internal
resources, waiting for the availability of message blocks, regardless
of priority or whether O_NDELAY or O_NONBLOCK has been specified.
No partial message is sent. On failure, errno is set to one of the
following values:

EAGAIN   A non-priority message was specified, the O_NDELAY
                or O_NONBLOCK flag is set, and the stream write
                queue is full due to internal flow control conditions.

ENOSR   Buffers could not be allocated for the message that
                was to be created due to insufficient STREAMS
                memory resources.

EFAULT   *arg* points, or the buffer area specified in ctlbuf or
                databuf is, outside the allocated address space.

EINVAL   One of the following: fildes in the strfdinsert
                structure is not a valid, open stream file descriptor;
                the size of a pointer plus offset is greater than the
                len field for the buffer specified through ctlptr;
                offset does not specify a properly-aligned location
                in the data buffer; an undefined value is stored in
                flags.

ENXIO   Hangup received on `fildes` of the `ioctl` call or `fildes` in the `strfdinsert` structure.

ERANGE   The `len` field for the buffer specified through `data-buf` does not fall within the range specified by the maximum and minimum packet sizes of the topmost stream module, or the `len` field for the buffer specified through `databuf` is larger than the maximum configured size of the data part of a message, or the `len` field for the buffer specified through `ctlbuf` is larger than the maximum configured size of the control part of a message.

I_FDINSERT can also fail if an error message was received by the stream head of the stream corresponding to `fildes` in the `strfdinsert` structure. In this case, `errno` will be set to the value in the message.

I_STR   Constructs an internal STREAMS ioctl message from the data pointed to by *arg*, and sends that message downstream.

This mechanism is provided to send user `ioctl` requests to downstream modules and drivers. It allows information to be sent with the `ioctl`, and will return to the user any information sent upstream by the downstream recipient. I_STR blocks until the system responds with either a positive or negative acknowledgement message, or until the request "times out" after some period of time. If the request times out, it fails with `errno` set to ETIME.

At most, one I_STR can be active on a stream. Further I_STR calls will block until the active I_STR completes at the stream head. The default timeout interval for these requests is 15 seconds. The O_NDELAY and O_NONBLOCK [see open(2)] flags have no effect on this call.

To send requests downstream, *arg* must point to a `strioctl` structure which contains the following members:

```
int     ic_cmd;
int     ic_timout;
int     ic_len;
char    *ic_dp;
```

`ic_cmd` is the internal `ioctl` command intended for a downstream module or driver and `ic_timout` is the number of seconds (-1 = infinite, 0 = use default, >0 = as specified) an I_STR request will wait for acknowledgement before timing out. The default timeout is infinite. `ic_len` is the number of bytes in the data argument and `ic_dp` is a pointer to the data argument. The `ic_len` field has two uses: on input, it contains the length of the data argument passed in, and on return from the command, it contains the number of bytes being returned to the user (the buffer pointed to by `ic_dp` should be large enough to contain the maximum amount of data that any module or the driver in the stream can return).

The stream head will convert the information pointed to by the strioctl structure to an internal ioctl command message and send it downstream. On failure, errno is set to one of the following values:

ENOSR   Unable to allocate buffers for the ioctl message due to insufficient STREAMS memory resources.

EFAULT   *arg* points, or the buffer area specified by ic_dp and ic_len (separately for data sent and data returned) is, outside the allocated address space.

EINVAL   ic_len is less than 0 or ic_len is larger than the maximum configured size of the data part of a message or ic_timout is less than -1.

ENXIO   Hangup received on *fildes*.

ETIME   A downstream ioctl timed out before acknowledgement was received.

An I_STR can also fail while waiting for an acknowledgement if a message indicating an error or a hangup is received at the stream head. In addition, an error code can be returned in the positive or negative acknowledgement message, in the event the ioctl command sent downstream fails. For these cases, I_STR will fail with errno set to the value in the message.

I_SWROPT   Sets the write mode using the value of the argument *arg*. Legal bit settings for *arg* are:

SNDZERO   Send a zero-length message downstream when a write of 0 bytes occurs.

To not send a zero-length message when a write of 0 bytes occurs, this bit must not be set in *arg*.

On failure, errno may be set to the following value:

EINVAL   *arg* is the the above legal value.

I_GWROPT   Returns the current write mode setting, as described above, in the int that is pointed to by the argument *arg*.

I_SENDFD   Requests the stream associated with *fildes* to send a message, containing a file pointer, to the stream head at the other end of a stream pipe. The file pointer corresponds to *arg*, which must be an open file descriptor.

I_SENDFD converts *arg* into the corresponding system file pointer. It allocates a message block and inserts the file pointer in the block. The user id and group id associated with the sending process are also inserted. This message is placed directly on the read queue [see intro(2)] of the stream head at the other end of the stream pipe to which it is connected. On failure, errno is set to one of the following values:

EAGAIN	The sending stream is unable to allocate a message block to contain the file pointer.
EAGAIN	The read queue of the receiving stream head is full and cannot accept the message sent by I_SENDFD.
EBADF	*arg* is not a valid, open file descriptor.
EINVAL	*fildes* is not connected to a stream pipe.
ENXIO	Hangup received on *fildes*.

I_RECVFD   Retrieves the file descriptor associated with the message sent by an I_SENDFD ioctl over a stream pipe. *arg* is a pointer to a data buffer large enough to hold an **strrecvfd** data structure containing the following members:

```
int fd;
uid_t uid;
gid_t gid;
char fill[8];
```

fd is an integer file descriptor. uid and gid are the user id and group id, respectively, of the sending stream.

If O_NDELAY and O_NONBLOCK are clear [see open(2)], I_RECVFD will block until a message is present at the stream head. If O_NDELAY or O_NONBLOCK is set, I_RECVFD will fail with **errno** set to EAGAIN if no message is present at the stream head.

If the message at the stream head is a message sent by an I_SENDFD, a new user file descriptor is allocated for the file pointer contained in the message. The new file descriptor is placed in the fd field of the **strrecvfd** structure. The structure is copied into the user data buffer pointed to by *arg*. On failure, **errno** is set to one of the following values:

EAGAIN	A message is not present at the stream head read queue, and the O_NDELAY or O_NONBLOCK flag is set.
EBADMSG	The message at the stream head read queue is not a message containing a passed file descriptor.
EFAULT	*arg* points outside the allocated address space.
EMFILE	NOFILES file descriptors are currently open.
ENXIO	Hangup received on *fildes*.
EOVERFLOW	*uid* or *gid* is too large to be stored in the structure pointed to by *arg*.

I_LIST   Allows the user to list all the module names on the stream, up to and including the topmost driver name. If *arg* is NULL, the return value is the number of modules, including the driver, that are on the stream pointed to by *fildes*. This allows the user to allocate enough space for the module names. If *arg* is non-NULL, it should point to an **str_list** structure that has the following members:

```
int sl_nmods;
struct str_mlist    *sl_modlist;
```

The `str_mlist` structure has the following member:

```
char l_name[FMNAMESZ+1];
```

`sl_nmods` indicates the number of entries the user has allocated in the array and on return, `sl_modlist` contains the list of module names. The return value indicates the number of entries that have been filled in. On failure, **errno** may be set to one of the following values:

EINVAL   The `sl_nmods` member is less than 1.

EAGAIN   Unable to allocate buffers

I_ATMARK   Allows the user to see if the current message on the stream head read queue is "marked" by some module downstream. *arg* determines how the checking is done when there may be multiple marked messages on the stream head read queue. It may take the following values:

ANYMARK   Check if the message is marked.

LASTMARK   Check if the message is the last one marked on the queue.

The return value is 1 if the mark condition is satisfied and 0 otherwise. On failure, **errno** may be set to the following value:

EINVAL   Invalid *arg* value.

I_CKBAND   Check if the message of a given priority band exists on the stream head read queue. This returns 1 if a message of a given priority exists, or -1 on error. *arg* should be an integer containing the value of the priority band in question. On failure, **errno** may be set to the following value:

EINVAL   Invalid *arg* value.

I_GETBAND   Returns the priority band of the first message on the stream head read queue in the integer referenced by *arg*. On failure, **errno** may be set to the following value:

ENODATA   No message on the stream head read queue.

I_CANPUT   Check if a certain band is writable. *arg* is set to the priority band in question. The return value is 0 if the priority band *arg* is flow controlled, 1 if the band is writable, or -1 on error. On failure, **errno** may be set to the following value:

EINVAL   Invalid *arg* value.

I_SETCLTIME

                Allows the user to set the time the stream head will delay when a stream is closing and there are data on the write queues. Before closing each module and driver, the stream head will delay for the specified amount of time to allow the data to drain. If, after the delay, data are still present, data will be flushed. *arg* is a pointer to the number of milliseconds to delay, rounded up to the nearest legal value on the system. The default is fifteen seconds. On failure, **errno** may be set to the following value:

EINVAL   Invalid *arg* value.

I_GETCLTIME

Returns the close time delay in the long pointed by *arg*.

The following four commands are used for connecting and disconnecting multiplexed STREAMS configurations.

I_LINK   Connects two streams, where *fildes* is the file descriptor of the stream connected to the multiplexing driver, and *arg* is the file descriptor of the stream connected to another driver. The stream designated by *arg* gets connected below the multiplexing driver. I_LINK requires the multiplexing driver to send an acknowledgement message to the stream head regarding the linking operation. This call returns a multiplexor ID number (an identifier used to disconnect the multiplexor, see I_UNLINK) on success, and a -1 on failure. On failure, **errno** is set to one of the following values:

ENXIO   Hangup received on *fildes*.

ETIME   Time out before acknowledgement message was received at stream head.

EAGAIN   Temporarily unable to allocate storage to perform the I_LINK.

ENOSR   Unable to allocate storage to perform the I_LINK due to insufficient STREAMS memory resources.

EBADF   *arg* is not a valid, open file descriptor.

EINVAL   *fildes* stream does not support multiplexing.

EINVAL   *arg* is not a stream, or is already linked under a multiplexor.

EINVAL   The specified link operation would cause a "cycle" in the resulting configuration; that is, if a given driver is linked into a multiplexing configuration in more than one place.

EINVAL   *fildes* is the file descriptor of a pipe or FIFO.

An I_LINK can also fail while waiting for the multiplexing driver to acknowledge the link request, if a message indicating an error or a hangup is received at the stream head of *fildes*. In addition, an error code can be returned in the positive or negative acknowledgement message. For these cases, I_LINK will fail with **errno** set to the value in the message.

I_UNLINK   Disconnects the two streams specified by *fildes* and *arg*. *fildes* is the
                  file descriptor of the stream connected to the multiplexing driver.
                  arg is the multiplexor ID number that was returned by the I_LINK.
                  If *arg* is -1, then all Streams which were linked to *fildes* are discon-
                  nected. As in I_LINK, this command requires the multiplexing
                  driver to acknowledge the unlink. On failure, **errno** is set to one
                  of the following values:

  ENXIO   Hangup received on *fildes*.

  ETIME   Time out before acknowledgement message was
                  received at stream head.

  ENOSR   Unable to allocate storage to perform the I_UNLINK
                  due to insufficient STREAMS memory resources.

  EINVAL   *arg* is an invalid multiplexor ID number or *fildes* is
                  not the stream on which the I_LINK that returned
                  arg was performed.

  EINVAL   *fildes* is the file descriptor of a pipe or FIFO.

                  An I_UNLINK can also fail while waiting for the multiplexing driver
                  to acknowledge the link request, if a message indicating an error or
                  a hangup is received at the stream head of *fildes*. In addition, an
                  error code can be returned in the positive or negative acknowledge-
                  ment message. For these cases, I_UNLINK will fail with **errno** set
                  to the value in the message.

I_PLINK   Connects two streams, where *fildes* is the file descriptor of the
                  stream connected to the multiplexing driver, and *arg* is the file
                  descriptor of the stream connected to another driver. The stream
                  designated by *arg* gets connected via a persistent link below the
                  multiplexing driver. I_PLINK requires the multiplexing driver to
                  send an acknowledgement message to the stream head regarding
                  the linking operation. This call creates a persistent link which can
                  exist even if the file descriptor *fildes* associated with the upper
                  stream to the multiplexing driver is closed. This call returns a mul-
                  tiplexor ID number (an identifier that may be used to disconnect
                  the multiplexor, see I_PUNLINK) on success, and a -1 on failure.
                  On failure, **errno** may be set to one of the following values:

  ENXIO   Hangup received on *fildes*.

  ETIME   Time out before acknowledgement message was
                  received at the stream head.

  EAGAIN   Unable to allocate STREAMS storage to perform the
                  I_PLINK.

  EBADF   *arg* is not a valid, open file descriptor.

  EINVAL   *fildes* does not support multiplexing.

EINVAL   *arg* is not a stream or is already linked under a mul-
                  tiplexor.

EINVAL   The specified link operation would cause a "cycle" in
                  the resulting configuration; that is, if a given stream
                  head is linked into a multiplexing configuration in
                  more than one place.

EINVAL   *fildes* is the file descriptor of a pipe or FIFO.

An I_PLINK can also fail while waiting for the multiplexing driver
to acknowledge the link request, if a message indicating an error
on a hangup is received at the stream head of *fildes*. In addition,
an error code can be returned in the positive or negative acknowledgement message. For these cases, I_PLINK will fail with
errno set to the value in the message.

I_PUNLINK   Disconnects the two streams specified by *fildes* and *arg* that are con-
             nected with a persistent link. *fildes* is the file descriptor of the
             stream connected to the multiplexing driver. *arg* is the multiplexor
             ID number that was returned by I_PLINK when a stream was
             linked below the multiplexing driver. If *arg* is MUXID_ALL then all
             streams which are persistent links to *fildes* are disconnected. As in
             I_PLINK, this command requires the multiplexing driver to ack-
             nowledge the unlink. On failure, errno may be set to one of the
             following values:

ENXIO   Hangup received on *fildes*.

ETIME   Time out before acknowledgement message was
                  received at the stream head.

EAGAIN   Unable to allocate buffers for the acknowledgement
                  message.

EINVAL   Invalid multiplexor ID number.

EINVAL   *fildes* is the file descriptor of a pipe or FIFO.

An I_PUNLINK can also fail while waiting for the multiplexing
driver to acknowledge the link request if a message indicating an
error or a hangup is received at the stream head of *fildes*. In addition, an error code can be returned in the positive or negative acknowledgement message. For these cases, I_PUNLINK will fail with
errno set to the value in the message.

SEE ALSO
close(2), fcntl(2), getmsg(2), intro(2), ioctl(2), open(2), poll(2), putmsg(2),
read(2), signal(2), write(2), signal(5).
Programmer's Guide: STREAMS.

DIAGNOSTICS
Unless specified otherwise above, the return value from ioctl is 0 upon success
and -1 upon failure with errno set as indicated.

NAME

sxt – pseudo-device driver

DESCRIPTION

The special file /dev/sxt is a pseudo-device driver that interposes a discipline between the standard tty line disciplines and a real device driver. The standard disciplines manipulate virtual tty structures (channels) declared by the /dev/sxt driver. /dev/sxt acts as a discipline manipulating a real tty structure declared by a real device driver. The /dev/sxt driver is currently only used by the shl(1) command.

Virtual ttys are named by inodes in the subdirectory /dev/sxt and are allocated in groups of up to eight. To allocate a group, a program should exclusively open a file with a name of the form /dev/sxt/??0 (channel 0) and then execute a SXTIOCLINK ioctl call to initiate the multiplexing.

Only one channel, the controlling channel, can receive input from the keyboard at a time; others attempting to read will be blocked.

There are two groups of ioctl(2) commands supported by sxt. The first group contains the standard ioctl commands described in termio(7), with the addition of the following:

TIOCEXCL   Set exclusive use mode: no further opens are permitted until the file has been closed.

TIOCNXCL   Reset exclusive use mode: further opens are once again permitted.

The second group are commands to sxt itself. Some of these may only be executed on channel 0.

SXTIOCLINK   Allocate a channel group and multiplex the virtual ttys onto the real tty. The argument is the number of channels to allocate. This command may only be executed on channel 0. Possible errors include:

EINVAL   The argument is out of range.

ENOTTY   The command was not issued from a real tty.

ENXIO   linesw is not configured with sxt.

EBUSY   An SXTIOCLINK command has already been issued for this real tty.

ENOMEM   There is no system memory available for allocating the virtual tty structures.

EBADF   Channel 0 was not opened before this call.

SXTIOCSWTCH   Set the controlling channel. Possible errors include:

EINVAL   An invalid channel number was given.

EPERM   The command was not executed from channel 0.

SXTIOCWF	Cause a channel to wait until it is the controlling channel. This command will return the error, EINVAL, if an invalid channel number is given.
SXTIOCUBLK	Turn off the loblk control flag in the virtual tty of the indicated channel. The error EINVAL will be returned if an invalid number or channel 0 is given.
SXTIOCSTAT	Get the status (blocked on input or output) of each channel and store in the sxtblock structure referenced by the argument. The error EFAULT will be returned if the structure cannot be written.
SXTIOCTRACE	Enable tracing. Tracing information is written to the console on the 3B2 Computer. This command has no effect if tracing is not configured.
SXTIOCNOTRACE	Disable tracing. This command has no effect if tracing is not configured.

FILES

/dev/sxt/??[0-7]   Virtual tty devices

SEE ALSO

shl(1), stty(1) ioctl(2), open(2), termio(7)

NAME

timod – Transport Interface cooperating STREAMS module

DESCRIPTION

timod is a STREAMS module for use with the Transport Interface (TI) functions of the Network Services library. The timod module converts a set of ioctl(2) calls into STREAMS messages that may be consumed by a transport protocol provider which supports the Transport Interface. This allows a user to initiate certain TI functions as atomic operations.

The timod module must be pushed onto only a stream terminated by a transport protocol provider which supports the TI.

All STREAMS messages, with the exception of the message types generated from the ioctl commands described below, will be transparently passed to the neighboring STREAMS module or driver. The messages generated from the following ioctl commands are recognized and processed by the timod module. The format of the ioctl call is:

```
#include <sys/stropts.h>
        _
        _
struct strioctl strioctl;
        _
        _
strioctl.ic_cmd = cmd;
strioctl.ic_timeout = INFTIM;
strioctl.ic_len = size;
strioctl.ic_dp = (char *)buf
ioctl(fildes, I_STR, &strioctl);
```

Where, on issuance, *size* is the size of the appropriate TI message to be sent to the transport provider and on return *size* is the size of the appropriate TI message from the transport provider in response to the issued TI message. *buf* is a pointer to a buffer large enough to hold the contents of the appropriate TI messages. The TI message types are defined in <sys/tihdr.h>. The possible values for the *cmd* field are:

TI_BIND   Bind an address to the underlying transport protocol provider. The message issued to the TI_BIND ioctl is equivalent to the TI message type T_BIND_REQ and the message returned by the successful completion of the ioctl is equivalent to the TI message type T_BIND_ACK.

TI_UNBIND   Unbind an address from the underlying transport protocol provider. The message issued to the TI_UNBIND ioctl is equivalent to the TI message type T_UNBIND_REQ and the message returned by the successful completion of the ioctl is equivalent to the TI message type T_OK_ACK.

TI_GETINFO   Get the TI protocol specific information from the transport protocol provider. The message issued to the TI_GETINFO ioctl is equivalent to the TI message type T_INFO_REQ and the message

returned by the successful completion of the ioctl is equivalent
to the TI message type T_INFO_ACK.

TI_OPTMGMT   Get, set or negotiate protocol specific options with the transport
protocol provider. The message issued to the TI_OPTMGMT ioctl
is equivalent to the TI message type T_OPTMGMT_REQ and the
message returned by the successful completion of the ioctl is
equivalent to the TI message type T_OPTMGMT_ACK.

FILES

<sys/timod.h>
<sys/tiuser.h>
<sys/tihdr.h>
<sys/errno.h>

SEE ALSO

tirdwr(7).
Programmer's Guide: STREAMS.
Programmer's Guide: Networking Interfaces.

DIAGNOSTICS

If the ioctl system call returns with a value greater than 0, the lower 8 bits of
the return value will be one of the TI error codes as defined in <sys/tiuser.h>.
If the TI error is of type TSYSERR, then the next 8 bits of the return value will contain an error as defined in <sys/errno.h> [see intro(2)].

NAME

tirdwr – Transport Interface read/write interface STREAMS module

DESCRIPTION

tirdwr is a STREAMS module that provides an alternate interface to a transport provider which supports the Transport Interface (TI) functions of the Network Services library (see Section 3N). This alternate interface, allows a user to communicate with the transport protocol provider using the read(2) and write(2) system calls. The putmsg(2) and getmsg(2) system calls may also be used. However, putmsg and getmsg can only transfer data messages between user and stream.

The tirdwr module must only be pushed [see I_PUSH in streamio(7)] onto a stream terminated by a transport protocol provider which supports the TI. After the tirdwr module has been pushed onto a stream, none of the Transport Interface functions can be used. Subsequent calls to TI functions will cause an error on the stream. Once the error is detected, subsequent system calls on the stream will return an error with errno set to EPROTO.

The following are the actions taken by the tirdwr module when pushed on the stream, popped [see I_POP in streamio(7)] off the stream, or when data passes through it.

push –   When the module is pushed onto a stream, it will check any existing data destined for the user to ensure that only regular data messages are present. It will ignore any messages on the stream that relate to process management, such as messages that generate signals to the user processes associated with the stream. If any other messages are present, the I_PUSH will return an error with errno set to EPROTO.

write –   The module will take the following actions on data that originated from a write system call:

- All messages with the exception of messages that contain control portions (see the putmsg and getmsg system calls) will be transparently passed onto the module's downstream neighbor.

- Any zero length data messages will be freed by the module and they will not be passed onto the module's downstream neighbor.

- Any messages with control portions will generate an error, and any further system calls associated with the stream will fail with errno set to EPROTO.

read –   The module will take the following actions on data that originated from the transport protocol provider:

- All messages with the exception of those that contain control portions (see the putmsg and getmsg system calls) will be transparently passed onto the module's upstream neighbor.

- The action taken on messages with control portions will be as follows:

□ Messages that represent expedited data will generate an error. All further system calls associated with the stream will fail with **errno** set to EPROTO.

□ Any data messages with control portions will have the control portions removed from the message prior to passing the message on to the upstream neighbor.

□ Messages that represent an orderly release indication from the transport provider will generate a zero length data message, indicating the end of file, which will be sent to the reader of the stream. The orderly release message itself will be freed by the module.

□ Messages that represent an abortive disconnect indication from the transport provider will cause all further **write** and **putmsg** system calls to fail with **errno** set to ENXIO. All further **read** and **getmsg** system calls will return zero length data (indicating end of file) once all previous data has been read.

□ With the exception of the above rules, all other messages with control portions will generate an error and all further system calls associated with the stream will fail with **errno** set to EPROTO.

— Any zero length data messages will be freed by the module and they will not be passed onto the module's upstream neighbor.

pop — When the module is popped off the stream or the stream is closed, the module will take the following action:

— If an orderly release indication has been previously received, then an orderly release request will be sent to the remote side of the transport connection.

SEE ALSO

streamio(7), timod(7).
intro(2), getmsg(2), putmsg(2), read(2), write(2), intro(3).
Programmer's Guide: STREAMS.
Programmer's Guide: Networking Interfaces.

NAME

xt – STREAMS-based multiplexed tty driver for AT&T windowing terminals

DESCRIPTION

The xt driver provides virtual tty(7) circuits multiplexed onto STREAMS-based device drivers. STREAMS-based xt is a streams upper multiplexor pseudo-device driver that sits between the stream head and a STREAMS hardware device driver.

Virtual tty(7) circuits are named by character-special files of the form /dev/xt/???. Filenames end in three digits, where the first two represent the channel group and the last represents the virtual tty(7) number (0-7) of the channel group. Allocation of a new channel group is done dynamically by attempting to open a name ending in 0 with the O_EXCL flag set. After a successful open, the tty(7) file onto which the channels are to be multiplexed should be passed to xt via the I_LINK streamio(7) request. Afterwards, all the channels in the group will behave as normal tty(7) files, with data passed in packets via the real tty(7) line.

The xt driver implements the protocol described in xtproto(5) and in layers(5). Packets are formatted as described in xtproto(5), while the contents of packets conform to the description in layers(5).

There are four groups of ioctl(2) requests recognized by xt. The first group contains the normal tty ioctl(2) request described in termio(7), with the addition of the following:

TIOCGWINSZ   Requires the address of a winsize structure as an argument. The window sizes of the layer associated with the file descriptor argument to ioctl(2) are copied to the structure.

The second group of ioctl(2) requests concerns control of the windowing terminal. Request from this second group which involve communication with the terminal are described in more detail in layers(5). These requests are defined in the header file <sys/jioctl.h>. The requests are as follows:

JTYPE, JMPX   Both return the value JMPX. These are used to identify a terminal device as an xt channel.

JBOOT, JTERM   Both generate an appropriate command packet to the windowing terminal affecting the layer associated with the file descriptor argument to ioctl(2). They may return the error code EAGAIN on STREAMS buffer allocation failure.

JTIMOM   Specifies the timeouts in milliseconds. Invalid except on channel 0. This may return the error code EAGAIN on STREAMS buffer allocation failure.

JWINSIZE   Requires the address of a jwinsize structure as an argument. The window sizes of the layer associated with the file descriptor argument to ioctl(2) are copied to the structure.

JTRUN   Requires the address of a string of the form channel, UNIX system command as an argument. Run the UNIX system command in the specified channel (layer). It may return the error code EAGAIN on STREAMS buffer allocation failure.

JZOMBOOT   Generate a command packet to the windowing terminal to
                      enter download mode on the channel associated with the file
                      descriptor argument to ioctl(2), like JBOOT; but when the
                      download is finished, make the layer a zombie (ready for
                      debugging). It may return the error code EAGAIN on STREAMS
                      buffer allocation failure.

JAGENT   Send the supplied data as a command packet to invoke a win-
                      dowing terminal agent routine, and return the terminal's
                      response to the calling process. Invalid except on the file
                      descriptor for channel 0. See jagent(5). It may return the
                      error code EAGAIN on STREAMS buffer allocation failure.

JXTPROTO   Set xt protocol type [see xtproto(5)]. It may return the error
                      code EAGAIN on STREAMS buffer allocation failure.

The third group of ioctl(2) requests concerns the configuration of xt, and is
described in the header file <sys/nxt.h>. The requests are as follows:

XTIOCTYPE   Returns the value XTIOCTYPE. Identical in purpose to JMPX.

XTIOCHEX   Specifies that ENCODING MODE should be turned on.

XTIOCTRACE   Requires the address of a Tbuf structure as an argument. The
                      structure is filled with the contents of the driver trace buffer.
                      Tracing is enabled. See xtt(1).

XTIOCNOTRACE   Tracing is disabled.

XTIOCSTATS   Requires an argument that is the address of an array of size
                      S_NSTATS, of type Stats_t. The array is filled with the con-
                      tents of the driver statistics array. See xts(1).

The fourth group of ioctl(2) requests concerns configuring streamio(7) multiplexor. The requests are as follows:

I_LINK   Links the hardware driver underneath xt. The arguments to
                      the ioctl are documented in streamio(7).

I_UNLINK   Unlinks the hardware driver underneath xt. The arguments to
                      the ioctl are documented in streamio(7).

FILES

/dev/xt/??[0-7]   multiplexed special files
/usr/include/sys/jioctl.h   packet command types
/usr/include/sys/nxtproto.h channel multiplexing protocol definitions
/usr/include/sys/nxt.h   STREAMS-based driver specific definitions

SEE ALSO

layers(1), xts(1M), xtt(1M)
ioctl(2), open(2)
jagent(5), layers(5), xtproto(5)
streamio(7), termio(7), tty(7).
Programmer's Guide: STREAMS

G | Appendix G: Hardware Examples

Hardware Examples   G-1
3B2 Computer Configuration Mechanism   G-1

3B2 STREAMS-based Ports Driver   G-2
Data Structures   G-2
Open and Close Routines   G-4
Write Put Procedure   G-5
Write Service Procedure   G-7
Interrupt Procedure   G-8
Read Service Procedure   G-9

3B2 STREAMS-based Console Driver   G-10
Data Structures   G-11
Open and Close Routines   G-12
Read-Side Processing   G-12
 ■ Interrupt Level Processing   G-12
 ■ Service Procedure Processing   G-13
Write-Side Processing   G-13
Daemon Mode   G-14

3B2 STREAMS-based XT Driver   G-15
Data Structures   G-21
Open Processing   G-24
Close Processing   G-26
Data Flow   G-26
Read-Side Processing   G-28

Write-Side Processing   G-28
Multiplexing   G-32
Flow Control   G-32
■ STREAMS Flow Control   G-32
■ XT Driver Protocol Flow Control   G-32
Scanning   G-33
Cyclic Redundancy Check   G-33
Encoding   G-33

Extended STREAMS Buffers G-35

Hardware Examples

This appendix provides information pertaining to certain hardware types. These are only examples and their inclusion does not preclude using the STREAMS mechanism in hardware not mentioned here.

3B2 Computer Configuration Mechanism

The 3B2 computer configuration mechanism differentiates STREAMS devices from character devices by a special type in the *flag* field of master files contained in /etc/master.d [see master(4)]. The c flag specifies a non-STREAMS character I/O device driver. The f flag specifies that the associated cdevsw entry will be a STREAMS driver. The special file (node) that identifies the STREAMS driver must be a character special file, as is the file for a character device driver, because the system call entry point for STREAMS drivers is also the cdevsw table.

STREAMS modules are identified by an m in the *flag* field of master files contained in /etc/master.d and the configuration mechanism creates an associated fmodsw table entry for all such modules.

 Any combination of block, STREAMS drivers and STREAMS modules may be specified. However, on the 3B2 Computer, it is illegal to specify a STREAMS device or module with a character device.

3B2 STREAMS-based Ports Driver

The AT&T 3B2 computers support asynchronous RS232 communication with its PORTS and HIPORTS boards. In UNIX® System V Release 4.0, the device driver for the 3B2 ports board is a STREAMS-based asynchronous driver. Each model in the 3B2 series supports PORTS and HIPORTS boards, and each board supports four asynchronous ports and one parallel Centronics line printer port. The basic difference between PORTS and HIPORTS is that PORTS polls the **uart** for input, whereas HIPORTS gets input on an interrupt basis. In this section an expression *ports board* is used collectively for PORTS and HIPORTS.

The *ports board* is driven by an Intel® 8186 microprocessor. The board is made operational by downloading (pumping) the firmware on the board. This is done by the **/sbin/npump** command invoked by **/sbin/ports** which determines the number and locations of each *ports board* installed. **/sbin/ports** is called from a script that is invoked by **/sbin/init** from the **/sbin/inittab** file when going to an initial state 2 or 3.

From the file system perspective, each port is named **/dev/term/MN** where M is the physical board slot number on the backplane of the 3B2 and N is 1, 2, 3, 4, or 5 identifying the port. The port position 5 is for the Centronics port.

The *ports board* communicates via interrupts with the 3B2 host. Typical interrupts are acknowledgements of receipt of data buffer from the host, data arrival from a port, connection and disconnection to/from the host, an acknowledgement of option setting on the port, etc. The *ports board* also performs some **termio(7)** processing on the board.

Data passing between the 3B2 host processor and the *ports board* is performed in units of 64 bytes that is the size of data silos on the *ports board*.

Data Structures

Data local to the ports driver is stored in the *npp_tty* array that is an array of the structure **strtty**. **strtty** has the following format:

```
struct strtty
{
    struct t_buf    t_in;           /* input buffer information */
    struct t_buf    t_out;          /* output buffer information */
    queue_t         *t_rdqp;        /* pointer to tty read queue */
    mblk_t          *t_ioctlp;      /* ioctl block pointer */
    mblk_t          *t_lbuf;        /* pointer to a large data buffer */
    int             t_dev;          /* tty minor device number */
    long            t_iflag;        /* input setting flag */
    long            t_oflag;        /* output setting flag */
    long            t_cflag;        /* physical setting flag */
    long            t_lflag;        /* line discipline flag */
    short           t_state;        /* internal state */
    char            t_line;         /* active line discipline */
    char            t_dstat;        /* internal state flags */
    unsigned char   t_cc[NCCS];     /* settable control characters */
};
```

The *struct t_buf t_in* and *struct t_buf t_out* are buffers used for incoming and out-going messages to and from a *ports board*. The format is:

```
struct t_buf
{
        mblk_t          *bu_bp;         /* message block pointer */
        unsigned char   *bu_ptr;        /* data buffer pointer */
        ushort          bu_cnt;         /* data buffer character count */
};
```

where *bu_bp* is a pointer to a 64-byte message block and *bu_ptr* contains the physical address of the data part of the *bu_bp* message block, and *bu_cnt* is a data byte count in the buffer.

t_ioctlp is used to store **ioctl** data until the firmware acknowledges that the **ioctl** command has been performed. *t_rdqp* is a pointer to the driver's queue. *t_lbuf* is a large buffer used to store input data. The *t_dev* entry is a minor device number. The **termio** flags *c_iflag, c_oflag, c_cflag, c_lflag, c_line*, and the array *c_cc* are stored in *t_iflag, t_oflag, t_cflag, t_lflag, t_line*, and *t_cc* entries respectively. The *t_dstat* and *t_state* fields are used to store internal driver states.

The following lists the *t_state* flags used by the ports driver code:

- WOPEN - the driver is waiting for an open to complete.

- ISOPEN - the driver is open.

- TBLOCK - the driver has sent a control character to the terminal to block transmission from the terminal (input flow control).

- CARR_ON - set if a carrier has been detected by the driver.

- BUSY - the driver is transmitting data.

- WIOC - wait for an **ioctl** to complete.

- TTSTOP - output has been stopped by a control-s character received from the terminal (output flow control).

- TIMEOUT - set if timeout is in progress, for handling delays.

- TTIOW - a user process is sleeping awaiting for the driver to, for example, drain output, wait for a carrier, get buffers.

The list below gives the *t_dstat* flags used by the ports driver code:

- SPLITMSG - set if the buffer to be transmitted is greater than the maximum size the board can handle. The message is transmitted in PPBUF-SIZ (64-byte) units.

- WENTRY - set if waiting for transmit a queue entry on the board.

- SUPBUF - set if a port has received allocated STREAMS buffers.

- OPDRAIN - wait for output to drain in the open routine.

Open and Close Routines

The open routine is called whenever the port is opened. It allocates a *sizeof* (structure **stroptions**) buffer and in this buffer assigns the Stream head's read queue high and low water marks to 512 and 256 bytes respectively and also indicates whether a controlling terminal is assigned (see M_SETOPTS message). It also assigns initial values to the local *iflag, oflag, cflag, lflag,* and *c_cc* elements. The open allocates a STREAMS message block and uses this buffer to assign a set options message using the local *iflag, oflag, cflag, lflag,* and *c_cc* values. The open also sends a connect message to the *ports board*, and the port is marked as open (i.e., ISOPEN is set in the *t_state* field).

On the first open, five 64-byte buffers are allocated; these buffers are used as input buffers for incoming data. On subsequent opens, four 64-byte buffers are allocated per port.

If the device is not opened with O_NDELAY or O_NONBLOCK and there is no carrier detected, the sleep occurs until a carrier is detected or until the open is interrupted by the calling application. Otherwise, the open routine proceeds without waiting for a carrier.

The driver's close routine is called on the last close of a port. It drains the output queue by reading from the driver's write queue and transmitting the data to the board and frees the current input buffer and the transmit buffer. The close routine decrements the number of input buffers by 5 or 4 depending whether the buffers were allocated on the first or subsequent opens of a port.

The device is marked closed and the carrier flag is taken off. Finally, a disconnect message is sent to the *ports board*. In the disconnect sequence the host will be interrupted the same number of times as there are buffers to be freed (deallocated) on the board.

Write Put Procedure

The driver's write **put** procedure is called when a message is sent to the *ports board*. If the carrier is not on, data are held on the queue. The **put** procedure processes M_DATA, M_IOCTL, and M_CTL messages.

M_DATA messages are unbundled, thus a message is composed of linked *n* data blocks that are "broken" into *n* separate messages and put into the driver's write queue. Zero length messages are discarded.

The driver's write queue is read and message data are written to the *ports board*. If the data block is greater than 64 bytes (the maximum buffer size for the *ports board*), the data are "broken" into at most 64-byte blocks and transmitted.

If data are to be transmitted to the device that currently does not have Data Terminal Ready set high (e.g., the terminal is powered off), Terminal Ready signal goes high and data that were enqueued are written to the device.

For M_IOCTL the following **ioctls** are handled handled by the driver [see also **termio(7)**]:

- TCSETAW, TCSETA, TCSETSW, TCSETS - if the *ports board* is busy, the message is put back onto the driver's write queue. If the *ports board* can take the message, the *iflag, oflag, cflag, lflag,* and *cc_c* array are copied into a local data area, terminal parameters are set, and an M_IOCACK message is sent upstream. If terminal parameters can't be set because of lack of STREAMS buffers, the original message is put back on the head of the write queue for TCSETA and at the end of the write queue for TCSETAW. When the buffer becomes available the parameters are set. If the terminal parameter setting fails for any other reason, the negative acknowledgement is sent.

- TCSETAF, TCSETSF - these are treated like TCSETAW except that before the terminal parameters are set on the *ports board*, the board's input queue and the driver's read queue are flushed.

- TCGETA - a STREAMS buffer of size **struct termio** is allocated and *iflag, oflag, cflag, lflag,* and *cc_c* array values are copied from the local buffer area to this allocated buffer, and the buffer is sent in the M_IOCACK upstream.

- TCGETS - a STREAMS buffer of size **struct termios** is allocated and *iflag, oflag, cflag, lflag,* and *c_cc* array values are copied from the local buffer area to this allocated buffer, and the buffer is sent in the M_IOCACK upstream.

- PPC_VERS - this determines if there is a HIPORTS or PORTS board in a particular I/O slot.

- P_RST - this is called by **/sbin/npump** to reset ROMware.

- P_SYSGEN - this is called by **/sbin/npump** to "sysgen" the *ports board* (see note below for further details).

- P_LOAD - this is called by **/sbin/npump** to download the pump code to the board.

- P_FCF - this is called by **/sbin/npump** to "jump start" RAM code. The execution of the code starts on the board.

- EUC_MSAVE, EUC_MREST, EUC_IXLOFF, EUC_IXLON, EUC_OXLOFF, EUC_OXLON - the driver sends an M_IOCACK message upstream upon receipt of these **ioctls**, the module upstream acts upon them to handle multi-byte characters.

- **ioctls** type LDIOC are acknowledged and all other **ioctls** receive a negative acknowledgement.

 NOTE "sysgen" means system generation. First, **/sbin/npump** code sends a Reset, downloads the firmware, and then does an FCF (Force Call Function) call. **/sbin/npump** supplies the board with an address at which to begin execution of the downloaded program. After the FCF call, **/sbin/npump** does a "sysgen" which jump starts the the board.

termio(7) processing is shared between the line discipline module and the board. This is done using line discipline functional negotiation. The ports driver handles the M_CTL command MC_CANONQUERY sent by the line discipline module. Other commands are freed. The convention used between the ports driver and the line discipline module is that an M_CTL message has the same format as that of an M_IOCTL message. The returned command field is set to MC_SOME_CANON. The M_CTL message is generated by the line discipline module that queries the ports driver for **termios** flags, c_iflag, c_oflag, or c_lflag values the driver is handling. The bit value of 1 is assigned for c_iflag and c_oflag to indicate that the driver handles these flags. The value of 0 is assigned to c_lflag to indicate that the driver does not handle this flag.

Write Service Procedure

The only purpose of the write-side **service** procedure is to handle flow control. If the state of the *ports board* is BUSY or WIOC, nothing can be sent until the state becomes clear. If the board is not busy, the message is read from the driver's write queue. If there are no data to send, the sleeping process is awaken to receive input. When there are data to send, type of data is checked before processing starts. M_DATA messages are transmitted in 64-byte units and M_IOCTL messages are handled in the same way as in the write **put** procedure. All other messages are freed.

Interrupt Procedure

There is no **put** procedure in read-side. An interrupt procedure queues data for later processing by the **service** procedure in order to avoid interrupt stack overflows. Therefore, the ports driver should not call the **putnext** utility routine from the interrupt routine, but use its input queue to store incoming messages.

 NOTE The interrupt stack is usually small, and at STREAMS priority there are many devices that can interrupt. By avoiding the use of the **putnext** utility routine (that puts a message to the next queue) from the interrupt routine helps to keep the stack from overflowing.

On the 3B2s, the interrupt stack size and queue stack size are 1000 in UNIX System V Release 4.0.

The ports driver's interrupt routine is invoked whenever there is any communication to/from the *ports board*. The following values are returned when the interrupt routine is called:

- PPC_RECV - data have been received from the *ports board* to the host. If the buffers on the *ports board* were flushed or disrupted in any way, the buffers are freed if the Stream is closed. Otherwise, a zero length message is sent upstream. If a break is received, an M_BREAK message is sent upstream. Data will be read off the queue by the **service** procedure.

- PPC_XMIT - data have been transmitted from the host to the *ports board*. The wake-up process waiting for the port is freed and data are transmitted. Data are transmitted in units of 64 or less bytes. After all data have been transmitted, the message block is freed and the driver's write queue is read and sent to the board.

- PPC_ASYNC - the following are the *ports board* asynchronous interrupts:

  □ AC_BRK - a break is detected from the ports line.

  □ AC_DIS - asynchronous disconnection. If the Stream is open, an M_HANGUP message is sent, and both the read and write queues on the *ports board* are flushed.

  □ AC_CON - asynchronous connection. All processes are awaken when the line becomes active.

      □ AC_FLU - the board's read and write queues are flushed.

■ PPC_OPTIONS - an acknowledgement that options have been set on the board. The buffer that passed options to the board is freed and any processes waiting the options to be set are awaken.

■ PPC_DISC, PPC_CONN - an acknowledgement report for port open and close.

■ PPC_DEVICE - an express job is issued.

■ PPC_BRK - a break has been sent to the board from the host.

■ SYSGEN - the port is set in "sysgen" state. Firmware has finished the initialization process.

■ NORMAL, FAULT, QFAULT - NORMAL (command returns successfully), FAULT (illegal instruction), QFAULT (job placed on the queue has an unknown operation code).

If the data queued by the interrupt routine go beyond {MAX_INPUT}, all data in the queue are thrown away.

 NOTE The system may impose a limit, {MAX_INPUT}, on the number of bytes that may be stored in the input queue. If data enqueued exceed {MAX_INPUT}, all data enqueued will be thrown away.

Read Service Procedure

The driver's read-side **service** routine passes data upstream. If the queue upstream from the driver is full and there are ordinary messages to be delivered upstream, these messages are placed back on the driver's queue for later transmittal. High priority messages are delivered upstream. If the queue is full due to the flow control limits, a message is sent to the *ports board* to suspend transmission to the host and the messages are put back at the head of the driver's read queue.

3B2 STREAMS-based Console Driver

The console in the 3B2 UNIX System is similar to an ordinary user terminal but has some differences such as the ability to halt the system. The console can be considered a "dumb" terminal controller because it does not do any **termio** processing but requires a line discipline module in the host to do that processing. UNIX System V Release 4.0 includes a STREAMS-based console driver.

This section describes the operation of the console driver using the STREAMS mechanism. It does not consider the function of the console driver outside the STREAMS environment, except for brief descriptions of console related terms used in various places in the code and documentation.

UNIX System V has four special file names in **/dev** associated with the 3B2 console device driver: **contty**, **systty**, **syscon**, and **console**.

- **contty** is a 3B2 specific device that refers to the second port on the system board. It is driven by the console device driver.

- **systty** is the *physical system console*. It can refer to any device that is to be accessible to the system at early initialization time. It would normally be linked to the device that is built-in to the kernel as the target for kernel **printfs**. **systty** stays linked to a particular device and it can be used as a login device.

- **syscon** is the *virtual system console*. It is used by the initialization routine to communicate to the user. **syscon** starts off linked to **systty** and will get linked back to **systty** if the initialization routine can't communicate with **syscon**.

  When a user goes to a single-user mode, the initialization routine relinks **syscon** to the user's terminal, and **syscon** will now communicate to the user at the terminal where the user started the shutdown.

  An interrupt from **systty** while the initialization routine is waiting for a response from **syscon** will cause **syscon** to be switched back to **systty**.

  syscon can be thought as the boot time and single-user-mode system console. Anything sent off from **inittab** during this period interfaces with **syscon** since the initialization routine will have made sure that **syscon** can be accessed. **syscon** is moved around by the system and, therefore, it should not be explicitly relinked by users. Since **syscon** is the *virtual device* that becomes attached to other normal terminal, it should not be used as a login device.

■ **console** is the *real system console*. It is the device to which daemons send their output and where other processes send messages to system administrators. **console** is normally used as the console login device.

The 3B2 system board integral **uart** driver (also called **iuart**) uses a 2681 Dual Asynchronous Receiver/Transmitter (DUART) for serial communication. The DUART communicates with the console and contty ports on the 3B2. From the file system perspective, each port is named **/dev/console** and **/dev/contty**. One channel of the integral Direct Memory Access (DMA) controller is assigned to each **uart** channel. DMA is only done for output operations. The **uart** generates an interrupt as each character is received.

Data Structures

The **iuart** uses the *iu_tty* array to maintain state information. The *iu_tty* array is of type structure **strtty** that is used by all STREAMS-based terminal drivers. The format of the **strtty** is given in the section describing the 3B2 STREAMS-based ports driver.

The **iuart** uses the *t_out.bu_bp* field as the place to hold data that are being DMA'ed for the output operation. The *t_in.bu_bp* field is used to buffer input data until data are sent upstream either when the buffer is full or the buffering timeout period has elapsed. The *t_dev* entry is the minor device number. There is a one-to-one correspondence between the minor device and the port number. For the 3B2, a minor device 0 corresponds to the console and a minor device 1 corresponds to the contty line. The **iuart** handles only the **termio** flags *c_iflag* and *c_cflag*, which are stored in the corresponding *t_iflag* and *t_cflag* fields of the structure **strtty**. The other fields are used in the same way as with the ports driver.

Open and Close Routines

The open and close routines of the console driver are nearly identical to those of the ports driver. As with the ports driver, the open routine allocates a *sizeof* buffer, assigns high and low water marks to the Stream head, and indicates whether a controlling terminal is to be assigned. The console driver will also sleep until a carrier is detected or the open routine is interrupted by the calling application, if the device is not open with O_NDELAY or O_NONBLOCK; otherwise the open routine proceeds without waiting for a carrier.

The open routine is called whenever the console or contty is opened. The open routine also assigns initial values to the local *iflag*s. The initial *iflag* values are IXON|IXANY|BRKINT|IGNPAR, and all other flags are set to zero. The default contty setting (*t_cflag*) is SSPEED|CS8|CREAD|HUPCL. The port is marked as open (ISOPEN is set in the *t_state* field). For the first open, if the line opened is the system console, the control modes are taken from the nonvolatile RAM (nvram).

The close routine is called on the last close close of the port. The close drains the output queue by reading from the driver's write queue and transmitting the data to the board. If HUPCL is set in the *cflag* field, a command to hang up the line is sent.

Read-Side Processing

The console driver's read-side processing is split between the interrupt level routines and the **service** procedure.

Interrupt Level Processing

The minor device number of the device interrupting is derived from the inter-rupt vector. The private data structure for the minor device is also obtained. If the received interrupt character is a special character (STOP, START) the driver specific routines are called to suspend/restart output. The incoming character is then checked for framing error, parity errors, and overruns. If a break condition is set in the DUART status registers and the BRKINT flag is set in the *iflags*, an M_BREAK message is sent upstream to the module above. If the ISTRIP flag is set, the left most bit (most significant bit) will be stripped off the incoming char-acter. The received character is then put into a STREAMS buffer and kept in the buffer until:

- Three clock ticks have elapsed since the last character was received, or

- READBUFSIZE (defined to be 128) characters have been received by the **iuart**.

When either of the above conditions have been satisfied, the STREAMS buffer containing the characters will be enqueued on the **iuart**'s read queue. The eventual handling of input by the **service** procedure is provided to avoid problems with interrupt stack overflows (also see note in "Interrupt Procedure" of the ports driver description).

Service Procedure Processing

The **service** procedure removes the message waiting in the read queue and if there is no flow control blockage upstream, the message is sent upstream. Otherwise, the **service** procedure enqueues the message back on the read queue and returns.

If **ldterm**'s read queue is full and input flow control is in effect, then a command is sent to the **uart** to block input. If the character count exceeds {MAX_INPUT}, data are dumped without warning and the read queues are flushed.

Write-Side Processing

The **put** procedure handles all processing on the write-side. The write-side handles the same messages as the **ldterm** module (see Chapter 12, the section "Write-Side Processing" under "Line Discipline Module").

M_DATA messages are processed by the **put** procedure that splits a complex M_DATA messages (message with several blocks attached) into individual blocks. If DMA is currently underway, the message is put back on the read queue and are examined when the DMA complete transmit interrupt is received.

The **iuart** handles M_IOCTL messages and recognizes the following **ioctls**: TCGETA, TCGETS, TCSETA, TCSETS, TCSETAW, TCSETSW, TCSETSF, and TCSETAF [see **termio**(7)]. The **ioctl** TCFLSH is converted to an M_FLUSH message that causes the read and write queues of the **iuart** to be flushed. In addition, if the FLUSHR flag is set in the M_FLUSH message, the message will be looped around. The **iuart** expects the line discipline module to handle the

TCXONC **ioctl** and generate an appropriate M_START/M_STOP or M_STARTI/M_STOPI message, which is then handled by the **iuart**. For EUC **ioctls** that support of multi-byte characters, an M_IOCACK is sent. All other **ioctls** requests receive an M_IOCNAK message from the **iuart**.

If activated from upstream by generation of M_STOP and M_START messages, the **iuart** disables/enables transmit interrupts from the DUART so that momentary lapses in output can be produced. M_START and M_STOP can be used if additional, settable characters are used for output flow control. If activated from upstream by the generation of M_STARTI and M_STOPI messages, the **iuart** enables/disables transmit interrupts from the DUART so that momentary lapses in input can be produced.

On receipt of the M_DELAY message upstream, the **iuart** causes a real time delay to be introduced in the data stream. The time value for the delay is the argument of the M_DELAY message.

All other messages received by the driver are freed.

Daemon Mode

Daemon mode is useful to those doing kernel debugging and driver development on the 3B2, if one has access to the daemon debugger. Sometimes there is a need to turn off daemon mode (^P) on the console. The console driver is set up so that one can turn off access to daemon mode by setting the control character to null. The following example shows how to do it:

```
/* setting the 2nd argument to 0 retrieves the current daemon character */

current = sys3b(S3BCCDEMON, 0);

/* setting the 2nd argument to 1 and the 3rd argument to 0 sets the daemon to 0 */
/* it can also be set to other than 0, if so desired */

sys3b(S3BCCDEMON, 1,0);
```

The driver only tries to enter daemon mode if the entry character is not null. If daemon mode is entered and **layers**(1) is used on the console, the terminal should be in encoding mode. Otherwise, the system may panic.

3B2 STREAMS-based XT Driver

The STREAMS-based xt driver is a multi-channel multiplexed packet driver that provides a windowing environment for all the AT&T windowing (dmd) terminals. This driver can be used over the STREAMS hardware drivers like the console and ports driver, and also over several networks such as Starlan® and Datakit®.

The STREAMS-based xt driver supports several AT&T windowing terminal such as the 5620, 615, 620, and 630. It runs under the control of the **layers** command [see **layers**(1), **layers**(5)]. The **layers** command initiates the windowing session, creates and kills processes as windows are created and deleted, and shuts down the session.

After a user has logged into a windowing terminal, the **layers** command does the following to set up the STREAMS-based xt driver:

- The control channel (xt/000) is opened (see Figure G-1).

- The standard input line is set to raw mode so that raw data can be received over the control channel.

- The **ldterm** module is popped from the standard input.

- The hardware driver is linked under the xt driver using the **ioctl** I_LINK [see **streamio**(7)]. Figure G-2 shows the STREAMS-based xt after I_LINK.

- The **layers** command then stays in a loop and reads the commands on the control channel xt/000.

- When the first window (xt/001) is opened with a mouse device, the **ldterm** module is pushed on the Stream (Figure G-2).

- More windows (maximum of seven) can now be created using the mouse device.

Figure G-3 shows a typical STREAMS-based xt driver architecture with one control channel and up to seven windows along with the line discipline module pushed on each window.

Data coming from the windows (channels) is multiplexed (N-to-1) onto a single Stream by the xt driver and data coming from the windowing terminal is de-multiplexed (1-to-N) and sent to the appropriate window. The **ldterm** module does the **termio**(7) processing for each window.

Figure G-1: STREAMS-based XT Driver (before link)

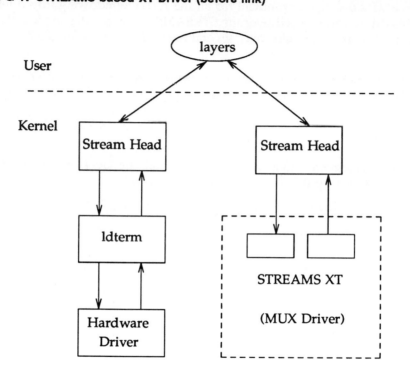

Figure G-2: STREAMS-based XT Driver (after link)

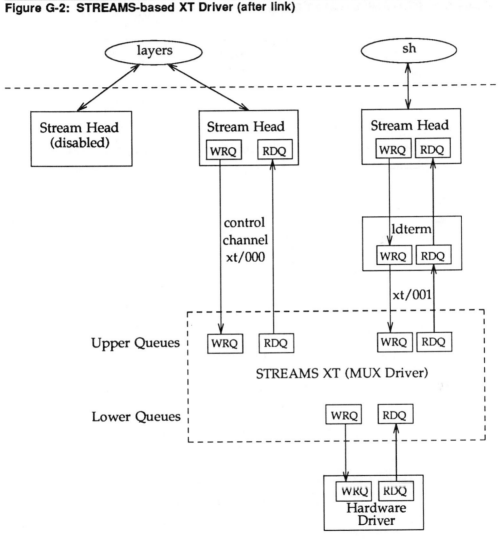

Figure G-3: STREAMS-based XT Driver

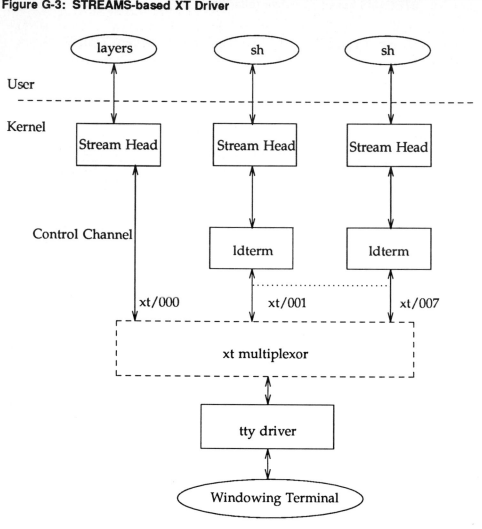

Figure G-4 shows the STREAMS-based xt driver over Starlan using the Network Access Unit (NAU) box. After logging into the machine via the NAU box, if the **layers** is invoked, the Starlan protocol stack is linked under the xt multiplexor. The same scenario can be achieved when logging into the host remotely from another machine.

Figure G-4: STREAMS-based XT Driver over Starlan

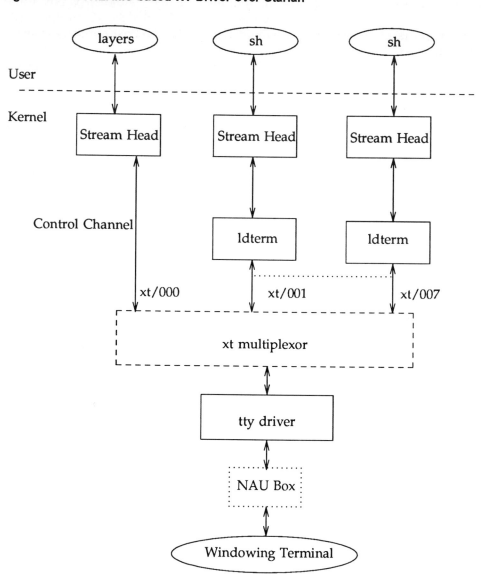

The protocol used by the STREAMS xt driver is the following:

<1:1|cntl:1|seq:3|cbits:3> <dsize:8> <dsize bytes of data> <crc1> <crc2>

where the notation <> signifies a byte and x:n signifies n bits of x (for example, cbits:3 signifies 3 bits of cbits). Bits are numbered from high bit of the byte. The *crc* is sent low byte first and applies to the entire packet except the two *crc* bytes.

The protocol uses packets with a 2-byte header containing a control flag, 3-bit sequence number, 3-bit channel number, and data size. The data part of the packet may not be larger than 32 bytes. The trailer contains a CRC-16 code in 2 bytes. Each channel is double buffered. See **xtproto**(5) for more protocol details.

Data Structures

The STREAMS-based xt driver is a multiplexing driver and hence has both the normal and multiplexing **qinit** structures. The following are the **qinit** structures:

```
struct qinit xtrinit = { nulldev, xtupisrv, nxtopen,
      nxtclose, NULL, &xt_iinfo, NULL };

struct qinit xtwinit = { putq, xtosrv, nxtopen, nxtclose,
      NULL, &xt_oinfo, NULL };

struct qinit m_xtrinit = { xtiput, xtisrv, nulldev,
      nulldev, NULL, &xt_iinfo, NULL};

struct qinit m_xtwinit = { nulldev, xtwsrv, nulldev,
      nulldev, NULL, &xt_oinfo, NULL};
```

The *xtrinit* and *xtwinit* structures are used for upper multiplexing and *m_xtrinit* and *m_xtwinit* structures are used for lower multiplexing.

The xt driver data structures also include the **module_info** and **streamtab** structures.

The STREAMS-based xt driver also has the private data structure to maintain the control and status information. Its private data structure xtctl has the format:

```
struct xtctl {
    struct queue    *xt_ttyq;          /* downstream write queue */
    struct xt_chan  xt_chan[MAXPCHAN]; /* channels per active tty */
    unsigned char   xt_next;           /* schedule this channel next */
    unsigned char   xt_lastscan;       /* channel that got canput failure */
    short           xt_ctlflg;         /* control flags */
    mblk_t          *xt_inbp;          /* block for incoming packet */
    mblk_t          *xt_pendjagent;    /* pending JAGENT ioctl packet */
    unsigned short  xt_insize;         /* # of data bytes expected */
    unsigned short  xt_incount;        /* # of data bytes left*/
    clock_t         xt_intime;         /* time stamp for input timeout */
    short           xt_instate;        /* state of incoming packet */
    unsigned char   xt_inchan;         /* channel # of incoming packet */
    unsigned char   xt_maxpkt;         /* max packet data size to terminal */
    unsigned long   xt_ttycflag;       /* dummy c_cflag - termio structure */
    unsigned char   xt_hex;            /* 1 if 6-bit path, 0 if 8-bit path */
    unsigned char   xt_firstchar;      /* 1st char in packet on input */
    unsigned char   xt_inpktcmd;       /* input packet command byte */
    unsigned char   xt_outpkts;        /* total outstanding packets waiting
                                          an acknowledgement */
    short           xt_recvtimo;       /* receive timeout in HZ for current
                                          baud rate */
    short           xt_HZperpkt;       /* time in HZ to transfer in outgoing
                                          packet at current baud rate */

    struct Tbuf     trace;             /* trace strings stored here */
    Stats_t         stats[S_NSTATS];   /* usage statistics */
};
```

The *xt_ttyq* field is used to save the downstream write queue. The *xt_chan* structure contains information on the active windows. The *xt_next* is used to do round robin scheduling of the upper write queues. The *xt_ctlflg* can have the following flags:

- XT_INUSE - xt device is in use

- XT_NETACK - processing incoming network xt acknowledgement packet

- XT_ININPUT - don't scan in input routines

- XT_EXIT - C_EXIT in progress

- XT_UNLINK - UNLINK in progress

The *xt_inbp* field stores the incoming packet until it is processed. The *xt_pendjagent* indicates that there is a pending JAGENT **ioctl** packet to be received from the terminal. The fields *xt_incount, xt_insize, xt_intime,* and *xt_instate* are used to store information during the processing of an incoming packet. The *xt_instate* can have the following values:

- PR_NULL - a new input packet is expected.

- PR_SIZE - expecting data byte count.

- PR_DATA - expecting actual data.

- PR_GETBUF - get a buffer for putting the received message.

The *xt_hex* field indicates if the transmissions are encoded. The *trace* and *stats* fields are compile time options and are used for tracing and statistics information. Tracing and statistics won't be available if they are not compiled in.

One **xtctl** structure is allocated for each instantiation of the STREAMS-based xt driver.

One *xt_chan* is allocated for each window on the user's terminal. It has the following format:

```
struct xt_chan {
    queue_t            *xt_upq;       /* upstream read queue */
    struct xtctl       *xt_ctlp;      /* pointer to ctl structure */
    struct jwinsize    xt_jwinsize;   /* layer parameters for
                                         JWINSIZE/TIOCGWINSZ ioctl */
    short              xt_chflg;      /* flags */
    pid_t              xt_pgrp;       /* process group of 1st opening process */
    short              xt_channo;     /* channel number for easy reference */
    short              xt_outbufs;    /* slots for outpackets */
    struct xt_msg      xt_msg[2];     /* outpacket awaiting acknowledgement */
    unsigned char      xt_inseq;      /* expected inpacket sequence number */
    unsigned short     xt_bytesent;   /* for flow control in network xt */
};
```

The *xt_upq* is used to store the upstream read queue of the window and the *xt_ctlp* points to the control structure. The *xt_jwinsize* stores the window size information. The *xt_chflg* can have the following flags:

- XT_CTL - the channel is a control channel.
- XT_ON - the channel is open.
- XT_WCLOSE - the channel is in process of being closed.
- XT_IOCTL - the channel is processing an **ioctl**.
- XT_NONETFLOW - network xt flow control is disabled.
- XT_M_STOPPED - a channel stopped by user ^S (control-s).

The *xt_channo* stores the channel number and *xt_outbufs* stores the number of output buffers (default is 2). The *xt_msg* is used to store the output packet awaiting a positive acknowledgement (ACK) from the terminal. It is defined as:

```
struct xt_msg
        {
        mblk_t *mp;                       /* pointer to message */
        clock_t timestamp;                /* stamp for ACK/NAK timeout */
        unsigned char seq;                /* sequence number */
        unsigned char xt_saveoutpkts;     /* outpkts when packet was sent */
        };
```

Open Processing

The open routine allocates and initializes the private data structures. It differentiates between a normal window open and a control channel open (channel 0). The control channel open is the first open and normal window opens are the subsequent open calls when a new window is opened with a mouse device. On a control channel open, the allocation and initialization of structures for all windows is done.

The following steps are taken on a control channel open:

- Only one layers process is allowed at a time. This is done using O_EXCL flag. If more than one layers process is invoked, EBUSY is returned.

- Opening of the control channel is regarded as one instantiation of the STREAMS-based xt driver and an xtctl structure is allocated. The control channel is then marked as being used (XT_INUSE is set).

- A window channel structure *xt_chan* is allocated and marked as control channel being used (XT_CTL|XT_ON).

- A window structure element *xt_upq* of the control channel is initialized with the upper read queue address.

- A window structure *xt_chan* is initialized for each window.

- The *q->q_ptr* of the upper read and write queues are initialized with the window structure address *xt_chan*.

- Scanning is initiated.

The following steps are taken on a normal window open:

- A check is made to ensure that a channel number is in the legal range.

- A window structure *xt_chan* is assigned and marked as being used (XT_ON).

- A window structure element *xt_upq* is initialized with the read queue address.

- The *q->q_ptr* of the read and write queues is initialized with the window structure address *xt_chan*.

- The Stream head is notified to allocate a controlling tty, if not already done.

If the open routine fails, the following *errno* values are returned:

- EINVAL - xt being opened as a module, or the first channel opened is not a control channel.

- EBUSY - xt control channel opened with the exclusive flag previously.

- ENXIO - channel number of range.

- EAGAIN - someone is closing the supplied channel.

On success, 1 is returned.

Close Processing

The close routine cleans up the allocated structures and pointers. It differentiates between a normal window close and a control channel close (channel 0). The control channel closes all the channels and dismantles the entire multiplexor.

The following steps are taken on a control channel close:

- All the channels are looped through and the entire multiplexor is dismantled.

- Enqueued messages are freed.

- All the structures are freed (deallocated).

- A hang up message is sent to all open windows.

- The control channel is released.

The following takes place in the normal window channel close:

- The structures are deallocated.

- The data on the write-side are flushed.

- The channel is released.

Data Flow

Figure G-5 shows the data flow in the STREAMS-based xt driver. The data on the output (write-side) are processed by the upper write-side queue **service** procedure and passed directly to the write-side **put** procedure of the hardware driver linked under the multiplexor. The lower multiplexor write processing is bypassed. Similarly, data on the input side (read-side) are processed by the lower read queue **put** and **service** procedures and passed directly to the input side **put** procedure of the **ldterm** that is pushed on the top of the multiplexor. The upper multiplexor read processing is bypassed.

Figure G-5: STREAMS-based XT Driver Data Flow

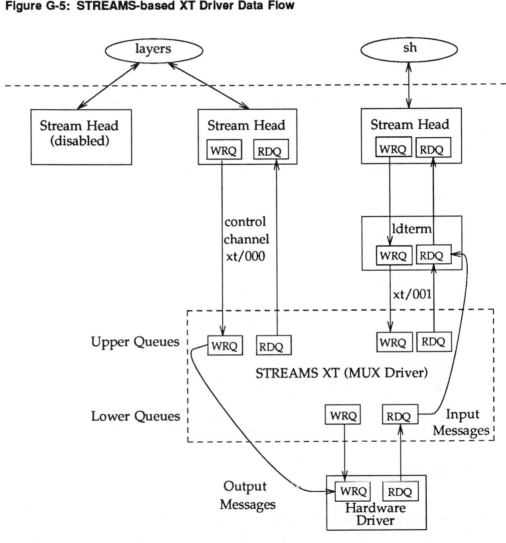

Read-Side Processing

The read-side **put** procedure only queues messages when the allocation fails or when other messages are already enqueued. Otherwise, all messages are processed right away.

The read-side **put** procedure sends M_SIG, M_PCSIG, M_BREAK, M_ERROR, and M_HANGUP messages coming from downstream up to the control channel. M_DATA is processed by the input processing routine at bottom of the multiplexor.

The read-side input processing routine also does the following processing:

- It checks if the current mode is encoding. If so, it decodes the data (that is, it converts the 6-bit data path to 8-bit data path).

- It processes PR_NULL state that indicates that new packets are expected.

- It processes PR_SIZE state which indicates that the next byte in the buffer is the *dsize* byte of the xt protocol.

- It processes PR_DATA and calls a routine to decipher the incoming packet and to check and process three xt messages types (control packet, data packet, and error packet).

The control packet processing is done by the routine processing positive and negative acknowledgements received from the windowing terminal. The data packet processing is done by the routine dealing with commands specified in **layers**(5) (e.g. C_NEW). The windowing terminal commands processed are: C_SENDCHAR, C_SENDNCHARS, C_UNBLK, C_EXIT, C_DELETE, C_NEW, C_RESHAPE, C_DEFUNCT, C_NOFLOW, C_YESFLOW, and JAGENT.

Write-Side Processing

There is no **put** procedure processing done by the upper write queues. All messages are queued for the **service** procedure.

The **service** procedure processing causes all the upper write queues to be emptied in a round robin fashion. If a channel was blocked before because the downstream terminal driver queue was full, then the output is started from that channel. Otherwise, output is started from the channel that is passed in to the **service** procedure. The result is that a write on any channel will start emptying of other channel queues that were blocked before. This method provides a *fair share processing* for all windows.

Each channel is double-buffered (*xt_msg*), so a process writing on a channel does not block unless both packet slots on that channel are awaiting acknowledgements. When a positive acknowledgement is received, the packet slot is made available.

Write queues are emptied one at a time in the following way:

- M_DATA - messages are packetized into maximum of 36 bytes and sent to the windowing terminal. Each packet has a 2-byte header, up to 32 bytes of data, and 2 bytes of *crc* error correction code. If the write is more than 32 bytes, the read pointer of the outgoing message buffer is incremented and the message is enqueued back on the queue.

- M_FLUSH - read and write queues are flushed depending on the argument to the message. If the argument is FLUSHR, the message is turned around with only the FLUSHR flag set.

- M_IOCDATA - this message is received in response to a previous M_COPYIN/M_COPYOUT request. Transparent **ioctl** processing is continued.

- M_IOCTL - There are four groups of **ioctl** request processed by the STREAMS-based xt driver. The first group contains all the normal tty **ioctls** described in **termio**(7). The **termio**(7) **ioctl** processing is done assuming I_STR style of **ioctl** because the Stream head does the conversion from transparent **ioctls** to I_STR format. The second group of the **ioctls** (J type) request concerns control of the windowing terminal (described in the header file <sys/jioctl.h>). The third group of the **ioctls** (X type) request concerns the configuration of the xt (described in the header file <sys/nxt.h>). The **ioctls** (J and X type) are processed using **ioctl** transparency. The fourth group of the **ioctls** requests concerns **streamio**(7) multiplexing setup.

The EUC **ioctls** are sent an M_IOCACK message upstream to support multiple byte character handling.

BSD/Xenix/V7 **ioctls** can be supported by pushing the **ttcompat** module on each window.

All other messages are freed and **ioctls** are sent an M_IOCNAK message upstream.

The following **termio(7) ioctls** are handled by the STREAMS-based xt driver:

- TCGETA, TCGETS - returns a **termios** structure in the M_IOCACK response to TCGETS, a **termio** structure in the M_IOCACK response to a TCGETA.

- TCSETA, TCSETAF, TCSETAW, TCSETS, TCSETSF, TCSETSW - sets the *xt_ttycflags* in the *xt_chan* private structure and sends an M_IOCACK response upstream.

- TCSBRK, TCFLSH, TCXONC - sends an M_IOCACK response upstream.

TIOCSETP, TIOCGETP, TIOCEXCL, and TIOCNXCL handling can be done by the **ttcompat** module.

The STREAMS-based xt driver also handles the following windowing **ioctls:**

- JTIMO, JTIMOM - sets the timeout parameters for the protocol by sending an IOCDATA packet to the terminal. The packet contains four bytes in two groups; the value of the receive timeout in milliseconds (the low 8 bits followed by the high 8 bits) and the value of the transmit timeout (in the same format). The JTIMO **ioctl** is converted to JTIMOM **ioctl.**

- JMPX, JTYPE - sends an M_IOCACK message upstream.

- TIOCGWINSZ, JWINSIZE - returns a **winsize** structure in the M_IOCACK response to TIOCGWINSZ and a **jwinsize** structure in the M_IOCACK for response to JWINSIZE.

- JBOOT - sends an IOCDATA packet with the command and the channel number to the terminal. It prepares the terminal to a new terminal program into a designated layer. Also an M_IOCACK message is sent upstream.

- JZOMBOOT - actions are similar to JBOOT, but the terminal does not execute the program after loading.

- JTERM - sends an IOCDATA packet with the command and the channel number to the terminal. This command kills the layers program, restores the default window program, and exits **layers.** Also an M_IOCACK message is sent upstream.

- JTRUN - runs a UNIX system command in the specified channel (layer). Also an M_IOCACK message is sent upstream.

- JAGENT - sends a command byte string to the terminal and waits for a reply byte string to be returned. The command bytes are described in **jagent**(5).

- JXTPROTO - sets xt protocol type [see also **xtproto**(5)].

The following xt (X type) **ioctls** are handled by the STREAMS-based xt driver:

- XTIOCHEX - turns on the encoding mode and sends an M_IOCACK message upstream.

- XTIOCTRACE - copies out the trace record and sends an M_IOCACK message upstream.

- XTIOCNOTRACE - turns off the tracing mode and sends an M_IOCACK message upstream.

- XTIOCSTATS - copies out the stored xt statistics and sends an M_IOCACK message upstream.

- XTIOCTYPE - sends an M_IOCACK message upstream (similar to JMPX **ioctl**).

The following **streamio**(7) **ioctls** are handled by the STREAMS-based xt driver.

- I_LINK - links a hardware driver underneath the STREAMS-based xt driver. It saves the hardware driver queue address in the private structure and the private structure address in the q->q_ptr of the queue. After link processing, JTIMOM **ioctl** processing is done to initialize the timers and to send an M_IOCACK message upstream.

- I_UNLINK - nulls out all the structure elements initialized by the I_LINK **ioctl** and sends an M_IOCACK message upstream.

Multiplexing

Multiplexing in the STREAMS-based xt driver is done with the help of the protocol information and using information stored in private structures during open and link time. The packets that are sent to the windowing terminal are packaged with a channel number. This channel number is obtained from the xt driver's private data structure that is stored in q->$qptr$ during open of a window. Similarly, data coming from the terminal come with a channel number. Using the channel number the upper window queue can be derived.

Flow Control

The flow control of data is done using both the STREAMS flow control and the STREAMS-based xt driver flow control.

STREAMS Flow Control

On the write-side, the **canput()** routine is used to determine if the driver's queue downstream is full. If it is full, the data are put back on the upper write queue. When the flow control is relieved, the lower write **service** procedure is called by the STREAMS mechanism, which enables the upper write **service** procedure to start sending the data again. The purpose of lower write **service** procedure is only to enable the upper queues in case of flow control.

If the data cannot be sent upstream because of **canput()** failure, the data are freed. The protocol is expected to recover from this situation. Since a positive acknowledgement is not sent to the data packet that was freed, the protocol retransmits the data after a timeout interval.

XT Driver Protocol Flow Control

The windowing terminal controls the packet flow using the UNBLK command in a positive acknowledgement packet. A control packet from the terminal to the host contains ACK and UNBLK as data characters. If UNBLK is sent with the ACK, the host assumes that more data could be sent to the channel. If UNBLK is not accompanied with the ACK, the host slows the data flow to that channel and stops all the data when a second ACK with no UNBLK is received. Two UNBLK packets directed to the blocked channel are required to restore the channel to full throughput. There is no UNBLK command from the host to the terminal and, therefore, no explicit flow control of data packets exists from the terminal to the host. However, the host controls the data flow by not acknowledging the packets and just freeing them, expecting the protocol to recover.

Scanning

The STREAMS-based xt driver has routines for scanning the time-out input and output packets. Since the timeout functions are called at a high priority, the scanning has been split between a routine calling a high priority and a routine calling at a **service** procedure priority.

The routine calling at a high priority is triggered off from the open routine and is run at regular time intervals. This routine schedules the upper write **service** procedure to be run if there is activity on channels. The write **service** procedure invokes its scanning routine to scan for timed-out input and output packets. First, the routine checks if the input packet is received within the timeout interval. If not, the routine resets the input state and performs clean-up functions. Next, it runs through all the channels awaiting an output ACK and if it notices any timeout situations, it resends the output packets.

Cyclic Redundancy Check

The STREAMS-based xt driver does error checking on the transmissions using cyclic redundancy check (*crc*) byte generation. Two *crc* bytes are generated using the polynomial $x^{**}16 + x^{**}15 + x^{**}2 + 1$ that has a 64 byte look-up table. These two bytes are added to the end of each output packet sent to the windowing terminal with the lowest byte first.

Encoding

The STREAMS-based xt driver supports encoded transmissions. Encoded transmissions are required when using a binary protocol with certain local-area networks and data switches. The encoding hides the ASCII XON and XOFF character, which the transmission system misinterprets as flow control.

When using **layers** on the 3B2 console, encoded transmissions should be done by turning the encoding option *ON* on the terminals. Daemon mode (control-P) cannot be used when using **layers** on the console.

When **layers** or the xt is used on the console, the console device (a Stream) goes into a state where it cannot be opened since it is linked under the xt multiplexor. Therefore, console messages don't go through, and writes to the console (**dev/console**) fail. Console logging mechanism will redirect the console messages.

Extended STREAMS Buffers

STREAMS maintains its own memory resources for message storage. However, system developers need not be constrained to allocating STREAMS buffers, because it can be done dynamically or by taking advantage of a system supporting extended buffers.

An ability to share data buffers between the kernel and I/O cards is supported by some hardware. If the a module or driver so chooses, the shared buffers can be attached to a data block and processed as if the data were part of a normal STREAMS message, thus eliminating a copy of the buffer into kernel space.

With the hardware supporting extended buffers, data received from the network are placed in the dual access RAM (DARAM) section of the I/O card. Since DARAM is shared memory between the host and the card, data transfer by the controller from I/O card to kernel is eliminated.

The following two figures show pictorial views of extended buffers. (Chapter 5 describes how to allocate and free extended STREAMS buffers.) They show the copies necessary to transfer data from the network to user space and from the user space to the network. In each case, the I/O card receives data from the network and places data into an internal buffer on the card. Figure G-6 differs from Figure G-7 in that it makes use of DMA to transfer data from the I/O card to a kernel resident data buffer. The I/O card interrupts the host computer acknowledging data are present and ready to be read. The network access unit (NAU) driver allocates enough STREAMS buffers to hold data. It passes the address and length of the buffers to the I/O card and from there the card transfers data from its buffer to the data buffer resident in the kernel. The data are sent upstream for processing. Once data reach the Stream head, data are copied to the user space via **copyout()**.

A similar process occurs when data are transmitted from user space to the network. Data are copied into the kernel via **copyin()**, packaged into a message block and sent downstream. The driver issues an interrupt to signal the I/O card that data are ready to be read. The I/O card then transfers the data from a kernel buffer and places data into a buffer on the card itself, and on to the network.

Figure G-6: UNIX I/O on 3B2

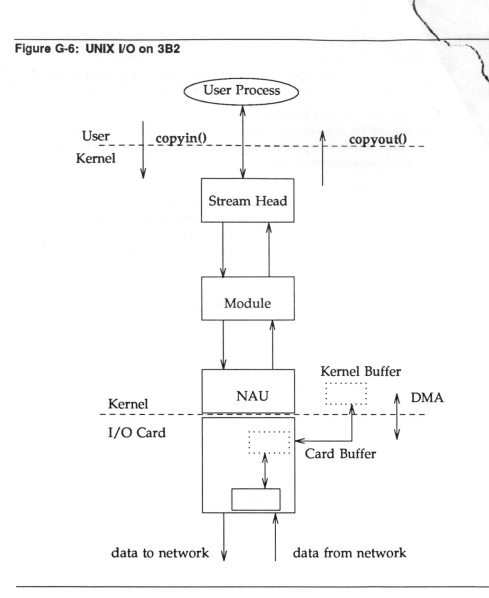

In Figure G-7, data are also received from the network by the I/O card. However, unlike in the previous figure, data are placed in a section of the I/O card that is shared between the kernel and the card. The card interrupts the host computer when data are ready for manipulation. Since DARAM is shared memory, there is no need for the driver to allocate a data buffer and pass its address to the card. Instead, it packages the buffer located in DARAM into a STREAMS message using the STREAMS utility routine **esballoc()**, and sends it upstream for processing.

On the other hand, the transfer of data between the kernel and a user resembles the previous example. A **copyin()** and **copyout()** are issued to copy data from user space to kernel and from kernel to user, respectively. On the write-side the driver still has to copy data from a STREAMS buffer to DARAM.

Figure G-7: UNIX I/O on a 386 Box

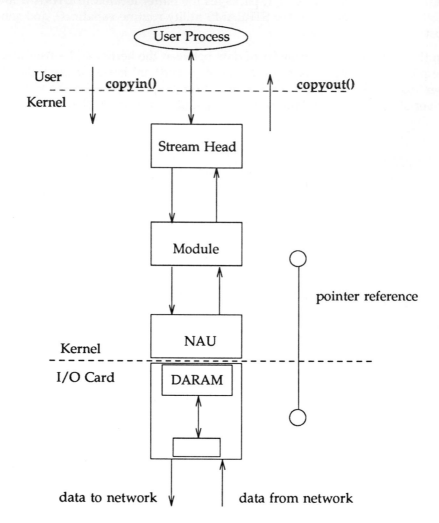

GLOSSARY

Glossary

autopush	A STREAMS mechanism that enables a pre-specified list of modules to be pushed automatically onto the Stream when a STREAMS device is opened. This mechanism is used only for administrative purposes.
back-enable	To enable (by STREAMS) a preceding blocked queue's **service** procedure when STREAMS determines that a succeeding queue has reached its low water mark.
blocked	A queue's **service** procedure that cannot be enabled due to flow control.
clone device	A STREAMS device that returns an unused major/minor device when initially opened, rather than requiring the minor device to be specified by name in the **open**(2) call.
close routine	A procedure that is called when a module is popped from a Stream or when a driver is closed.
controlling Stream	A Stream above the multiplexing driver used to establish the lower connections. Multiplexed Stream configurations are maintained through the controlling Stream to a multiplexing driver.
DDI	Device Driver Interface. An interface that facilitates driver portability across different UNIX system versions on AT&T hardware.
DKI	Driver–Kernel Interface. An interface between the UNIX system kernel and different types of drivers. It consists of a set of driver-defined functions that are called by the kernel. These functions are entry points into a driver.
downstream	A direction of data flow going from the Stream head towards a driver. Also called write-side and output side.
device driver	A Stream component whose principle functions are handling an associated physical device and transforming data and information between the external interface and Stream.

driver	A module that forms the Stream end. It can be a device driver or a pseudo-device driver. It is a required component in STREAMS (except in STREAMS-based pipe mechanism), and physically identical to a module. It typically handles data transfer between the kernel and a device and does little or no processing of data.
enable	A term used to describe scheduling of a queue's **service** procedure.
FIFO	First-In-First-Out. A term for named pipes in UNIX System V. This term is also used in queue scheduling.
flow control	A STREAMS mechanism that regulates the rate of message transfer within a Stream and from user space into a Stream.
hardware emulation module	A module required when the terminal line discipline is on a Stream but there is no terminal driver at the end of a Stream. This module understands all **ioctls** necessary to support terminal semantics specified by **termio**(7) and **termios**(7).
input side	A direction of data flow going from a driver towards the Stream head. Also called read-side and upstream.
line discipline	A STREAMS module that performs **termio**(7) canonical and non-canonical processing. It shares some **termio**(7) processing with a driver in a STREAMS terminal subsystem.
lower Stream	A Stream connected below a multiplexor pseudo-device driver, by means of an I_LINK or I_PLINK **ioctl**. The far end of a lower Stream terminates at a device driver or another multiplexor driver.
master driver	A STREAMS-based device supported by the pseudo-terminal subsystem. It is the controlling part of the pseudo-terminal subsystem and is also called **ptm**.

message	One or more linked message blocks. A message is referenced by its first message block and its type is defined by the message type of that block.
message block	A triplet consisting of a data buffer and associated control structures, an **msgb** structure and a **datab** structure. It carries data or information, as identified by its message type, in a Stream.
message queue	A linked list of zero or more messages connected together.
message type	A defined set of values identifying the contents of a message.
module	A defined set of kernel-level routines and data structures used to process data, status and control information on a Stream. It is an optional element, but there can be many modules in one Stream. It consists of a pair of queues (read queue and write queue), and it communicates to other components in a Stream by passing messages.
multiplexor	A STREAMS mechanism that allows messages to be routed among multiple Streams in the kernel. A multiplexing configuration includes at least one multiplexing pseudo-device driver connected to one or more upper Streams and one or more lower Streams.
named Stream	A Stream, typically a pipe, with a name associated with it via a call to **fattach**(3C) (i.e., a mount operation). This is different from a named pipe (FIFO) in two ways: a named pipe (FIFO) is unidirectional while a named Stream is bidirectional; a named Stream need not refer to a pipe but can be another type of a Stream.
open routine	A procedure in each STREAMS driver and module called by STREAMS on each **open**(2) system call made on the Stream. A module's open procedure is also called when the module is pushed.

packet mode	A feature supported by the STREAMS-based pseudo-terminal subsystem. It is used to inform a process on the master side when state changes occur on the slave side of a pseudo-tty. It is enabled by pushing a module called **pckt** on the master side.
persistent link	A connection below a multiplexor that can exist without having an open controlling Stream associated with it.
pipe	Same as a STREAMS-based pipe.
pop	A term used when a module that is immediately below the Stream head is removed.
pseudo-device driver	A software driver, not directly associated with a physical device, that performs functions internal to a Stream such as a multiplexor or log driver.
pseudo-terminal subsystem	A user interface identical to a terminal subsystem except that there is a process in a place of a hardware device. It consists of at least a master device, slave device, line discipline module, and hardware emulation module.
push	A term used when a module is inserted in a Stream immediately below the Stream head.
pushable module	A module interposed between the Stream head and driver. It performs intermediate transformations on messages flowing between the Stream head and driver. A driver is a non-pushable module.
put procedure	A routine in a module or driver associated with a queue which receives messages from the preceding queue. It is the single entry point into a queue from a preceding queue. It may perform processing on the message and will then generally either queue the message for subsequent processing by this queue's **service** procedure, or will pass the message to the **put** procedure of the following queue.

queue	A data structure that contains status information, a pointer to routines processing messages, and pointers for administering a Stream. It typically contains pointers to a **put** and **service** procedure, a message queue, and private data.
read-side	A direction of data flow going from a driver towards the Stream head. Also called upstream and input side.
read queue	A message queue in a module or driver containing messages moving upstream. Associated with the **read**(2) system call and input from a driver.
remote mode	A feature available with the pseudo-terminal subsystem. It is used for applications that perform the canonical and echoing functions normally done by the line discipline module and tty driver. It enables applications on the master side to turn off the canonical processing.
SAD	A STREAMS Administrative Driver that provides an interface to the autopush mechanism.
schedule	To place a queue on the internal list of queues which will subsequently have their **service** procedure called by the STREAMS scheduler. STREAMS scheduling is independent of the UNIX System V process scheduling.
service interface	A set of primitives that define a service at the boundary between a service user and a service provider and the rules (typically represented by a state machine) for allowable sequences of the primitives across the boundary. At a Stream/user boundary, the primitives are typically contained in the control part of a message; within a Stream, in M_PROTO or M_PCPROTO message blocks.
service procedure	A routine in module or driver associated with a queue which receives messages queued for it by the **put** procedure of that queue. The procedure is called by the STREAMS scheduler. It may perform

processing on the message and generally passes the message to the **put** procedure of the following queue.

service provider   An entity in a service interface that responds to request primitives from the service user with response and event primitives.

service user   An entity in a service interface that generates request primitives for the service provider and consumes response and event primitives.

slave driver   A STREAMS-based device supported by the pseudo-terminal subsystem. It is also called **pts** and works with a line discipline module and hardware emulation module to provide an interface to a user process.

standard pipe   A mechanism for a unidirectional flow of data between two processes where data written by one process become data read by the other process.

Stream   A kernel aggregate created by connecting STREAMS components, resulting from an application of the STREAMS mechanism. The primary components are the Stream head, the driver, and zero or more pushable modules between the Stream head and driver.

STREAMS-based pipe

A mechanism used for bidirectional data transfer implemented using STREAMS, and sharing the properties of STREAMS-based devices.

Stream end   A Stream component furthest from the user process, containing a driver.

Stream head   A Stream component closest to the user process. It provides the interface between the Stream and the user process.

STREAMS   A kernel mechanism that provides the framework for network services and data communication. It defines interface standards for character input/output within the kernel, and between the kernel and user level.

The STREAMS mechanism comprises integral functions, utility routines, kernel facilities, and a set of structures.

tty driver A STREAMS-based device used in a terminal subsystem.

upper Stream A Stream that terminates above a multiplexor. The beginning of an upper Stream originates at the Stream head or another multiplexor driver.

upstream A direction of data flow going from a driver towards the Stream head. Also called read-side and input side.

water mark A limit value used in flow control. Each queue has a high water mark and a low water mark. The high water mark value indicates the upper limit related to the number of bytes contained on the queue. When the enqueued characters in a queue reach its high water mark, STREAMS causes another queue that attempts to send a message to this queue to become blocked. When the characters in this queue are reduced to the low water mark value, the other queue will be unblocked by STREAMS.

write queue A message queue in a module or driver containing messages moving downstream. Associated with the write(2) system call and output from a user process.

write-side A direction of data flow going from the Stream head towards a driver. Also called downstream and output side.

Index

A

asynchronous input/output, in polling   6: 6
asynchronous protocol Stream, example   4: 4–11
autopush(1M)   E: 6

B

back-enable of a queue   5: 29
background job, in job control   6: 9
bidirectional transfer, example   7: 24–29

C

cloning (STREAMS)   9: 18
connld(7)   11: 12
console   G: 11
controlling terminal   6: 13
contty   G: 10
copyreq structure   A: 10
copyresp structure   A: 11
crash(1M), STREAMS debugging   D: 2–6

D

daemon mode, in STREAMS-based console   G. 14
data block (STREAMS)
   linkage   5: 6
   structure   5: 5
data flow, in xt driver   G: 26
device numbers   9: 5–6

downstream

downstream, definition   2: 3
driver
   classification   9: 1
   configuration   9: 2
   device numbers   9: 5–6
   entry points   9: 3
   interface to STREAMS   7: 37–41
   overview   9: 1–6
   STREAMS   2: 14, 9: 6–8
   STREAMS-based console   G: 10–14
   STREAMS-based ports   G: 2–9
   STREAMS-based sxt   12: 3
   STREAMS-based xt   G: 15–34
   writing a driver   9: 3–5

E

encoded transmission, in xt driver   G: 33
EUC handling in ldterm(7)   12: 8
expedited data   5: 3, 7: 35
extended STREAMS buffers   5: 60–61
   allocation   5: 60
   freeing   5: 61
   in different hardware   G: 35–38
external device number   9: 5–6

F

fattach(3C)   11: 7
fdetach(3C)   11: 8
FIFO (STREAMS)   11: 1
   basic operations   11: 1–6
   flush   11: 6
   queue scheduling   4: 2
file descriptor passing   11: 9

flow control   5: 28–32
  definition   2: 7
  in driver   9: 16
  in line discipline module   8: 12
  in module   8: 11–13
  in xt driver   G: 32
  routines   5: 29–32
flush handling
  description   7: 31–35
  flags   7: 31, B: 16
  in driver   9: 12
  in line discipline   7: 31
  in pipes and FIFOs   11: 6
  priority band data   7: 35
  priority band data example   7: 36
  read-side example   7: 34
  write-side example   7: 33
foreground job, in job control   6: 9

G

getmsg(2)   5: 10
getpmsg function   5: 12
grantpt(3C)   12: 25
  with pseudo-tty driver   12: 22

H

hardware emulation module
  12: 13–14

I

input/output polling   6: 1–7
internal device number   9: 5–6
interrupts
  in console driver   G: 12

  in ports driver   G: 8
iocblk structure   A: 9
  with M_IOCTL   B: 3
ioctl(2)
  console driver write-side   G: 13
  general processing   7: 10–12
  handled by ports driver   G: 6
  handled by ptem(7)   12: 17
  hardware emulation module   12: 13
  I_ATMARK   5: 19
  I_CANPUT   5: 18
  I_CKBAND   5: 18
  I_GETBAND   5: 18
  I_LINK   10: 6, B: 3
  I_LIST   7: 29
  I_PLINK   10: 32, B: 3
  I_POP   3: 10
  I_PUNLINK   10: 32, B: 3
  I_PUSH   3: 10
  I_RECVFD   11: 9, B: 6
  I_SENDFD   11: 9, B: 6
  I_SETSIG events   6: 6
  I_STR   3: 14, B: 3
  I_STR processing   7: 12–14
  I_UNLINK   10: 11, B: 3
  supported by ldterm(7)   12: 7
  supported by master driver   12: 24
  termio(7) handled by xt driver
    G: 30
  transparent   7: 14–29
  xt driver windowing   G: 30
isastream(3C)   11: 9

J

job control   6: 9–12
  terminology   6: 9–10

L

ldterm(7) 12: 3
ldterm_mod structure 12: 4
LIFO, module add/remove 3: 13
line discipline module
  close 12: 5
  description 12: 3–12
  in job control 6: 11
  in pseudo-tty subsystem 12: 15
  ioctl(2) 12: 7
  open 12: 5
linkblk structure A: 12
lower multiplexor 2: 17
lower Stream 2: 15

M

major device number 9: 5
master driver
  in pseudo-tty subsystem 12: 15
  open 12: 22
MAX_INPUT G: 9
M_BREAK B: 2
M_COPYIN B: 14
  transparent ioctl example
    7: 18–21
M_COPYOUT B: 15
  transparent ioctl example
    7: 22–24
  with M_IOCTL B: 6
M_CTL B: 2
  with line discipline module 12: 3
M_DATA 2: 10, B: 2
  xt driver write-side processing
    G: 29
M_DELAY B: 2
M_ERROR B: 15

message block (STREAMS) 2: 4
  linkage 5: 6
  structure 5: 4
message processing routines
    (STREAMS) 4: 1–3
  design guidelines 7: 44–46
message queue (STREAMS), priority
    5: 15–19
message (STREAMS) 2: 9
  allocation 5: 54
  control information 2: 10, 5: 47
  definition 2: 3
  freeing 5: 54
  handled by pckt(7) 12: 21
  handled by ptem(7) 12: 18
  high priority 5: 2, B: 14–21
  ldterm(7) read-side 12: 5
  ldterm(7) write-side 12: 7
  linkage 5: 6
  M_DATA 2: 10
  M_PCPROTO 2: 10
  M_PROTO 2: 10
  ordinary 5: 1, B: 2–13
  processing 5: 26
  recovering from allocation failure
    5: 57
  sending/receiving 5: 8
  service interface 5: 34–47
  structures 5: 4–6, A: 6–8
  types 2: 10, 5: 1
M_FLUSH B: 16
  flags B: 16
  in module example 8: 8
  packet mode 12: 21
  xt driver write-side processing
    G: 29
M_HANGUP B: 17
minor device number 9: 5

M_IOCACK B: 17
  with M_COPYOUT B: 15
  with M_IOCTL B: 4
M_IOCDATA B: 18
  xt driver write-side processing
    G: 29
M_IOCNAK B: 19
  with M_COPYOUT B: 15
  with M_IOCTL B: 4
M_IOCTL B: 3–6
  transparent B: 4
  with M_COPYOUT B: 15
  xt driver write-side processing
    G: 29
MORECTL 5: 47
MOREDATA 5: 47
M_PASSFP B: 6
M_PCPROTO 2: 10, B: 19
M_PCRSE B: 20
M_PCSIG B: 20
M_PROTO 2: 10, B: 7–8
M_READ B: 20
M_RSE B: 8
M_SETOPTS B: 8–13
  SO_FLAG B: 9–13
  SO_READOPT options 5: 13
  SO_WROFF value 5: 14
  with ldterm(7) 12: 5
M_SIG B: 13
  in signaling 6: 7
M_START B: 20
M_STARTI B: 21
M_STOP B: 20
M_STOPI B: 21
multiplexing
  in xt driver G: 32
  STREAMS 2: 15–19
multiplexor

building 10: 2–10
controlling Stream 10: 8
data routing 10: 12
declarations 10: 20
design guidelines 10: 37
dismantling 10: 11
driver 10: 19–31
example 10: 16–18
lower 10: 1
lower connection 10: 13–15
lower disconnection 10: 15
lower read put procedure 10: 28–31
lower write service procedure
    10: 28
persistent links 10: 32–36
upper 10: 1
upper write put procedure
    10: 23–26
upper write service procedure
    10: 27
multiplexor ID
  in multiplexor building 10: 6
  in multiplexor dismantling 10: 11

N

named pipe (see FIFO)
named Stream
  description 11: 7–9
  fattach(3C) 11: 7
  fdetach(3C) 11: 8
  file descriptor passing 11: 9
  isastream(3C) 11: 9
  remote 11: 10
NSTRPUSH parameter 3: 10, E: 5

Programmer's Guide: STREAMS

O

O_NDELAY
  close a Stream   3: 11
  with M_SETOPTS   B: 11
O_NONBLOCK
  close a Stream   3: 11
  with M_SETOPTS   B: 11

P

packet mode
  description   12: 21
  messages   12: 21
pckt(7)   12: 21
persistent link   10: 32–36
PIPE_BUF   11: 5
pipemod STREAMS module   11: 6
pipes, STREAMS (see STREAMS-
    based pipe)
poll(2)   6: 1
pollfd structure   6: 3
polling
  error events   6: 5
  events   6: 1
  example   6: 3–6
priority band data   5: 3, 7: 35
  flow control   5: 30
  flush handling example   7: 36
  ioctl(2)   5: 18
  routines   5: 16
  service procedure   5: 27
pseudo-tty emulation module
    12: 17–20
pseudo-tty subsystem   12: 15
  description   12: 15–26
  drivers   12: 22–25
  ldterm(7)   12: 15

messages   12: 18
packet mode   12: 21
remote mode   12: 20
ptem structure   12: 19
ptem(7)   12: 17, 19
ptm (see master driver)
pts (see slave driver)
ptsname(3C)   12: 26
  with pseudo-tty driver   12: 22
putmsg(2)   5: 9
putpmsg function   5: 11

R

read-side
  console driver service procedure
    G: 13
  console processing   G: 12
  definition   2: 3
  ldterm(7) messages   12: 5
  ldterm(7) processing   12: 5
  ports driver service procedure   G: 9
  put procedure   8: 1
  xt driver   G: 28

S

SAD (see STREAMS Administrative
    Driver)
scanning, in xt driver   G: 33
service interface   5: 35–37
  definition   5: 34
  library example   5: 38–47
  rules   5: 47
service primitive   5: 37
  in service procedure   5: 39
service provider   5: 37
  accessing   5: 40

closing 5: 43
receiving data 5: 45
sending data 5: 44
signal(2) 6: 1
signals
    extended 6: 8
    in job control management 6: 11
    in STREAMS 6: 7
slave driver
    in pseudo-tty subsystem 12: 15
    open 12: 22
SO_FLAG, in M_SETOPTS B: 9–13
strapush structure E: 8
strbuf structure 5: 10
strchg(1) 7: 29
strconf command 7: 29
STRCTLSZ parameter E: 6
Stream
    controlling terminal 6: 12
    definition 2: 1
    hung-up 6: 12
Stream construction 3: 3–11
    add/remove modules 3: 10
    close a Stream 3: 11
    define module/driver 3: 5
    example 3: 11–16
    open a Stream 3: 5
    queue structures 3: 3
Stream head
    definition 2: 1
    processing control 5: 12
STREAMS
    3B2 configuration G: 1
    basic operations 2: 5–8
    benefits 2: 20–24
    components 2: 9–14
    configuration E: 1–9
    definition 2: 1

header files 7: 48
manual pages F: 1–2
master.d E: 3
multiplexing 2: 15–19
system calls 2: 5, 3: 1
tunable parameters E: 5–6
STREAMS Administrative Driver
    E: 7–9
STREAMS data structures A: 1–13
    design 7: 47
    dynamic allocation 7: 47
STREAMS debugging D: 1–19
    crash(1M) D: 2–6
    dump module D: 6–17
    error and trace logging D: 17–19
STREAMS driver 2: 14, 9: 6–8
    accessible functions 7: 49
    cloning 9: 18
    close routine design 7: 43
    declarations 7: 2
    definition 2: 1
    design guidelines 7: 42–50, 9: 30
    environment 7: 1
    flow control 9: 16
    flush handling 9: 12
    interface 7: 40
    ioctl(2) 7: 9–30
    loop-around 9: 20–29
    open routine design 7: 43
    printer driver example 9: 9–16
    pseudo-tty 12: 22–25
    pseudo-tty subsystem master 12: 15
    pseudo-tty subsystem slave 12: 15
STREAMS message queues 2: 10
    priority 2: 11–12
STREAMS module 2: 12–14, 8: 1–10
    accessible functions 7: 49
    autopush facility E: 6, 9

close routine design   7: 43
connld(7)   11: 12
control information   2: 1
declarations   7: 2
definition   2: 1
design guidelines   7: 42–50, 8: 14
environment   7: 1
filter   8: 5
flow control   8: 11–13
ioctl(2)   7: 9–30
line discipline   12: 3
null module example   7: 6
open routine design   7: 43
ptem(7)   12: 17
read-side put procedure   8: 1
routines   8: 1–5
service interface example   5: 47–53
service procedure   8: 3
status information   2: 1
write-side put procedure   8: 3
STREAMS queue
   definition   2: 3
   equeue structure   5: 22
   flags   5: 21
   overview   2: 9
   qband structure   5: 22
   queue structure   5: 19
   structures   A: 1–6
   using equeue information   5: 24
   using qband information   5: 24
   using queue information   5: 21
STREAMS scheduler, in service procedure   4: 2
STREAMS utility routines   C: 1–21
STREAMS-based console driver
   description   G: 10–14
   open   G: 12
   read-side processing   G: 12

   read-side service procedure   G: 13
   write-side processing   G: 13
STREAMS-based pipe   2: 1
   atomic write   11: 5
   basic operations   11: 1–6
   creation   3: 8
   creation errors   11: 2
   definition   11: 1
   PIPE_BUF   11: 5
STREAMS-based ports driver
   close   G: 5
   description   G: 2–9
   interrupt procedure   G: 8
   ioctl   G: 6
   open   G: 4
   read-side service procedure   G: 9
   write-side put procedure   G: 5
   write-side service procedure   G: 7
STREAMS-based pseudo-terminal
   subsystem (see pseudo-tty subsystem)
STREAMS-based sxt driver   12: 3
STREAMS-based terminal subsystem
   (see tty subsystem)
STREAMS-based xt driver
   close control channel   G: 26
   close normal window   G: 26
   data flow   G: 26
   description   G: 15–34
   encoded transmission   G: 33
   error checking   G: 33
   flow control   G: 32
   open control channel   G: 24
   open normal window   G: 25
   scanning   G: 33
   set up   G: 15
   streamio(7)   G: 31
   termio(7)   G: 30

windowing ioctl   G: 30
X type ioctl   G: 31
strioctl structure   3: 15, A: 12
STRMSGSZ parameter   E: 5
stroptions structure   A: 13
STRTHRESH parameter   E: 6
strtty structure   G: 3
synchronous input/output, in pol-
    ling   6: 1
syscon   G: 10
systty   G: 10

T

t_buf structure   G: 3
termio(7)   6: 11
    default flag values   12: 3
    xt driver   G: 30
termiox(7), support   12: 12
transparent ioctl
    M_COPYIN example   7: 18–21
    M_COPYOUT example   7: 22–24
    messages   7: 17
    processing   7: 14–29
tty subsystem
    benefits   12: 1
    description   12: 1–14
    hardware emulation module
        12: 13–14
    ldterm(7)   12: 3
    setup   12: 2

U

unique connection (STREAMS)
    11: 11–13
unlockpt(3C)   12: 26

with pseudo-tty driver   12: 22
upper multiplexor   2: 17
upper Stream   2: 15
upstream   2: 3

V

virtual system console (see syscon)

W

windowing terminal commands
        G: 28
write-side
    console driver processing   G: 13
    definition   2: 3
    ldterm(7)   12: 7
    ports driver put procedure   G: 5
    ports driver service procedure   G: 7
    put procedure   8: 3
    xt driver   G: 28

X

xt_chan structure   G: 23
xtctl structure   G: 22
xt_msg structure   G: 24